African Religion, Philosophy, and Christianity in Logos-Christ

American University Studies

Series VII
Theology and Religion

Vol. 188

PETER LANG
New York • Washington, D.C./Baltimore
Bern • Frankfurt am Main • Berlin • Vienna • Paris

Emmanuel K. Twesigye

African Religion, Philosophy, and Christianity in Logos-Christ

Common Ground Revisited

PETER LANG
New York • Washington, D.C./Baltimore
Bern • Frankfurt am Main • Berlin • Vienna • Paris

BR
128
.A16
T93
1996

Library of Congress Cataloging-in-Publication Data

Twesigye, Emmanuel K.
African religion, philosophy, and Christianity in
Logos-Christ: common ground revisited/ by Emmanuel Kalenzi Twesigye.
p. cm. — (American university studies. Series VII,
Theology and religion; v. 188)
Rev. and expanded ed. of: Common ground. 1987.
Includes bibliographical references and index.
1. Christianity and other religions—African. 2. Africa—Religion.
3. Salvation. 4. Love—Religious aspects—Christianity. 5. Rahner, Karl,
1904– . I. Twesigye, Emmanuel K. Common ground. II. Title. III. Series.
BR128.A16T93   261.2'96—dc20   95-37315
ISBN 0-8204-3069-2
ISSN 0740-0446

Die Deutsche Bibliothek-CIP-Einheitsaufnahme

Twesigye, Emmanuel K.:
African religion, philosophy, and Christianity in logos-Christ: common ground
revisited/ Emmanuel K. Twesigye.–New York; Washington, D.C./Baltimore;
Bern; Frankfurt am Main; Berlin; Vienna; Paris: Lang.
(American university studies: Ser. 7, Theology and religion; Vol. 188)
ISBN 0-8204-3069-2
NE: American university studies/ 07

The paper in this book meets the guidelines for permanence and durability
of the Committee on Production Guidelines for Book Longevity
of the Council of Library Resources.

Printed in the United States of America.

FOR

All God's People
Everywhere in the World

and

BULASIO and ESTHER JOY KALENZI
My Beloved Parents

Who

TAUGHT ME
LOVE and RESPECT
for
COMMUNITY, HUMANITY, NATURE
and
THE COSMIC CREATOR-GOD

CONTENTS

PREFACE

This book is a result of major revisions and expansion of *Common Ground: Christianity, African Religion and Philosophy*. This book has been written as a scholarly book for other scholars, advanced university/college, and graduate students in the fields of Religion, Theology, Philosophy and African Studies. The book is a result of many years of research, writing, reflection and revisions. The funding for research work and travel to Africa was obtained from several important sources. I am indebted to all of them. Without this essential funding and other kinds of practical support the original book and this revised work would not have been possible.

I am grateful to many people and organizations in the United States of America, Europe, and Africa who originally made it possible for me to undertake programs of study leading to graduate degrees in Communications, Theology, and Philosophy, in addition to the provision of funds for the various research projects and publications. In Europe, the Africa Theological Fund deserves special mention, and in Africa, the National Research Council of Uganda and Makerere University also deserve special acknowledgement.

Special thanks are also extended to my supportive colleagues here at OWU, and also to my former philosophy and theology professors and advisors at Vanderbilt University, of whom the following deserve special mention: Eugene TeSelle, Walter Harrelson, Peter Hodgson, Jackson Fortsman, Michael Hodges, John Lachs, and Donald Sherburne. They read and critiqued the original parts of this work as part of my PhD dissertation which utilized academic methodologies and resources in Philosophy, Theology, African Religion and Anthropology.

I am very indebted to Bishop David Birney, the late Urban T. Holmes, former Professor of Theology and Dean of The School of Theology, University of the South for having introduced me to the late Karl Rahner and his thought on which much of this book is based. I am also grateful to both the Rt. Rev. David Birney and the late Very Reverend Professor Urban T. Holmes for making arrangements for my program of study in the U.S.A. and for obtaining the needed funding. I now realize that this was indeed, a rare opportunity and favor which they offered to me on behalf of Africa.

I am very thankful to the National Episcopal Church of the U.S.A., the Episcopal Church Women of Tennessee, The University of the South, Sewanee; Vanderbilt University, the Sisters of St. Mary's Convent, Sewanee; and some "anonymous friends," for their moral and fiscal support.

Some of these organizations and people contributed significant funds needed for my various degree programs. These programs of study led to graduate degree awards of MA (Hons.) in Crosscultural Communications from Wheaton College Graduate School in 1978, STM in Systematic Theology from The University of the South in 1979, MA and PhD in Theology and Philosophy from Vanderbilt University in 1982 and 1983, respectively. Without this support and education, this research would not have been undertaken, and this book would not have been written.

I am also greatly indebted to Professor John S. Mbiti, my former teacher and colleague at Makerere University. He introduced me to the critical study, appreciation, and interpretation of the African Religion. He also secured for me a research fellowship in 1971 which led to the study and publication of "The Concept of Death Among the Bakiga of Western Uganda" in Byaruhanga (Ed.), *Research Occasional Papers*. Vol. II, Kampala: Makerere University Press, 1973. My study of the African Traditional Religion was shaped by Mbiti, Tempels and Alexis Kagame. My STM thesis entitled, "The Concept of Sin and Atonement Among the Balokole of Uganda." The work covered soteriology within African context.

This present work is heavily based on the original research for *Common Ground: African Religion and Philosophy* (Peter Lang, 1987). The revisions include new material and perspectives gathered in recent research trips to Africa, the reviews of *Common Ground* and discussions with fellow professors at local, national and international professional meetings in religion, philosophy and African Studies. This book represents another serious academic effort by an African scholar in philosophy, theology and ethics, to contribute to research and scholarship in these areas of academic interest. This work contributes some new research data, critical analysis and interpretation of the existing data in this previously neglected academic field.

I am also grateful to Vanderbilt University for giving me funds to carry out research at the Harvard Center for the Study of World Religions. However, this book is heavily based on original research carried out in Africa. These Research trips were carried out in 1982, 1987, 1992, 1994 and 1995. I am very thankful for Ohio Wesleyan University's funding for two of my recent research trips to Africa.

Without this essential support for research work in Africa, this book would not have been possible. Due to the unfortunate past Eurocentric White-supremacy and overt prejudice against Black Africa and its people, the Western academy has in the past also tended to denigrate Africa and its history, philosophy, religion, culture and languages. These were often derogatorily described as "primitive" and "pagan," and not being worthy of serious research or study. In religion, African Religion and culture were considered pagan, therefore, to be repudiated in favor of conversion to Western Christianity.

Whereas Western Christian and Arab Muslim missionaries tried to convert Africans to Christianity, and Islam, Africa was largely ignored by most Western scholars and researchers. As a result, with the exception of ancient Egypt (which was for many prejudiced Eurocentric scholars erroneously thought to be a European nation) and Ethiopia, little has been written on African metaphysics, ethics, ontology, and philosophical-theological anthropology which constitute the African material and background grounding. This African material is significantly important in the same way Karl Rahner's concept of the "Anonymous Christianity" is important for the book.

Equally important, and deserving of special acknowledgement and thanks, are my African informants and research assistants, particularly, those in East Africa where most of my field research work was carried out and most of the material was gathered. These include the Rev. Canon Wilson Baganizi, who was then the Provincial Secretary of the Church of Uganda for the special help and hospitality he rendered to me, when I went for research in Uganda. He showed me some private research material, made travel and accommodation arrangements for me comfortable when I could hardly afford them! I am also grateful to his kind wife for the warm hospitality which was generously extended to me as a guest in their home.

I am most thankful to Mrs. Mary Howard Smith for typing the original drafts of the manuscript, and Professor Dianne Harper for the invaluable hours spent in typing and proofreading the various versions of the manuscript. Riva Colvin, Mona Lisa Wellington, and Linda Dixon also deserve thanks for retyping and proofreading portions of the revisions of this book.

I am grateful to Beatrice, Joy, Grace, Gloria and Peace Twesigye for helping with various tasks regarding the manuscript in its several stages of development and revisions. These various tasks, include typing, proofreading and assembling the index. Gloria and Joy were kind enough to retype portions of this revision, and compile the index. I am grateful to them.

I am deeply indebted to Ohio Wesleyan University for supporting my research trips to Europe and Africa, in the summers of 1992 and 1994. The material obtained on these trips has been essential for the extensive revisions and rewriting of this book. Ohio Wesleyan also provided me with a computer and support which made this revision easier to carry out. For this institutional support, I am most especially indebted to Professor William Louthan the Provost, Dr. Kathryn Ogletree the Director of Student Minority Affairs and Professor Richard Fusch who is currently serving as an Associate Dean for Academic Affairs, for their support. Ultimately, I am truly grateful to all the people who helped in to make this book possible, even when their names are not cited.

Last, but not least, I am grateful to Trent Collier whose research paper appears in the appendix of this book. It is a good illustration of the best students whom I have had the pleasure to teach here at Ohio Wesleyan University, or supervise in their own independent study or honors' degree research projects. Trent's paper presents a good illustration for the universal validity of the concept of "anonymous Christianity" and supernatural salvation outside the Apostolic Church (*salus extra ecclesiam vs. extra ecclesiam nulla salus*), which is the central theme of this book.

Professor Emmanuel Kalenzi Twesigye
BA (Hons.); Dip. Th; Dip. Ed;
MA (Hons.); STM; MA & PhD

Department of Religion and Philosophy
and Director of Black World Studies,
Ohio Wesleyan University,
Delaware, Ohio, 43015, USA.

Summer 1995

I

INTRODUCTION

This book is both a major expansion and revision of the original work which was published in 1987 by Peter Lang. The revisions have taken into account the book reviewers' evaluations and comments. Three new chapters and two important appendices have been added. Most chapters have undergone major restructuring. As such, this book should be read as a new book, even when one has already read *Common Ground: Christianity, African Religion and Philosophy*, on which this present book is based.

The original basic material and central thesis have remained unchanged. Major revisions were made to the original work in order to strengthen some theological and philosophical arguments. This work also includes new additional collaborative and integrative global theological material in Appendix A. This appendix illustrates the universal validity of the central theological theory of the universal meaningfulness and application of "anonymous Christianity."

Ultimately, this work itself is a result of many years of serious research, and intense theological-philosophical reflection. The book has been primarily written for scholars, teachers, and advanced college students in the fields of Theology, Philosophy, African Studies, African-American Studies, African Traditional Religion, Ecclesiology, Missiology, Comparative Religion, Cultural Anthropology and Sociology. Subsequently, the language employed in this book is explicitly academic and technical in nature. Footnotes are intentionally extensive and very detailed in order to provide more information, and support. In some cases, there are sub-arguments in footnotes which could not be well covered in the main text of the book!

The notes are intended for the more serious reader who wishes to gain the maximum impact of the arguments in light of their total academic theological and philosophical context. However, I realize that some readers will find such a method of presenting the research data, argumentation and writing distracting or heavy. Nevertheless, this manner of writing was made necessary by the complex academic and controversial theological nature of the material discussed in this book.

The central arguments in the book, and the extensive footnotes along with some secondary sub-arguments in some notes, were also made in light of the highly sensitive theological Christian dogma of *"extra ecclesiam nulla salus"* (there is no salvation outside the [Roman Catholic] Church). Extensive notes were required to cite scholarship data, and substantiate arguments on this very controversial theological subject, and exclusive ecclesial dogma.

This religious bigotry is universal. Therefore, it is not limited to Christianity, Judaism and Islam. It is inherent in the universal tendency for most religions to teach mutually exclusive doctrines of God's grace, special election as God's unique people destined for heaven whereas others are destined for God's judgement, rejection and hell. This becomes self-evident when one defines hell as the exclusion from heaven or fellowship with God. nature of the central theme and thesis of this book.

I have also included long quotations from primary works not generally available to the ordinary readers. All this is done in order to provide sufficient support for positions taken on extremely controversial theological and the correlative moral or ethical issues. These are the ethical issues regarding the reality, and logic of the efficacious existence of God's universal salvation and God's kingdom, beyond the confines of the traditional Apostolic Christian Church.

In this theological and philosophical context, God's universal salvific will is positively viewed as being inseparable from God's essence as Creator-Redeemer or positive creativity, "Sola Gratia" and Agape. As such, God's activities of grace, agape and salvation, are both intertwined and inseparable from other God's free cosmic activities. This is impossible, since God's work and cosmic activities are mutually inclusive of one another, being twin activities of a single divine continuous process, namely, the unconditional creation and redemption of the cosmos and all its creatures.

This essential divine process of cosmic creation and redemption is carried out by God by virtue of God's own unmerited free and efficacious redemptive grace in the cosmic Logos as the eternal omnipresent Cosmic Christ and Agape, is positively explored and reaffirmed. Correlatively, God's universal free supernatural salvation is positively viewed as being inseparable from nature and history. That is to affirm that God's supernatural salvation is bestowed by God to creatures, everywhere in the world and its events.

In short, God's extraordinary purposes are ordinarily mediated to creatures through the world, nature and historical processes. The apparent natural processes in nature and the world are the authentic universal vehicles for the extraordinary and the supernatural or the divine.

The ordinary world, nature, human mind or moral agency and history are the divine arena of God's self-communication, revelation, grace, agape, and concrete temporal historical personal and societal processes, by which God is both working indirectly and incognito in the world. This divine indirect process of cosmic creation and redemption, appears to many secular human viewers as mere "the natural law," and to the scientists as "evolution." Nevertheless, to study nature and science is also to study God's work in creativity, order, complexity, mystery and efficacious revelation in nature.

Therefore, nature as the "*a priori*" ordered being as the cosmos (world or creation), biological evolution, the human community and history, are in this study positively portrayed as part of God's special process of creation and salvation in the world. Natural law, the human community and history are the concrete temporal ordinary and historical processes and events, through which God works incognito to effect his extraordinary events and special supernatural activities of creation and redemption.

The ordinary events and natural processes of life in the world are also both correlative and coextensive with God's special events and extraordinary processes of eternal life in the world. This is the essence of the Divine Incarnation into humanity, finite nature, culture, the world, history, time and space. God achieves this perpetual historical process of special divine Incarnation in the world and humanity by means of the Logos or Christ. Through the Logos and the Incarnation, God as the Cosmic Spirit, Force and Creative Energy, is efficaciously omnipresent, and also effectively, redemptively present everywhere, in the cosmos and its processes.

The ordinary or the natural instrument in the world is also the bearer or the divine vehicle, instrument and divine sacrament for the mediation of extraordinary and the supernatural. For instance, Agape, and authentic humanity is the incarnation of God in the world and historical processes. Likewise, the loving or agapic and harmonious community, anywhere in the world, regardless of whether, it is in traditional Africa, Native America, India, China, Japan, Saudi Arabia and Israel, is both coextensive and correlative with God's election, redeemed people, the Church of God in the Logos or Cosmic Christ, salvation and the kingdom of God.

To this end, God as the Cosmic omnipresent Creator, Sustainer and Redeemer, works patiently and incognito, through an apparently ordinary, everyday human events and processes of the family, the community or society, to create, redeem or positively socialize, humanize and fulfill each individual human being as his or her own adopted son or daughter (*imago Dei*), in the cosmos.

Everywhere, and in every human society, and in every age, God gratuitously works incognito in his unmerited universal free efficacious grace, unconditional love and freedom, to create, persuade and positively transform each human being into the very unique obedient, caring and loving human being, that he or she was uniquely created by God to become.

Therefore, just like in any well organized social community, such as that of bees and ants, in God's orderly community or the kingdom, each human being in the cosmos is positively viewed as having a special place in the world, and unique role to fulfill in God's eternal cosmic plan and divine providence. As such, each human being as a free moral agent, thinking, and problem solving complex creature, is both created unique by God in his own image and mystery.

Characteristically, the finite human being is also constantly redeemed by God from evil, particularly, in the form of chaos and hate. This evil includes dysfunctional self-destructive tendencies, negative self-image, ignorance, rebellion, hate, and existential anxiety or fear of premature death. In this respect, both creation and redemption are essentially linked together in a single process of creation and fulfillment as a God's historical correlative context of the uniqueness of his unfathomable essence of cosmic Agape, free grace and creativity and transcendent infinite mystery. Accordingly, each person is also valued and loved unconditionally by God. In return, God requires each human being also to value and love each human being unconditionally, as a fellow child of God or as a sister or brother in God's cosmic family.

Furthermore, since this process of divine creation and humanization is historically visible as universal process, subsequently, it will also be argued that God's free activity in both creation and redemption, is also universal free process. This divine cosmic creative-redemptive process takes place universally, by virtue of God's unmerited free loving grace. Therefore, both creation and redemption are presented as indivisibly correlatively intertwined universal twin processes of creation and continuing creation or transformation (salvation or redemption). This is God's process of "*kairos,*" creative and positively transforming "*Sola Gratia*" or "Agape."

In God's right time (*kairos*) and scope of grace, this process coincides with this historical, universal human phenomenon and self-consciousness as moral agents living in God's loving omnipresence and moral obligation to serve as responsible divine ambassadors and stewards of God's creation and the world. Consequently, divine salvation will be positively viewed, analyzed and presented as the ultimate divine process of creaturely positive fulfillment, completion of the creation or humanization process, regardless of wherever, and whenever this positive process occurs in cosmic history.

Subsequently, the authentic universal evidence, standard measure and criterion measure for divine salvation has been identified as "unconditional love for God and the neighbor." This unconditional love is required of all well socialized ("inculturated" or civilized), educated (informed in civic arts or skills and virtues), and humanized individuals (*homo sapiens*) as a prerequisite condition for complete self-actualization, fulfillment and divinization as a complete and humane human being as "*imago Dei.*"

This *theosis* or divine redemption as liberation from evil and human divinization or deification, is achieved anywhere in the world, both inside and outside the Christian Church, through the praxis of agape, under the inspiration and guidance of the Logos. The observance of Agape and its good works are universally redemptive, since to love unconditionally is, also to fully participate in God. This is the case, since God is himself, this creative, redemptive and divinizing Cosmic Agape and Infinite Transcendent Mystery. As such, Agape and good works are a universal criteria of an true holy path to God, salvation and heaven. Agape in this respect is an equivalent of the combination of "*karma yoga*" and "*bakti yoga*" within Hinduism and Buddhism or "*Li*" and "*Jen*" within Confucianism.

In essence, the doctrine of God's universal salvation in unconditional loving free grace is not new. It can be found both in the Old and New Testaments, especially in the teachings of Isaiah, Jesus, John and Paul. Some of the leading thinkers and famous Church Fathers, such as Justin Martyr and Origen taught this doctrine very explicitly whereas many others taught it implicitly.

The main trouble of teaching this doctrine implicitly, is a lack of systematic development of the doctrine and its serious implications for Christian theology, ethics, philosophy, ecclesiology and missiology. Fortunately, this doctrine of free supernatural salvation was taught by Karl Rahner (S.J.). He was a leading Catholic theologian until his death in 1984. Rahner taught this old doctrine under the ill-advised term of "anonymous

Christianity." He made it quite clear that he used this term for lack of a more inclusive appropriate Christian term.

Nevertheless, after considerable reflection, I have chosen to adopt Rahner's terminology and teaching, despite its shortcomings in some areas. I have employed Rahner's Christian teaching on "anonymous Christianity" as a radical representative of Western Christianity to non-Western religions and the non-Christian religions. I have also attempted to show how Rahner's criterion for "anonymous Christianity" is adequately met and fulfilled by some members of the African Traditional Religion, as represented by John Mbiti.

I have re-affirmed the Patristic Fathers' Christian teaching that God's free creative, redemptive and fulfilling process, was also efficaciously at work in pre-Christian and pre-colonial Africa, in the same way it was at work in ancient Israel before the ministry of Jesus of Nazareth.

Consequently, the central theological claim made in this book is that for Africans, the African Traditional Religion has the same kind of redemptive efficacy, fundamental societal moral value and validity which Judaism has for the Western Christian, and Islam for the Arab. Analogously, the African is akin to both a Jew and Arab who are shaped as such by their respective religions.

Apparently different religions, such as Judaism, Christianity, Islam, Buddhism, Hinduism and African Religion or various religious traditions, at a more religiously mature, transcendental unitive monotheistic universal ethical, spiritual, mental and redemptive effectiveness rooted in the same cosmic Logos (or pre-existent and Cosmic Christ) of the one cosmic Creator-Redemptive God.

Therefore, different religions and various religious traditions and just different paths (*ethos* and *yogas*) of responding to God's invitation of life; and various paths to God, life, ultimate meaning, happiness, Agape, forgiveness of sins, peace and salvation. God's free process of cosmic creativity, redemption and fulfillment is universal and inclusive of all God's people. Therefore, God's grace, salvation and heaven are not limited to any group of people in time or space. Consequently, in this work and theological objective, Africa and the Africans are only used studied in order to illustrate this global theological inclusiveness theory, and universal inclusive salfivic principle of God's unmerited universal free and efficacious revelation and redemption. Africa provides the best example, since in the past, it was always singled out as "the benighted continent," "pagan" and "primitive."

I have tried to remain objective and fair to the African Tradition even when I have approached this study as a Christian. However, the fact that historical Christianity is currently growing at a very fast rate in Africa, is good theological, religious and cultural evidence that the necessary adequate religious ground, has indeed, already been sufficiently prepared, by God's redemptive free grace in prior readiness for the Apostolic Church's explicit world Christian missions, and evangelization. As a result, Apostolic Christianity in its Catholic expression has become a meaningful fulfillment of the African Religion. "Inculturation" becomes the African Religion's process of expanding and adopting Christianity as its own new adaptation.

Nevertheless, this does not mean that unless, Africans convert to this new Apostolic Christian missionary Western based Church, they will be excluded from God's universal salvation and the kingdom. On the contrary, only, those who fail to abide by God's moral law and to produce the necessary good works of Agape and social justice, will be eternally condemned to damnation, hell and self-destruction, by their own unloving, negative and life-negating evil and antisocial deeds (cf. Matt. 5-7; 25:31-46; Jam. 2:1-26; 1 John 4:7-21; 1 Cor. 13; Rom. 1:17-32; 13:7-12).

Since creation and redemption are God's free unconditional cosmic activities, therefore, these divine activities are also universal in scope and essential nature. As such, supernatural salvation as obedience to God's invitation to accept a free gift for a fuller life and more fulfilling life salvation as a life in heaven on earth.

This heavenly life on earth requires human conversion from a mode of destructive evil or negative modes of life to a positive mode of unconditional love or agape and goodness. The human being is universally invited to repent of evil or sin. Therefore, God's Word/Logos is efficaciously omnipresent in the universe. The Logos-Christ is universally active teaching and leading men and women everywhere (John 1:1-6) into the narrow redemptive path of goodness, justice and the renunciation of the destructive evils of greed, selfishness, malice and hate (John 3:16-20).

This human moral or spiritual conversion and repentance enables human beings anywhere and in any era and religion or philosophical system, become God's redeemed saints, ambassadors and true vehicles of grace and redemption in the world. This positive response to God's universal offer of life, love, redemption and happiness redeems and empowers the imperfect and sinful human being to live in love with other people and damnation as opposite, can both effectively take place simultaneously in the world and inside and outside the Apostolic Church.[1]

In reality, both salvation and damnation represent two different voluntarily chosen concrete existential modes or paths (*yogas*) of life as measured by the nature and quality of social relationships, mental attitudes, nature of choices and deeds.

Ultimately, God does not judge and sentence one to damnation or hell. God as Agape of infinite universal unmerited redemptive efficacious grace, does not delight in sentencing people to damnation in hell or to such a predestination as Calvin and his followers erroneously taught. On the contrary, it is because human beings possess superior minds that they are thereby enabled to become cosmic and temporal agents of self-transcendence, causal freedoms and moral agency in the world. Because of intelligence and mind human beings have truly become the apex of creaturely biological evolution, thus becoming "*imago Dei*" or "*homo sapiens.*"[2]

When the ape (ordinary animal) spoke, it became human or a supernatural being (*imago Dei*). Speaking and story telling or abstract communication is the evidence of thinking and intellectual life. Therefore, to speak is also to become a divine being and a special adopted child of God, the Cosmic Speaker of the Eternal Word of life, creation and redemption (cf. Gen. 1:1-31; John 1-3). Therefore, as *imago Dei*, the human being, is the finite hearer of God's Word/Logos for both true humanization, mental or spiritual guidance, enlightenment and salvation. Logos, mind, thought and language are certainly the divine gifts implanted by God in human beings so that they could transcend themselves, and be enabled to hear God and become fully divinized into more God-like beings, which they all aspire to become (Gen. 3:1-24).

This affirmation is true in as much as language is rightly considered as the evidence and unique tool of human abstract thought, mind, knowledge, truth, self-consciousness, self-transcendence and communication with God and other people in the network of the linguistic and social community. Therefore, in this context, to think and speak is to be both human and divine or God-like (*imago Dei*). As such, both mind and language enable the human being to become an active participant in God's Word or Logos of creation and redemption. That is, human beings are essentially, co-speakers, co-creators and co-redeemers with God in this physical and evolutionary world.

As the "*homo sapiens*" or "*imago Dei*," all human beings have universally become effectively able to both efficaciously and consequentially determine their own personal eternal destiny and fate through their own actions. This is achieved by either choosing God's goodness and salvation or sentencing themselves to damnation and hell, by rejecting God's universal free offer of the gift of redemptive grace to live in unconditional love, forgiveness, peace, fellowship with the neighbor, respect for nature and the cosmos as God's own holy dwelling temple and kingdom.[3]

NOTES

1. Language as abstract and symbolic communication as seen in speaking or story telling is the evidence of creative or analytical thinking is the primary distinguishing mark of a human being. Abstract thinking and symbolic communication or language, set the human creature apart from the other animals, especially the higher primates such as chimpanzees and other apes. Animals lack the necessary mental, spiritual, moral, linguistic and self-contemplative capabilities for freedom, abstract thinking, self-consciousness, self-transcendence, religion and morality, apart from the natural programming for self-preservation, procreation and survival.

These mental capacities are present if a creature asks the ultimate universal self-transcendental and existential questions of life, and its ultimate value, source, destiny and meaning. According to Socrates, Plato, Aristotle, Augustine, Aquinas, Tillich, Whitehead, Rahner, Sam Keen, Mbiti and others, the ultimate universal questions of life include the following: Who am I? Where did I come from? Where is my existence heading? If or whenever these ordinary animals ask these kinds of profound ultimate questions of life and meaning, then they will cease to be mere animals. They have become supernatural (*imago Dei*). For a human being is a creature that possesses the capacity to ask these self-transcending questions (cf. Gen. 1:26-31).

2. Anthropology is the fundamental starting place for both African Religion and Christianity. Human beings are the temporal mirrors and mediators (*imago Dei*) of God in the material world. As a result, God himself has become a real human being in the Incarnation. See: Imbelli, Robert P. "Karl Rahner's *Itinerarium Mentis in Deum*" *Dunwoodre Review* 12 (1972), 76-91. McCool, Gerald A., S.J. "The Concept of the Human Person in Karl Rahner's Theology," *Theological Studies* 22 (1961), 537-562. Karl Rahner, *The Theology of Karl Rahner* (Albany, N.Y.: Magi Books, 1969). Rahner, Karl, "Theology and Anthropology" in Patrick T. Burke, (ed.) *The Word in History* (New York: Sheed and Ward, 1968).

From the *Theological Investigations*, see: "Philosophy and Theology," VI, 71-81; "Theology and Anthropology," IX, 28-45; "Philosophy and Philosophizing in Theology," IX, 46-63; "The Historicity of Theology," IX, 64-82; "Theology and the Church's Teaching after the Council," IX, 83-100; "Christian Humanism," IX, 187-204; "Man (Theological Anthropology)," IV, 365-370; "Person (Theological)," IV, 415-419; "Philosophy and Theology," V, 20-24;

This is God's prior gratuitous orientation of the human being in creation toward the supernatural destiny in the beatific vision. See Rahner: *Foundations of Christian Faith*, 75-80; "The Experience of Self and the Experience of God," *Theological Investigations* 13:122-132; *Hearers of the Word* (New York: Seabury Press, 1960), chs. 5 and 11; "The Existential," *Sacramentum Mundi: An Encyclopedia of Theology*, ed. Karl Rahner et al, (New York: Seabury Press, 1968-1970) 2:304-307. Rahner affirms that the human being is a spirit because of the intrinsic divine gifts or qualities of personal freedom and self-transcendence.

This spirit the human being is evolutionary, historical and a finite being because it is emergent in time and history.

3. See: Twesigye, *The Global Human Problem*, 75-134; Twesigye, *Common Ground*, 1-50; 110-170 and Sullivan, *Salvation Outside the Church? A Catholic History of the Doctrine*, 5-150. An analysis of the doctrine of *"Extra Ecclesiam Nulla Salus"* is central to this work. Rahner's doctrine of the "Anonymous Christianity" constitutes critique and rejection of ethnocentric, bigoted and exclusivist Christian traditional doctrine of *"Extra Ecclesiam Nulla Salus."* See also: Charles N. Bent, S.J. *Interpreting the Doctrine of God* (Glen Rock, N.J.: Paulist Press, 1968), 140-224. Rahner, *Inspiration in the Bible* (New York: Herder and Herder, 1966). Also printed in *Inquiries* (New York: Herder and Herder, 1964). Rahner and Joseph Ratzinger, *Revelation and Tradition* (New York: Herder and Herder, 1966). Rahner, K. *Kerygma and Dogma* (New York: Herder and Herder, 1969).

See also the *Theological Investigations,* "The Development of Dogma," I, 39-77; "Considerations on the Development of Dogma," V, 3-35; "Theology in the New Testament," V, 23-41; "What is a Dogmatic Statement?" V, 42-66; "Exegesis and Dogmatic Theology," V, 67-93; "Reflections on the Notion of 'Jus Divinum' in Catholic Thought," V, 219-243; "Scripture and Theology," IV, 89-97; "Scripture and Tradition," VI, 98-112. In the *Sacramentum Mundi,* see: "Bible (Theology)," I, 171-178; "Dogma," II, 95-98; "Development of Dogma," II, 98-108; "Dogmatics," II, 108-111; "Revelation," V, 342-355, 358-359.

II

PROLEGOMENA: AN OVERVIEW
OF CONTENT AND
PHILOSOPHICAL-THEOLOGICAL METHOD

This book is a major revision of the original work which was originally published in 1987. These revisions have taken into account the major scholarly book reviewers' comments, praises and criticisms.[1] However, the original central thesis has remained unchanged. Instead, arguments for the thesis have been strengthened.

1. The Primary Background and Broad Context
for this Philosophical-Theological Work

The original arguments which were considered to embody either major deficiencies or errors in the original work have been corrected according to the central thesis and what was thought necessary or appropriate. As a result, this work reads like a new and different book when compared to the original work. Nevertheless, the central thesis and the main arguments for it have remained the same. In addition, the original scholarly objectives for research and objective academic interpretation of existing data have also remained unchanged in this revised work.

Since it is difficult to achieve total agreement and consensus in matters of theology or philosophy, predictably some scholars and theologians both in the West and Africa, have appreciated the works of Karl Rahner, whereas others have not. Those who have appreciated the works of Rahner will also appreciate the choice as the respective primary representative spokesman for the mainline Western Christianity. On the African scene, Professor John Mbiti has been chosen as the respective spokesman for the African Religion and philosophy in Africa. Again, some African scholars may criticize this choice, since they may prefer some other scholar, such as Alex Kagame.

Some Western and African scholars have negatively viewed Rahner and his explicit universal methodological theological comparative and analytical approach as a theological handicap and weakness for this present work. This group and its criticism have not been taken seriously. This is because this group of scholars is also guilty of both implicitly or explicitly of fostering either the Western Darwinist form of White supremacy, or on the other hand, promoting a divisive destructive neocolonial form of African tribalism.

The tribalists affirm that there is no such entity as "Africa." For this group there is no "African culture," or "African Religion." Instead of speaking collectively of African people, these tribalist scholars positively affirm that one can only speak of the Yoruba people, the Hausa, Ibo, Baganda, the Zulu, Masai, Kikuyu, Luo and the Fulani.

This kind of African division, was in the African colonial past promoted vigorously promoted by the European colonial masters in Africa. This was part of their "machiavellian colonial policy of divide and conquer." It worked well. In the present neocolonial Africa, this policy and Western denigration of African material continues. African people and systems are negatively presented as being merely local and limited tribal cultural expressions.

Subsequently, the alleged African tribal systems are then, arbitrarily declared not being worthy of serious academic study or material for serious university or college course content. This is because they are misrepresented as being limited in scope, cultural relevancy, and academic value. In this manner, both the Western racist White supremacists, and the misguided ethnocentric African tribalistic scholars, have formed a convenient "unholy alliance." This alliance has resulted in the familiar trivialization of the African Religion as mere African religious forms of cultural parochialism, and tribalism by some Africanist scholars is repudiated as being fundamentally Eurocentric, ethnocentric, colonialist or neocolonialist, imperialistic, racist and disparaging to Africa.[2]

These cultural parochialists or tribalists and misguided Africanists have claimed that the African religious, philosophical or cultural content can only be truly studied in its narrow tribal cultural, historical, religious, and local social context, using tribal methods. As such, it can be affirmed that these Eurocentric and African tribalistic scholars are, either inadvertently or deliberately, divisive neocolonialist agents of both the Western White supremacy and African inferiority.

These kinds of scholars are also effective indirect agents of Western cultural or explicit religious missionary imperialism. It was this kind of Western or Eurocentric approach that resulted in the devaluation and denigration of the African Religion and cultures by the major and influential Western scholars and philosophers, such as, George Friedreich Hegel[3] and Arnold Toynbee[4] and their disciples.

These kinds of prejudiced, ethnocentric or Eurocentric, Hegelian and Darwinist White supremacist and racist scholars have generally tended to view Africa negatively as just a benighted or dark continent without any history or civilization of any value. As a result, it was either erroneously or falsely alleged by these Eurocentric scholars and historians that Africa had in reality "contributed nothing to world history and human civilization." Again, this was also partly due to the narrow understanding and definition of history, philosophy, religion, and civilization to refer only to the European or written texts.

As a tragic consequence, African history and civilizations which the Europeans found there, such as those in ancient Egypt, Nubia and Ethiopia one which predate the Western civilization was credited to the Greeks, and later to the Romans. This constituted academic fraud and falsification of African history.

Therefore, this erroneous misrepresentation of African history, civilization and religions, inadvertently led to the misrepresentation and falsification of the world history. Ironically, this moral evil and distortion of truth took place in the European academy, largely unchallenged even when the Jews (Hebrews) and the Greeks themselves, had been the pupils of the Egyptian scholars and masters in mathematics, philosophy, religion, medicine, natural sciences, including engineering and architecture.[5]

This Eurocentric or Western academic distortion of African history and led to other distortions of African material. The correlated historical truths affected the presentation of African religious truths from Alexandria in Egypt to the Cape of Good Hope in South Africa.

In time, both African and Western scholars were led to revise the historical truths to fit the new understanding of Africa or operating philosophy. As a result, in the eighteenth and nineteenth century, many Western scholars employed the new racist or Darwinist and White supremacist theories and Eurocentric paradigms of the new epistemological structures. Accordingly, many Eurocentric, White-supremacist, colonialist and neocolonialist scholars in Europe and America tried hard to deconstruct history from a Eurocentric perspective in order to justify both slavery and colonialism.

Inadvertently, this endemic Eurocentric, White supremacist and intrinsic racist quest for the revision of world history from a European perspective led to the invention of the ancient Egypt as a White and European nation. This position affirms that Egypt was occupied by the European people, even prior to the conquest of Alexander the Great in 322 BCE (before the common era or before the Christian Era), as an acceptable form of academic fraudulent distortion and even deliberate falsehood.

Understandably, many Africans and Afrocentric African-American scholars, such as Mulefi Asante, Josef ben Jochannan, Mulanga Karenga and Stanford Lewis are beginning to take serious offense at Eurocentric records and misinterpretations of African history, religion, philosophy and values. Characteristic of this Afrocentric school of thought is the following:

> If one is a critical reader, one can immediately see the reluctance of the author to admit that the facts have forced the scientific community to acknowledge that Afrikan humanity is the oldest currently known to science. But while popular journalism resists the truth, serious scholarship unequivocally affirms it. Says UNESCO: "The whole human race had its origin, just as the ancients [our Afrikan ancestors] had guessed at the foot of the mountains of the Moon" in the great lakes region of Central/East Afrika at the source of the Nile.
>
> "Africa was the main setting both for [humankind's] emergence as the sovereign species of the planet and for the development of political society. ... all the evidence suggests that the continent was the first - and indeed the principal - centre of human development." In addition, it "emerges from a great many studies that the blacks [the only humans on the earth at this time] came into being on the continent some 120,000 years ago...The 'whites' [who could only have come from "the blacks"] appeared on the planet much later - about 55 000 years ago."
>
> The total cultural impact of Afrikan genius and creativity in the world experience is both staggering and revolutionary. Many of the advanced ideas of our Kemite ancestors were created in a search for divinity or Amon ("the hidden one"). The Kemites believed that they would resurrect or "raise like Ra" into eternal life. Therefore, they prepared the body and its organs by embalming them. This technique was so advanced that contemporary science still has not solved the mystery of how it was done and what was used in this process. Likewise, the priests invented a 365-day calendar...is still used today. They created the calendar by watching the positions of stars, thereby establishing a calendar of absolute chronology about 4236 years ago.

Pharaonic Kemet, or the reign of the priest king, began about 3400 BCE (Before the Christian or Common Era). It brought political and national unity as well as the pyramid building age, which was made possible by previously accrued wealth. Imhotep (3200 to 3000 BCE), who is worshipped as the Greek god Asclepius, the god of medicine and healing, lived during this period. He is identified as the world's first multigenius. He lived 2500 years before Hippocrates, who is falsely called the father of medicine. The art of writing also evolved in Kemet in the Nile Valley region (it may have also simultaneously developed in the Levant). Diop maintains "the Egyptians taught writing to all the people they colonized, especially the Phoenicians who later carried it to Greece and through the Mediterranean in alphabetical form."

As an Afrocentric scholar, Stanford Lewis goes on to write as follows:

Both the development of a calendar and hieroglyphic writing allowed the Kemites to document the events and culture of their time. They established excellent libraries, and like all other civilizations, they developed folklore, mythology and theology, which was used then - as they currently are - for the "immortalization of their heroes and heroines and descriptions of the origins of their civilization." These are merely some of the many reasons that Afrikans must re-examine all ideas and concepts that are so "benevolently given" to us by white scholars.

For those of us who study both history as written by the Europeans, it becomes apparent that the writing on the history of ancient Kemet has constituted a cultural theft intended to denigrate the accomplishments and humanity of Afrikan peoples and to inflate the accomplishments and humanity of European peoples. Bernal makes this plain when he writes that even in the contemporary study of ancient Kemet "modern archaeologists and ancient historians of this region are still working with models set up by *men who were crudely positivist and racist* [emphasis is mine]."

Carruthers' response is to call for a thorough rejection of this historical falsification. "It is now time for us to stand on our own feet as men and women and see the world rightly constructed." This moral obligation for correctly reconstructing the world extends to Afrikan Americans. This is not merely to the study of ancient Kemet, but to every aspect of our history and existence. This is a mammoth task for people who believe that the very liars, cheaters, thieves and murderers who have established white hegemony are holy people of high moral caliber.

In fact, until Afrikan Americans can look at George Washington and Thomas Jefferson in the same way that Jewish Americans look at Adolf Hitler and Joseph Spengler, we as a people will not have assessed our story properly and we will, subsequently, remain mentally enslaved. And to be mentally enslaved is to be enslaved indeed.[6]

The Western invention of the "myth of Africa as a dark continent" was thought to be the ideal political and academic solution of this African dilemma in global history. It was invented to mitigate the cruel and tragic manner, in which Africa and its people had been, characteristically savagely treated by the Europeans.

This was self-evident in Western literature which had been written by prejudiced scholars, as well as in the history of the inhumane trans-Atlantic tragic commerce in her people, by the unethical, European materialistic and cruel slave-traders. Later, after the Europeans had stopped trading in Africans as human cargo and valuable slaves or cheap labor, the Europeans resorted to land-grabbing in Africa. This was done by those we now call colonialists, settlers and precious mineral prospectors.

However, this prejudiced Western ethnocentric or Eurocentric White-supremacist solution of the African problem and history, deliberately further harmed Africa by distorting African geography and history. For this purpose, the Eurocentric scholars invented a new view of mythical Africa. Accordingly, they divided a new mythical Africa into European Africa, north of the Sahara and another Africa south of the Sahara. Africa north of the Sahara was allegedly White and civilized. Conversely, Africa south of the Sahara was the impenetrable, Black and alleged to have been both historically and culturally permanently cut off from the north and therefore, uncivilized.

All forms of African civilizations, such as the presence of divine kingships in Uganda, and great empires in West Africa, were supposed to have diffused from Europe through Egypt. In this Eurocentric diffusion theory, ancient Egyptian civilization, was itself erroneously misrepresented and identified as White or European, both in its origin and basic nature. For that matter, according to this "hamitic myth" the Ethiopians, the Somalis, the Bahima and Batusi, who were the ruling classes in Eastern Africa, were generally affirmed to be Europeans in black skin.

These Eurocentric scholars could not accept the possibility that the reverse could be the case. For instance, these prejudiced Western White-supremacist scholars had great difficulty conceiving of the possibility of Africa being a civilized place or accepting the fact that all human beings and their civilization had actually originated in Africa.

Later, many of these biased academicians found it difficult to accept the scientific and archeological data which proved that humanity and civilization had first evolved in Eastern Africa. Human beings had evolved in Africa. As such, biblical "Garden of Eden," was actually in East africa. Human beings had evolved there by God slow process of human creation. Subsequently, these Africans as the original human beings, successfully created a basic human civilization which was later bestowed on the rest of the world, including religion, kingship, cattle-keeping and the humanocentric values.

Accordingly, humanity and human civilization originated around the lake Victoria in the interior of Africa, and flowed down along the Nile through Nubia, Egypt to the Mediterranean Sea and the rest of the world. Thus, the "Nile Civilization" is an African civilization and gift to the rest of the world. This includes Moses, strict monotheism and Judaism which he founded.

These theocentric-humanocentric values are community based and find maximum expression in the social moral obligation and practice of agape as unconditional love for the neighbor, since one's own meaningful existence, self-fulfillment, peace, well-being and happiness, are intrinsically intertwined with that of the neighbor and the community. The individual's fate, happiness, redemption and damnation take place within the community.

According to this African theology-philosophy, no human being ever gets saved without his or her neighbor. Nobody is ever saved outsider and apart from his or her community, and the world in which he or she lives. This is the case since the individuals and their own fate or destiny are inseparable from that of the neighbor, and the rest of the community.

Therefore, wholesome existence and well-being of the individual is contingent on the well-being of the community of which individuals are inseparably bound as integral members of that given community. This being as such, it then follows that, the destiny and fate of the community is also, both correlative and coextensive, with the fate and destiny of its respective constitutive individual members.

The reverse, is also the case. What happens to the individual member happens to the community. Conversely, whatever happens to the community, also happens collectively to individual members of that respective community. This is the case, irrespective of the individual members and their own personal moral or social condition.

Furthermore, as a result of the Eurocentric world-view and Darwinist or racist White-supremacism, all non-White or non-European cultures and religions, particularly, that of the Sub-Sahara Africans, were often deliberately distorted and misrepresented. This was sometimes done in order to make them fit the prevailing racial stereotypes or preconceived Darwinist notions and paradigms. This was also undertaken in order to justify the inhuman European history of violence against non-Whites, global imperialism, and other evil or cruel practices, such as those of the morally reprehensible slave-trade, cruelty of colonialism, and genocide in Africa, and America.[7]

To this end, the African and the Native American cultures and religions, were projected to the world as mere primitive relics of the past with no value for the world as forms of knowledge or relevancy for the civilized world. Tragically, therefore, in order for non-Europeans, such as Africans, Asians and Native Americans to be considered civilized, one had to become Christian, and westernized. For instance, one had to speak a European language, and correlatively, also to dress, eat and act like the Europeans.

As W.E.B. DuBois, Western educated Africans in French Africa and the Native Americans would soon discover, even this assimilation into the European culture (or White inculturation) would not in itself be considered an adequate qualification and guarantee for full acceptance by the Whites or the Europeans into their society with its privileges of power, wealth, civil rights and liberties. Tragically, despite the religious and cultural inculturation of the non-Whites, they remained unacceptable to the Whites on racial grounds. This was the case, since the skin pigment and hair texture could not be assimilated into the European looks![8]

Within this context, the misguided tribalizing or parochialist Africanist scholars are rejected and presented as destructive allies of the racist White-supremacists and cultural or religious imperialists, in the case of the missionaries. Within the Christian tradition, they are, both analogous and theologically, akin to the exclusivist and tribal Judaisers in the early Church who opposed St. Paul's more universalist and inclusive approach to the message of Jesus, as the Christ of God. The bigoted, "electionist," tribalistic, ethnocentric and misguided Judaisers erroneously saw Jesus as a mere Jewish Messiah whose primary divine liberation mission was to the Jews and their salvation.

However, in St. Paul's tireless fundamental divine mission and quest for the most meaningful universalization of Christianity, which was in his time still largely a Judaic tribal sect of Judaism, modified the message of Christianity and its essential audience. Consequently, he proclaimed Jesus as the Cosmic Christ of God whose primary mission was to save all humankind, regardless of tribe, nationality, culture, and creed or philosophy, beginning with the Jews (members of the Mosaic Covenant), and then, the gentiles (non-Mosaic Covenant members).

Therefore, in this book, I have deliberately adapted and followed the inspiring great Christian inclusive universalizing theological example of St. Paul. Subsequently, I have reaffirmed the central message and teachings of Jesus-Christ and his message for the modern world, using the Pauline example and inclusive paradigm (cf. Matt. 5-7; 25:31-46; Rom. 1-6; 13:8-12; 1 Cor. 13:1-14:1).

In this fundamental Christian philosophical-theological work, I have also elected to follow the early Church's Fathers' great scholarly examples. Remarkably, most of the great theologians or philosophically influential Patristic and other later Church Fathers and saints, such as Justin Martyr, Clement, Tertullian, Origen, Athanasius, Antony and Augustine were from Africa. It is self-evident that almost all these major Western Christian Fathers, theologians and philosophers, actually came from the ancient Alexandrian African Church in Egypt and North Africa.[9] This being the case, then, this work stands at the center of, both Western and African mainline Christian theological tradition.

Today, Judaisers are represented by the White supremacists, ethnocentric or racist Western colonialists. They are also equivalent to religious bigots and other cultural and religious imperialists. This has been more historically and concretely self-evident, in the case of some colonialist and tribalist African scholars who have rejected the idea of there being either Africa as a cultural region with any African systems, such an African Religion. These tribalistic people and scholars are also anti-pan-Africanism. They would argue that there is no identifiable or homogeneous cultural group, region or state, such as the Nigeria, Uganda, Ghana, Somalia, South Africa, Egypt or Kenya.

As we have already seen, for tribalistic Africanist group, one can not speak of African and Africans. For them, it is positively affirmed that one can only truly speak of specific African groups, such as the Zulu, Shona, Ndebele, Baganda, Ibo, Yoruba, Akan, Ashante, Banyoro, Kikuyu, Luo, Somalis, Masai, and Batusi. After all, for these kinds of African tribalists, God is both essentially conceived and affirmed as being the primordial human ancestor and Cosmic Father, God was also akin to the respective divinely "elected people." Consequently, God may also become tragically localized, tribalized and exclusively identified with the local people and their ethnic group. The Yoruba Orishas and pantheon of gods is a good example.

However, no academically sound African theologian or philosopher, would in good conscience, propose this kind of divisive narrow tribalism, xenophobia and absurdity. Nevertheless, these tribalist Africanist scholars almost convincingly argue that one should not collectively speak of the Africans, without any qualification, since there are no such people.

These kinds of tribalistic scholars also almost convincingly argue that, in reality there is no African cultural or racial homogeneous group in africa, which identifies itself as "African." They argue that there is no such a group of people, in Africa, which identifies itself being "the Africans." However, this is analogous to the category variously known as "American Indians" or "Native Americans." Just because Columbus erroneously called the people he found on this new continent Indians and just because they were recently referred to as Native Americans even when they never referred to themselves as such, does not mean that there is a group of people who are collectively referred to by those inadequate names or terms.

Furthermore, just because the Native Americans belong to different and diverse nations which variously call themselves names such as the Navajo, Cherokee, Hopi, Delaware, Cheyenne, Sioux and others, does not mean that they are culturally and ethnically interrelated. Despite these apparent superficial divisions and cultural diversity, the truth remains self-evident, namely, that all Native Americans, actually, share a common basic underlying unifying racial or characteristic cultural heritage that is recognizable as being uniquely Native American.

Indeed, for the Europeans, non-Europeans groups such as Africans and Native Americans, were considered to have identifiable common characteristics which transcended regions and local linguistic, cultural differences and diversity. This is also true for the Africans in the diaspora, especially America, where most of them are found outside Africa. Africans in the USA have recently decided to reaffirm their own common identity and historical heritage with Africa. This explicitly stated in their own positive process of historical and cultural self-consciousness development, and public self-identification with the African continent as the motherland by freely renaming themselves as "African-Americans," instead of "Negroes," "Coloured," "Afro-Americans" and more recently, "Black-Americans."

Analogously, just because these African people (in diaspora) did not call themselves Africans, that did not make them more American and less African. That is like fish may not know that it is actually fish, or that it actually lives in the water. However, that "invincible ignorance" does not change the fact that it is fish which is by given essential nature a water dweller.

Names of objects in themselves are sometimes not important, apart from the essence of the object, which they point and refer to. Some names are not intrinsic to the real essence of the object, since they mere conventional labels and price tags on merchandise, in a shop of life, or the world. For instance, Beethoven the "dog" would still be a dog regardless of whether you called it "dog," "god" or another name. Significantly, for the dog, the master is still known, and recognized and "loved" as its master and friend, despite the fact that the dog has no "name" for its master.

In traditional African cultural, social, religious, social, and political life, ethnic, tribal and clan identities still dominate and overshadow the Pan-African or African collective self-consciousness as Africans. Moreover, as the recent tragic example of military inter-clan conflicts in Somalia most clearly illustrated to the world, not even the same ethnic groups in Africa would almost exclusively identify themselves with their own primary clans, "tribes" or ethnic groups. As such, to the outsiders they may call themselves a local ethnic or tribal name, such as Somalis, Kikuyu, Luo, Chewa, Ngoni, Fulani, Ewe, Ashante, Kru, Baganda, Banyoro, Zulu, Yoruba, Ibo, Akan or Masai.

However, for most Africans the most preferred form of identity, essentially, remains with that of kinship of the extended family, village or the parochial community and clan. As such, the non-tribalizing, inclusive, and African epistemological universalization of knowledge and other kinds of pragmatic Pan-Africanism would cover any and all groups of Africans in Africa and in the diaspora or abroad in Asia, Europe and America. That is any true Pan-African systems of knowledge, ideas, cultural practices, religion and philosophy can be validly affirmed to transcend the local tribal or ethic group, linguistic borders, regardless of state, regional cultural sameness or affinity.

In reality, true Africanity transcends the superficiality of the current state boundaries. These were externally imposed on Africa by the former European colonial masters as they divided the continent among themselves without any regard for the well-being of the Africans or the natural African linguistic or cultural lines for borders. Therefore, the present African political boundaries do not reflect any naturally binding ethnic, cultural, linguistic, religious, historical and epistemological homogeneity.

Likewise, these borders are no serious barriers to a pan-Africanist unity. This includes African religious, philosophical, political and economic positive and inclusive redefinition and reconstruction of the Africa. This pan-African process has to be undertaken as part of the "vision quest" and search for true African spiritual, moral, economic and political liberation and rehabilitation. Therefore, this process cannot occur if it follows those enslaving, self-negating and alienating colonial and externally imposed alien modes on thinking and negative mental conditioning of the African minds and history from the European ethnocentric and a White supremacist perspective.

If one accepts the latter colonial or neocolonial Eurocentric paradigm for Africa and the rest of the non-Western world, then, it follows that everything would have to be measured by the European standards including culture, language, religion, philosophy, values and societal systems.[10] Tragically, this has disastrously happened both in the colonial and precolonial Africa.

In this prevailing Eurocentric world-view and measure of things, the more alien a person, culture, idea, value system or religion is to the European systems, the less developed, inferior and more primitive that person's cultures, ideas, values and religious systems, were judged to be. As a result, the more liberal and philanthropic French, followed a colonial policy of education, civilization and assimilation of their colonial subjects, including the Africans. This was in contrast to the more racially conscious and prejudiced British who believed in Darwinism and the inherent racial inferiority of non-Whites, particularly, the Africans. The French believed that the Africans were true human beings who could be truly "civilized and humanized" by being assimilated into the French culture with its language, values and Christian religion!

Whereas this French colonial policy of assimilation was benevolent, and grounded in good intentions it was misguided. This is because, it rested on the rejection of African people and their cultures as primitive. As a truly cultured African, the African was devalued as a human being in as much as he or she remained an adherent of the African culture and religion. For such misguided White-supremacist and Eurocentric cultural and religious imperialists, and Western Christian missionaries in Africa, the local African cultures and religion were condemned as outdated heathen relics of the primitive and pagan past from which to be delivered in God's holy name and superiority of Western redemptive religion or Christianity.

For the French, the African mission of civilization, redemption and divine salvation consisted in the Europeanization and Christianization of Africa. Africans had to be given a French education. They were supposed to be converted to Christianity along with its Western dualistic values.

On the other and, for the Protestants, missionary work in Africa meant the inculturation of the Africans in the victorian European values, which were grounded in sexual asceticism and puritanism. Later, this Protestant sexual puritanism clashed with African Religion and culture, which positively sanctioned sex and polygamy, as God's life-giving and life-enhancing special gifts of love and therefore, essentially good and sacred. Therefore, since for the traditional African, an active sex life, many children and multiple spouses were positively considered to be God given gifts, and special blessings, subsequently, these perceived divine gifts were to be positively socially and religiously celebrated. They were to be truly enjoyed within the guidelines established by both God and the local society.[11]

Nevertheless, the African society was enriched with the great natural diversity of cultures and religious practices. Remarkably, in precolonial Africa, no African culture or religion ever claimed to be superior to that of the other people, so as to require missionary work to convert the other people.

Given lack of modern technology and the limitations of local transportation, Africa accepted the primacy of local identity based on extended families, clan and "tribe." As a result, local identity and affairs became the prevailing microcosmic representations of society, the cosmos, God and his kingdom. Despite this prevailing African parochialism as epitomized in tribal or ethnic identity, kingdoms or the community such as the Masai one, as the arena of God's primary activities and meaningful human fulfillment, there is also an awareness and acceptance of cultural human diversity as God's work in the world.

Subsequently, and probably more than any other racial group in the world, the Africans are aware of languages and cultures pluralism, since they often come into contact with people of different languages, customs and values which exist across the neighboring mountains, rivers or lake. Just like the diversity of animal and plant life is God's holy work, and divine gifts to the world, based on the folk stories told in many parts of Africa, many Africans also positively view, both the human cultural and linguistic pluralism and diversity, as gifts of God. The more sophisticated ones are aware that these differences have come about as the results of migrations over vast distances or due to prolonged human isolation of one group of people from other people, due to the natural barriers of mountains, forests, or across the rivers, lakes, seas and deserts.

As a result of this traditional African pragmatic ethnic parochialism and tribal isolation, for the traditional Yoruba of Nigeria, the Muganda or Kikuyu of East Africa may feel actually as foreign or at home as the Ibo. Yet, the Ibo lives only next door from Eastern Nigeria and south of the cattle keeping Muslim Fulani from northern Nigeria. Significantly, these people coming from different African ethnic groups would have to speak to one another in English, which a foreign colonial language. This is necessary in order to communicate with one another, even when they are all Africans and non-English! But, speaking English does not make them less African.

Therefore, these English-speaking Africans are generally more at home with one another than with an English person whose language they have borrowed or adopted in order to communicate with one another! As a result, the English language or French is the conventional medium of the African message, education, African cultural content, self-consciousness, meaningful self-examination, values, religion and philosophy within the Pan-African and global academic or universal context.

However, in this context and perspective, the foreign language is not part of the primary African cultural content or the message. Despite the universal usage of foreign languages in the research and study of African Religion and philosophy, the African languages truly remain the essential tools and inseparable intrinsic component parts of the African content, religion and philosophy. As such, some key, African words, such as "*NTU*," "Katonda" and "*Ozovehe*" have been retained.

Accordingly, some of these important African words have been employed in this book to fulfill that essential cultural, epistemological, theological and philosophical function. These words are used in the same way that many Western scholars employ Latin and Greek languages in order to go back to the essential root meanings of some important theological or philosophical concepts.

In this respect, Greek or Latin has no more religious intrinsic holiness or theological validity, relevance, truth value or academic sophistication than the African Bantu languages employed in this work. The primary cultural and epistemological function of language is just that of serving as a conventional societal system of symbols for the purpose of coding and decoding information. In short, language is a channel and vehicle of personal and societal communications.[12]

Therefore, in contradiction to Ludwig Wittgenstein's linguistic ontological claims, for the Africans, language is a human created imperfect channel of communication as opposed to being reality in itself. On the contrary, language itself is the local or international societal conventional symbol and channel for the abstract or intangible mental reality of which it is the conventional mental and societal symbol.

Subsequently, apart from holy silence, there is no definitive or universal divinely revealed holy or special language or culture. Therefore, Hebrew,

Latin, Arabic, Greek, Sunscript and King James English may have been languages of holy scriptures an liturgy, but these languages are not special or God's sacred languages and divinely preferred linguistic media for religion or more acceptable modes of worship. Ultimately, all cultures, languages and religions are mundane as well as sacred expression of both humanity and the divine.

Language and religion along with their respective inseparable correlative cultures, are essentially part of the ongoing, universal, coextensive process of human intellectual evolution, mind, mental abstraction, thinking, and creativity. As human creations, all languages are finite, local, culturally conditioned and imperfect. As such, all languages and cultures are imperfect vehicles for God's revelation, truth, knowledge and human worship.

To some degree, God speaks both personally and universally to all his people everywhere in the cosmos. God speaks uniquely, and personally through their own human language, culture, religion and scriptures. This is the ultimate universal message of the "good news" and primary meaning of the divine Incarnation in both humanity and correlatively, also the coextensive human history. Each human being can therefore, hear God speak personally from within his or her own language, culture, condition, history and unique experience.

In this respect, Latin has no advantage over English, French, Swahili, Luganda, Yoruba, Ibo, Zulu, Hindi, or Japanese, as a special medium for Christian worship, the liturgical celebration of the holy Mass or the Eucharist and theology. Likewise, in Islam, Allah can be validly worshipped in Swahili, Luganda, Luo, Zulu, Ibo, Fulani, Yoruba as in Arabic. There is no human culture or language that is "ever more holy" or "purer" for the worship of God than any other given human culture or language.[13] To claim otherwise is mere ethnocentrism and bigotry, which underlie much of the Western global cultural and religious imperialism.

Consequently, cultures, religions, languages and their correlative and co-extensive constituent "man-made" or conventional systems of symbols are relative and imperfect. They are only useful and effective to the degree and acceptable practical extent to which they both most conveniently or relevantly embody and convey the message most accurately and meaningfully. This being the case, then, it also follows that there is no human language, which is in itself, is better than another one. However, languages differ and can be judged on the basis of their capacity for function in the work place and society in general. For instance, languages can be judged as vehicles, modes and media for functions, or capacity for better symbolization of complex ideas, scientific data or clear instructions for performing complex tasks with precision.

Subsequently, like human culture, language is ever in a perpetual fluid state of being created, refined, reshaped, re-tooled and revamped. Ultimately, both culture and its correlative language or complex living medium for self-consciousness, self-reflection, thought, ideas and communications, exist in the living process of ongoing creation, growth, transformation or redemption and change. This ongoing process of creation and transformation of both the human culture and language, does not to take place in a vacuum. The processes occur "*sui causa*" in correlation to the human evolution, and sophistication in both mind and level of technological skills.

The historical processes for the evolution and creation of culture, language and religion, and their transformation are inseparably intertwined concurrent processes. This is because culture, language and religion are both correlative and co-extensive with the development, growth, and changes in human evolution, history, experience, geographical location, climate, education, technology, ideas, knowledge, trade and cross-cultural interaction.

However, since the usage of language is intrinsically fundamentally cultural, social, and political, as well as being a moral choice, therefore, one has to be careful with his or her usage of language. Language and its usage have great implications for the speaker and the hearers of the eternal cosmic "Word of God" (Logos-Christ) or the divine message. Therefore, the speaker has to become consciously aware of the primary message, objectives for the message, the target audience or intended recipients of the message. This context can give the speaker the appropriate criteria, and moral or in this case, the theological basis for his or her choice of language for communication, especially when he or she can speak several languages.

In its verbal and non-verbal usage, language both implicitly and explicitly reveals the intrinsic speaker's identity, status, power, mind, creativity, values and personality. Therefore, to speak is not only to be like God (*imago Dei*), but also to become the true temporal co-creator and co-redeemer with God. To utter the "Word of God" (Logos), and speak good words of love, kindness, peace and positive life-affirmation, is also to participate in God's cosmic processes of creation and redemption.

Through the act of language, and speaking the Word of God (Logos), like God in primordial creation, the human or divine author or speaker of the word, inevitably initiates and sets in cosmic motion either a positive chain of creativity or the negative power of chaos and destruction (cf. Gen.

1:1-31; 3:1-12:6). Therefore, to speak or write is to participate in God's primordial Logos and his divine processes of cosmic creative and redemptive power. This divine cosmic gift of Logos in the form of creative and redemptive power which can be positively appropriated, and effectively employed by all human beings as "*imago Dei*."

Ultimately, God's Word or Logos of life, Agape, wisdom and virtue is a potent universal free gift of God. It has been indiscriminately, freely bestowed by God, on all human beings, everywhere in the cosmos, as an intrinsic part of his inseparable twin cosmic activities of creation and redemption. This is God's gratuitous cosmic work of "*sola gratia*" and agape. Therefore, it is both universally and eternally unmerited, and non-negotiable by any human beings. God's unconditional universal activities of grace in creation and redemption can only be accepted in love, joy and thanksgiving. This human acceptance of God and his or her works finds its best positive expression in acts of explicit faith in God, worship, and obedience to agape and God's moral laws.

However, in practice, some individuals, groups of people or nations have from time to time tried to tap into this power and attempted to both amass, and harness it, in order to use it at the expense of the other people in the world. Modern examples include Adolph Hitler and Idi Amin. The ancient Hebrew prophets and Jesus, like many benevolent African medicine-persons and priests, used this cosmic intrinsic divine imminent power for God's purposes in the world.

In general, the culture, religion, and language of the most dominant group or person becomes adopted by the less powerful groups of people or subjects in self-defense and survival mechanism as the most preferred standard and measure of values. Correlatively, the most culturally, politically, economically and militarily dominant group's native language, becomes adopted as the "*lingua franca*."

Likewise, the religion of the most dominant group is also generally proclaimed as being, also both correlatively and co-extensively superior to that of the less powerful groups of people. For instance, the English king's or queens's versions of the English language became the universal standard and measure of the true usage of the English language for all the people in the British empire and territories, all over the globe.

To this end, Kings Henry VIII and James of England, Adolph Hitler of Nazi Germany and Idi Amin of Uganda, provide us with some of the best examples of how the power and influence of the most powerful person or group of people can shape and transform culture, language and religion in society and the wider world. The fact that the English were at one time the most economically, politically and militarily dominant ethnic or linguistic group in the world, by their power they made English the major international language.

This being the case, then, English is not any better than Swahili or Yoruba, as a language for this work. However, English speakers wield more military, political, economic, academic, religious, cultural and philosophical power in this world, and therefore, it is more appropriate to use the English language, in order to reach the appropriate audience. This audience is composed of the wider international academic community in Africa, America, Asia, Canada and Europe.

In this unique state of African affairs, there is the unconscious tendency to identify nationhood and cultural identity with ethnic grouping along the tribal or clan lines. Tragically, this has also unconsciously resulted in the denial and rejection of the intrinsic trans-cultural, religious, racial and philosophical commonality shared by all Africans on the continent or in the diaspora.

Therefore, despite the serious complexity of the apparent African cultural, and linguistic differences, pluralism and diversity, it is still obvious to a keen external well trained wholistic observer of African affairs that in reality there are identifiable African racial, cultural, religious, philosophical and epistemological characteristic unity which transcends regional distance, ethnic grouping, language and colonial experience. In some cases, tribalist Africans have first to travel abroad in Europe or America in order to discover this basic truth, namely, that they are all essentially "Africans."

Some pan-Africanist Scholars and leaders, such as W.E.B. DuBois, President Kwame Nkrumah of Ghana and Professor Ali Mazrui, have been among the most vocal commentators and writers on this important subject.[14] For that matter, those scholars who have rejected either DuBois' or Mazrui's inclusive pan-Africanist unitive approach to Africa, her people, culture, ideas, history, religion, philosophy and values, will also inevitably find objectionable both the universal or pan-Africanist methodological approach, and universalization of African theological-philosophical ideas, which are positively represented in this book.

It is true that the term or name "Africa" is an artificial Eurocentric invention, but that is not unique. Names evolve are given by those who wish to name or talk about the object of reference. This is one function of language, and all the terms or names we use were given or invented by someone.

Language itself is just a series of conventional codes to encode and decode information or meaning. It does not matter whose codes are used. What matters in communications is the correct information and meanings are conveyed from the speaker or primary originator of the message to the target audience or intended hearers of the message; and that the original message is properly and correctly decoded without any distortions or background noise interferences. As such, although language is culturally and historically conditioned, with due care, it can be reliably employed to communicate cross-cultural information, truths, knowledge and values.

Therefore, I will employ the English language to translate, discuss and communicate to my fellow Western and African scholars, the primary African ideas which are found in traditional African theology, philosophy and religion, and show how they relate to the Western Christian ideas of Christ, Logos, Agape, grace, revelation, salvation, true humanity, the saints, an acceptable redeemed life of virtue, happiness and God's kingdom.

In pre-colonial or traditional Africa, "Africa" was not a form of reference in respect to culture, skin color, race or identity. That is to say that in traditional Africa no Africans identified themselves as the "Africans." This is not unique to Africa. The Europeans themselves did not identify themselves as "Europeans" until they came into contact with non-Europeans. These ancient Europeans, like the ancient Africans, just referred to themselves by their own villages, towns, manors, and farms. Later, they also identified themselves by their own kingdoms and languages, such as "English," "French," "Spanish" and "Italian."

Obviously, when the other groups began to learn to speak the foreign languages as requirement for foreign relations, diplomacy and trade, identity began to be more defined in terms of birth and ethnicity. This form of self-identification or identity was later extended to include color, race, culture, ideology and religion. For instance, in twentieth century America, if you were identified either as "communist" or "atheist," you were generally treated as being both a moral and religious deviant and as a public enemy of the nation.

Traditionally, Africans primarily identify themselves by family kinship, then followed by the clan, tribe, linguistic or ethnic group. In this context, nation is more akin to ethnic group and state. Accordingly, modern African states are not nation states nor empires. They are mere Western colonial political artificial construction.

However, this alien and European colonial political partition and reconstruction of Africa has taken on an African perspective and a strained measure of local or regional African identity. The colonial African states have remained the main frames of power and self-identity despite strong tribal or ethnic feelings which have threatened the existence of such states as tribal violence and wars in Nigeria, Liberia, Uganda, Rwanda, Kenya, South Africa, Sudan and Ethiopia have tragically demonstrated.

Nevertheless, despite the explicit or self-evident African diversity and cultural pluralism, on the more underlying African fundamental cultural level, there is both an implicit and explicit African cultural unity and inter-regional cultural continuity. This basic general cultural and historical unity and continuity stretch from Egypt in the north to South Africa in the south; Somalia in East Africa to Liberia in West Africa.

As result, the Africans, generally, share more in common many primary or fundamental characteristic universal African non-dualistic, wholistic, cultural, religious, philosophical, racial, historical, political, psychological and behavioral similarities or world-view than they share with their White-supremacist European colonizers.

In general, the European colonizers of Africa were White, Christian, philosophically dualistic, Greek-based, materialistic and greedy for quick gain, and other forms of wealth. Tragically, this excessive Western greed and materialism also led to tragic, and morally reprehensible practices of fraud and genocide. These evils were committed in quest for land, minerals in places like Kenya, South Africa and Rhodesia (Zimbabwe).

In the light of the above phenomena, I will treat Africa both as a cultural and religious unit, despite their distinctive cultural diversity and tribal linguistic pluralism. As such, African unity consists in its characteristic, unique constitutive tribal and ethnic diversity. That is, Africa is an inclusive diverse, flexible cultural and religious umbrella that encompasses many different constitutive cultural and religious elements which have shaped it and continue to shape it into the very unique continent that it is. That is an African continent which fully accepts and recognizes as her own, the various different races of people that it has given birth to.

This unique African diversity of races includes not just Black people, but also the Arabs, Whites and others, as permanent natives and citizens of that continent. In the same way, parts of what are considered to be Western, namely, Jewish, Greek, Arab and Asian religions and philosophy, particularly, Christianity, Judaism and Islam are also traditionally linked to Africa through Moses, Muhammad, Athanasius, Tertullian, Cyprian and Augustine.[15] Consequently, these religions are inseparable from Africa. As such, there are groups of Africans, such as the Falasha in Ethiopia and the

Bayudaya of Uganda, which have traditionally claimed to be Jews and to practice some Africanized version of Judaism and the Mosaic Law.

For that matter, Christianity has been in Africa, shortly, after the Christ-event in Jerusalem. However, African Christianity in having produced great theologians such as Clement, Origen and Athanasius at ancient Alexandrian University in Egypt; and Tertullian, Cyprian and Augustine, in North Africa, later disappeared because of the Islamic invasion in 641 CE. Islam was more willing to become more African and less foreign in its outlook and practices. Egyptian, Nubian, and Ethiopian Christianity became so Africanized and tribalized as "Coptic," that it became part of the African non-missionary traditional religion.

Therefore, as both a Western and a post-modernist pan-Africanist Christian theologian and philosopher, the author rejects the colonialist and neocolonialist isolation of the African Religion from the global arena of God's gratuitous interrelated and inseparable cosmic activities of uncondi-tional love and unmerited free grace both in creation and redemption. To reject the cosmic, historical, metaphysical and universal theological truth, as the true starting point of an truly global and inclusive Christian theology, will inevitably lead to the kind of religious divisions and theological bigotry which have characterized the world, since the time of Moses.

Human sins of hubris, tribalistic or cultural ethnocentrism, and exclusiveness or claims to God's special election; claims of the scriptural, theological or papal infallibility and special divine favors are responsible for most tragic forms of human religious divisions and bigotry. This includes the different competing religions, denominationalism, mutual hate, and exclusions of one another from life, the community, God's presence, and heaven. This religious division, mutual hate, rivalry and religious intoler-ance have negatively resulted in hell on earth, instead of God's salvation and his kingdom.

Consequently, God's world and the human history are filled with "hellish" and destructive acts of violence, war, intolerance, hate and cruelty, which are tragically perpetrated in God's holy name. In right-wing Augustinianism and Calvinism this has manifested itself in the form of the fundamentalist doctrines of God's limited, grace, conditional love, favoritism and election.

Sin does not permit human beings to perceive the holy and impartial Cosmic loving God as a non-divided holy cosmic transcendent Creative and Redemptive Agapic reality or divine Spirit. Instead, universal human endemic sins of greed, selfishness, division, hate, favoritism, exclusiveness are anthropomorphically ascribed the holy transcendent God. Then tragically, these human evils are then projected into essence, as the origin and sanctioner in the form of human conditional election and the familiar Calvinist dogmas of double predestination.

This is the kind of ill advised theological, ethnocentric and culturally conditioned erroneous colonial mentality that corrupts the true revelation of God, as an essentially impartial Agapic Cosmic Creative and Redemptive Spirit or Energy that creates and energizes all life and human beings, everywhere, without any prior conditions or favoritism. It is the human sin of hubris, exclusiveness, greed, selfishness, egocentrism, racism, tribalism, bigotry, xenophobia, ethnocentrism, and self-deification that give credence to human sins of finitude and failure to love others without any condition that get projected on God's own essence, and universal truth and basic revelation of God in scriptures and religions.

Obviously, this corrupt understanding of God as a finite and partial being who does not love all his creatures equally and without any prior conditions, leads to the rejection of non-Christian, and therefore, non-Western religions of the world as being truly revelatory of God, and redemptive. In Africa, this has very inadvertently, both negatively and destructively, resulted in the study of African Religion not as a revealed religion cable of redeeming the African, but as a mere form of African cultural anthropology, magic and witchcraft. In this colonial process the African Religion is divided along the cultural and linguistic lines, so as to bring out the mere essential cultural parochial tribal rituals and primitive heathen superstitious practices.

This approach should be positively perceived as an appropriate attempt at the overdue theological venture and delicate task for the universalization of African theological content, into a mainline academic, global Christian theology. The same academic rigorous methodologies, and scrutiny for both truth claims in respect to content and validity of conclusions, should also be brought to bear on this theology, in the same way it is applied on the other kinds of theologies. In other words, traditional Western theological methods should be appropriately redesigned and modified or "re-tooled" in order to be also relevantly applicable to African theology if it is both sound and academic in both approach and content.

Ultimately, this book represents a deliberate venture in global theological universalization of both African theology and its academic significance. Therefore, such a methodological universalization of tribal African concepts should be positively viewed as a positive epistemological and theological strength as opposed to the colonial and neo-colonial devaluation, tribalization and trivialization of African Religion and theology.

2. The Academic Style of Writing

This is an academic book which has been written for scholars and advanced college students or other interested serious readers. The language, content and style of writing are designed to meet that primary objective.

The introduction and conclusion have been rewritten. Two chapters have been added to the original work. Some chapters have undergone some major restructuring, whereas others have only undergone minor revisions and modifications.

However, the basic material and central thesis remain unchanged. Revisions were needed to make some arguments clearer and stronger. This revision has also some new additional collaborative material in the appendices. The material was researched and written by Trent Bryce Collier. The material was written as papers for fulfillment of the requirements of my courses in theology, under my supervision and direction. It adds new insights into the basic theological theme of this book.

This book is a result of many years of serious research and reflection. It has been written primarily for scholars, teachers, and advanced college students in the fields of Theology, Philosophy, African Studies, African-American Studies, African Traditional Religion, Ecclesiology, Missiology and Comparative Religion. Accordingly, this is an academic and technical book in both its content and terminologies.

This is also is a book in contemporary, global, systematic Christian theology and philosophy. Africa which has been largely previously ignored by Western scholars, including both the theologians and philosophers has been employed as the main example of this inclusive post-modernist global Christian theology. As a result, the book has been both ambitiously designed and written as a scholarly contribution both to Western and African theology and philosophy.

The book has been written from a Christian Logos-Christological perspective, and post-modernist, inclusive epistemological view of global, theological and religious pluralism, as God's will. Ethnocentric, universalist monolithic theological structures, and Christian claims to exclusive possessions of God's definitive redemptive revelation are repudiated as forms of Western cultural religious White-supremacy, cultural and religious imperialism in non-Western cultures, such as Asia, Africa and among the

Native Americans. Nevertheless, the main area of focus is Africa, because Africans were for so long treated as primitive "pagans," and as people without religion, even when nobody described them as being "atheists!"

Since this is an academic book, which has been written primarily for scholars and advanced students, therefore, the language employed is also explicitly academic and technical in nature. The original extensive footnotes have been kept in their original format. They were originally deliberately written in this very detailed manner, in order to provide more information, support and even sub-arguments not covered in the main text of the book!

Therefore, the notes should be read carefully along with the text. I realize that some readers will find such a method of writing disjointed and distracting. However, this manner of scholarly approach and writing style has been adopted in order to deal more adequately and competently with the very complex nature of the material and content of this book.

Extensive footnotes and sub-arguments in the notes were also made in light of the highly sensitive theological Christian dogma of *"extra ecclesiam nulla salus"* (there is no salvation outside the [Roman Catholic] Church).[16]

I have included some long quotations from primary works not generally available to the readers. The main purpose of these quotations is to furnish the necessary outside detailed academic evidence of secondary arguments in support of my central thesis, and position on these very controversial, sensitive, theological, dogmatic and the correlative or coextensive moral or ethical issues.

3. The Theological and Philosophical Scope of the Book

This book represents a serious Christian theological-philosophical post-modern Africanist effort to deconstruct Christian systematic theology and reconstruct it more meaningfully. This task is essential in order to liberate traditional Christian theology from its antiquated soteriological and exclusive sacramentalist system. This venture is also desirable in order to liberate theology from its outdated systematic, sectarian, Eurocentric Western, elitist and xenophobic Christian theology and positively reconstruct it in an inclusive, global and evolutionary manner.

By this method I will be able to demonstrate that both cosmic creation or generation and sustenance as both redemption and fulfillment or completion are God's quintessentially interrelated Agapic simultaneous and coextensive twin gratuitous cosmic processes of God. Both processes take place within God himself, as both the arena, ground, playwright and chief actor in this divine cosmic drama (cf. Acts 17:28: "God is the dimension and reality in which we both exist and have our being.")

In other words, both creation and salvation or redemption are inseparable correlative and coextensive free cosmic activities. That is to affirm that wherever God's processes of creation take place, there also is the presence of God's free cosmic redemptive agape and free grace at work actively engaged in the creation process persuading free, intelligent and moral creatures to choose those options in life that bring the best or maximum positive results. This also implies that it is the vehicle or mode of human existence that best facilitates a practical agapic way of life, that is most satisfying personal and societal meaning fulfillment, peace and well-being.

As an intrinsic free moral agent and obedient participant in God's concrete or temporal and yet, ever ongoing supernatural cosmic process of creation and salvation, the human being everywhere as a moral agent is ever invited by God to make concrete free moral positive choices and to do good works as a contribution to God's temporal processes in which the human being as a moral agent is a co-creator and co-redeemer with God. Therefore, the positive moral and redemptive choices are those made in faith in God's agapic goodness, creation and the sacredness of all life, both human and non-human.

Accordingly, these God-centered and agapic redeeming choices and redemptive good or agapic humanocentric actions are those which are made in the intention and spirit of Agape. Consequently, when these agapic moral choices are positively and diligently correctly acted upon, one's good actions or deeds, should also both correlatively and coextensively lead to positive results and goodness. This includes the enhancement of life, love, health, peace, happiness and both personal and societal harmony and well-being. This positive state of human existence is positively affirmed to be constitutive of God's concrete supernatural salvation and the kingdom of God on earth. Christ as the eternal Logos and God's cosmic agent of primordial creation is also affirmed to be the agent of cosmic salvation as continuing creation and renewal of creation.

Therefore, all salvation anywhere in the cosmos is God's work through the Logos who is known to the Christians as both the pre-existent and the Incarnate Christ and founder of historical Apostolic Church or Christianity two thousand years ago. However, God's processes of both creation and salvation predate the Incarnation and they remain cosmically valid and effective in the cosmos as inseparable coextensive processes.

The divine Incarnation was explicitly for the purpose of temporal, historical and social embodiment of the exemplary processes of life, healing, agape, peace, God's free forgiveness of sins, liberation from evil and to effect concrete historical salvation in the world. This being the case, then it follows that the divine Incarnation as the historical incarnation of God's creative and redemptive eternal Logos into the world, and each human being in the cosmos. This was both symbolically and historically accomplished by God through his mystical Incarnation and union with Jesus, the man of Nazareth, the carpenter who was later variously hailed by his followers as a rabbi, prophet and the Christ of God, was meant to positively illustrate and enhance these processes rather than to negate them.

In this perspective, the primary divine purpose of the divine Incarnation was God's free choice to become united in unconditional love, history, identity and personal experience by becoming one of them. Furthermore, God's purpose in the incarnation was to effect free human response to him as their free loving creator and to persuade them to fulfil themselves more positively by following the quintessential universal moral principle of agape and living in mutual peace.

To this end, God chose to become historically incarnated into the world. That is, God chose to become a human being in the temporal world, and its history. By this venture God sought to serve humanity as a fellow human being or God incognito. In the incarnation, God has decided to become a historical being, and to become one of us, namely, to become identified with his free intelligent, and moral creatures. He took this venture in order to show them by example how to live a more obedient and agapic life, which is fully open to God, in unconditional love and forgiveness for all one's fellow human beings as the beloved children of God as "*imago Dei*" (cf. 1 John 1:1-18).

In the light of the above affirmations and since God is a Creative and Redemptive Agape (cf. I John 4:4-21), Agape will be placed at the center of this work as both God and a means of fellowship with God and as evidence of the presence of God, his reign, true godliness, sainthood, supernatural salvation and God's kingdom. As such, hate, violence, war, greed and injustice as concrete negations of agape will be treated as temporal characteristics and concrete evidence of the existence of conditions of hell.

Therefore, in the context of this book, I have unconditionally accepted the centrality of the Gospel as "Good News" for the salvation of every human being in the universe that hears within the Word of God (the Christ or Logos of God). In addition, it is positively affirmed that such a person implicitly or explicitly believes in God, and that he or she also obeys God's will for him or her in creation. Furthermore, it is also positively affirmed that person also practices practical faith in God's redemptive agape, which is in obedience to the definitive commandment of God through the incarnate Christ. God's universal commandment is that human beings should love the neighbor without conditions.

Therefore, whoever, and wherever this divine commandment of agape is fulfilled, there is God's also saint and God's true salvation or the eternal kingdom of God. As both a Christian theologian and philosopher, I have also both consciously and deliberately grounded my research work, hypothesis, analysis and the interpretation of the research data in the traditional Catholic and mainline Protestant Christian positive monotheistic affirmation that there is only one Triune Cosmic Creative, Redemptive and Fulfilling Transcendent Eternal Mystery.

This is the essentially nameless Transcendent Cosmic Mystery, that is universally referred to variously as God, Yahweh, Allah, Deus, Theos, Katonda, Mungu, Ngai, Unklunkulu, Ruhanga, Leza, Amun, Amen-Ra, The Great Spirit, Shango, Brahma, Imaana, and the like. All these names refer to the same unnameable, transcendent, and ultimate cosmic reality. As such, these names are equally valid, relevant and meaningful in the relative local culture, linguistic and religious context in which they were invented in order to talk about the transcendent unnameable ultimate Cosmic Creative and Redemptive Mystery or God.

An attempt to name God is analogous to human attempts to definitively define and determine the shape of the clouds. Clouds and their functions are real. However, the shapes of the clouds are unreal and mere illusions. They are mere figments of our own imaginations, which have been projected up into the heavens or the sky as reality. This is analogous to our attempts to know God's essential nature or to possess a revealed religion that would reveal to us God in his or her definitive essence. This also applies to various human claims to most definitively "name God," or to possess special access to God's special revelation and essence apart from God's universal, essential explicit self-disclosure, as the free cosmic Creator, Redeemer and Fulfiller.

Consequently, no name or term for God, is ever better than another term for God that has been coined in another language and culture for the same Ultimate Reality. This is the same nameless reality that some Western philosophers like Martin Heidegger and Karl Jaspers, have also respectively and variously, referred to, as "Being," and "the all encompassing."

Likewise, this is also the same ultimate reality that theologians like Paul Tillich and Karl Rahner also variously referred to as the "Ground of Being" and "The Transcendent Mystery," the "Horizon of Being," "Being in-itself," the "Ultimate Reality," "the Abyss" and "Cosmic Creator."

Just like the African thinkers, theologians and Traditional Religion, the Western thinkers and theologians, are in full harmony that regardless of name, God is this essentially nameless Transcendent Cosmic Creative and Redemptive Mystery. It is the cosmic spirit and reality, that is all encompassing, living, thinking and intelligent non-visible primordial reality that enables other realities or beings to occur and have any meaningful existence as long as they remain anchored in this cosmic Ultimate Reality, as the source and medium of their continuing existence.

Since this is the case, then, names or terms for God are just mere relative and local terms for this universal creative and redemptive force who has universally revealed himself variously in creation, or nature, the prophets, culture, language, mind, values, religion and history. This is the same reality that has revealed God to the Western Christian thinkers and their religious experience as the eternal Triune God who is ever the Cosmic Creator as the Father, Redeemer as the Son/Christ or Logos, and the Fulfiller or Comforter, as the Holy Spirit.

God's universal salvific will, as it effectively operates in the world freely, by means of efficacious redemptive grace and agape, will be positively affirmed. Correlatively, God's universal free supernatural salvation, will be positively viewed as the concrete temporal historical personal and societal process, by which God works incognito, both in the temporal affairs and processes of the world and the entire cosmos.

Specifically, God works indirectly in the world through "natural law." That is to affirm that God actually works implicitly and incognito, through the ordinary every day events and life to effect the extraordinary, supernatural events of eternal life, salvation and his kingdom. Accordingly, God works incognito through the ordinary human family, the community or society, as his special and chosen arena and temporal historical social, divine media to create, and redeem or positively socialize, humanize and fulfill each individual human being as his own special son or daughter, both in the world and his kingdom.

Everywhere, and in every human society, and era, God has faithfully been fully present to carry out his activities of grace in creation and redemption. God has always worked incognito in his unmerited universal free efficacious grace, love and freedom, to create, persuade and positively transform each human being into the very unique human being, that he or she was uniquely created by God to become.

In this context, each person in the cosmos is positively viewed as "*imago Dei*," God's adopted child and ambassador of God in the world. Each human being is viewed as having a special place in the world, and a unique role to fulfill in God's eternal cosmic plan and providence. As such, each human being is both created unique by God in his own image and mystery. Therefore, he or she is also redeemed in that intrinsic correlative context of uniqueness and mystery. Accordingly, each person is also valued and loved unconditionally by God. In return God requires each human being also to value and love each human being unconditionally, as a fellow child of God or as a sister or brother in God's cosmic family.

Furthermore, since this process of divine creation and humanization is historically visible as universal, subsequently, it will also be argued that God's free activity in both creation and redemption, in free loving grace is likewise to be viewed as indivisible and correlatively universal in scope so as to coincide with this historical, and universal human evolutionary historical phenomenon.

This creative and evolutionary process is initiated and energized by God. It takes place in God's cosmic animating, living and agapic creative omnipresence. Consequently, divine salvation will be viewed as the process of divine completion and fulfillment of the human being. Therefore, God's unmerited grace in universal creation and redemption is present and at work in this creative, and humanization process. God's omnipresence, reign or kingdom and supernatural salvation are fully present and effective wherever, and whenever this process occurs in this cosmos.

Subsequently, the authentic criterion and reliable visible concrete evidence for divine salvation has been identified as "unconditional love for God and the neighbor." As a result, this unconditional love is required of all well socialized and humanized individuals as a prerequisite condition for full self-actualization, fulfillment and divinization, as a complete human being as "*imago Dei*." This process of *theosis* involves a positive completion, humanization, and positive transformation of any obedient human creature (*homo sapiens*), into the true "*imago Dei*" and God's redeemed child. This process of God's positive human transformation from an animal into his beloved son or daughter is coextensive with God's free creative process of complete humanization of the human being into an agapic, caring, loving, humane, good, compassionate, virtuous, hardworking, wise, intelligent, peaceful, social and responsible moral being.

These noble virtues are God's free gifts which are universally bestowed by God on each human being and accepted and appropriated in faith. This positive dynamic and living faith is the energy and grounding of true Agape and all good deeds which are acceptable to God. The positive intrinsic implicit and explicit faith of the human being both in God and the goodness of life or creation is demonstrated in visible human obedience to God through the concrete praxis of agape and good works as the concrete visible fruits of the indwelling supernatural gift of God's redemptive grace (cf. Matt. 7:16-21; 25:31-46).

Therefore, since God's cosmic creation is gratuitous, then, God's cosmic salvation or redemption of creation is also correlatively gratuitous and unmerited. Salvation or redemption is this essential free divine gift for re-creation or positive transformation. As such, God's efficacious redemptive grace is part of God's own unconditional love or agape, and it is universally free. God's free grace in creation and redemption is not for sale! God is not a greedy or corrupt capitalist who requires payments or bribes for his essential cosmic services of either creation or redemption!

Therefore, whoever has the faith to believe in this "Good News" of God's unconditional love, in both creation and redemption, and responds positively to God's universal free invitation to live an authentic agapic life in social harmony and happiness. This universal free divine invitation, is a divine call to all human beings in the world, to live positively, in a path (yoga) of life of agape, just works, holiness, and peace. This positive social mode of life is based on Agape, and obedience to God.

In this understanding, any human that truly unconditionally loves his or her neighbor, or performs the altruistic or self-sacrificial good works of Agape, both correlatively and coextensively, he or she also, thereby, fully participates in God. That person also fully participates in God's salvation, heaven and eternal kingdom, since these belong to God who is also this eternal cosmic Agape, Creator and Redeemer. This being the case, then entrance to God's salvation and eternal kingdom, are God's agape and grace alone. Therefore, they are open to all human beings everywhere, irrespective of gender, ethnic grouping, race, nationality, color, culture, language, religious affiliation, economic system, socio-economic class, era, political ideology and level of development.

4. The Intrinsic Unity of God's Cosmic Free Activities
of Creation and Redemption

From beginning to the very end, the activities and processes of cosmic creation and salvation, are God's free works of gratuitous unmerited grace and unconditional love. In addition, both creation and redemption, constitute God's cosmic free intertwined and inseparable twin or bipolar temporal agapic, and unconditional activities processes. As a result, creation requires redemption.

In turn, redemption both requires and presupposes God's continuing process of creation, recreation or new creation and positive transformation of evolutionary or intelligent moral agents. Redemption and divine salvation as forgiveness and new beginnings, are God's process of all morally thinking and responsible creatures. This is the case, since consequential creaturely freedom, is part of the factor in God's temporal world and its secondary creative processes, in the form of the historical long chain of cause and effect, and the reverse.

Significantly, the human being as a creature of God, in the temporal world, exists in an imperfect moral condition of hubris, self-centeredness, rebellion and alienation from God. As such, all human beings in the world exist in sin and guilt. They have fallen from the primordial perfection and happiness as the original unspoiled *"imago Dei."* In order to return to this primordial divine and human perfection, the human being can only be restored to the definitive primordial essence by God the creator when he acts as redeemer. Therefore, in this divine process of cosmic creation and redemption, the human being can only respond positively by cooperating with God in these processes, out of gratitude and obedience to God's will and explicit commandments, as found both in nature and in the scriptures.

The human mind, conscience, reason, history, cultures and science, can also become other alternative sources of God's true divine guidance for positive and agapic moral action in the world. As such, in this work the traditional Protestant dogmas of *"sola fide"* (salvation by faith alone) and *"sola scriptura"* (salvation based on scriptures alone) are repudiated as bigoted and meaningless partisan and divisive antiquated theologically fallacious dogmas.

On the other hand, the doctrine of *"sola Gratia"* (salvation by God's Grace alone), has been amplified as the theological truth and existential religious paradigm. *"Sola Gratia"* has been expanded into *"sola Agape"* (cf.

1 John. 4:7-21), who acts freely to create and redeem the world without any prior conditions. God as both "Agape" and "*Sola Gratia*" have been used interchangeably in this work since God's free creative agape and unmerited redemptive grace are intrinsically intertwined and truly inseparable in time, space, design or any divine activity.

Therefore, both God's true and efficacious creative agape and redemptive grace are inseparably universal in nature, scope and free divine activities. They are both found in all places, and in every cultural or religious group. God offers his free gifts of efficacious grace and agape to the world, and all its inhabitants, without any divine preferences to creed or religious favoritism.

As result, God is equally present in Islam, Christianity, Judaism, African Religion, Hinduism, and Buddhism as in the Native American Religion and Shintoism. The only main difference is how these various people, and cultures have experienced God's activities and presence in their own experiences and history, as both individuals and as a group. For instance, Israel came into being as a nation, as the Hebrew people had experienced God's concrete acts of redemption, both in their liberation and exodus from Egypt under the messianic and prophetic leadership of the secessionist, rebellious African prince and prophet Moses.[17]

Later on, the familiar Jewish apocalyptic messianic expectations were based on this liberation and the benevolent theocentric reign of King David. As such, historical, Jewish theological apocalyptic messianic political expectations were essentially, uniquely and exclusively "tribal" or "ethnic" in origin, nature and essential collective public expression.

As a result, the mainline messianic expectations were essentially rooted in Hebraic and exclusive Jerusalem-centered Palestinian Judaism. This Mosaic Judaism regarded Yahweh as Israel's tribal God. As such, Yahweh was supposed to favor Israel and the Jews as his special elect people, against other peoples (gentiles) or (pagan) non-Mosaic covenant nations.

Despite the fact that Yahweh's throne was considered to be physically and geographically located in heaven or the sky, as the infinite space above, nevertheless, God's is omnipresent and the world is God's kingdom in process of perfection. The Hebrews also, anthropomorphically, regarded God as a King and "*Primordial Father*," or heavenly ancestor of human beings (cf. Luke 3:23-39). whose physical-spiritual mighty and beneficial special presence was to be found on holy Mount Sinai, and the city of Jerusalem. Subsequently, the physical altar and sanctuary in the holy temple in Jerusalem, were later religiously and superstitiously regarded, as the concrete holy temporal places on earth, where God's redemptive presence, and atonement for sins could be truly experienced and obtained by the repentant sinners, who diligently observed the Mosaic Law.

In order to appease an angry God, whose moral law had been transgressed, and thus positively facilitated this desired ideal positive state of human atonement for sins, and the divine forgiveness of sins and redemption, animal sacrifices and prayers were offered to God in the temple. This Jewish central theological belief and religious practice were similar to those found in Africa. For instance, they were almost the same as the Kikuyu's affirmation that Ngai their God lived in heaven and his earthly presence could be visible in the form of a cloud and fire on holy Mount Kenya.

Accordingly, the Kikuyu worshipped the Transcendent, holy Creator, Sustainer and Redemptive God, while facing the holy Mount Kenya.[18] Likewise, the Masai generally faced the holy Mount Kilimanjaro Or "Olinyo Ngai" (the holy Mountain of God), as part of their worship of Ngai, the cosmic Creator, the cattle-giver, benevolent, and holy God.

Consequently, it would be wrong for the Kikuyu to change the name of God to Yahweh and worship facing Mount Sinai or Jerusalem or Mecca, unless, they are already Jews or Arab Muslims. God as Ngai, Yahweh and Allah is present today on holy Mount Kenya as he was also present for Moses on Mount Sinai and for Muhammad in the cities of Mecca and Medina.

Unlike finite and limited physical beings, God is transcendent, omnidimensional and therefore, simultaneously omnipresent everywhere in the cosmos. Therefore, unlike finite human beings, the transcendent God has no limitations or preference for places, cities, rivers, colors, foods, houses, people, gender, cultures, languages, religions, philosophies, rituals, and music. Likewise, God has no preference for specific religious rituals, sacraments, ceremonies, special dwellings, holy places of worship, modes of worship, and procedures in liturgical worship.

Preference is itself a function of prioritization which is a result of finitude, chronological or linear time and limitations imposed on all finite things by the dimensions of time and space. For instance, the cyclical processes of birth, growth, bloom, decline, death, decay and rebirth, is in it self a law of God regulating the function of time or life of finitude and the evolution and refinement of creation, including human beings as physical embodiments of portions of God's own mind or Logos, creativity, and self-consciousness. As *imago Dei*, human beings are both temporal "Bearers of God" and "mirrors of God" in creation.

Therefore, if anyone desires to know or see God, one has to seek a true human being or saint of God, in order to catch a glimpse of God and even to know God. This is why Adam, Moses, Buddha, Mary, Jesus, Muhammad, Gandhi, Mother Theresa and the other saints of God reveal God to us, and to know them is also to know. And to follow their teachings and practice them is both to find, and know God.

Ultimately, everything which God has made, is intrinsically both good and holy in itself (cf. Gen. 1:31). Therefore, as God's essentially good creation, every place and each creature manifests God's special work in creation and is therefore, not to be profaned, abused or polluted. As such, God does not make trash or junk for creation.

Nevertheless, human beings as moral free creative moral agents can rebel against God, and goodness in creation. Then, these rebels and other ignorant or sinful greedy people can carelessly exploit, trash, pollute and destroy God's wonderful creation. Human revolt against God is the source of moral evil in God's creation, such as chaotic discord, strife, conflict, malice, hate, violence and war in society. Examples are ethnic and religious wars in the Rwanda, Burundi, Kenya, Angola, Mozambique, Uganda, Nigeria, the Middle East, Northern Ireland, El Salvador, Bosnia and much of former Soviet Union empire.

Ironically, wars in South Africa, Rwanda, Bosnia, the Middle East, Somalia and Liberia clearly indicate, most human violence and wars in the world originate from erroneous theological and false anthropomorphic religious conceptions of God and divine election. The supposed divine racial, ethnic or religious election by God leads ethnocentrism and intolerance of others as the non-elect of God. Concepts of divine election lead to racial or ethnic pride as God's special elect people and religious bigotry. The extreme intolerance, excessive cultural ethnocentrism and nationalism attached to this concept of election and exclusion of other people as outsiders or enemies of the elect people, and therefore, enemies of God may lead to violence, war, and genocide or "ethnic cleansing" as clearly illustrated by ethnic wars in Bosnia and Rwanda.

Christ as the new Moses, was later expected to come and to liberate Israel from evil and military oppression by the neighboring more powerful states, and later, degradation and ritual pollution of the colonial occupation of the Roman empirical forces. A messiah or the Christ was expected as a form of God's gracious intervention in Israel's misery and political history in order to save and redeem his people from evil.

Evil and hell, were real existential and historical experiences. Evil and the kind of existential hell it caused to the people, the community and society, were real. This evil took place, in various forms. These concrete forms of evil included falsehood, strain and harmful stress or distortions of human relations, and failure to love the neighbor without conditions. This form of evil and sins also in turn lead to the development of both personal and societal evil in the form of conflict, violence, corruption, hate, malice, injustice, selfishness and greed.

In reality, evil as both a passive absence the maximum good or as an active rejection and negation of the good, was real to the people and their respective world. Evil was visible everywhere in the temporal processes of life, politics, human cultures, exclusive religious practices, strife, hate, violence and war. Therefore, the presence of evil was concretely experienced. It was externally manifested in historical, military, social, moral and economic processes.

This evil affected the individuals personally, and collectively as members of the community, nations and the world, in which this evil was taking place. Tragically, if left unchecked, this societal evil was producing more destructive secondary evils or consequences, such as poverty, suffering, pain, disease and premature violent deaths. As such, non-Jews had no Hebraic context in which to expect a Jewish messiah. However, they still needed God's special intervention in history in order to liberation from the oppression of evil forces and evil people.

Therefore, like the Jews, the non-Jews, such the Africans, Asians and Native Americans, had their own locally relevant context of experiencing both the demonic oppression of evil and divine liberation from this oppression of evil forces. This includes cultural, economic, political, societal and social religious contexts, in which they required God's direct intervention in order to bring about a change of direction, effect supernatural salvation. This God's universal supernatural salvation, is both freely effected by God and correspondingly experienced by human beings, as both ordinary and extraordinary liberation or deliverance from evil, guilt, oppression, strife or conflict, chaos, violence and threat to life or collective well-being.

Subsequently, the non-Jews still had a valid understanding of God as their own gracious benevolent Creator and Redeemer or Protector from evil. They also had the special awareness or "intuitive special divine revelation," that they were sinners who were now fallen from God's grace and primordial perfection. The were now in possession of God-consciousness and holiness, as well as the contrast of human being as an imperfect sinful and morally rebellious being.

Traditional Africans were aware that they were living in a state of sin, guilt, and moral imperfection or alienation from God. And therefore, deserved God's judgement, wrath and punishment for sin. This was the theology and philosophy that governed life and rituals of taboos, atonement and sacrifice in Islamic, pre-Christian and pre-colonial Africa.

Obviously, all human groups of people, including the traditional Asians, Native Americans and Africans, had a form of God-consciousness, religion, myths of God's primordial perfect creation, human disobedience, the fall or imperfection and guilt, which are analogous to those of the Hebrews as recorded in the biblical book of Genesis.[19] Those stories of Adam and Eve are found in the Bible are just samples of the stories of creation and the fall as told by the peoples of the world. Beyond that, there is nothing special about them. God did not reveal them nor write them. This also applies to the cherished "*Kintu and Nnambi*" accounts of creation in Uganda.

Stories of creation and the fall are universal. They are exist in hundreds. Unlike the scientific account of creation by evolution, these other stories and myths of God's creation of the cosmos and the human rebellion due to misuse of freedom, ignorance and defiance of God's moral commandment, they provide functional spiritual and moral road maps life and the world as it is perceived and experienced now.

These stories and myths also provide a spiritual map and religious geography of the world. For instance, in Asian and Western mythical geography allows for the existence of heaven as God's abode, the world as the imperfect and dangerous place where human beings live God in eternal quest for God's unconditional merciful intervention and salvation from evil as chaos and premature death. Hell as the realm of evil forces and destiny for evil doers.

In this religious geography God, perfection and happiness or peace exist in heaven above. Human beings aim at heaven since, they are in the world from which they seek to escape by going to God in heaven. This escapism is desired by many since they are ever battling demonic evil or forces of chaos and destruction. Unlike African religious and metaphysical monism, where the world is treated as God's kingdom and abode, in Western and Asian traditions, the religious myths as spiritual maps of life, also provide clues and keys to God's mysteries and paths back to God, goodness, and happiness in the world. This stories of creation and the fall of humanity are more concerned with redemption from this life than giving the historical and scientific accounts of creation or how life got here, except that it originated from God to whom and whose fellowship, the world separated and should now find correct means or paths to return, for its salvation.

Therefore, myths and stories of creation and the fall are more concerned with primordial past in God the prescription of how to return to fellowship with the primordial Creator-God in heaven. This human quest and prescription for salvation is expressed in the teaching found in all religions which affirm that by diligently following specific the paths to God, obedience to the Torah, *Shari'a*, agape or practice of *"yogas"* or other prescribed, commandments, rituals as the vehicles for the mediation of the secrets of the meaning of life, virtue, and a fuller life.

It is self-evident, therefore, that the Hebrews are not the only people in of God's special possession or revelation. As a result, there many stories which are similar to those found in the biblical book of Genesis. In the case of Africa, these primordial stories or myths of creation and the fall make it very clear that many people in Africa and other places had the consciousness that they had been created perfect by God to live in harmony with God, the relatives, neighbors, and the rest of God's creation or nature.

However, the original human beings had unfortunately, tragically revolted against God's primordial will and breached his moral commandments. Therefore, *"original sin"* as the intrinsic human consciousness moral imperfection, and the primordial human transgression of the natural or intrinsic God given moral law or limits, and the consequent intrinsic correlative guilt are universal human characteristics.

Consequently, God's revelation and the free gift of grace for agape, forgiveness of sins, removal of guilt and salvation are also correlatively universal and free. This being the case, then, God's free universal revelation, grace, election, agape, and forgiveness are, also God's own unmerited free transcendent gifts. These are God's free gifts, which, also have been, indiscriminately, universally and freely bestowed on all humanity, everywhere in the cosmos, without any prior condition for God's dispensing or human receiving of these free divine gifts. As a result, God's redemptive love, gratuitous efficacious grace, deifying revelation and supernatural salvation, can never be truly limited to the Hebrews, or any single or groups of special elect people, since there is no such an elect group of people as a special favored people of God.

Ultimately, the entire human race as *"imago Dei"* stands collectively together before God as its free Creator-Redeemer. Humanity is God's creation and special elect, among other creatures. With these divine gifts of mind, freedom, thinking, language, God-consciousness, moral responsibility, creativity and agape, the human being as "*imago Dei*" and God's special cosmic ambassador or representative in the world, remains a special creation and an elect creature of God in the rest of the unthinking cosmic matter and among the other less intelligent creatures, on this special living planet.

Therefore, for the non-Jews, such as the Africans, all finite creatures everywhere, and particularly, the more intelligent ones, such as the human beings, God gave them his true redemptive revelation and provided salvation to them in their own context. This divine supernatural salvation was offered by God, and both directly and indirectly experienced, by the human beings, as concrete temporal liberation from their own genuine local forms of troubling forms of evil and imperfections, and dangers to be unconditionally saved from by a loving and merciful God.

For human beings, evil is reality. Evil is not an illusion which can be dismissed as a mere mental concept, or mere philosophical idea construction or abstraction. Therefore, many of those people are experience the threat of evil in their own personal lives and in the community or the world, may sometimes, consciously seek to escape from it. Many people have tried to escape it by seeking for salvation in God as the most powerful cosmic Creator-Redeemer. Most of these people who resort to the practice of religions and other related rituals are often do so in quest for God or a divine power to deliver them and liberate from the threats of evil or predicament of chaos, powerlessness, pain, loneliness, suffering and untimely death. However, only the Creator-God can truly save his creatures from evil and a path of self-destruction.

The catalogue of evils from which people seek God or his various agents, messiahs, angels and others to save them includes the following: disasters, ignorance, imperfections the self, incomplete natures, inadequacy, dangers, oppression, threats to chaos, imperfections of life, poverty, injustice, oppression, starvation, violence, loneliness, disease, suffering, pain, evil habits, guilt, inner-emptiness, and existential personal and collective anxiety, which make life less perfect and less fulfilling.

This intrinsic universal human imperfection and incompleteness demand the omnipresence of a creator God in order to sustain the process of life; and also to redeem creatures from evil in both self-imposed or external predicament. The essential divine process of cosmic creation is through the delicate and finite processes of evolution, of the rhythms of birth, growth, maturation and death. Death serves as the gate and means for enabling life to be sustained as in nurture, purified and pruned of impurities, and thereby, both improved and renewed. In this understanding, death serves as a positive essential function in God's processes of life. Therefore, death is positive and part of God's will. For instance, death as God's natural process of both purifying and renewing life, works in the world to facilitate rebirth or resurrection in a new and more sophisticated form.

However, because life and its processes are evolutionary and in constant process of change, it becomes threatening to the intelligent creatures who are aware of these changes but are unable to control them sufficiently to their own advantage, especially those of self-preservation, self-enrichment, and fulfillment in happiness and a long healthy and rich life.

Tragically, the human being is universally aware that he or she is finite and transitory or travelling on a one way road to death. This is the "*a priori*" universal condition of all created life, including that of all human beings, regardless of whether they are good or evil, religious or atheistic.

All life follows the intrinsic universal, divine guiding principle of the natural law, of which birth and death, are the most important and definitive events, as entrances and exits to this life. As such, life is both appreciated by living things, and at the same time, it is also feared by most intelligent beings because they know how unique, complex, fragile, and transitory God's divine special gifts of life happen to be rare in this vast cosmos. Life is also feared due to its great complex mysteries, uncertainties and transitoriness.

These mysteries are embedded and hidden deep within its intrinsic impenetrable complex nature of flux, evolution, and finitude, alarm the more intelligent creatures who then yearn for static perfection in the form of pure reality, and eternal static life, which is sometimes erroneously equated with heaven and immortality! Tragically, for many Christians, and other religious people this kind of utopian static perfection in the form of this kind of permanent, unchanging reality is erroneously equated with heaven and the kingdom of God!

On the contrary, God's kingdom is as universal and omnipresent as God himself. That is to say that God's kingdom is wherever God is present, and wherever his will is obeyed. That means that God is as present here and now, in the midst of the chaos, strife and confusion of the world, as effectively and lovingly, as he or she was in the primordial Garden of Eden. As result, each human being in the world, effectively serves as an Adam or Eve in the present moment and in respective to the fate of the world, or that of the other people and creatures, who are affected by our moral choices. As such, each human being freely chooses not to sin or to sin, and bring more evil, imperfection, suffering, and premature death into God's good world.

God's universal gratuitous grace to energize, empower, and positively transform any obedient people into loving, morally upright, good and benevolent child of God as the true *"imago Dei"* is unconditional and unmerited. It is both free and efficaciously universal in scope. That is to affirm that it is truly free for all obedient moral agents, everywhere, in the cosmos and in every age. Accordingly, all human beings are eternally, universally freely elected to become the heirs of God's kingdom and eternal life or salvation. All they need is faith and good works in obedience to God's will.

Good works in obedience to God, is itself a concrete evidence to the free acceptance of God's own free grace, since no good works can be performed apart from faith and the power of God's grace. This universal free divine grace is also required in order to live according to God's will in a life of agape and good works. Therefore, any true practical faith in God, or obedience to God is universally measured by Agape and altruistic good deeds on behalf of God. These good works are freely performed in love to aid the poor, assist the helpless, or serve those in need, regardless of who they are, or the reasons why they are in that particular predicament.

Therefore, within this universal human existential context of *"angst"* or finitude, and theological methodology, all human beings everywhere experience an existential intrinsic form of primordial imperfection and predicament. Consequently, human beings everywhere, desire find God. They actively do so explicitly in worship or implicitly do so through the moral choices they make in daily. In general, human moral and moral consciousness consists in the life of moral (religious) quest for God's intervention in their own lives and that of the world, so as to effect concrete salvation.[20]

God's creative and redemptive power or grace is universally desired by human beings to help them overcome their problems in life and save them from despair, evil, imperfection, inadequacy, inner-emptiness, chaos and the threat of premature death. As such, non-Jews do not have to have similar enemies and evils like those of the Jews in which the apocalyptic messianic expectations, and theological doctrines were very narrowly culturally conceived.

These Jewish messianic concepts were later both developed and systematized in the form of the Prophets such as Isaiah and Jeremiah, in order to appreciate the mission and moral teachings of Jesus-Christ as God's incarnate Logos. Jesus-Christ's ethical teachings and centrality on unconditional love and forgiveness for the neighbor have a universal validity, appeal, relevancy and redemptive value. As such, Agape and its praxis is the practical means by which God can turn this world into his concrete kingdom.[21]

Agape restores openness, harmony, unity and fellowship with God, the neighbor, and the community. It is the only practical, moral and ethical form of justice and harmonious relationship with one's fellow creatures in God's creation as our fellow beings and co-inhabitants of the earth. This is the essence of Noah's story. God cares about the whole world, and all his creatures and desires to save them without condition. This being the case, God's salvation is an inclusive open reality, which includes all creatures and all obedient and loving human beings, regardless of their creed or lack of it.

In this theological and philosophical perspective, God's process of salvation is both coextensive with creation and this temporal life on earth. This is the very concrete life and world which God loves so much, that he sent his own Son or the Logos in order to save it from rebellion and self-destruction (John 3:16-20). All societies tell stories of this universal human rebellion against God's primordial will and commandment.

Rebellion against God is also a rejection of God and the correlative satisfying holy, agapic and harmonious life with the neighbor, God and creation or nature. Thus, all human societies possess an intrinsic knowledge of this moral rebellion, and guilt. Subsequently, all human beings are aware of how moral rebellion against God leads to a reckless life of egocentric idolatrous self-deification, greed, hate, malice, violence, chaos, existential anxiety, despair, vice, war and self-destruction. Consequently, all human beings everywhere, live in an implicit or explicit perpetual existential quest for God, and his salvation as concrete temporal (categorial) or existential liberation from this human moral rebellion and the correlative life of evil, discord, violence and self-destruction.[22]

As such, all human beings in every society have had their own fears, and threats to life, self-fulfillment, and happiness from which they desired God's supernatural liberation or salvation. That is, human beings, everywhere have hoped for God's free redemptive grace and the unconditional intervention of God to come in and liberate them and empower them to overcome the threats of evil and chaos both in their own lives and the collective life of the community, the nation and ultimately, the whole world. In this respect, evil is analogous to human sickness, whereas god is analogous to the physician, and salvation or God's liberation the medicine or cure from this moral or physical sickness.

Therefore, God's salvation as concrete redemption from evil and chaos as relative to what kind of evil and chaos some seeks to be liberated from. As such, it is as wrong to be treated for cancer by the doctor because he or she is an expert oncologist, as it is to be liberated from the sin of adultery or disbelief whereas the real spiritual destructive malady, is that of disobedience to God, and failure to practice agape.

As a result of Israel's original special experience of God's redemptive grace and power, as experienced both in the "Passover" and the "Exodus," Israel developed an exclusive and ethnocentric dogma of election and soteriological theological bigotry of "*extra Israel* [Mosaic Covenant] *nulla salus.*" Later, Christianity itself as a self-proclaimed successor of Judaism also naively appropriated the exclusive doctrines of election, and soteriological superiority to all other religions by affirming the now familiar bigoted and exclusive ethnocentric doctrine of "*extra ecclesiam nulla salus.*" This was basically a non-violent crusade and Western cultural imperialistic form of religious coercion of non-Christians to become Christians and Western in culture.

5. African Religion as a Form of an Anonymous Christianity: A case for God's Universal Salvific Will and Kingdom

In essence, the doctrine of God's universal salvation in unconditional loving free grace is not new. It can be found both in the Old and New Testaments, especially, in the teachings of Isaiah, Jesus, John and Paul. Some of the leading thinkers and the famous Church Fathers, such as Justin Martyr and Origen, taught this doctrine very explicitly, whereas many others taught it implicitly. The main trouble of teaching this doctrine implicitly, is a lack of systematic development of the doctrine and its serious implications for Christian theology, ethics, philosophy, ecclesiology and missiology.

Fortunately, this doctrine of free supernatural salvation has recently been taught by Karl Rahner (S.J.). He was a leading Catholic theologian until his death in 1984. Rahner taught this old doctrine under the seemingly ill-advised Christocentric and Christian term of "anonymous Christianity." This was partly because he wanted to fulfill the Christian theological dogma, which that all God's salvation is through Christ (cf. John 14:6: "I am the way the truth and the life, and no one comes to the Father except through me").

However, Rahner wanted to achieve this central Apostolic Church's Logos-Christocentric soteriological affirmation without insisting that God's salvation was only universally available to the world, and every human beings through the Apostolic Church. This was what was essentially wrong with the traditional Christian doctrine of *"extra ecclesiam nulla salus."*

Nevertheless, Rahner made it quite clear that he used this term for lack of a better and more appropriate Christian inclusive theological term. However, I have adopted both his terminology and teaching as it stands, without much modification. This has been deliberately done, so that the arguments and results of my study, would not be overlooked or clouded by my modification of Rahner's teaching.

In this book, I have chosen Karl Rahner as the main spokesperson for the Western Christian tradition. For the African tradition, I have chosen Professor John Mbiti as the main pan-African representative and spokesperson. Rahner's inclusive theological Christian paradigm, will be adopted and adapted for the practical working model in this work in Christian philosophical-theology from an Africanist, global or universalist Christian perspective.

This inclusive Christian theological model is ideal for this task, because it does not treat radically different religions, or the various different branches in the diverse Christian denominations within Christianity, such as Roman Catholicism, and the extreme non-liturgical congregationalist Protestants, such as the Baptists and Pentecostal as different Christian religions. I will also treat the diversity of the African traditional religious beliefs, rituals and practices, as mere branches or denominations within the African Religion. In addition, the African Religion is co-extensive with the authentic life of any African. Therefore, it both logically and naturally follows, that African Religion is intrinsically and essentially, inseparable from the African's mode of authentic existence, of which it is the central cohesive social, moral and cultural force.

This is the authentic nature of primary, universal Africentric theocentric-human social, and cultural existential context, regardless of whether that African is consciously aware of it or not. Those who are not conscious of this fact, are analogous to fish in the sea which may at the same time be unaware that they exist in the water or existing unaware that water is essential for their own existence, until they have been fished out of the water. To some extent, this is analogous to what has happened to Africa with the cruel and inhuman phenomena of the African slave trade and the subsequent Western attempts to de-Africanize, Europeanize and inculturate the African slaves and other free Africans in the diaspora, or the colonial agent and the Christian missionary Africa.

Therefore, I have positively affirmed the sacredness of all human life, as having been created in the image of God, regardless of race, color, gender, class, culture, language, creed, and technological level of development. In this book I reaffirm the universal positive truth of God's unconditional creation and redemption, in God's unconditional and unmerited universal free grace, agape and salvation, for all those who believe and obey.

I have deliberately employed Rahner's Christian teaching on "anonymous Christianity" as being representative of Western Christianity and attempted to show how Rahner's criterion for "anonymous Christianity" is adequately met and fulfilled, by some members of the African Traditional Religion. Subsequently, I have made the claim that God's free creative, redemptive and fulfilling process, was also efficaciously at work in pre-Christian and pre-colonial Africa, in the same way it was at work in ancient Israel before the ministry of Jesus of Nazareth.

Therefore, the main claim being made in this book is that for the Africans, the African Traditional Religion has the same kind of validity which Judaism, and Christianity, have for the Western people, or Islam has for the Arabs and Hinduism has for the Indians.

Ultimately, the central thesis and fundamental Christian theological and Christocentric soteriological claim, is that God's free process of creativity, loving, redemption and fulfillment is universal, and therefore, not in any way limited to any group of people in time or space. As such, precolonial and Christian missionary Africa is used in this work as the best example to illustrate this global theological principle and divine truth. This is primarily because unlike Hinduism, Buddhism, Judaism and Islam, which were respected and positively studied by both Western scholars and missionaries, the African Religion and the Native American Religion, were in the past always the ones left out of the academy as being irredeemably primitive, "pagan" and "anti-Christian."

As an African Christian professional systematic theologian and philosopher I have tried to be objective and fair to the African Tradition. Nevertheless, my own standpoint as both a Christian philosophical-theologian and an Anglican priest is both consciously and unconsciously bound to have some indirect subjective bearing and both implicit and explicit influence on my academic work, including the gathering of data, its analysis, interpretation, and presentation in this book. Obviously, this state of affairs has shaped my view of the African Religion and its treatment in this book.

Nevertheless, the fact that historical Christianity, particularly, Roman Catholicism, is currently growing at a very fast rate in Africa, is sufficient theological and cultural evidence for the position I which have taken in this work in respect to African Religion as being sufficiently revelatory of God and good preparation for the historical message of the Gospel of the Incarnate God in Christ-Jesus.

For many traditional Africans, it is good news, indeed, to hear that God the Creator and Redeemer has in the past become incarnate in a real human being. This is understandable, since Africans have defied ancestors into god and the charged them with mediation to God as advocates and high-priests for the living. Jesus-Christ becomes a better model for this African theological and ontological world-view, divine-kingship and sacerdotal priesthood.

In modern Africa, the historical Apostolic Christianity, has been conveyed to Africa in the form of Western missionary Christianity. Roman Catholicism has taken root almost immediately as evidence that the ground for the sowing of the Gospel of the Incarnate and Risen Christ, had been already adequately prepared, by God through the African Religion. This adequate preparation for the Incarnation, was also redemptive for the people, who both lived faithfully according to God's moral as revealed to them, in the positive life-enhancing and agapic ordinances and practices of the African Religion.

God was present in the Logos, calling all human beings, including the Africans, to come to him or her for divine redemption. In Africa, God called his through the African Religion. Therefore, the pre-Incarnate cosmic Logos-Christ was equally present in Africa, as he was in Israel, Asia, America and Europe. God's Logos is omnipresent, and works in the entire cosmos, in order to effect God's unmerited free universal acts of creation, and God's universal salvific will.

In this understanding, all world religions exist as various paths to God. In this respect, all religions point to God and embody various degrees of God's effective redemptive historical revelation. All religions which stress love and peace are varied cultural forms of the revelation of God, incognito through the cosmic Logos-Christ. Therefore, these religions are different "Christian forms" of "anonymous Christianity." As such, they are vehicles of God's historical redemptive processes in the world. Accordingly, the African Religion is not only adequately equipped by God's redemptive grace to become God's concrete medium of efficacious supernatural redemptive grace, and divine salvation in the world.

Ultimately, there is no single religion, which has been exclusively, and universally elected by God for the salvation of all human beings in the world. In God's redemptive plan there are no preferred or "special elect" groups of people, liturgical procedures, ministers of special mediators apart from the eternal Logos, as both cosmic and Incarnate in the world.

God has no single, universal, special or ordained, favored or infallible religion for all his children, as both Christianity and Islam have most ethnocentrically, imperialistically, fallaciously and tragically claimed to be the infallible case. These exclusive, ethnocentric and bigoted theological claims are, therefore, negatively viewed and rejected as antiquated, misguided concretized fanatic societal religious and cultural perceptions of God's limited revelation and selective activities in their own local communities as microcosms of the world.

Religion is an inseparable component part of the society which creates it, or in which it functions. Therefore, much of the religious doctrines and practices have a local cultural or philosophical connection and basis. As a result, much of the traditional Western Christian theological dogmas, creeds, and teachings of Judaism, Christianity, and Islam are deeply rooted in the prevailing local cultural conditions, in which they were originally created or developed. That is to say that these religions are, both implicit and explicit, in the cultural and political expressions. These negative expressions or evils, include: self-centeredness, ethnocentrism, bigotry, ignorance, xenophobia, religious intolerance, exclusiveness, and global religious imperialism.

In the final analysis, it can be positively, and universally affirmed that the cosmic Creator, Transcendent infinite God is completely just, and impartial. Accordingly, unlike finite imperfect human beings, this transcendent God does not any special preferences or favorites. This includes preference for any human religion, creeds, doctrines, rituals or sacraments, philosophy or universal codes of ethics except those that promote Agape, harmony and peace in the world. This being the case, then the African Religion is one of God's imperfect temporal channels for his redemptive activities in the world, blessings, and salvation. Therefore, the African Religion is God's effective primary channel and means for the concrete societal and personal acquisition and mediation of virtue, well-being, agape, peace, and societal harmony.

The African Religion is the means of establishing God's concrete kingdom and theocracy on earth. It is also the most effective societal vehicle for effecting social and political unity and the redemption of African traditional cultures, values, identity, self-worth, direction and meaningful self-fulfillment. Finally, in this respect, the African Religion is also an adequate preparation for God's activities of grace, and redemptive readiness for new era of global Apostolic Christian missions, to proclaim to the world, the fullness of self-fulfillment, in the explicit nature of an Agape-centered Apostolic Christianity, and the explicit for the post-modern peaceful global intra-racial human community, and harmonious mutual interdependence.

In the light of the above, Apostolic Christianity, is then, only considered to supersede and fulfill the African Religion only in as much as Christ in the temporal and historical Incarnation of God's Agape, universal gratuitous grace in cosmic creation and unconditional universal redemption. In this understanding, the divine incarnation is God, consists of the incarnation of the Logos-Christ into humanity and positive human relationships.

This means that it is God's agape and Logos that become transmitted and embodied in humanity and society as the "*obuntu/buntu*" (humaneness). Therefore, it is by God's creative and redemptive grace in traditional Africa working through God's Word as the incarnate Logos-Christ that both the complete societal "concretization" and historicization of "*obuntu*" or agape as the basis of authentic humanity, peace and societal harmony are enabled to occur.

In this African theological and philosophical metaphysics and systematic theological construction, the divine incarnation into the world is coextensive with God's universal self-disclosure to his creatures, as both their concrete primordial eternal Creator, and benevolent Cosmic Primordial Ancestor. This is the "*Cosmic Abba*" who is also simultaneously both their loving creator and savior. The incarnation is also the historicization and concretization of Agape, and God's universal kingdom on earth and beyond.

As such, according to this research and its presentation, Christianity is only to be validly promoted, or defended as a superior to the other world religions including the African Religion, if it is better at promoting the praxis of societal Agape and peace within both the local communities, and the in the global human community or the world. This includes peaceful human mutual coexistence with one another, and the rest of God's creation, such as the trees, the animals, land, water and space.

Therefore, the misguided familiar characteristic Protestant evangelical theological principles of "*sola fide,*" "*sola scriptura,*" and more fallacious fundamentalist or literalist "inerrancy of scriptures" both implicitly and explicitly examined. Subsequently, they are rejected as invalid and fallacious defenses of Apostolic Christianity and its uniqueness. These confessional doctrines and dogmas do not prove the erroneously formulated dogmatic claims of the definitive superiority of Christianity, and the Apostolic Church as God's exclusive vehicle of supernatural conditional, selective or elective grace and exclusive means of salvation for the world, outside which, there is no salvation (*extra ecclesiam nulla salus*).

On the contrary, both "sola Agape" and sola Gratia," are proposed as the new principles of any sound and redemptive religion or other authentic and godly, life-affirming, positive life-enhancing, good modes of life. Secondly, Christianity is superior to other religions or supersedes them, only if it offers and facilitates a better societal, and interpersonal system of life. That is Christianity has to promote superior modes of life, both in the community and the world. As such, true agapic Christianity has to provide positive societal values of Agape, and empower the people to live together harmony and peace.

In short, true Christianity, like any other true religion, is that which is based on Christ's definitive and non-negotiable commandment to love God and the neighbor, without any conditions or reservations. This supernatural dynamic or practical faith and redemptive obedience to God, both supernaturally and naturally, lead to a concrete human life in the world, which is more harmonious with social life within family, community, nation, and the world as the international community of nations and communities of non-human beings. This is, the intrinsic theological and philosophical wholistic messages of non-Western religions, such as the African Religion, Hinduism, Buddhism and the Native American Religion.

Finally, what is universally and positively affirmed for the African Religion is also implicitly affirmed as true for those religions, too. Consequently, Trent Collier's paper has been included in the appendixes in order to provide an insightful illustration of this fundamental point. It will help to illustrate that God's creative and redemptive free grace, are as efficaciously inclusive, universal and free. The paper illustrates how these divine activities are inseparably bound together, as correlative and co-extensive cosmic creative processes of God's universal free acts, of gratuitous grace and unconditional love (Agape), in concrete divine self-embodiment and self-disclosure to the cosmos.

This process of God's cosmic free activities of Agapic and gratuitous universal creation and redemption, are also both correlative and coextensive with God's own free revelation in both nature or creation and humanity, as revealed both in every human being as "imago Dei" and more authentically or clearly, in the divine Incarnation. For Christians, humanity represents God's ultimate special presence in the historical and temporal world. This is both firmly believed and positively affirmed in the creeds and other statements of faith.

This confession of faith, in turn based on the faith and mystical beliefs in humanity as God's chosen and special medium for the divine temporal self-embodiment, in the incarnation, and concrete historical God's cosmic self-disclosure to the historical world of matter, and particularly, the human beings, as the most intelligent creatures. However, if this is the case, then it also naturally follows that this God's self-disclose to the world is essentially universal, free and efficacious for all human beings without any prior qualifications or conditions.

This divine self-communication and self-disclosure to the world, both in nature or creation and redemption, is universal, gratuitous, unmerited, and unconditional in its divine cosmic expression or effective universal impartial operation. Consequently, all human beings and their religions, are simply imperfect finite and partial agencies of this divine transcendent macrocosmic process of both unmerited free creation and redemption.

This gratuitous cosmic and impartial process of both God's creation and redemption, is gratuitously universally effected, by the eternal divine Creative and Redemptive Logos, and historically as the Jesus-Christ. This cosmic divine process is of both free creation and salvation, is particularly, significant pre-requisites for the universal creaturely self-completion, self-consciousness as "*imago Dei*."

This self-consciousness as "*imago Dei*" is essential for the creaturely quest, for the ultimate self-completion and self-fulfillment, in the holy Agapic fellowship with the neighbor and the beatific fellowship with God, on earth as God's concrete kingdom and heaven. As such, God-conscious-ness, and God's supernatural self-disclosure in nature and the cosmos, are necessary for the well-being of the more intelligent, free moral agents or thinking and responsible creatures or human beings.

As "*imago Dei*," all normal human beings, everywhere in the cosmos are by quintessential "*homo sapiens*." This is God's unique gift to human beings everywhere. Mind, language, self-transcendence or spirit, freedom and moral agency are God's universal free gifts to all human beings as his adopted children, and created minds in the cosmos of unintelligent and non-self-reflective matter.

As the children of God, God's mind in created matter, temporal free moral agents, all "normal" human beings everywhere in the cosmos, are unique creatures and natural citizens of the kingdom of God in the cosmos, unless they chose to exclude themselves from it by rebellion, living in vice, and doing evil even when they possess correct factual and ethical knowledge what is good, and right in the situation. Therefore, human beings are thinking unique creatures, moral agents, and special ambassadors of God in the world. Irrespective of the process of evolution, and sharing in common, the world of matter, with other animals, the human beings are the only divinized creatures into the special, divine and supernatural creatures, and ambassadors of God in the world.

Therefore, all normal and obedient human beings, are God's concrete moral agents who perpetually ask the ultimate questions of their primordial origins, destiny, their ultimate and the right way to live or fulfill themselves in the present in order to effect the positive destiny of their own lives, friends, neighbors, the community, the nation, and ultimately, the entire world.

Accordingly, God's supernatural salvation and the kingdom are variously experienced by different human beings as both individuals and as members of distinct cultural groups. The experience of God or God's ultimate answer to a need for salvation, is locally experienced differently, by people depending on what kind of ultimate answers or divine interventions, are locally sought from God. God answers questions, and gives to the people an appropriate supernatural response to prayers and the respective local human quests for otherwise, ultimate answers to ultimate universal human questions of life and meaning.

In short, the universal existential and implicit religious human quest for salvation is both local and universal. This search and quest for God and supernatural salvation is, both implicit and explicit, in the correlative and co-extensive with the universal human quest for meaning, fulfillment and general conditions of peace, as both personal, and the societal well-being in the community and the world.

Consequently, the universal human quest for God and salvation are inseparable from the universal human existential quest for the ultimate concerns and answers is very often experienced and expressed as concrete local quests for divine salvation as concrete intervention in a local situation. Therefore, such divine intervention in a local situation is clearly understandable as God's supernatural salvation. Some good examples include: the Passover and exodus event; the supernatural birth of Krishna, the Buddha experience; the reported Virgin birth of Osiris, Buddha, and Jesus; the crucifixion, alleged bodily resurrection and physical ascension of Jesus into heaven; and the Hegira or flight of Prophet Muhammad from Mecca to Medina.

Nevertheless, despite the kind of local miracles, religious sentiments, mythical religious value and sophisticated universal theological meaning, which may be locally attached to such a local historical event of God's redemption, it should never be validly universalized as the exclusive universal paradigm and *"modus operandi"* for all God's true redemptive actions in the world. Nor should any religious group be allowed to claim that itself, alone constitutes God's exclusive, and true redemptive path to God's happiness, truth, Agape, heaven, eternal peace and the kingdom.

This is analogous to the claim that one's view, and naming of constellations of stars or the clouds, or claim to know the authentic permanent shapes of these clouds. This is also akin to the claim that there is only one road and one way to travel to Washington, in D.C. or to London, regardless of one's own location in time and space, and means of available travel or lack of it. There is no one road or path to these cities. Analogously, unlike an ancient castle, precariously situated on a cliff, with little or limited access, the city of God must have many roads and entrances leading to it from every nation, village, cultural group, race, tribe, creed and religion.

Unfortunately, the crude and false anthropomorphic analogy of God's city has been that of the small boat of Noah or the castle on the mountain cliff with limited space and access to the world and the people. This fallacious analogy has led to the absurd fallacies and tragedies of the traditional Western Apostolic Christianity, and its Eurocentric ethnocentric Church, and theological bigotry. These include the destructive Christian historical ethnocentric teachings and exclusive divine redemptive claims expressed in the dogma of *"extra ecclesiam nulla salus."*

This work represents a systematic rebuttal and repudiation of this kind of false Christian teaching. Following the reformation and inclusive positive Christian teachings of Vatican II, and guidance of the teachings of Rahner, this exclusive dogma is rejected. It is racist, Eurocentric, imperialistic, and unacceptable antiquated dogmatic Christian doctrines steeped in bigotry, sinful exclusive xenophobia, religious and cultural imperialism.

The "good news" or the Gospel of God's universal free salvation in his unmerited gratuitous grace and unconditional love remains the universal true Gospel of God and the academically proclaimed message of this book. The Gospel is reaffirmed in the traditional Christian pure essence as taught by Jesus Christ and his apostles and as understood by the New Testament writers and the Fathers of the early Church. In this original theocentric soteriological understanding, and Christocentric mediation and proclamation of the Gospel, as the good news of God's free unmerited grace and unconditional love working in the world incognito through the Logos as the incarnate Christ God desires and wills to save every obedient human being in the cosmos from evil, self-centeredness, hate, ignorance and the rebellious path to self-destruction.

This is the universal Gospel of God which is freely proclaimed to the world in both natural revelation in nature and special revelation in the prophets, scriptures and the Incarnation. This good news is universally variously directed and efficaciously freely proclaimed everywhere, and anywhere by God, and his special designated agents in the world. This Gospel of God's unconditional love in creation and unmerited free grace in redemption is addressed to each human being in the cosmos, irrespective of era, class, race, color, education, nationality, language, culture, religion or creed, gender, level of technological development, age, marital state, and sexual orientation. God is the ultimate impartial and just equal opportunity, agapic, free cosmic Creator and Redeemer.

Therefore, regardless of what the Apostolic Church and exclusive Christianity dogmatically and falsely claim, teach or proclaim to the world as the Gospel of God in Christ, God's universal inclusive creative and redemptive truth remains unchanged and still efficaciously cosmic at work. It is working in the universe to effect both unmerited free creation and redemption. These free divine cosmic activities cannot be nullified by human ignorance, malice, and sins of the human beings and the Church. Despite human sin, God remains the same in his infinite unconditional love and gratuitous universal grace both in undeserved creation and redemption.

Ultimately, in his free grace and agape, God is constantly at work everywhere, in the universe to effect cosmic creative and redemptive eternal Word or the eternal Logos, and the Incarnate Christ. These free and universal activities of God's unconditional, and unmerited free grace, and universal salvation for all those with faith and obedience to God's universal commandment of Agape, has been most vigorously theologically and philosophically presented, explained and defended at those two levels. It has also been correlatively theologically upheld, as the universal inclusive, and temporal existential and living social truth of God's reign, and his temporal kingdom in the world.

This state of supernatural salvation, and the kingdom of God, is efficaciously universally mediated, in the temporal world and the human society, by concrete positive practical saintly practice, of the redemptive and divinizing, altruistic moral values of Agape. To this end, any religion or Church, becomes the most effective true channel for the mediation of God's redemptive grace and salvation in the world, in as much as it becomes the true temporal embodiment of God's Agape, and the agency for the mediation of God's free universal unconditional love, unmerited redemptive grace, forgiveness of sins and removal of human existential guilt, and its correlative hellish state of anxiety and despair (*angst*). Such a Church or religion, becomes the concrete efficacious sacrament of God to the world.

To this end, Buddhism, Hinduism, the African Religion and the Native American Religion are good pointers to inclusive Transcendent Cosmic God. These religions are also examples of non-Western efficacious sacramental channels and effective redemptive supernatural instruments for God's efficacious mediation of his inclusive unconditional love, unmerited free grace and universal salvation for all God's obedient people, regardless of conditions or who they are.

These universally redemptive free divine gifts of grace, virtue and moral values of Agape as universally expressed by the altruistic good deeds, are considered as the universal concrete or temporal criteria measure and definitive universal visible evidence of any redeemed, godly and obedient saintly life. This is true for God's salvation inside the historical Apostolic Church in the Incarnate Christ as well as the universal salvation outside the Church through the universal mediation of the pre-Incarnate Cosmic Christ as the Primordial Creative and Redemptive eternal Cosmic Logos of God (cf. Gen. 1:1-31; John 1:1-18).

Therefore, it can be definitively and positively affirmed that as the unconditional Agape and free Cosmic Creator and Redeemer, God's true redemptive Church is by essential nature cosmic, inclusive, multi-religious, multi-cultural, multi-racial, nondenominational, and universal in its pluralistic inclusive nature and interreligious scope. God's free universal salvation and the kingdom, are efficaciously universal and omnipresent in the cosmos through the gratuitous mediation and free universal cosmic creative and redemptive activities of God through the divine eternal Cosmic Logos.

Ultimately, agape and its praxis or correlative altruistic good deeds, are also the universal explicit and concrete existential evidence of the real efficacious temporal supernatural presence of God's universal supernatural salvation. Therefore, the altruistic good deeds of Agape, are supernatural temporal signs and symbols of the efficacious mediation of God's free extraordinary universal salvation, and presence of God's eternal kingdom, in the midst of the ordinary temporal processes of this concrete world. Good deeds of agape are also the universal true manifestations and temporal evidence of God's concrete reign. They are the holy sacraments and seasoning ingredients of God's kingdom, in this world of greedy people and constant strife. Therefore, agape and its true altruistic praxis or good deeds of redemptive Agape, grace and faith, constitute the universal incontrovertible concrete and visible evidence of God's transcendent activities of creation and salvation.

Agape and its praxis efficaciously mediate or transmit to the temporal world God's goodness, positive action, and divine salvation. Agape and positive action (praxis), are God's efficacious, universal temporal holy channels, and efficacious sacraments of God's gratuitous redemptive grace, unconditional love, unmerited free forgiveness and salvation to the world. God's grace and Agape working through all the loving men and women of good-will, reveal God's supernatural presence and his work in the world. The obedient, morally upright, just, and loving men and women as the true saints of God, represent God in the world as his ambassadors, ministers and high-priests of love, creation and redemption in the world.[23] Agape and its practice both embody and mediate God and his concrete supernatural agapic and unconditional activities of creation and redemption in his world and kingdom.

The loving cosmic transcendent God works in his unmerited, universal efficacious grace, and unconditional love, in a simultaneous divine process, to create the world and then transform it into his free, inclusive and agapic kingdom, of redeemed saints and sinners. God's universal kingdom and salvation are found everywhere, and anywhere in God's vast cosmos. This is because God's creation, redemption, kingdom and salvation are akin to God himself in whom they all originate and coexist and have their ultimate fulfillment.

Therefore, by quintessential divine nature and essence, agape, salvation and God's kingdom are both transcendent and universal gifts. God's creation, redemption or salvation and kingdom are inseparably linked and interrelated. They are both universal in intrinsic essential nature and scope. Consequently, they are correlatively and coextensively, both found everywhere, and anywhere in the world wherever God's will is done. This is, especially true, in a condition where God's will is done in unconditional love and positive faith, without any coercion. Rather, working in free reciprocal love, and not because of any threats of hell-fire, and or fears of divine punishment, such as disease, pain, poverty, social rejection, suffering, misfortunes, disasters and premature death.

In God's world, and kingdom, there is one central divine principle of true religion, redemption and salvation, namely, Agape. It is also the only commandment which was given to the world by Jesus as the Christ of God. It is both the path to God and salvation. Failure to hear God calling us, and inviting us to come to salvation as the divine cosmic banquet and agapic celebration of life leads to self-alienation from God, an impoverished insecure life of dread (*angst*) and moral paralysis due to existential anxiety. God's Word or the Logos is, therefore, ever present in the world and each human being as the omnipresence of the Cosmic Creator-Redeemer God.

God's eternal Word of life or the Logos is heard speaking within each obedient human being, speaking the words of life, love, peace and forgiveness. God's Logos is the indwelling Word of God that calls us into being and into the fullness of life through the practical application (praxis) of Agape. God's eternal Word of unconditional love, life, creation and redemption is heard from within in silence, calling silently, persuading and gently luring each person to a positive response to God. This must be a voluntary response freely made in personal freedom, and in love. This is also a positive response to God's Word of invitation to a fuller life of faith, justice, holy, obedience, good deeds and positive self-fulfillment. Positive human responses to God empowers the human being to live in harmony with the neighbor.

This heavenly mode of life or "*Nirvana*" is achieved on earth (cf. Matt. 6:9-10) through faith and diligent praxis of agape. This is God's universal invitation and God's gospel of salvation to the world. Thus, agape leads to heaven, for those who live by it. It is also the gate and criterion by which all human beings are judged by God as being either worthy or unworthy of salvation and heaven. The rejection of agape is also a self-imposed sentence a hell as a negative life of hate, chaos, discord, evil works and destruction (cf. Matt. 5-7; 25:31-46; 1 John. 4:7-21). Agape rejects Darwinism.

Ultimately, both Agape and the correlative "*shalom*" (peace) of God, constitute God's universal concrete salvation and the kingdom in the cosmos. Therefore, those people who carry out the missions of love, mercy and charity, are God's concrete temporal ambassadors, saints, and angels in the world. Agape is regarded as the ultimate divine gift for the completion and maximum humanization, and divinization of the human an evolutionary animal in the world. Agape represents the apex of human evolution. In short, agape is the tangible form of human divinity.

Agape is the divine medium through which the natural and ordinary human-animal is both positively and supernaturally transformed from a mere brute (beast or an animal) into a supernatural heavenly being as a morally responsible loving divine being or "*imago Dei.*" As such, the truly authentic human being as a responsible, caring and loving creature of God in the temporal world, is also both by God's free unmerited grace, the temporal incarnation and epiphany of God in the world, and its temporal and historical processes.

Jesus as the Christ was this true divine manifestation of God in history, as a prototype and example for other obedient, caring and peace loving saints of God to follow. As such, anybody who promotes love, ethnic or religious mutual tolerance and peaceful coexistence, in war-torn or divided countries like Somalia, Rwanda, Liberia, Nigeria, Uganda, Sudan, Angola, Mozambique, Kenya, Burundi, South Africa, Zaire and Algeria is such a saint and an ambassador of God in the world (cf. Matt. 5-7; 1 John 4:7-21).

NOTES

1. This includes the reviews of professors Jacob Olupona, Benjamin Ray and S.K. Kisirinya. I have also taken into account the constructive comments given by Professors Olupona, Ray and other scholars on November 20, 1993 given in response to my paper entitled, "African Religion as the basis for Religious and Societal Ethics in Africa." The paper was presented at the annual meeting for the American Academy of Religion and the Society for Biblical Literature. The paper was based on the material, and central thesis in this book. The Rev. Dr. Kisirinya's analytical and critical book review appeared in the *Journal of African Religion and Philosophy*, Vol. 2, No. 1, 1991:167-169.

2. Some examples of this kind of research and literature includes the works of Levy Bruhl and Authur Jensen. Bruhl believed that the African culture and language were so primitive based on gestures for meaning and communication to the extent that the Africans could not understand themselves in the dark. The other demeaning example research and works to Black people are those of the White supremacist professors Authur Jensen and Charles Murray the coauthor of the infamous *The Bell Curve* (New York: Random House Press, 1994). Jensen both erroneously believed and taught that the Africans were akin to the chimps due to similar quick locomotor when compared to the Whites. See: Stephen Jay Gould, *The Mismeasure of Man* (New York/London: Norton, 1981), 1-344; Ronald Segal, *The Race War* (New York: Viking, 1967), 9-119; George M. Fredrikson, *The Black Image in the White Mind*, (Middletown: Wesleyan University, 1987), 1-311; Emmanuel Kalenzi Twesigye, *God, Race, Myth and Power: An Africanist Corrective Research Analysis* (New York: Peter Lang, 1991), 1-58; 213-220.

3. See Frederick Hegel's *Philosophy of History* and the demeaning section on Africa in terms of the negative evaluation of its culture, history and civilization.

4. See Anorld Toynbee's negative comments on Africa and its history in influential and monumental works, *The History of Civilizations*, 12 vols.

5. For some examples, see following works: Karl W. Luckert, *The Hebrew Light and the Egyptian Fire: Theological and Philosophical Roots of Christendom in Evolutionary Perspective* (New York: New York University Press, 1991); Grace Beardsley, *The Negro in Greek and Roman Civilization: A Study of the Ethiopian Type* (Baltimore: Johns Hopkins Press, 1929); Yosef A. A. ben-Jochannan, *The African Mysteries System of Wa'Set, Egypt, and its European Stepchild: "Greek Philosophy"* (New York: Alkebu-lan Books and Educational Materials, 1986); Yosef ben-Jochannan, *Abu Simbel-Ghizeh: Guidebook/Manual* (New York: Alkebu-lan Books and Educational Materials, 1986); Yosef ben-Jochannan, *Africa: Mother of Western Civilization* (New York: Alkebu-lan Books and Educational Materials, 1971); ben-Jochannan, *Black Man of the Nile and His Family* (New York: Alkebu-lan Books and Educational Materials, 1981); ben-Jochannan, *We the Black Jews: Witness to the White Jewish Race Myth* (New York: Alkebu-lan Books and Educational Materials, 1983); Lerone Bennett, *Before the Mayflower: A History of Black America* (Chicago: Johnson Publishing Co., 1982).

Other notable works include: Martin Bernal, *Black Athena: The Afroasiatic Roots of Classical Civilization, Volume I: The Fabrication of Ancient Greece 1785-1985* (New Brunswick, NJ: Rutgers University Press, 1987); Cheikh Anta Diop, *Civilization or Barbarism: An Authentic Anthropology* (Translated by Yaa-Lengi Meema Ngemi. Edited by Harold J. Salemson and Marjolijn de Jager. New York: Lawrence Hill, 1991); Cheikh Anta Diop, *The African Origin of Civilization: Myth or Reality* (Edited and translated by Mercer Cook. New York: Lawrence Hill, 1974); Stanford Lewis, "The Falsification of Ancient Kemet: From 3400 BCE to 500 BCE" MPS thesis, Cornell University, August, 1993; Emmanuel K. Twesigye, *The Global Human Problem* (New York: Peter Lang, 1988), 184-204; Twesigye, *God, Race and Myth*, 1-40.

6. See Stanford Lewis's MPF thesis (Cornell, 1993), 149-150. This thesis is a good guide for those who seek a good post-modernist Africanist or Afrocentric understanding of Egypt, African civilization, and history or its vast Eurocentric literature. Predictably, Lewis most provocatively concludes his research and interpretation of the African material in his thesis in a manner that will probably alarm most Eurocentric scholars.

7. For sample literature, see: Ronald Segal, *The Race War*, 1-407; Jay Gould, *The Mismeasure of Man*; George Fredrickson, *The Black Image in the White Mind*; Bob Blauner, *Black Lives and White Lives: Three Decades of Race relations in America* (Berkeley: University of California Press, 1989); Edward H. Flannery, *The Anguish of the Jews: Twenty-Three Centuries of Antisemitism* (Mahwah: New Jersey, 1985); Twesigye, *God, Race, Myth and Power*, 1-50; Twesigye, *The Global Human Problem*, 249-294; James M. Jones, *Prejudice and Racism* (Reading /London:Addison Wesley Publications, 1972), 1-177; Nicholas Lemann, *The Promised Land: The Great Black Migration and How it Changed America* (New York: Knopf, 1991); Paula S. Rothenberg, *Racism and Sexism: An Integrated Study* (New York: Martin Press, 1988); Joseph Barndt, *Dismantling Racism: The Continuing Challenge to White America* (Minneapolis: Augsburg Fortress Press, 1991).

8. Based on this observation, W.E.B. DuBois was predict that the twentieth century would be characterized by struggles and violence along racial and color lines. See, *The Souls of Black Folk*, (Nashville: The Fisk University Press, the Diamond Jubilee Edition, 1979), 1-20. White people are threatened by the color and non-Caucasian features of the non-

Whites. This is more visible in the case of the Africans both in africa and in the diaspora. As a consequence, Blacks in any part of the world have been subjected to more racial discrimination, harassment, enslavement and segregation more than any other group of people, including Jews. Jews have suffered a great deal not just because of their race or color, but mainly for voluntary self-segregation in order to keep themselves religiously pure. See Flannery, *The Anguish of the Jews*.

As wars in Liberia, Rwanda, Somalia and Eastern European have clearly demonstrated the new world disorder is characterized by atavistic tribal and ethnic consciousness, ethnocentrism, exclusive ethnic pride, cultural nationalism, xenophobia, and neurosis of destructive racism. See, *Time Magazine*, (January 3, 1994), 34-59. There are also the positive movements for peace which are universally applauded by the men and women of good-will.

The *Time Magazine* (Jan. 3, 1994) honored Yitzhak Rabin the President of Israel, Nelson Mandela, now the President of South Africa, F.W. de Klerk, and Yasser Arafat the President of the Palestinian Organization (PLO) as the men of the year. They received this honor for their role as the peace-makers. Mandela and de Klerk were also the joint recipients of the Peace Nobel Prize for their own efforts at bridging the racial gulf and ending racial violence in South Africa. These are concrete examples of agapic, divine mission of peace-making in the world as part of God's cosmic salvation.

9. See: Justo L. Gonzalez, *The History of the Christian Thought* (Nashville: Abingdon, 1971) Vol. 1:125- 360; vol. 2:13-73; and EuGene TeSelle, *St. Augustine of Hippo*, 1-67.

10. This cultural ethnocentrism and idolatry is what is referred to as Eurocentrism. In this respect, Europe usurps the place of God as the measure of humanity, religion, civilization, culture, language, beauty, technology, education and values. Tragically, in a crude White supremacist theological understanding to be a "*imago Dei*" is be White and European. This form of crude form of idolatry is found in the White supremacist teachings of Ku Klux Klan and other White supremacist organizations in the USA, South Africa and Germany. See: Twesigye, *God, Race, Myth and Power*, 1-50; and note 7 above. Subsequently, failure to accept any human being just because of his or her color, race, gender or any other natural physical feature, such as sexual orientation, is a serious sin against both god and the neighbor.

11. See, Twesigye, "The African Religion as the Basis of Religious and Societal Ethics," *Zumari: The Journal of Black World Studies*, (Ohio Wesleyan University), December, 1993, 1-9. Unlike the puritanical Victorian negative view of sexuality, the Africans celebrated sex a good gift from God for the life enhancement processes creation of new human beings as a means positive social interaction, alliances and social bonding. To this end, polygamy and other socially sanctioned sexual activities and marriage were traditionally positively viewed as good. However, AIDS and other sexually transmitted diseases, have brought Africans to the reaffirmation of faithful monogamous marriages are now promoted as God's new revealed will. See, also, Oswald Ndolerire, "In Search of Lost Values: The African's Quest for Self-Development," *The Journal for African Religion and Philosophy*, Vol. 2 No. 2:1-16.

12. See, Twesigye, *The Global Human Problem*, 126-146; and *God, Race, Myth and Power*, 145-170. The human being speaks because he or she is a divine being or "*imago Dei.*" Therefore, whatever speaks qualifies to be either a human being, God's ambassador or God. God is the Primordial Speaker of the Word and the human being the is the cosmic Hearer of God's Word. All creation, including humanity exists as a result of God's Creative Word. Therefore, creation exists as God's a materialized, and concretized living speech or

song of love and drama. Creation also exists as form of God's own symphony for self-entertainment.

13. See, "Sacrosanctum Concilium" 54, *The Documents of Vatican II* edited by Walter M. Abbot, S.J. and translated by the Very Rev. MSGR. Joseph Gallagher (Chicago: Association Press/Follet, 1966), 156. Liturgy can be validly conducted in the local language as in Latin. However, the conservatives have preferred Latin Mass. Since most of these people could not understand Latin, the Latin Mass truly sounded more magical, holy, mystical and mysterious or God's own incomprehensible special language. Likewise, many conservative Baptists still prefer the King James version and the conservative Episcopalians, have rejected the introduction of the new and revised *Common Prayer Book* of 1978 and preferred the 1928 *Book of Common Prayer*. Some Roman Catholics, have also negatively viewed mass in the local language as a "vulgarization the mass" and the liturgy! Likewise, the ancient Christians who also resisted St. Jerome's original translation of the holy scriptures from Greek and Hebrew into the Latin, and had contemptuously referred to his translation *"The Vulgate."* Now it is respectable. "Christianity" was also "invented" as a derogatory term to describe the "idolatrous worshippers of a man called Jesus the Christ!"

14. For some examples, see: Ali Mazrui, *The African Condition* (New York: The University of Cambridge, 1980); Mazrui, *The Africans: A Triple Heritage* (Boston/Toronto: Brown & Co, 1986). The documentary films based on this work were welcomed by many pan-Africanists, but rejected by the Eurocentric scholars.

15. For sample literature, see: Martin Bernal, *Black Athena: The Afroasiatic Roots of Classical Civilization, Volume I: The Fabrication of Ancient Greece 1785-1985* (New Brunswick, NJ: Rutgers University Press, 1987); Cheikh Anta Diop, *Civilization or Barbarism: An Authentic Anthropology* (Translated by Yaa-Lengi Meema Ngemi. Edited by Harold J. Salemson and Marjolijn de Jager, New York: Lawrence Hill, 1991); Cheikh Anta Diop, *The African Origin of Civilization: Myth or Reality* (Edited and translated by Mercer Cook. New York: Lawrence Hill, 1974); Stanford Lewis, "The Falsification of Ancient Kemet: From 3400 BCE to 500 BCE" MPS thesis, Cornell University, August, 1993.See also: Karl W. Luckert, *The Hebrew Light and the Egyptian Fire: Theological and Philosophical Roots of Christendom in Evolutionary Perspective* (New York: New York University Press, 1991); Grace Beardsley, *The Negro in Greek and Roman Civilization: A Study of the Ethiopian Type* (Baltimore: Johns Hopkins Press, 1929); Yosef A. A. ben-Jochannan, *The African Mysteries System of Wa'Set, Egypt, and its European Stepchild: "Greek Philosophy"* (New York: Alkebu-lan Books, 1986).

16. See, Francis A. Sullivan, S.J., *Salvation Outside the Church? Tracing the History of the Catholic Response* (New York: Paulist Press, 1992), 1-155.

17. Cf. Bernhard W. Anderson, *Understanding the Old Testament*, 4th Edition (Englewood Cliffs: Prentice Hall, 1986), 54-58.

18. See, Jommo Kenyatta, *Facing Mount Kenya* (New York: Vintage Book/Random House, 1962). Moses and the Mt. Sinai experience sounds like the Kikuyu stories.

19. See: Sam Keen, "Personal Myths Guide Daily Life: The Stories We Live By," *Psychology Today*, December, 1988:44-47; Joseph Campbell and Bill Moyers, *Religious Myths*, (6 vols/parts on Video by PBS hosted by Bill Moyers).

21. In the New Testament God is Agape (1 Jn. 4:7-21). Therefore, to participate in Agape is to both participate in God and to experience the beatific vision in heaven.

20. For Example, see Paul Tillich, *New Being*; *The Shaking of the Foundations*; *Systematic Theology*, Vols 2 and 3.

22. According to John Mbiti, (*African Religions and Philosophy*) the African Religion the greatest evil is that of societal strife, social imbalance, and discord with the neighbor, ancestors, nature, spirit-world and God. Therefore, God's supernatural salvation consists in the restoration or establishment of love, cooperation, well-being, peace, harmony and balance in human relationships with the neighbor, the community, the ancestors, the spirit-world, God and nature. Also, see L. Njinya-Mujinya, "Zoroastrianism and Kinyankole Views of Good and Evil: A Comparative Study," *Journal of African Religion and Philosophy*, Vol. II, 2:95-113.

23. See 21 above. God is the cosmic Creative Mystery and Redemptive Agape. God is *Sola Gratia* in all his works of unmerited cosmic creation and redemption. With God, nothing is ever deserved; not creation nor redemption. All of created beings and life is by divine *gratis* as free gifts of God's Agape or Unconditional Love and Universal gratuitous Grace. This is the philosophical and theological hypothesis and basic foundation for this work. It is based on Scriptures, reason, tradition, comparative religion, science, history, theology, ethics, anthropology and linguistics.

III

GOD'S UNIVERSAL FREE GRACE IN CREATION AND REDEMPTION: THE PROBLEM OF THE EXCLUSIVE CHRISTIAN DOGMA OF *"EXTRA ECCLESIAM NULLA SALUS"*

It is now certain that Karl Rahner has been the leading and most influential Catholic theologian for this century.[1] Perhaps he is not the equal of either St. Augustine or Thomas Aquinas, but his impact on the Second Vatican Council, and on post-Vatican II Catholic theology is so great that it is difficult to assess it adequately at present.

However, it can be said that like both saints Augustine and Thomas Aquinas, he too, has defined and reshaped the nature of Catholic theological reflection and ecclesiality. He has also introduced a new universal, and inclusive fundamental soteriological base, with its correlative inclusive theological methodology. Both this inclusive soteriology and methodology are fully grounded in philosophical-theological anthropology and post-modern inclusive global epistemology.[2]

1. The Theological Starting Point: The Inseparable Nature of Creation and Salvation as God's Twin Cosmic Activities of Free Grace and Unconditional Love.

This theological starting point has enabled him to analyze and critique the well-established Western, traditional theology and ecclesiology. His innovative, post-modernist inclusive philosophical and anthropological-theological approach has led him to reject the traditional, narrow ecclesiastical, ethnocentric, exclusive, Western or Eurocentric bigoted soteriological dogmas, such as that of *extra ecclesiam nulla salus*.[3]

By his constructive use of an inclusive theological-philosophical Christian anthropology, Rahner has critically analyzed and reappraised these traditional Christian doctrines in a more constructive, positive, inclusive, ecumenical and contemporary, global existential theological, and philosophical manner. This inclusive, innovative global theological method and approach has yielded a very profound global Christian theology and inclusive universal soteriology based on the inclusive universality of God's creative and redemptive will, unmerited gratuitous grace, and unconditional love.

Rahner's theological method and approach universalist, inclusive of all God's people, and undogmatic. Rahner's fundamental inclusive universal Christian soteriology and *modus operandi* are grounded in seeing all human beings, everywhere, as the universal concern of one cosmic, eternal Creator-Redeemer God.

According to Rahner, both creation and salvation are inseparably viewed, and treated as one process which takes place in history as two simultaneous *"kairotic moments"* or "twin activities" of one divine act of creation and transformation of creation. This position rejects the traditional human finitization of God's activities of creation and redemption into two separate successive or "chronological divine events" which take place in concrete time or space, just because they appear to finite human minds and temporal history, to occur in that manner.

However, this is a mere mental illusion and distortion of God's transcendent eternal and *"kairotic events"* in the human mind and the historical world, which is unable to understand them fully. This apparent illusion and distortion of God's time and activities is due to the human problem of finitude and limitations. As such, the human being is unable to transcend the limitations of historical finite time, space, and mundane logical progression or historicization of God's eternal or *"kairotic events"* in historical and mental limitations which are imposed by finite categories of time and space. Therefore, it is a serious error, if we finitize God's unlimited eternal time and transcendence, in order fit his or eternal activities into the human conceptual framework of religious dogma, and philosophical or epistemological limitations of finite time, space, power, knowledge, creativity, mercy, freedom, intentions and will or capacity to act.

It is theologically, philosophically or epistemologically important to note that these limited finite temporal categories are the human mental epistemological basic structures which the human being employs to apprehend, decipher, analyze, process, and understand God and his activities in the cosmos. In this humanizing and historicization process of God, the transcendent holy God is not only incarnated in culture, history and the world, but also inadvertently mundanized by this imperfect humanocentric process and anthropocentric theological epistemology.

Tragically and unconsciously, God is philosophically, theologically, culturally, religiously, and idolatrously mentally created in the respective local human image, instead of the converse. Unfortunately, in most cases, human beings are blind to the truth and unaware of their idolatrous illusions of God, and the co-extensive correlated distorted theological or philosophical ideas of God and his creative and redemptive work in the world. This contributes to the theological formulation of erroneous and exclusive bigoted doctrines, such as "*extra ecclesiam nulla salus.*"

This being the case, Rahner then goes on to argue that the Agape-God or "Sola Gratia," is the one who created all human beings out of his free, unmerited grace, and because he also loves them all unconditionally, he also redeems them unconditionally. In short, the Loving-Creator-Redemptive-God gratuitously creates and redeems all human beings everywhere in the cosmos, and in every age. God does this by virtue of his free, unmerited universal grace, which is efficaciously salvific by His unconditional love, and universal redemptive will for all human beings He has created.[4]

God's redemptive efficacious grace enables human beings everywhere, and in every age, to become more fully humanized and humane. This process of humanization is correlative with human deification and salvation. Both of these are the intention of God in both creation and salvation which are correlative with the divine act of calling humanity into being, and the constant divine action of calling human beings to become more humane and more loving.

It is very insightful of Rahner and theologically accurate to refer to this divine process of completing the humanization of the human being as "divine salvation." This humanization process is synonymous and co-extensive with *theosis*. This is God's divinization process of the human creature into God's obedient child (*imago Dei*), ambassador or saint and entry to God's kingdom or the attainment of divine salvation. This is positively and soteriologically affirmed to be God's universal's will, and benevolent activity, regardless of conditions, such as color, race, gender, creed, and religious affiliation.

Nevertheless, Rahner being both a Catholic priest, and a leading modern Western Christian theologian, had already acquired a given specific Western Christian context, and as such a Western Christian standpoint from which to discuss this central issue of humanity and salvation. Since according to the traditional mainline Christian Christocentric soteriological dogma of *"extra ecclesiam nulla salus"* (there is no salvation outside the Church), therefore, in order to remain within the traditional Church and its teachings, Rahner still affirms that all God's supernatural salvation is God's work of unmerited universal grace.

For Rahner, God effects this inclusive cosmic redemption through the eternal and cosmic Logos-Christ (cf. John 1:1-18; 14:6). The historical Church is just a small part of God's vehicles of cosmic grace and salvation. Therefore, it erroneous for the historical Christian Church to claim either a monopoly of God's redemptive grace or to fail to realize that God's activities of cosmic creation and redemption are universal, free and not limited to the Christian historical Church's work, sacraments or membership.

However, in some broad understanding of the Logos-Christ, and the correlative "Cosmic Church," we can still affirm this dogma, and yet, still affirm the God's free universal salvific will and free grace. Both positions presuppose God's existence and his works of creation, moral evil or sin and the necessary universal divine, free, sufficient and efficacious grace through the eternal Cosmic Christ to effect salvation in the world and positive transformation, for those with faith in God or who love life and their neighbors. This Cosmic Christ and Universal Savior is also the same eternal Logos. According to Christianity, this God's Logos/Word, the second person of the Trinity. As such, the Christ-Logos is eternal, divine in nature and the inseparable dual agent of God's cosmic creation and redemption.

Therefore, the systematic study, definition and explanation of the mysteries of God's cosmic free activities of unmerited universal grace and agape, in both creation and redemption should be the main tasks of theology. Since a good, and meaningful applied Christian theology, like a good scientific theory, should present a practical model of God in the context and relationship of God's inclusive free cosmic activities of free creation and universal free supernatural salvation.

For the sake of a inclusive working theological model, and evaluation of temporal or existential religious truth, God's supernatural salvation or redemption, are defined as being coextensive, and synonymous or correlative with God's cosmic temporal creative and redemptive activities.

These are concrete divine activities in terms of creation and any activities which lead to positive human moral transformation, justice, agape, peace, harmony, general well-being for humanity, the community, creation, and the world. These are God's actual historical divine activities which constitute God's cosmic work of free creation and redemption. These apparent ordinary divine activities in the world are miracles to be discerned by the wise, the prophets and the saints of God.

For those with the eyes and insight to see at deeper spiritual and religious level, the world and its ordinary events and history constitute God's supernatural arena for creation and redemption. The apparent ordinary arena and its natural historical or evolutionary processes become correctly viewed as God's chosen humble, but appropriate extraordinary vehicles for the supernatural mediation of God's unmerited free gifts of efficacious free of grace, agape, forgiveness and salvation as both the evolutionary improvement and humanization of the temporal world.[5]

Consequently, the central thesis and argument of this book is that Rahner's more inclusive Christian teaching on humanity, universal divine redemptive grace, and "anonymous Christianity are very meaningful and attractive Christian concepts which are at the same time compatible with the teaching, and the lived life in the African tradition.

The central focus as well as the central thesis of this book is that God's activities of cosmic creative and redemptive are both free and universal. They are carried out by God in his own free universal unconditional love or agape, and the unmerited universal divine salvific will. Both of these divine cosmic inseparable twin activities of free cosmic creation and redemption are efficaciously indiscriminately carried out by God in the whole cosmos. God carries out his work of cosmic creation and salvation freely, without help from his creatures.

Both creativity and redemption are eternally interrelated, and irrevocably intertwined in God's eternal bipolar or twin dynamic evolutionary[6] creative motion and processes of God's free functions of grace, agape, creative self-expression and self-embodiment in the genesis and sustenance of the orderly, and yet, non-static, active processes that constitute the intricate, living, growing and self-conscious cosmos as an orderly and well-balanced system.

This cosmic divine work is universally carried out through the divine Mind or the *Logos* (the Word of God) described in the Bible (cf. John 1-3; 10:9; 14:6-11; Acts 4:12). As such, all human beings everywhere in the cosmos and in every age, right from the beginning of humanity, are created, redeemed, and fulfilled by God's free and unmerited universal gratuitous efficacious grace and agape, working in everywhere in the cosmos through the Logos or the Christ.

Therefore, no person is created to be truly redeemed from the threat of evil, hate, malice, finitude, existential anxiety, chaos, and fear of death, apart from God's grace and agape working through Christ as the divine eternal Logos. Universally, this is the case. The Logos or the eternal Cosmic Christ is the essential eternal embodiment and source of God's primordial cosmic life, order, harmony, meaning, peace, happiness and all fulfillment of creaturely life.

This being the case, therefore, the traditional Christian dogma of "*extra ecclesiam nulla salus*" can be validly repudiated in as much as the "*ecclesiam*" is defined as the "Apostolic and holy [Roman] Catholic Church." But it can be affirmed positively in the inclusive Christian global context of this book, if "ecclesiam" is more broadly defined as God's universal (catholic) community of the redeemed," or if it is defined as "the universal (catholic) community of the family and obedient children of God."

2. The Problem of the Term "Anonymous Christianity"

The Christian affirmation is that all human beings are saved by God's free universal, supernatural grace through Christ. St. John affirms that the incarnate Christ was also the pre-existent Logos of God who is also God's eternal agent of creation (John 1:1-18; Gen. 1:1-3). Subsequently, for lack of a better and more inclusive Christian terminology, Rahner calls all those people "anonymous Christians"[7] who experience divine salvation outside the conventional Christian fellowship, and outside the explicit Apostolic Christian Community or Church. This is theologically important and central to this work.

This is the case because the major Christian theologians and Church leaders such as Cyprian, Augustine, Aquinas and Calvin saw the necessity of membership in the Church as being essential and mandatory for all those elected and destined for supernatural salvation. This membership was viewed to be essential, since the Church was supposed to possess the special gifts of God's redemptive grace and power for salvation in the form of the sacraments which are duly administered by the Apostolic Church.

Within the theological and framework of this work, God's redemptive Church presented as universal fact or reality. It exists universally and efficaciously in God's eternal Creative and Redemptive Word, the eternal Logos prior to the Incarnation. Membership in this universal and inclusive pre-Incarnation Cosmic Church is also membership in God's kingdom, since both are co-extensive divine realms, realties and positive agapic modalities of peaceful, socially harmonious, just and agapic human existence in the local community, and in the world.

The true universal sacrament of this Church of God is Agape and its praxis. To participate in Agape and practice it, is to participate in God and his kingdom. In this respect, Agape being identical with God and being God (cf. 1 Cor. 13; 1 John 4:7-21) is analogous to the Apostolic Church's doctrine of the incarnate Logos being identical to God and also being God, and as such, the eucharistic sacrament being the mystical channel of participation in the Christ or the Logos and therefore, the mystical union with the incarnate God. However, this is a faith based passive union with God, which may not result in necessary correlative redemptive agapic good works of God's redeeming grace in the world (cf. John 15:1-17; Matt. 7:15-27; 25:31-46; James 2:1-26).

3. The Problem of the Necessity of Church Membership and Sacraments for Salvation

Traditionally, membership in the mainline Apostolic Catholic Church (and not the heretic or schismatic), and diligent partaking of its essential principle sacraments of baptism and the eucharist, was viewed and politically emphasized by the Church, and its confessional denominational dogmatic theologians as being the primary necessary prerequisite or mystical holy ritual for salvation.

The Church and the sacraments were naively theologically narrowly viewed in literal and physical terms. As a result, they were perceived wrongly as the concrete physical means or vehicles by which God's efficacious redemptive and salvific grace was supposed to be conferred upon the baptized people or the initiates. The baptized or the initiates were considered to be mystically and supernaturally [or magically] united and incorporated into Christ through the power and the mysteries of the saving grace of God's Church.[8]

Nevertheless, Aquinas and other Catholic theologians themselves found this doctrine too restrictive and exclusive. As a result, Aquinas, taught that non-baptized holy people of faith and charitable works, would be saved by God based on their implicit desire for baptism and the eucharist. Later, Rahner built an inclusive systematic Christian theology on this Thomistic profound inclusive theological foundation of the sacraments.

However, most Christians including theologians, have tragically remained mentally, and theologically ethnocentrically enslaved to this exclusive soteriological literalism, and erroneous physical understanding of the sacraments. This is based on a biblical literalism interpretation of the book of Genesis, and the soteriological paradigm of the exclusive, small redemptive Ark of Noah in a vast perishing rebellious evil world of doubt, hedonism, pride and corruption (Gen. 1-12).

According to this theologically tragic, narrow traditional Christian ecclesiology and soteriology, the exclusive or special Christian administration of the rite of the sacrament of holy baptism, is miraculously or magically supposed to cleanse away the original or Adamic sin. As such, it is supposedly universally required in order to regenerate the sinner, and to initiate the baptismal candidate into the holy mysteries of God's salvation and eternal life through Jesus as the Incarnate Christ. This ecclesiology and soteriology sounds good, but it is short sighted, culturally and religiously ethnocentric, bigoted and exclusive. It has little tolerance for religious and cultural diversity and pluralism.

Traditional Western ecclesiology, especially in its Roman Catholic expression is essentially monolithic in ecclesiological understanding, polity, doctrine, liturgical formulation of worship, and in procedure of ritual and sacraments.

Subsequently, this ethnocentric and exclusive monolithic traditional Eurocentric Christian Church, in its traditional theology and world-view, has no room for tolerance and inclusion of non-Christians in the fellowship with God on earth or heaven, and God's kingdom. For these kinds of bigoted exclusive Christians, God's kingdom is only for the baptized saints and not for all God's saints and obedient people everywhere, and in every age, unless they are members of an acceptable mainline historical Apostolic Christian Church, namely, the Roman Catholic Church or the "Balokole" (those born again) in the case of East Africa.

Therefore, traditional mainline Apostolic Christian Church exclusive ecclesiology and its correlative collaborative theology, particularly, the various forms and degrees of exclusive incarnational soteriology, are inadequate in today's religious diversity and culturally pluralistic society. These ancient and antiquated exclusive dogmas are stumbling blocks to Christian ecumenism, interreligious dialogue and mutual cooperation in working on common tasks and ventures for peace and well-being of all God's people in the world, irrespective of creed, class, gender, race, nationality and ideology.

4. God's Universal Activities of Grace, Human Cultural and Religious Diversity and Need for an Inclusive Theology of the Church and Sacraments

Narrow and exclusive dogmatic systems of ecclesiology and soteriology, are theologically unacceptable, since they are too restrictive of God's universal salvific will and universal efficacious grace which is both mystically and visibly working in the whole cosmos as God's free and unmerited creation of grace and agape working through the pre-Incarnate Cosmic Christ or the Logos.

Moreover, within the context of human evolution the literal theological affirmation of the original or Adamic sin, which needs to be washed away by the sacrament of baptism, becomes theologically absurd and false. Likewise, the familiar Augustinian and Thomistic analogies of the Church to Noah's ark, outside of which there is no salvation,[9] becomes both historically and theologically false. Based on both history, human evolution and archeology, we know for a fact that there was no single man (Adam) and his wife (Eve) who were created about 5000 years ago by God as fully adults. There is also a lack of evidence for a literal historical event, such as Noah's ark, and the legendary cosmic flood which, allegedly, destroyed all disobedient and sinful human beings who were not members of Noah's family (Gen. 5-11).

Therefore, to insist on the literal existence of a historical Adam, Eve and Noah in order to formulate an exclusive soteriology, sexist or racist ecclesiology, is theologically destructive and malicious. It is a mockery of God's universal activities of free grace in both cosmic creation and redemption. Therefore, an adoption and narrow interpretation of the dogma of *extra ecclesiam nulla salus* to exclude Jews, Muslims, Hindus, Buddhists, Native Americans and members of the African Traditional Religion, is both theologically unwise and religiously fraudulent.

God does this work effectively by his own power which works by means of God's own unmerited infinite gratuitous grace and unconditional love. All that creatures can do is to respond in faith, love, thanksgiving and worship. This is the appropriate human response. In addition, the human being can also cooperate with God in the free holy cosmic activities of creation and redemption. In this venture, the human being as *imago Dei* can effectively become a co-creator and co-reader with God in the world.

Nevertheless, the human being has to become obedient to God's will in the cosmos and be positively oriented to God's cosmic mysteries and free divine activities of grace in creation and redemption, so as to cooperate with God's will which works through the power of persuasion through love, grace and humility. Then the obedient people of God and his saints anywhere in the world will be able to come to God's eternal holy beatific presence through agape, and respect for God's cosmic creation, which is God's universal temporal temple where, God's universal and free efficacious holy creative and redemptive presence is concretely experienced, and seen at work (cf. Rom.1:17-32).

Therefore, it is the positive Christian affirmation that anyone, anywhere and in every age, can know God and gain access to supernatural salvation through the eternal Logos as both the cosmic pre-Incarnate, and the Incarnate or historical Christ. Subsequently, all human beings in the cosmos have been created by God with an intrinsic inner efficacious redemptive grace and positive orientation to God's saving mysteries of grace and salvation. The human being was also freely endowed by God with the supernatural grace, power and effective capacity to gain positive faith in God's mysteries, goodness, love, peace, and to respond to God in voluntary activities of thanksgiving, praise and worship.

Consequently, in this book, God's free cosmic activities of both creation and redemption are viewed, as being just merely two inseparable divine simultaneous dual or bipolar activities in God's time as "*kairos*." However, to the finite minds which are limited by finite chronological time and space, God's simultaneous events of "*kairos*" which take place in God's eternal time, are processed chronologically in human finite linear time. As a result, these divine events of *kairos* are distorted in finite human minds. Subsequently, they are "finitized" in history as two separate events of which one is always prior to the other, as cause and the other, as the secondary consequent and effect. It is because of this logic, and illusion due to the confusion of God's *kairos* and human *chronos*, that for human finite minds everywhere, creation and redemption appears as two independent and separate historical events of God's agape, grace, and power in the world and within the world's categories of time, space, chronological sequence of cause and effect.

Nevertheless, God being eternal and "*ahistorical*," in God's time of both eternity and *kairos*, there is no limitation of cause and effect or actuality and potentiality are the same in terms of knowledge and experience. God exists in the timeless, multi-media, transcendent and omnidimension of eternity. Therefore, God as this eternal and Transcendent, can also in a single glance or unbroken moment, see the entire dimension of finite time and history, both past and future or potential events, as a present reality.

Therefore, for God, all past and potential future events constitute one single category of actuality in the present or "eternal the now." Accordingly, for God, there is no division of events into past, present and future events or potential events, since they all subsist in him, as their single present reality, and creative ground in the ever present, cosmic omnipresent or the "eternal now." Like a cosmic time traveller, the Cosmic Transcendent Creative Spirit as God the Creator, Sustainer and Redeemer, can simultaneously be in all places and eras, to effect events in the past as in the future. Accordingly, contrary to the naive claims of some process theologians, God is unlike finite limited human beings, who are limited by dimensions of time and space. Therefore, the transcendent God as an eternal creative comic Creative Spirit or Energy is not bound nor limited by finite dimensions, such those of location, space or chronological time and its correlative sequence of cause and effect.

Due to the omnipresence, non-linear and fluid nature of eternity, for God, an effect can be validly and causetively prior to its apparent chronological cause, as after the cause. It is the process of becoming and or entering the temporal world that events assume a chronological or sequential order. This order is to permit proper creaturely evolution from the simple to the complex forms of life. This includes the evolution and proper functioning of human beings as moral agents, emerging in the world in their chronological, finite historical time and the temporal, historical and material world.

Both historically and theologically, these inseparable cosmic twin activities of God in creation and redemption, are universally, erroneously apprehended by the finite human being. The limited historical finite human observers have a distorted perspective of God's time or kairos as it manifests itself in both creation and redemption. In this human distortion of God's infinite time of eternity and kairos, both creation and redemption appear to the finite historically conditioned human mind, as being separate or as two different discrete divine activities in linear time and sequential human history.

Therefore, being a finite theologian-philosopher writing for other finite Christian theologians and philosophers, I will employ the finite theological language and the applicable temporal epistemological limited structures in order to speak about God's transcendent nature and activities in the world.

As a result, in this work, I will treat creation and redemption as God's inseparable twin activities, which in human chronological time and process are to be treated as two moments in time and space of the same free divine, universal, single, historical and continuous process of creation and redemption.

This being the case, then, God's redemption as divine universal gratuitous salvation is also correlatively viewed as the moment of the supernatural transformation, modification, reformation, sustenance, nurture, maturation and fulfillment of the initial historical process of creation. Therefore, redemption as continuing creation, sustenance, and fulfillment involves the person's positive growth through the events of life as they continually unfold through the daily processes of life.[10]

Creation, life and salvation or redemption are not separate, static and discrete events which take place in a given place in time and history. On the contrary, these events are intrinsically interrelated as contemporaries, and as components of the same divine on going process of God's creation sustenance, and re-creation, transformation, completion or fulfillment.

Therefore, God's supernatural redemption or salvation, as continuing divine creation and transformation by God and the human obedience and positive cooperation with God, is achieved by means of the respective person's use or misuse of personal freedom, nature and quality of choices, responsibility, experience, love, knowledge, failures, dissatisfaction, despair, fear, anxiety, sin, self-examination, repentance, forgiveness, transformation, growth and maturation.[11]

5. God as Agape and God's Work as "*Sola Agape*" in "*Sola Gratia*"

Whereas in the Old Testament or Hebrew Scriptures God is defined primarily as the cosmic holy Creator (Gen. 1-12), Infinite Mystery and Redeemer (cf. Exod. 1-4) in the New Testament God is positively affirmed as Creative and Redemptive Agape (cf. 1 John 4:7-21; John 1:1-18; 3:16-21; 14-17; Matt. 5-7; 25:31-46).

God is still engaged in the process of creation and redemption of the cosmos and all its beings. God does this gratuitously, out of his unmerited grace, free and unconditional agape (cf. Gen. 1:1-31). This is also the paradigm for God's universal salvation to the world. It is unmerited, unearned and undeserved by any creature, including the saints. For instance, Moses was not chosen or elected by God to become his saint, messiah and prophet in the world due to his own holiness. On the contrary, Moses is said to have been actually a political rebel, and a murderer on the run and in exile (cf. 2:11-15) when God confronted him and called him to become his servant.

It was Creator God that did all the work of creation and salvation. In the case of Moses, in his own grace, God created and saved Moses as a child. Later, "God went out into the wilderness" to seek out the fallen and exiled Moses. By his unmerited free grace and unconditional love, God carried out his characteristic universal free creative and redemptive activities in redeeming, and positively transforming Moses into his obedient servant, messiah and law-giver. All that Moses can do in positive response to God supernatural activities is cooperate with God in faith, hope, love and obedience.

This example of God, Moses and Israel, is a characteristic example of God's free cosmic redemptive grace at work in the world to redeem in unconditional love or agape. In this case God is Agape, functioning in the world as both "*Sola Gratia*" and "*Sola Agape*" in both creation and redemption. God redeems, recreates and transforms Moses into a new being. The rebel and the murderer, Moses is positively transformed into God's holy, obedient saint, liberator of the oppressed Jews, and law giver. Likewise, the liberated Hebrews were not morally or spiritually worthy of salvation before God. They were not morally superior to their Egyptian oppressors, but, God intervened and redeemed them just because he is Sola Agape and Sola Gratia.

Likewise, Mary the holy mother of Jesus did not have any special merits before God. God as "*Sola Gratia*" and "*Sola Agape*" chose her among other women to become the vessel of the incarnation as the mother of Jesus-Christ. Mary choice was out of unmerited grace and unconditional love. Therefore, equally validly, for this holy purpose, and mission, God could have also chosen another woman, such as Mary Magdalene, despite the fact that she had been possessed the devil. After all, she too, by this same unmerited redemptive grace and God's unconditional love, got redeemed, healed, and was positively transformed into God's saint, apostle and citizen of the kingdom of God (cf. Luke 8:2; John 20:11-18).

God's choice of Moses, Simon Peter the ignorant fisherman, the bigoted and murderous Saul (Paul) as his special ambassadors of redemption and salvation in the world, clearly illustrates that redemption or salvation, is God's work from beginning to end. Salvation is a result of God's undeserved work of free grace and agape alone. Therefore, no human being is ever good enough, apart from God's grace to have enough faith, good works and agape to merit God's reward of salvation, heaven, eternal life or God's kingdom.

Like the rebellious and murderous Moses, Saul was a devout Pharisee, patriarchal, sexist and notorious persistent persecutor of the Christians before his dramatic encounter with God on the road to Damascus and subsequent conversion to Christianity (cf. Acts 8:1-3; 9:1-31). In God's free and unmerited universal redemptive grace, and unconditional love, God working through his cosmic Logos-Christ confronted him and transformed him into his saint and Christian missionary on that "unholy road and unholy mission" to Damascus, where he was going to persecute and kill innocent people just, because they had become Christians.

In this redemptive event, God was the primary actor as Redeemer and Savior. Saul did not even have faith worth any merit for God's salvation. Nevertheless, Saul was knocked down from his "high horse," blinded, and humbled by God. When his eyes were re-opened by God, they were spiritually opened to the new inclusive religious reality and truth of God's free redemptive grace, and the need for faith to believe in this new divine salfivic revelation.

Subsequently, Paul converted to the very "Christocentric religious path" (Christianity) to God, even when he had previously sought to persecute and eliminate (cf. Acts 9). As a result, by God's characteristic free universal redemptive grace, God transformed Saul a murderer into Paul the saint, apostle and greatest missionary and theologian of the New Testament and the Christian Church. It is almost impossible to imagine any global Christianity without the missionary journeys of Paul or his global theology, writings and letters which helped to establish it (cf. Acts 15), as such, from a narrow Jesus-cult of the early Jewish Christians.

Indeed, without Paul's missionary work, theological writings, the Apostolic Church would have probably remained another sect in Judaism or died out, all altogether! Thus, Saul the notorious intolerant religious bigot and persecutor of Christianity, was without merit before God. Yet, God acted in his undeserved free grace and unconditional love to redeem him, nurture and transform him into his saint, apostle (missionary) and globalist Christian theologian. As a result, St. Paul founded the gentile Christian inclusive Apostolic Church and wrote more than twenty five percent of the New Testament, despite the fact that he was not a direct disciple or an eyewitness of Jesus and his teaching ministry.

By God's redemptive grace, and his unconditional love alone, Simon Peter, the uneducated and ignorant fisherman of Galilee was called to become the follower of Jesus as the rabbi and the Christ. Despite the fact that Simon Peter promised to be faithful and defend Jesus as his master, when confronted by a maid who identified him as a disciple of Jesus, he denied ever knowing him. Regardless of the fact that Peter denied Jesus three times on the same night, God still redeemed him from evil and guilt. Subsequently, following the resurrection Peter became the obedient saint of God, and most zealously proclaimed Jesus as the crucified and risen Christ. He also proclaimed that Jesus was innocent of sin, but had been wrongly put to death, due to human injustice and sin.

Because Jesus had chosen Peter to succeed him as the leader of the disciples, and having given him the powers or keys to do so, the Popes are known as the successors of St. Peter, whereas the bishops are also regarded and esteemed in the Catholic Church, as the historical, visible successors of the original apostles of Jesus (cf. Matt 16: 17-19; 18:17-20; John 20:21-23). Although these Christian doctrines, and ecclesiological systems of the "Apostolic Succession" and the "Apostolic Faith," are supposed to guard against heresy, they are nonetheless non-efficacious, and theologically meaningless, if they are divorced from the universal unmerited, free redemptive grace of God through his unconditional love, in which they are rooted, and of which they should proclaim as the "good news" of salvation.

Ultimately, this good news should consist in the positive proclamation that in reality the Creator-Redeemer-God loves all human beings unconditionally, and seeks to save them without any prior conditions. That is God in his unmerited grace and love comes to us wherever we are in order to save us from evil, wrong choices in life, and a path of self-destruction.

God's salvation does not wait until we die. That would be too late. That is analogous to a doctor who waits to treat the patient until the patient had already died! Likewise, God's salvation is for the living. Accordingly, God is ever at work of creation, recreation, salvation or redemption and positive creaturely transformation in the world. Therefore, through the Logos-Christ, God is ever calling inviting all human beings, and gently persuading them to actualize ourselves daily in more loving and positively meaningful and satisfying ways as part of that divine salvation and life in the kingdom of God on earth.

Therefore, within this theological context, the praxis of agape is the universal definitive criterion for any truly obedient, holy and saintly life which is pleasing to God. This is because God is creative and redemptive

Agape (cf. 1 John 4:7-21). Accordingly, since, God is Agape, therefore, to practice agape is to be truly like God. Correlatively, to practice agape, is also, to participate in God, and to become a member his kingdom.

Agape and its praxis, both completely humanizes and divinizes all those who practice it. By faith and obedience to the definitive commandment of God to love God and the neighbor unconditionally, as we love ourselves is the universal redemptive divine truth, and most reliable path to God, saintliness, salvation, societal peace, harmony and the concrete kingdom of God on earth. Accordingly, St. Paul identified the supernatural gift of agape as being superior to all other divine or charismatic gifts, including that of faith (cf. 1 Cor. 12-14).

Agape as the universal criterion and primary form of any true godliness is analogous to a "good fruit tree" which is only known by the quality of its good fruits, as opposed to mere green leaves or faith (cf. Matt. 7:15-27; 25:31-46; James 2:1-26). Therefore, any truly redemptive religion should also affirm altruistic good deeds which build about social or societal goodness in the form of justice, harmony, peace, well-being and happiness, as being the outward positive explicit expressions of the inward implicit state of positive faith, obedience to God, holiness and salvation. As both St. Paul and John Wesley also taught, these good deeds are the required positive fruits of grace and growth in the life of sanctification (cf. Rom. 1-6). Immanuel Kant also positively taught that love is the only acceptable foundation for moral grounding of sound ethics, virtue and authentic moral action.

6. Common Ground between Christianity and the African Traditional Religion and Theocentric Humane Modes of Social Existence

To some extent this book is largely a detailed Africanist, theological and philosophical demonstration that the previously degraded and disparaged African Traditional Religion as mere primitive paganism, actually possessed God's free efficacious universal gifts of supernatural redemptive grace and supernatural salvation. In this respect, the African Religion was God's concrete and efficacious channel of grace and salvation to its African adherents or any other person who diligently practiced its positive theocentric and co-extensive agapic community centered stipulations.

Therefore, this books also provides support for Rahner's and the Catholic Church's broad Christian affirmation that the concrete, temporal and historical human existence is the very divine universal arena of creation and salvation. That this is also the arena of God's self-communication to all human beings in His unconditional love, and universal gratuitous efficacious grace, regardless of creed, color, ethnic origin, race, nationality or level of technology.

Rahner uses the technical term of "*categorial*" to denote concrete, temporal, spatial and historical dimensions of human existence in contrast to the transcendental or spiritual ones, which he regards as infinite, and unlimited, unlike these categorial dimensions of matter, time and space which characterize our own limited finite existence and the temporal world in which we live. In this work, I have also employed the term "temporal" in this Rahnerian sense. However, "categorial" is also sometimes used in this same Rahnerian sense and usage of the term.

Obviously, this Rahnerian Christian inclusive doctrine and teaching that the whole cosmos constitutes God's real arena of God's unconditional and universal gratuitous efficacious grace in both creation and salvation is very meaningful, and "good news" to be welcomed by traditional Africans, as for the Hindus and Native Americans. This is an inclusive and powerful Christian teaching, for all people, most especially those who are traditionally non-Christian, such as the Africans and Asians, whose major percentage of the population is still non-Christian.

Therefore, it will be shown in this work that the African modality of authentic human existence (*Obuntu*) is in harmony with Rahner's Christian teaching that whoever accepts God's implicit or explicit revelation, wherever it is given, and within its given mystery accepts both God (*Ruhanga/Katonda/Mungu/Imaana* or *Amun*) and himself/herself as a finite special creature "Omuntu" of God whose well-being and salvation lies in this very Incomprehensible, Creative, Infinite Mystery that Rahner calls God.

Consequently, an attempt has been made in this book to demonstrate that Rahner's Christian teaching on God, humanity and supernatural salvation as the divine humanization of the human being, is in fact similar to the African understanding of authentic human existence (*Obuntu*) as the fullness of loving, humane, godly human life lived by individual human beings in the right social or communal living in full openness, love, and fellowship with God, the neighbor as a fellow human being, and both the living and the departed, most especially the ancestors.

This subject is especially significant and attractive to me as an African theologian and philosopher, because conventional Christianity in Africa South of the Sahara is still new. Although some countries like Uganda,

South Africa, Kenya, Rwanda, Burundi, Zimbabwe, Liberia, Ghana and Zaire are predominantly Christian, in much of Africa, Christianity still remains, largely nominal or a minority religion. Christianity is almost absent in a number of predominantly Islamic African nations, particularly, those in North and West Africa. Therefore, it is important for us to study and adopt this previously unexamined, yet constructive Christian concept and teaching on "anonymous Christianity" in and for the African religious and philosophical systems of thought, teaching and practice.

7. "Anonymous Christianity" as a Theological Tool for Building an Inclusive, Tolerant, Interreligious Harmonious Global Community

Religion has divided people and caused conflict, enmity, hate, wars and violence in the world. Therefore, instead of religion being redemptive and nonviolent, it has often taught it members the vice of bigotry, discrimination, ethnocentrism, xenophobia, exclusivism, sectarianism, intolerance for differences and *jihadism.*

However, the inclusive teaching of "anonymous Christianity" and the theological world-view which proceeds from the axiom that all human beings are God's beloved children to be loved and served without condition, will negate and reverse these apparent evils and shortcomings within Christianity, the Church and other exclusive religions.

By this venture, I hope to create more room in African Christian theology and philosophy for a more sympathetic understanding of both our departed ancestors, who died before hearing the historical and Apostolic Gospel of Incarnate Christ. This is the Gospel which has been proclaimed and witnessed to, by the Apostolic Church, both in word and deed. Since the historical Church is finite and limited in time and space, therefore, the historical Church had to have a beginning in history. That does not mean that God had favorites whom he elected for heaven and others for hell, for lack of access to Apostolic Christianity, the Church and her sacraments.

In addition, God has not rejected those of our relatives, countrymen, and friends, who just happen to be non-Christians, such as Jews, Hindus, Muslims and African traditionalists. Nor has God rejected those to whom Christianity has been misrepresented, and therefore, have rejected it as evil due to the abuses associated with it, such as slavery, materialism, imperialism, racism, sexism and the oppression of women. Nor has God rejected those people who just look at Christianity as just another "foreign religion" to choose from.

Furthermore, in some countries like Uganda, on which much of this book is empirically based, there have been in the past, serious wars which were fought in the name of God and Religion! Here Rahner's inclusive Christian teaching can become a corrective, and therefore, a harbinger of God's true salvation and peace in the current conflicts which are largely grounded in ethnic and religious sectarianism, bigotry and intolerance.

This study confronts this kind of religious hostility, bigotry and intolerance with the Rahnerian inclusive teachings on "anonymous Christianity," with emphasis on God's universal redemptive activity in gratuitous grace which is appropriated in faith and whose chief fruit is obedience to Jesus Christ's commandment of unconditional love for the neighbor (the neighbor being each human being; cf. Luke 10:25-37; Matt. 25:31-46; John 13:34-35.) By this method, it is made very explicit that these kinds of religious conflicts and wars have been misguided.

It will also be demonstrated that jihads, crusades or other holy wars do not endear anybody with God, despite the fact that they are religious crusades or holy wars fought in the holy name of God. On the contrary, in negation of holy wars and righteous violence, God's commandment in Christ is that of agape or the unconditional love and forgiveness for the neighbor, including one's enemy. God is like a compassionate parent who does not desire the death of a sinning child. On the contrary, as Agapic or Loving, compassionate, merciful and forgiving Cosmic Parent, God desires the repentance and salvation of each sinner as his alienated and lost child.

Therefore, such an infinitely good, benevolent, merciful and loving God, desires and wills all his children to be reconciled to him in freedom. Consequently, such a loving and gracious God, cannot will some people to go to heaven and others to go to hell. God does not will nor desire any of his beloved children or people to be lost or injured in any way, including war and violence. War and violence, including holy wars and all religious violence or crusades are never sanctioned by God.

War and violence are evil. They are negative, destructive, societal consequences of human disobedience against God and sin. This is self-evident, since wars and other forms of violence negate agape, goodness, peace and harmony. They are uncharitable, violent and brutal in nature, and therefore, very contradictory to God's unconditional love for all human beings, which is also required of all God-loving human beings. They negate God's agape, forgiveness and peace which are the very basis and quintessence of the supernatural human salvation in Christ (cf. John 3:16, 17; Rom. 5:5-11.)

The new religious understanding sought and portrayed in this book is one rooted in God's universal divine salvific will, the unconditional love of God and universal sufficient free efficacious creative and redemptive grace. This understanding of God has led to the characteristic soteriological doctrines of the inclusiveness of God's kingdom and salvation for Christians and non-Christians. It has also led to the advocacy for global religious tolerance for diversity, unconditional love, and free forgiveness for all people as one's neighbors in Christ and fellow brothers and sisters in the cosmic family of God.

In addition, there is also the appeal for the acceptance of life as God's free gift is freely bestowed on all creation. God has freely given life and redemption as one whole package. As such, it is non-negotiable complexity and diverse riches, glories and mosaic of humanity composed of different colors of racial, ethnic, cultural, ideological diversity and religious pluralism. Diversity is positively affirmed as God's gift to the world.

Conversely, the rejection of diversity, particularly, that of gender, culture, language, religion and race, is denounced as sin against both God as the creator of all different races of people and against the neighbor, since he or she is rejected instead of being accepted unconditionally and loved as a child of God. This is the case regardless of whether this sinful rejection of the neighbor is carried out in the name of God, Christ, the Church, jihad, crusade, economy, politics, ideology, class gender or nationalism.

Rahner's challenge and inclusive Christian teaching have great relevance for the world and Africa, today. For instance, his challenge can be restated as follows: that those engaged in religious discrimination, conflicts, hatred, violence or wars in the name of God, have in fact already lost Him/Her in so doing. For our God is the God of love, who commands us all to love one another without conditions, and to do this by our manner of living as it finds its definitive expression in both word and deed. Subsequently, our own human worth and godliness or Christianity (both explicit and anonymous), are to be measured by our love for the neighbor as viewed by and through our acts of charity both spiritual and material.

Since God creates all human beings freely out of his gratuitous loving grace, the argument is that he also freely sustains them in this grace, and seeks to bring them to fulfillment in himself through his Word (Logos), who is the very divine medium of both creation and salvation, as the authentic human existence in universal divine redemptive grace and creative love (cf.

John 1:1-5, 14.) This means that salvation also consists in our own free, positive self-actualization and fulfillment as finite creatures in this life as it is lived in the presence of God, the very Mystery of life as both its origins, and absolute future.

According to Professor John Mbiti's well documented study of the African religions and philosophy, there is already some fertile ground for rooting this new religious and philosophical understanding. For instance, Mbiti observes that for the African, God is regarded as both the ultimate human origin and destiny.

The present, as the "now," is regarded as the perpetual divine unfolding of this ultimate destiny, and mystery of life as the absolute future with God, who is both the absolute beginning and the end of the human being. For the African, the human being cannot change this givenness of God-oriented life. It can only be either accepted in its givenness and mystery or be rejected by the rebellious sinner. Rejection of God's grace for a fuller life and salvation lead to serious consequences of such a rejection. This rejection of God's grace is also correlative with the rejection of God, goodness, peace and God's will or providence in creation.

An attempt has been made to show that, despite Rahner's strong emphasis on this theme of anonymous Christianity, unlike Frederick Dennison Maurice or Origen, he does not teach that everyone is or will be saved. For Rahner, it is only those who obey God and practice agape, that are saints who are saved by God. It will be clearly demonstrated in this theological-philosophical Christian study of God and the inclusive Christocentric soteriology that there is still room for becoming eternally lost in Rahner's schema of inclusive universal soteriology and "anonymous Christianity."

Although God's salvific will and efficacious redemptive grace are universally freely offered to all human beings, not all human beings will positively respond to God's invitation for a fuller life and appreciate the divine gifts of grace and agape. Accordingly, I agree with Rahner that both those conventional Christians and non-Christians who fail to love their fellow human beings are lost to God and his kingdom of the fellowship of agape, peace and happiness.

Therefore, Rahner's anthropology, Logos-Christology and soteriology are faithful in their exposition of the true inclusive Gospel of Jesus as the Christ. After all, Jesus as the Christ of God himself summed up the necessary criterion of godliness and righteousness definitively in the commandment to love, unconditionally, both God and the neighbor.

Like St. John and St. Paul, Rahner says that our own free unconditional love for one another, and our positive orientation or openness to the mysteries and fullness of life in thankfulness, as a divine gift, just as it is freely given to us by God, and in awe to celebrate it with our neighbor in concrete acts of love, joy, thanksgiving and the ever present mystery which is ever hidden in the God's own impenetrable transcendence and Cosmic Mystery of his essential being, is the evidence for true godliness and presence of God's supernatural salvation or the kingdom of God.

Rahner affirms that missionary work is still to be undertaken by the Church, contrary to Balthasar's claim that Rahner does away with missionary work, declaring pagans to be anonymous Christians! This mission is to proclaim God as both Love and Mystery, who desires that all human beings should love one another as part of their *raison d'etre*.

Most of all, missionary work is to be undertaken in order to bring anonymous Christians to the more desirable explicit confession of their hidden faith in God, and wherever possible, to bring them into the conventional Church. This venture in mission is viewed positively, since it is essential if these non-explicit Christians are to be strengthened and nurtured in the fullness of Agape, free forgiveness, and brought to spiritual maturity. This is best done and achieved through the Church fellowship, teaching, and above all by participation in liturgical worship and the celebration of the sacraments, particularly penance and the Eucharist. Anonymous Christianity, though salvific, is still a deficient mode of Christianity, as Anita Roper and Klaus Riesenhuber clearly document.

Karl Rahner's concept of the anonymous Christian in relation to the African situation raises a number of serious questions for Christian theology, the Church and her mission in Africa. For instance, should the Church in predominantly Islamic nations like Nigeria try to convert the Muslims, who far outnumber the Christians? Should the Church in Africa develop denominational traditions inherited from the missionaries, and should it repudiate them and try to create an African ecumenical Church based upon the uniqueness of their heritage and experience? Is polygamy a sin that excludes those engaged in it from salvation of the Church? Which one of these rival missionary churches is the true Church of God? Are all "pagans" and Muslims lost to God? What should one do to be sure of salvation? How should we live a good and satisfying life? These questions are significant for African spirituality and ecclesial life.

We shall undertake a study of Karl Rahner's theory of explicit and implicit anonymous Christianity, understood within his philosophical-theological anthropology as a whole, and try to relate this to the African religio-philosophical background. Such an inquiry will enable us, I hope, to answer these questions in a constructive manner.

In undertaking this study, I have briefly outlined the history of narrow and exclusive soteriological views in contrast to the inclusive ones. I have also outlined Rahner's concept of anonymous Christianity in its anthropological and philosophical-theological aspects, and have also examined the African religio-philosophical thought in its traditional expressions in regard to the question of authentic human existence and salvation.

Finally, the two systems of thought are brought into dialogue and synthesis, with Rahner's Christian teaching being tentatively regarded as the most suggestive statement of the case, and one that is at the same time most meaningful, attractive, inclusive and compatible with the African experience.

This is not "to sell out" the African Religion and tradition. On the contrary, this approach is designed to give it universal validity, and credibility by demonstrating that what the West has already accepted as sound philosophical and Christian religious teaching, is in harmony with the pre-colonial and pre-Christian African traditional teaching and practice. This makes some of us question whether Africa itself might not be the actual origin of the main religious ideas which were later developed and systematized fully by the Hebrews, the Christians, and the Muslims.

However, when conflict arises between Rahner's Christian exposition of either human existence or salvation and the African religious viewpoint, I will attempt to follow the Scriptures. I will also let Rahner's inclusive Christian position address and challenge the African religious viewpoint. I also let the African tradition critic and challenge Rahner's Western, Christian and Catholic radical theological view. Whenever necessary, I have also referred to other relevant views held by other major thinkers, both Christian and non-Christian, on the key issues under examination.

The scope of this book is broad, but the actual empirical data tends to be taken from the Bantu ethnic groups of Central and East Africa. This approach is necessary to give the book a particular regional or ethnic focus, since Africa is so vast and varied. Uganda has received special attention mainly because that is where most religious and ethnic wars have been seriously fought, both in the colonial era, and in the modern post-independence period. The Martyrs of Uganda, and Idi Amin and his legacy, are all part of that unfortunate mutually intolerant, exclusive, hostile and violent religious tradition.

My ability to speak and work with nine Bantu languages, including Swahili, Luganda and Runyarwanda has been a great asset, since word study has been necessary in order to unveil the African ontology and metaphysics denoted by some African terms which might otherwise be missed, especially by foreign scholars.

Since much of the African ontology and metaphysics is still oral, the study of local vocabulary, as well as the world-view, is imperative for this kind of book in order to arrive fully at both the explicit as well as the implicit African religious and philosophical understanding or consciousness on this important subject of what it means to be human "*Omuntu*", and the required process needed in order to create or transform imperfect human beings into authentic humanity or to understand what it is like to be an authentic human being possessing the completeness of humanity (*Obuntu*).

8. Vatican II and the Rejection of the Exclusive Dogma of "*Extra Ecclesiam Nulla Salus*"

Since the Roman Catholic Church by its councils and various papal bulls had both formulated and sanctioned the doctrine of "*extra ecclesiam nulla salus*" into dogma, it is therefore, extremely important to note that Vatican II having very carefully evaluated this antiquated exclusive central Christian dogma, and weighed its merits and demerits, it repudiated it. The reversal of the doctrine of "*extra ecclesiam nulla salus*" is found in the council's explicit new positive decrees on ecumenism and the non-Christian religions. It was almost a new divine revelation for the world which came in the form of the council's positive affirmation of the soteriological efficacy of both non-Catholic Churches as well as that of the non-Christian religions.

However, this was not considered good news by many conservative theologians and priests in the Catholic Church. As a result, Vatican II has caused some discomfort among many Catholics. It has also led others to question the coextensive and correlative dogmas of the Infallibility of the Pope and the Church in the formulation of eternal truths regarding God, the Church, grace, sacraments and salvation.

Nevertheless, there are many theologians who affirm the positive inclusive theological value, practical religious wisdom and divine guidance of God's truth as they formulated in the teachings which are contained in the documents as released by the holy Vatican Council of 1962-1965, therefore, their teachings should be heeded by the mainline Christian Churches. Vatican II reaffirmed the ancient Apostolic broad Christian theological inclusive soteriological view of God's universal salvation. As a result, the holy Vatican Council decreed the following regarding God's universal salvific will and efficacious universal free divine sufficient grace which effects the supernatural salvation of the obedient and loving members of non-Christian religions:

> Finally, those who have not yet received the gospel are related in various ways to the People of God. In the first place there is the people to who the covenants and the promises were given and from whom Christ was born according to the flesh (cf. Rom 9:4-5). On account of their fathers, this people remains most dear to God, for God does not repent of the gifts He makes nor of the calls He issues (cf. Rom 11:28-29).

> But the plan of salvation also includes those who acknowledge the Creator. In the first place among these there are the Moslems, who, professing to hold the faith of Abraham, along with us adore the one and merciful God, who on the last day will judge mankind. Nor is God Himself far distant from those who in shadows and images seek the unknown God, for it is He who gives to all men life and breath and every other gift (cf. Acts 17:25-28), and who as Savior wills that all men be saved (cf. 1 Tim 2:4).

> Those also can attain to everlasting salvation who through no fault of their own do not know the gospel of Christ or His Church, yet sincerely seek God and, moved by grace, strive by their deeds to do His will as it is known to them through the dictates of conscience. Nor does divine Providence deny the help necessary for salvation to those who, without blame on their part, have not yet arrived at an explicit knowledge of God, but who strive to live a good life, thanks to His grace. Whatever goodness or truth is found among them is looked upon by the Church as a preparation for the gospel. She regards such qualities as given by Him who enlightens all men so that they may finally have life.

> But rather often men, deceived by the Evil One, have become caught up in futile reasoning and have exchanged the truth of God for a lie, serving the creature rather than the Creator (cf. Rom 1:21,25). Or some there are who, living and dying in a world without a God, are subject to utter hopelessness. Consequently, to promote the glory of God and procure the salvation of all such men, and mindful to the command of the Lord, "Preach the gospel to every creature," the Church painstakingly fosters her missionary work *(Patrologiae cursus completus, series latina, 16).*

Ultimately, our acceptance and positive affirmation of God's universal salvific grace, and redemptive will, which also leads us to the acceptance and affirmation of anonymous Christianity and divine universal salvation, does not in-itself negate nor nullify the validity of the existence of the historical Apostolic Church, and its co-extensive Christian missionary activities in the world. Christian missionary activity is validated as a historical vehicle to bring implicit Christianity to explicit self-awareness and better praxis of Agape.

NOTES

1. Karl Rahner has written more than three thousand individual articles and scores of books. The articles have been collected in more than twenty volumes, *Theological Investigations*. He has written far more than his protestant rivals, namely, Paul Tillich, and Karl Barth. Likewise, Rahner's theological and philosophical influence is far more than that of any of his protestant rivals and other theologians of this century. Rahner influenced the proceedings of Vatican II and radicalized its theology.

2. Anthropology is the starting place for Rahner's theology, including, soteriology. Human beings are the temporal mirrors and mediators of God in the material world. As a result, God himself has become a real human being in the Incarnation. See the following selected readings: Imbelli, Robert P. "Karl Rahner's *Itinerarium Mentis in Deum*" *Dunwoodre Review* 12 (1972), 76-91. McCool, Gerald A., S.J. "The Concept of the Human Person in Karl Rahner's Theology," *Theological Studies* 22 (1961), 537-562. Karl Rahner, *The Theology of Karl Rahner*, Albany, N.Y.: Magi Books, 1969. Rahner, Karl. "Theology and Anthropology" in Patrick T. Burke, (ed.) *The Word in History*. New York: Sheed and Ward, 1968.

3. See ch. 2, notes, 1-4. See also: Sullivan, *Salvation Outside the Church? A Catholic History of the Doctrine*, 5-150. The discussion of the doctrine of "extra ecclesiam null salus" is at the center of this work. The doctrine of the "Anonymous Christianity" constitutes the critique and rejection of the traditional doctrine of "extra ecclesiam nulla salus." See also the following important references: Bent, Charles N., S.J. *Interpreting the Doctrine of God* (Glen Rock, N.J.: Paulist Press, 1968), 140-224. Rahner, Karl. *Inspiration in the Bible*. New York: Herder and Herder, 1966. Also printed in *Inquiries* (New York: Herder and Herder, 1964); Joseph Ratzinger. *Revelation and Tradition* (New York: Herder and Herder, 1966).

4. Rahner's radical concept of God universal salvific will and his correlative free universal efficacious redemptive grace for each human being is the center of his soteriology. The Logos as Christ in both pre-Incarnate and post-Incarnate states makes it necessary to affirm that each redeemed person is a Christian regardless of whether he or she knows and accepts it as such or not. Those who are not aware of this fact are "anonymous christians."

See the following Rahner's writings: *Belief Today* (New York: Sheed and Ward, 1967); "The Faith of the Priest Today," *Woodstock Letters* 93 (1964), 3-10; in the *Theological Investigations* see the following: "Intellectual Honesty and Christian Faith," VII, 47-71; "The Need for a Short Formula of Christian Faith," IX, 117-126; "Christianity and the Non-Christian Religions," V, 115-134; "What is Heresy?" V, 468-512; "Anonymous Christians," VI, 390-398; "Atheism and Implicit Christianity," IX, 145-164; "On The Theology of Hop," X, 242-259; "The Commandment of Love in Relation to the Other Commandments," V, 439-467; "Reflections on the Unity of the Love of Neighbor and the Love of God," VI, 231-249; Nita Roper, *The Anonymous Christian* (with an afterward "The Anonymous Christian According to Karl Rahner" by Klaus Riesenhuber, S.J., New York: Sheed and Ward, 1966); Eugene Hillman, C.S.P. "Anonymous Christianity and the Missions," *Downside Review* 85

(1966), 361-380. Donald Maloney, "Rahner and the Anonymous Christian," *America* 123 (1970), 348-350.

See also Karl Rahner, *Foundations of Christian Faith* (New York: Seabury Press, 1978), pp. 44 ff, 85-89; *Spirit in the World* (New York: Herder and Herder, 1968), pp. 406-408; *Grace in Freedom* (New York: Herder and Herder, 1969), pp. 183-196, 203-207 and 229 ff. Rahner argues that the proper name or term given to the Infinite Mystery is not considered important. What is considered important is our attitude and response to this divine Cosmic Mystery. That is why the rejection of the term "God" does not necessarily lead to atheism as long as the person remains open to life, the world and its mystery. Cf. Rahner, "Atheism and Implicit Christianity," *Theological Investigations* 9:145-164.

5. Salvation is wholistic. It is viewed as God's free cosmic work or any divine and correlated human positive activities in the world which thwart the negative threats of chaos and nothingness. It is a daily process which is coextensive and correlative with life, order, peace, well-being, agape, forgiveness, peace and harmony. It is analogous to God's free rain which falls on both the righteous and the wicked! However, in this case, salvation becomes personal when it is received and the person lives a new life by the new moral law of agape and good works, instead of living destructively by greed, selfishness, malice, hate and evil works (cf. Matt. 7:13-32; 25:31-46: 1 Jn 4:7-22).

See also Rahner: "The Appeal to Conscience," *Nature and Grace* (New York: Sheed and Ward, 1964), 39-63; "On the Question of a Formal Existential Ethics," II, 217-234; "On the Dignity and Freedom of Man," II, 235-263; "The Theology of Freedom," VI, 178-196; "Practical Theology Within the Totality of Theological Disciplines," IX, 101-114; "The Experiment with Man," IX, 205-224; "The Problem of Genetic Manipulation," IX, 225-252; "Practical Theology and Social Work in the Church," X, 349-370; James F Bresnahan, "Rahner's Christian Ethics," *America* 123 (1970), 351-354. Donald J. Dorr, "Karl Rahner's Formal Existential Ethics," *Irish Theological Quarterly* 36 (1969), 211-229; Fuchs, Josef, S.J. *Human Values and Christian Morality* (Dublin: Gill and MacMillan, 1970); Michael Moga S.J. "The Existential Ethics of Karl Rahner," *Focus* (Spring, 1965); William Wallace, O.P. "The Existential Ethics of Karl Rahner: A Thomistic Appraisal," *Thomist* 27 (1963), 493-515.

6. For this work, human biological evolution will be regarded as God's historical and temporal method for creating human beings. However, the primordial conditions of Aden and primordial sin will be retained in Tillich's metaphorical sense. That is, the fall as the awareness of the difference between the human authentic essence as what ought to be and what is. See also the following: Kenneth Baker, S.J. *A Synopsis of the Transcendental Philosophy of Emerich Coreth and Karl Rahner* (Spokane: Gonzaga University, 1965); Vincent P. Branick, *An Ontology of Understanding: Karl Rahner's Metaphysics of Knowledge in the Context of Modern German Hermeneutics* (St. Louis: Marianist Communications Center, 1974); Joseph Donceel, S.J. *The Philosophy of Karl Rahner* (Albany: Magi Books, 1969); Donceel, "Rahner's Argument for God," *America* 123 (1970), 340-342; Gerald A. McCool, S.J. "The Philosophical Theology of Rahner and Lonergan: in Robert J. Roth, S.J. (ed.), *God Knowable and Unknowable* (New York: Fordham University Press, 1973), 123-157; Edward MacKinnon, "The Transcendental Turn: Necessary But Not Sufficient," *Continuum* 6 (1968), 225-231.

See also: Rahner, Karl. *Spirit in the World* (New York: Seabury Press, 1968); *Hearers of the Word* (New York: Seabury Press, 1969); "The Concept of Existential Philosophy in Heidegger," *Philosophy Today* 13 (1969), 126-137; Bernard Tyrrell, S.J. "The New Context of the Philosophy of God on Lonergan and Rahner" in Philip McShane (ed.), *Language, Truth, and Meaning* (Notre Dame, Ind.: University of Notre Dame Press, 1972);

Alfred North Whitehead, *Process and Reality* (Edited by David Ray Griffin and Donald Sherburne. New York: The Free Press, 1978).

7. "Anonymous Christianity" is a Christian ethnocentric and bigoted theological critique of the exclusive doctrine of "extra ecclesiam nulla salus." See note 4 above. See Also the following: Rahner, "The Order of Redemption within the Order of Creation," *The Christian Commitment* (New York: Sheed and Ward, 1963), 38-74; "Nature and Grace," *Nature and Grace* (New York: Sheed and Ward, 1964), 114-149; From *Theological Investigations*: "Concerning the Relationship Between Nature and Grace," I, 297-317; "Some Implications of the Scholastic Concept of Uncreated Grace," I, 319-346; "The Theological Concept of Concupiscentia," I, 347-382; "Reflections on the Experience of Grace," III, 86-90; "Nature and Grace," IV, 165-188; From *Sacramentum Mundi*: "The 'Existential,'" II, 304-307; "Grace," II, 412-427; "Potentia Obedientialis," V, 65-67; "Salvation (Universal Salvific Will)," V, 405-409.

Charles R. Meyer, *A Contemporary Theology of Grace* (New York: Alba House, 1971); William C. Shepherd, *Man's Condition: God and the World Process* (New York: Herder and Herder, 1969, a study of Rahner's theology of grace and the Supernatural Existential); Regina Bechtle, "Rahner's Supernatural Existential," *Thought* 48 (1973), 61-77; Kenneth D. Eberhard, "Karl Rahner and the Supernatural Existential," *Thought* 46 (1971), 537-561; Kenny, J.P. "Reflections on Human Nature and the Supernatural," *Theological Studies* 14 (1953), 280-287 and "The Problem of Concupiscence: A Recent Theory of Karl Rahner," *The Australasian Catholic Record*, 29 (1952), 290-304; 30 (1953), 23-32; Thomas Motherway, "Supernatural Existential," *Chicago Studies* 4 (1965), 79-103; Carl J. Peter, "The Position of Karl Rahner Regarding the Supernatural: A Comparative Study of nature and Grace," *Proceedings of the Catholic Theological Society of America* 20 (1965), 81-94.

See also Rahner's following Christological works: "Current Problems in Christology," I, 149-200; "On the Theology of the Incarnation," IV, 105-120; "Dogmatic Questions on Easter," IV, 121-133; "History of the World and Salvation History," V, 97-114; "Christology Within an Evolutionary View of the World," V, 157-192; "Dogmatic Questions on the Knowledge and Self-Consciousness of Christ," V, 193-215; *Sacramentum Mundi:* "Resurrection of Christ," V, 323-324.

8. The Church as the community of God's redeemed people is Catholic, that is universal. However "Catholic" has been misrepresented as Roman Catholic. God's cosmic true community of the saints constitutes the true Church. It is inclusive of all God's obedient people regardless of creed or cultural religious rituals, and symbols, such as the Christian rituals of baptism and the Eucharist.

See Rahner's following works on Church and Sacraments: *Free Speech in the Church* (New York: Sheed and Ward, 1960); *The Episcopate and the Primacy* (New York: Herder and Herder, 1962); Also printed in *Inquiries* (New York: Herder and Herder, 1964); "The Significance of the Order of Redemption within the Order of Creation," *The Christian Commitment* (New York: Sheed and Ward, 1963), 75-113; "The Individual in the Church," *Nature and Grace* (New York: Sheed and Ward, 1964), 9-38; *Theology for Renewal: Bishops, Priests and Laity*. New York: Sheed and Ward, 1964; *The Dynamic Element in the Church* (New York: Herder and Herder, 1964); *The Christian of the Future* (New York: Herder and Herder, 1967); *The Church and the Sacraments* (New York: Herder and Herder, 1963); Also printed in *Inquiries* (New York: Herder and Herder, 1964); with Angelos Haussling, O.S.B. *The Celebration of the Eucharist* (New York: Herder and Herder, 1968).

From *Theological Investigations:* "Freedom in the Church," II, 89-107; "The Church of Sinners," VI, 253-269; "The Church and the Parousia of Christ," VI, 295-312; "The New Image of the Church," X, 3-29; "The Presence of the Lord in the Christian Community at

Worship," X, 71-83; "On the Presence of Christ in the Diaspora Community According to the Teaching of the Second Vatican Council," X 84-102; Dialogue in the Church," X, 103-121; "The Bishop in the Church," VI, 313-389; "On the Relationship Between the Pope and the College of Bishops," X, 50-70; "On the Teaching of the Second Vatican Council on the Diaconate," X, 222-232; "Peaceful Reflections on the Parochial Principle," II, 283-318.

"The Sacramental Basis for the Role of the Layman in the Church," VIII, 51-74; "The Position of Woman in the New Situation in Which the Church Finds Herself," VII, 75-93; "The Eucharist and Suffering," III, 161-170; "On the Duration of Christ in the Sacrament of the Lord's Supper," IV, 287-311; "On the Duration of the Presence of Christ after Communion," IV, 312-320; "Forgotten Truths Concerning the Sacrament of Penance," II, 135-174; "The Meaning of Frequent Confession of Devotion," III, 177-189; "Problems Concerning Confession," III, 190-206; "Penance as an Additional Act of Reconciliation Within the Church," X, 125-149; "The Renewal of Priestly Ordination," III, 171-176; "Marriage as a Sacrament," X, 199-221; "Personal and Sacramental Piety," II, 109-133.

9. See note 3 above. See also the following works of Rahner, *Encounter with Silence* (Westminster, Md: Newman Press, 1960); *Spiritual Exercises* (New York: Herder and Herder, 1965); *Servants of the Lord* (New York: Herder and Herder, 1968); *On Prayer* (New York: Paulist Press, 1968); *Watch and Pray With Me* (New York: Herder and Herder, 1969); *The Identity of the Priest* (New York: Paulist Press, 1969); *Leading a Christian Life* (Denville, N.J.: Dimension Books, 1970); *The Priesthood* (An Ignatian Retreat for Priests, New York: Seabury Press, 1973).

10. See note 5 above. God's salvation is coextensive with creation and therefore, it is an ongoing historical and evolutionary process. The right time for salvation or "kairos" is the present moment. Both God and eternal life are coextensive with the present moment or *"kairos."* In other words, this temporal life is correlative with the eternal life, and correlatively, this world is also coextensive with the kingdom of God and heaven for God's obedient and loving saints. Conversely, this life and the world is also coextensive with hell for the rebels, the spiteful and hateful evil-doers (cf. Rom. 1:17-32; Jn. 1:1-3:21).

See also: Karl Rahner, *Theological Investigations:* "Reflections on the Problems of the Gradual Ascent to Christians Perfection," II, 319-352; "Justified and sinner at the Same Time," VI, 218-230; "The Ignatian Mysticism of Joy in the World," III, 277-293; "Behold This Heart!: Preliminaries to a Theology of Devotion to the Sacred Heart," III, 277-293; "The Passion and Asceticism," 58-85. "Reflections on the Theology of Renunciation," III, 47-57; "Self-Realization and Taking Up One's Cross," IX, 253-257; "On the Evangelical Counsels" VIII, 133-167; "On the Theology of Poverty," VIII,168-214; "Priestly Existence," III, 239-214; "The Consecration of the Layman to the Care of Souls," III, 236-2; *Theological Investigations* III and VIII (are devoted to Spiritual Theology). See also Rahner's treatment of death: *On The Theology of Death* (New York: Seabury Press, 1961).

From *Theological Investigations:* "The Resurrection of the Body," II,203-216; "The Hermeneutics of Eschatological Assertions," IV, 323-346; "The Life of the Dead," IV, 347-354; "Ideology and Christianity," VI, 43-58; "Marxist Utopia and the Christian Future of Man," VI, 59-68; "The Church and the Parousia of Christ," VI, 295-312. A Fragmentary Aspect of Evaluation of the Concept of the Future," X, 235-241; "The Theological Problems Entailed in the Idea of the 'New Earth,'" X, 260-388; "Immanent and Transcendent Consummation of the World, X, 260-272; "The Peace of Christ and the Peace of the World," X, 371-388. From The *Sacramentum Mundi:* "Beatific Vision," I, 151-153; "Death," II, 58-62; "Eschatology," II, 242-246; "Hell," III, 7-9; "Last Things," III, 247-276; "Parousia," IV, 345-346; "Resurrection," IV, 329-333.

11. Life and salvation being a process rather than static events which happen in time and space. As such process theology and philosophy have a positive contribution to make to theology within this context of evolution and the divine creative and redemptive process. For some examples see: Charles Winquist who has used Whitehead in *The Transcendental Imagination* (The Hague: Martinus Nijhoff, 1972), and *The Communion of Possibility* (New Horizons Press, 1975).

The first two specially Whiteheadian Catholic theological books are Bernard M.Lee, *The Becoming of the Church: A process Theology of the Structure of Christian Experience* (Paulist/Newman Press, 1974), and the introductory work by Robert B.Mellert, *What is Process Theology?* (Paulist/Newman Press, 1975). Richard Overman's book, *Evolution and the Christian Doctrine of Creation*; Don S. Browning, whose treatment of Erikson has received much attention, wrote in 1966 a Whiteheadian-Hartshornean study entitled *Atonement and Psychotherapy* (The Westminster Press). Eugene H. Peters has provided in *The Creative Advance: An Introduction to Process Philosophy as a Context for Christian Faith* (The Bethany Press, 1966). William D. Dean has called for a deeper religious appreciation of the primacy of the aesthetic dimensions in *Whitehead's Thought in Coming To: A Theology of Beauty* (The Westminster Press,1976).

David Ray Griffin produced a treatment of *Jesus as the Decisive Revelation of God in A Process Christology* (The Westminster Press, 973). He is also published a full-scale Whiteheadian treatment of the problem of evil as *God, Power, and Evil: A Process Theodicy* (The Westminster Press, 1976). John B. Cobb and David Ray Griffin, *Process Theology: An Introduction* (Philadelphia: Fortress Press, 1976). Finally, Whitehead's books, *Process and Reality*; *Adventures in Ideas; Religion in the Making*; and *Religion and Modern Science* must be read as keys for a good understanding of process thinking both in its various philosophical and theological forms.

IV

FINITUDE, EXISTENCE AND VULNERABILITY
AS CONTEXT FOR QUEST OF SALVATION
AND AGAPE:
PROBLEMS OF EGO AND UNCONDITIONAL LOVE

Human existence and its authentic value or meaning constitute the ultimate human quest for God, meaning, happiness and salvation. Religion and philosophy are mutual, universal complementary avenues and valid paths for self-transcendence in quest for God as the universal principle for goodness, reality, mind, value, creation, redemption or salvation and happiness.

As result, like Paul Tillich, Karl Rahner also correctly contends that the universal human quest for happiness and the ultimate questions of concern raised in the process of this quest for authentic human existence are universal questions of human ego and existence. Due to the universal existential human finitude, and vulnerability, human beings everywhere live in the threat of chaos and death. Human beings pose questions in their quest for ultimate meaning, and search for God as Creator-Redeemer and Destiny.[1]

These universal questions of existence are intricately intertwined with the universal human quest for God as the cosmic Creative and Redemptive Mystery. This universal human quest for God is rooted in the quest for salvation. Human minds perceive that God is the universal free Mystery who is the essential embodiment and source of life, meaning, fulfillment, peace or salvation and happiness. Christian theologians also affirm that this Infinite Mystery is also same cosmic Creator and Redemptive God who redeems creation, and all creatures from sin and evil: chaos, rebellion against God, hate, malice, alienation, imperfection and premature death. This cosmic Creative-Redemptive Spirit and Absolute Mystery is called God or other names, such as "Yahweh," "Allah," "Mungu" or "Katonda."[2] This is God the transcendent cosmic Creative-Redemptive Mystery, who unlike idols or "man-made gods" cannot be owned by human beings as their own property.

Subsequently, no group of people, nation, tribe, religious school, Church or person, regardless of whether he or she is a great saint, priest or prophet, such as Moses, Buddha, Jesus, Luther, or the "infallible Pope," can ever claim any special merit and access to this eternal, cosmic, impartial free cosmic Creator-Redeemer God. This cosmic Creator-Redeemer God is accessible to all human beings, everywhere, and anytime in the world. This is universally true, irrespective of race, class, education, religious creed or affiliation, gender, skin color, marital state, and other conditions. All human beings are God's adopted children, irrespective of whether they are obediently aware of it or not.

1. Finitude and the Universal Human Problem

The correlation of the human existence and the quest for the Absolute[3] as the Infinite, Unconditioned, and yet loving, Transcendent personal Being[4] necessarily arises from the human limitless self-transcendence, as a historical free spirit in the world.[5] The human being finds himself or herself surrounded by infinite mystery, beauty and occasional joyous experiences as well as being dismayed and threatened by the forces of evil and destruction.

These forces of evil are perceived by the human being to be operative in this same world inhabited by the human being. These evil forces are attributed with the creation of chaos, discord, confusion, enmity, pain, disease, death, and therefore, the cause of human insecurity and despair, especially among those who are already overwhelmed by this sense of prevailing evil, finitude and its vulnerability.[6]

This awareness and experience of finitude, vulnerability and insecurity in the world, leads the human being to the quest for salvation as primarily security, and well-being[7] in this wonderful world, yet infested with evil and its consequences in the form of pain, hatred, malice, finitude, destruction, death, and decay. Yet, the human being realizes that this is still the same world in which he or she is, nevertheless, called fully into active being.

2. Human Quest for Salvation and Exclusiveness
of the Elect

Wherever humankind exists in this world[8] whether in Africa or America, Asia or Europe, it faces the very same problem of human existence and its ultimate meaning. This is particularly the case since all human beings, regardless of who or what they are or where they are, are equally and radically threatened by guilt, evil, and most of all, they live in constant fear of the natural processes of finitude in terms of aging, disease, withering, pain, death and decay.

All human beings are to some degree, variously engaged in the same universal ultimate human quest for meaning, a fuller life, a future, love, happiness, well-being, success, harmony and peace. In short, all human beings, irrespective of creed, ideology, and religious affiliation, are all engaged in the same ultimate human quest for salvation.

Therefore, inasmuch as all human beings feel threatened by finitude, imperfection, chaos and death, they will always seek the infinite and merciful God for salvation. This universal human quest for God and divine salvation may not be explicit. For instance, it may be expressed in terms of looking for security, better ways of survival to old age, better health, economy, and politics that makes it possible, such as the observance of international peace, and global human rights and freedom.

All the people engaged in these different kinds of forms of quest for a more meaningful life, peace and fulfillment are, also both correlatively, and coextensively, implicitly or explicitly, in quest for God, and divine redemption or salvation. Irrespective of creed or lack of one, all these people are validly engaged in this same religious quest for fulfillment in God, grace, agape, peace and salvation. This is the nature of universal and implicit human quest for God, meaning and salvation in its inclusive or broad scope, and nondiscriminatory wholistic dimensions.

This unique form of quest is as valid and sacred as for those hermits who live in a prayerful quest for God. However, this universal quest for God may take different locally appropriate forms, depending on the local cultures and religions. For some people, it may take the rebellious form of atheistic denial of transcendence or mystery, whereas for others it may take the opposite form in the self-explicit monastic expressions. These expressions include quests for supernatural salvation in the lonely deserts or mountain tops or more conventionally, behind the sacred walls of convents and monasteries.[9]

The Soviet Communists may undertake this ultimate quest in a seemingly very different manner, and under a very different label or terminology from the self-confessed Christian West, who themselves undertake the same ultimate quest under other labels or even under the variety of the bigoted stereotyped terms such as, "democracy," Christianity," "Evangelicalism," "Charismatic," and the like.[10]

On the other hand, the same quest for a more meaningful and a fuller life,which is the life of human existence in grace, and the right relationship with God as the Creator of the human being and the ultimate destiny,[11] may be undertaken differently by different peoples, such as the peoples of Asia and Africa because of their dissimilar historical, cultural and religious backgrounds. For instance, the Arabs might objectify their quest for the Divine and for salvation in their religion known as Islam,[12] (which translates as peace due to submission to God), whereas the Asians traditionally have done so through Hinduism and Buddhism.

In the same way, Africans have traditionally objectified their own ultimate quest for divine salvation and authentic human existence in their Traditional Religion which permeates all their life, and all human activities to the very extent that the sacred and the secular had merged into one sacred realm of human life, and its activities could never be divided into the sacred and the secular, like the case in the West.[13]

The result of this African hallowing of the cosmos, life and its "mundane activities" has led to the African perception as that of being "incurably religious,"[14] as well as "superstitious"[15] and "animist,"[16] since most Africans seemed to believe that the divine power or Spirit could dwell everywhere and whenever it chooses, manifest itself anywhere, even including "mundane things," such as tops of mountains, gigantic trees, huge rocks, lakes, rivers, people and even animals.[17] This theophany was always understood to have a very specific meaning, directive and purpose for the people and the community.[18]

It is clear that all human beings are aware of their vulnerability as human beings[19] and that they are variously engaged in dealing with this problem of meaning and concern for a fuller life.[20] Some of the solutions which have been prescribed have been political, economic, medical, philosophical and religious in nature. For instance, the enlightened Greek thinkers and philosophers, such as Socrates, Plato and Aristotle, taught that the main goal of human life was happiness;[21] whereas happiness was itself regarded as the result of the disciplined human life lived in the sober, contemplative state of virtue.[22] However, virtue itself was viewed as the result of the knowledge of the ultimate good[23] and its relentless pursuit.[24]

Implicit in this teaching is the idea that the untutored ignorant masses were almost lacking in virtue and its correlative divine life, since they lacked the necessary knowledge required to enable them to become wise and virtuous.[25] This Platonic exclusion of the ignorant masses from happiness and salvation as union with God in intellectual or mental contemplation, and the virtuous life[26] resulting from it, also led Plato to exclude these same untutored, ignorant masses from responsible political process, and self determination in the exercise of their human and political rights to vote or hold office in a democracy.[27]

Therefore, for Plato the philosopher-king is the ultimate representative of God in society. Subsequently, Plato like the African tradition assigned the philosopher, a divine position which made him the ideal, wise, divine king and high priest, since he is the one close to God by virtue of possessing the divine secret of knowledge of the good which is the divine quintessence of God.[28]

In another sense, the philosopher as an agent of knowledge, truth, wisdom and positive values, is God's human elect, prophet and missionary in a given society. Therefore, in each era and in each cultural or ethnic group, God has efficaciously acted in unmerited agape and universal redemptive grace and revealed himself as Creator, Redeemer and Sanctifier-Fulfiller. Accordingly, God has given each society a local prophet to warn the people of worldliness, evil, and to recall them to holiness through self-denial, purification, self-discipline, charity and doing the good works which enhance the common good, and the general welfare of humanity and the world.

The Hebrews, on the other hand, had a different experience. They believed that they were the elect people of God out of all the peoples that God had created.[29] The writers of the biblical book of Genesis correctly inclusively perceived that the election of Israel in Abraham as the "archpatriarch" of the believers, was also an election of all believers. Therefore, Abraham's call was for the redemptive purpose of the whole world, and not just for Abraham's descendants or Israel's election and salvation alone. Accordingly, God is understood to be saying the following:

> Now the Lord said to Abraham, "Go from your country and your kindred and your father's house to the land that I will show you. And I will make you a great nation, and I will bless you, and him who curses you I will curse; and by you all the families of the earth will bless themselves." (Gen. 12:1-4).

Despite this election for mission to the world, Israel as a nation forgot the world-wide mission that it had been entrusted with and had been elected to. Ironically, circumcision, which had been given to her as a sign of the covenant identity, and the Torah, which had been given to her as a tutor and guide into a fuller life of right living with each other and righteous communion with God, became a stumbling block and a barrier in Israel's relationship with the non-Jews.

The non-Jews or Gentiles were supposed to be excluded from God's grace, election and the covenant. Accordingly, they were negatively viewed as a source of ritual uncleanliness. Subsequently, God's salvation and fellowship were then understood to include only those elect people of God or Israel. As such, for these exclusive Jewish soteriologists, for non-Jews, supernatural salvation was impossible, unless they converted to Judaism.

As a result, all those non-Jews who wanted to gain God's salvation were supposed to be duly initiated into the Mosaic covenant, since Jews believed and also dogmatically, exclusively and definitively affirmed that there was no salvation outside the Mosaic Covenant or Israel. This was also the case with the early Church until St. Paul did away with the Mosaic Covenant and circumcision as prerequisite for becoming a Christian (cf. Acts 15:1-31). Even then, within the covenant, salvation was only for those who remained faithful to God, by being loyal to their election, and also by keeping the Ten Commandments as the central moral law of the Mosaic Covenant.[30]

Inevitably, this position led to the kind of exclusiveness that was associated with Judaism in its claims to God and divine salvation. The Gentiles and all pagan nations were thought to be headed for perdition![31] Nevertheless, members of the Judaic religion positively affirmed of its superior revelation, and exclusive redemptive value. They claimed that God's ultimate knowledge had been to the world through the Torah and the prophets, made no effort to go out to convert the Gentile world in order to save them from perishing and barbarism.[32]

Judaism as a religion remained oblivious to its election to be God's universal salvific agency in the world. This remained generally true until the coming and ministry of Jesus of Nazareth about two thousand years ago. Jesus himself cannot be considered a religious revolutionary but rather a reformer and fulfiller of Judaism.[33] For instance, he recruited twelve men to represent the new Israel he was instituting. He did away with the burden of the law while keeping its essence.[31]

As a typical male Jew of his day, Jesus was too conservative to include a few women or gentiles in his inner circle of the twelve Apostles as agapic tokens of God's dawning inclusive kingdom or his own gender and racially inclusive universal redemptive mission in the world. Obviously, these inclusions would have been a revolutionary symbol of the universal nature of Jesus' message and ministry; but most likely these inclusions would have rendered Jesus' own historical ministry unacceptable and ineffective in the Jewish nation.[35]

However, Jesus himself did not do any significant "foreign missionary" activity during his earthly ministry to the non-Jews.[36] Nevertheless, his willingness to go to the Gentile world constitutes the post-resurrection ministry, as his commandment to the Apostles to make disciples of all nations, and to baptize them, clearly illustrates:

> And Jesus came and said to them, "All authority in heaven and earth has been given to me. Go therefore and make disciples of all nations, baptizing them in the name of the Father, and of the Son and of the Holy Spirit, teaching them to observe all that I have commanded you, and lo, I am with you always, to the close of the age" (Matt. 28:18-20).[37]

Nevertheless, it appears that if it had not been for St. Paul's conversion, and vigorous missionary activity to the Gentile world, and stubborn refusal to allow his Gentile converts to observe the details of the Jewish religious law and ceremonies,[38] the religious reformation of Jesus would have probably been contained within the Jewish religious heritage just as another puritanical sect within Judaism, just like the Pharisees and the Essenes.[39]

Consequently, Christianity *qua* Christianity as we know it today would have been non-existent![40] It is also most likely that the books of the New Testament as we have them today would have been fewer and different, as they would have been dealing with different problems, and since there would be no Gentile Christian community uninitiated into the Mosaic Law, there would be no need either for the Pauline type of letters or the incipient treatment of issues of Christian contextualization of the Christian faith and ethics in a Gentile world of "paganism" and Greek philosophy.[41]

Some materials in the Gospels themselves, such as the commissioning of Jesus to the Apostles to preach and convert all the nations baptizing them in the triune God, or the claims we find in the Gospel According to John in regard to Jesus as the beloved "Son of God," the creative "Logos" of "God become flesh" as "the truth," "the true light that enlightens every man" and the only "way" to eternal life, would probably not have been written.[42]

In any case, if Christianity had not broken away from Judaism, most likely the gospels would not have been written. If the gospels had not been written, Christianity would not have emerged. On the other hand, if Christianity had emerged within the context of Judaism, it would have been different both in content and purpose. These gospels now found in the New

Testament, would have been unacceptable as they stand now. They would have probably been suppressed as both blasphemous and heretical.[43]

Since incipient Christianity was rejected and persecuted by the Jews, and was consequently forced to assert its own identity as a separate religion, distinct from Judaism by which it had been born and nurtured, the problem of the new and the old and how they relate to each other began to emerge.[44] It is clear that the Judaisers within the incipient Christian Church wanted Christianity subordinated to the old, namely, Judaism.[45]

However, radicals like Stephen and Paul saw a clear break between Christianity and Judaism, especially, as epitomized by the elaborate Mosaic Law. Christianity was regarded by the Christian radicals as "the new wine-skins,"[46] thus, stressing the necessity for the new wine or Gospel message, to have its own autonomous new existence independent of Judaism.

Paul and the radical hellenistic Christian group saw Christianity as both the fulfillment and replacement for Judaism. These hellenistic or Greek based Christians, saw Christianity in its Pauline exposition as the superseding the ethnocentric and exclusive Judaism and the Mosaic law. Paul had in his letters emphasized that Christianity had replaced Judaism, Jesus had superseded Moses and Agape had negated the Mosaic law of equal violence in relation ("lex talionis") as the basis of moral law and justice in God's community.

Most important of all, Christianity claimed to be superior to all other religions, including Judaism, because of its faith and historical affirmation that God had indeed, in Jesus as the Christ become Incarnate into humanity in human history as a unique gift of God himself to all humanity for their instruction and salvation.

It was also believed that through the Incarnation and the divine grace in the indwelling Holy Spirit, the holy Apostolic Church had become God's chosen special temporal vehicle of his efficacious redemptive grace and salvation for the world.[47] This divine gift of grace and the Holy Spirit enables humanity to live in a new era of the Christocentric abundant and fulfilling life in the love of God, and in the universal brotherly and neighborly love for our fellow human beings.[48]

3. The Idolatrous Theological Absolutization
of the Apostolic Church

At first, the Apostolic Church viewed itself as a reformation within Judaism. After all Jesus was a Jewish pacifist and radical ethicist rabbi who sought to reform the more strict and burdensome Mosaic Law and replace it with the more flexible moral law and path of agape (cf. Matt. 5-7). In addition, all his disciples and first followers were all Jews who still observed the Mosaic Law and regularly attended worship in the temple and the synagogue, just as Jesus himself had done.

However, as the Church became more gentile based and grew as a result of St. Paul's tireless missionary activities, the Christian community began to assume a new separate and characteristic hellenistic identity. Greek modes of thinking, philosophy in its neo-Platonic form and metaphysics began to dominate the new elitist Christian community, which had started off as a community of the poor, slaves, women, children and the ignorant lower status males.

When the Christians began to view themselves as the new creation, and as the obedient elect children of God, they inevitably began to view the non-Christians, whether Jews or pagans as lost, unless they were converted to the Apostolic Church and its explicit or confessional Christianity.[49] This was in their view, a revenge on the Jews who had rejected Jesus as their Messiah, and had trumped up charges of political sedition in order to get rid of him.[50] It is understandable, then, how strong anti-Semitic feelings would have arisen easily among the Gentile Christians.[51] Gospel passages like the following would have been negatively employed as justifications for the Christian hostile feelings against the Jewish people:

> So when Pilate saw that he was gaining nothing, but rather that a riot was beginning, he took water and washed his hands before the crowd, saying, "I am innocent of this man's blood; see to it yourselves." And all the people answered, "His blood be on us and on our children!"[52] Then he released for them Barabbas, and having scourged Jesus, delivered him to be crucified (Matt. 27:24-26).

Vatican II realized that much of anti-Semitic feelings arose from the hostile Christian attitude toward the Jews as responsible for the torture and cruel murder of Jesus on the shameful cross, and the Council repudiated this hostile attitude and misuse of scripture to justify it.[53] This is definitely a positive step in correcting this bad relationship that goes as far back as the very founding of Christianity itself by Jesus the Christ. It is also remarkable that the same Council, inspired by the spirit of Christ, nullified the old ecclesiastical bigotry of *extra ecclesiam nulla salus.*[54]

St. Paul was one of the most well educated, and philosophically sophisticated early Christian converts. Therefore, in his theological and pastoral letters to the Churches had founded, he struggled with the perennial theological question of the Jews, election, Judaism and the Mosaic Law in the Christian era.

Being also open minded, St. Paul fully realized that there was only one God who is Creator, Revealer, Savior, and Judge of all human beings, irrespective of wherever they are, and to whatever religion they belong.[55] For Paul, as for Karl Rahner, God's gratuitous and efficaciously salvific grace as God's self-disclosure or divine salvific self-communication has been gratuitously given universally to all human beings, in the same way all of them have been also the victims of sin without any exception.[56] This includes the Jewish people as the very elect people of God, with the special privilege of the Torah as a guide and the warnings of the prophets, but without limiting God's activity to them *vis-a-vis* the rest of the human world.

With the exception of philosophically inclined apologists like Justin Martyr and Clement of Alexandria, most of the Church Fathers, particularly the Latin ones such as Tertullian and Cyprian, tended to care less about non-Christians whether they were Jews, Greek philosophers, or mere pagans. For Tertullian, the Christian faith had nothing to do with the Greek Academy.[57] Philosophy was looked at as an enemy of faith and not as its ally, as Justin Martyr, Origen, Augustine and later St. Thomas, positively affirmed and taught.[58]

It is certain that, whereas the Greek fathers were interested in speculative, philosophical theology on controversial topics such as Christology, salvation and God's being, the Latin Church Fathers with a few exceptions, were less speculative, more dogmatic, and generally rather more concerned with Church structure, hierarchy and discipline.[59] The result was that the Latin Western Church was characterized by the preoccupation with ecclesiology, authority, unity and the threat of schism, whereas the Eastern Church was generally engaged in the intellectual quest for grounding and understanding of the Christian faith and doctrines.[60]

Given those main traits in the Church, it is not surprising, therefore, to find that Justin Martyr, Origen and Clement taught a broader and more inclusive view of Christian salvation.[61] For instance, Justin Martyr taught that Greek philosophy contained salvific truth for the Greeks, who adhered to it and lived faithfully in accordance with it like Plato and Socrates. He claimed that the truth found in this philosophy which men like Socrates and Plato taught was the same salvific truth of the cosmic divine Logos that was later made historically manifest in the incarnation of Jesus of Nazareth.

Since truth is the one divine, salvific grace in the divine Logos, who is the pre-existent Christ, Justin Martyr affirmed that all those who possess this divine truth and cherish it can be, therefore, termed Christians.[62]

However, as we have seen, the Latin Church Fathers such as Tertullian and later Augustine rejected such a view of salvation of non-explicit Christians, without accounting for the divine activity or lack of it outside the Christian Church. Bishop Cyprian made this view impossible to hold when he expounded *extra ecclesiam nulla salus* in his attempt to quell a Novatianist schismatic revolt that had sought unsuccessfully to dethrone him, and had consequently gone into schism in protest against his cowardice and flight into hiding during the severe mid-third century Roman imperial Christian persecution in North Africa.[63]

Although, the doctrine of *extra ecclesiam nulla salus*, was later ratified by the Church, should be viewed within its proper context of the Church's internal political rivalry, jurisdictional conflicts and discipline, rather than a broader theological spectrum of God's universal creative grace and salvation that is operative everywhere, inside and outside the historical Church. *Extra ecclesiam nulla salus* was even used by the Catholic Church for some time to exclude Protestant churches from divine salvation, as they were regarded as schismatic and lacking in efficacious salvific grace![64]

This doctrine illustrates the human problem of pride, egocentricity and bigotry that manifests the exclusive claim of truth and salvation. There are many contemporary examples of this religious or moral evil. For instance, Bailey Smith, the as the President of the American Southern Baptist Convention, said that "God does not hear the prayers of either the Jews or the Muslims!"[65] According to these kinds of exclusive ethnocentric Christians, Jews and Muslims are outside of both God's communion and divine salvation (unless they convert to Evangelical Christianity and become "born again.")

In economic and political systems, the East and the West discredit each other endlessly in the name of truth, freedom, religion, ideology and might.[66] The problem here does not seem to be primarily that of either faith in God or its absence. The real problem here, again, is that of human sin. The human sins of pride and bigotry make it hard and nearly impossible for one to love and accept the other as he/she is without any conditions or reservations and seek to live in mutual co-existence, harmony, and dialogue, rather than live in mutual suspicion, malignant competition, hatred and confrontation.[67]

The absurdity in this case lies in the fact that, whereas the West generally claims to be God-fearing and Christian,[68] often it forgets the very grounding and essence of Christianity, which is Jesus' commandment to love God and the neighbor as ourselves.[69] There is no doubt that the neighbor to be loved, in this case, includes the Soviets, Iranian fanatic shiite Muslims and "pagan" Africans.[70]

In the case of Uganda, which will serve the main African illustration of African Religion, and destructive negative Christian denominational religious politics, the neighbor includes the Catholics, Muslims, Anglicans, "Baloko-le," "pagans," and perhaps, most important of all, people of the different clans, "tribes" and members of different political parties.[71]

4. The Universal Problem of Human Finitude and Evil

The problem of human existence is the problem of meaning in the face of apparent prevailing evil and chaos in the world, in which, as finite beings, we are both created and called into being by the infinite and loving God. We are finite moral agents in the world.

God expects us to an authentic live as finite beings. This is in spite of vulnerable human being's nature and capacity of experiencing evil in the form of pain, loneliness, failure, despair and death, whereas he/she is also capable and aware of the possibility of joy, hope, happiness, friendship and fellowship with God and fellow human beings as the main objective and goal for human authentic life, or the human *raison d'etre*.[72] However, at the same time, because of human self-transcendence, and the subsequent moral self-evaluation, the human being realizes that there is a contrast in what one actually *is* as measured against what one *ought to be*.

This awareness causes internal guilt in addition to the external threats of pain, chaos, and extinction of one's being in the form of accidents, homicide, robbery, rape, hunger, poverty, disease, slander, broken relationships, isolation, loneliness, anxiety, crises of identity, and perhaps most of all the omnipresent threat of death. In short, this universal human experience of finitude and the threat of chaos, the universal human predicament arising out of finitude and entropy.

Finitude and the threats of chaos, pain, suffering, death and nothingness constitute the universal human problematic and the human existential condition. Many people take drugs as form of anaesthesia to life and escape from the awareness of pain and finitude. The drugs temporarily numb's minds and bodies to life and its joys and pains. By such escapism, many of these drugged up, semi-conscious people drift through life aimlessly, hopelessly and pathetically, as if they never lived! That is a great tragedy.

These people need to discover healing and redemptive teachings of Jesus-Christ and historical divine agent of God's life, forgiveness, and agape, or Buddha's great discovery and principle of life. Buddha formulated his new revelation in the first of the four noble truths. He had discovered that life is *"dukkha."* That is the positive principle which affirms life, in its givenness or *a priori* condition of finitude. Life is given to us, together with its inherent ingredient of natural characteristic sorrow, pain and suffering such as those of Job, to be part of life. Jesus himself experienced temptations, rejection, suffering, pain and finally crucifixion and death on a cross as a criminal.

However, in Africa, there are additional problems, which make life more difficult. These include poverty, dictatorships and abuse of human rights. There is also fear of evil spirits, witchcraft, and ostracism by the family or clan if one fails to behave in accordance with the culturally and religiously prescribed patterns of acceptable behavior. There is also the fear and hatred of strangers, such as the members of other tribes and races.[73]

There is also bitterness against some former Western imperialist and colonialist countries for their former harsh rule and, in some cases, previous cruel activities in Africa. The bitterness of slave trade has largely sunk into oblivion, though the Arabs and the Western nations that engaged in this inhumane trade have not been entirely forgiven. The colonial forced labor in Kenya and some other parts of Africa was resented by the Africans as a new form of slavery.[74] This was the case since its essence and objective was to provide either coerced or cheap African labor for the white settlers who owned vast plantations.

Until recently, Uganda, like most of Africa south of the Sahara, was largely non-Christian.[75] However, the people in this area had the understanding of God that enabled them to live humanely in the community. This pre-Christian understanding of both God and humanity still remains the very grounding of African values and the definitive guide for human interaction. This is still true at present for Uganda, which has now largely accepted Christianity, at least nominally.[76]

In this study I will employ Karl Rahner's Christian philosophical-theological anthropology, broad understanding of God and inclusive salvation, which explicitly includes unbaptized obedient people or godly, agapic and just non-Christians into God's kingdom. This Rahnerian inclusive broad understanding of God positively affirms God as *"Sola Gratia"* or the

Unconditional Loving free cosmic Creator and Redemptive Infinite Transcendent Mystery. Accordingly, God is understood as the Infinite cosmic Mystery, whose universal self-communication in efficacious gratuitous redemptive grace facilitates and effects universal divine gratuitous unconditional love, free forgiveness of sins, and salvation of all human beings everywhere in the cosmos.

This is both universally and positively affirmed to be the case, regardless of the finite dimensions of time and space, since these are themselves God's own creation. Just like a pregnant woman carries a microcosmic world of life in her womb, analogously, all finite beings and realities exist in God as the essential "creative" or "generative" "Cosmic-Mother" as the "All-Encompassing" or "Being" in the Tillichian and Heideggerian sense. God is the Ultimate Grounding Reality for all finite beings and transitory realities.[77]

This special agapic cosmic twin process of God's incognito activities of creation and supernatural salvation is also affirmed to be coextensive with both full humanization as also divinization into the child of God and true "*imago Dei.*" As such, whoever has accepted to become a truly humane "*Omuntu,*"[78] or a moral agent, that is, to become a responsible and/or an authentic human being, and has, therefore, accepted God's free universal supernatural invitation to authentic or meaningful human life which is coextensive with God's universal free creation and redemption.

In other words, such a redeemed person has visibly acquired the "*obuntu*",[79] or full humanity as manifested in being humane. Such a person has also both implicitly fully accepted God as the Creator and Christ as the divine cosmic Logos,[80] who is the full universal embodiment of authentic humanity (*Obuntu*) and the correlative God's own free cosmic supernatural salvation.[81] Karl Rahner contends that such a person has exercised personal faith, hope, and love for God and fellow human beings, and he/she is therefore truly an heir of divine gratuitous salvation through the divine cosmic Logos, who is similarly, the pre-existent cosmic Christ, and is therefore, a "Christian."[82]

However, since the described person may not even be aware of the existence of such a label,[83] and may even reject "Christian" as a description of his or her condition as a full human being fully open to the Absolute Mystery and life itself, which is the condition of grace and salvation, Karl Rahner affirms that he or she is, therefore, to be correctly termed an "anonymous Christian" and similarly, his or her state to be termed "anonymous Christianity."[84]

Divine salvation is properly viewed as a present condition of human life. This is because redemption or salvation is not a reward to be obtained in the future life for the good life lived on this earth.[85] Then, it is imperative for us to re-examine the world in order to see more of God's ceaseless activities of gratuitous grace in continuing creation, sustenance, transformation and renewal.[86] This is because both creation and salvation are God's freely willed and universally executed activities in the world by his unconditional love in gratuitous creative and salvific grace.[87]

Therefore, we are correct to reject the exclusive doctrine of *extra ecclesiam nulla salus*. Ultimately, human beings, regardless of who they are, including the members of the saints of God (such as Paul, Cyprian, Augustine, Aquinas), theologians, clergy and the Pope, cannot limit God's universal gratuitous salvation by our partisan exclusive theology to our own revival group, charismatic movement, church denomination, race, or political-economic ideological grouping or even East or West.[88]

God's free creativity pervades the whole universe. Similarly, God's gratuitous universal love and salvific will in gratuitous grace will act incognito in the universe to effect divine salvation[89] as well-being, wholeness, a peaceful life, joy, and hope for the abundant life. This universal and unrestricted salvation of God is for all people who truly positively respond to God's cosmic invitation to gratuitous supernatural salvation that presupposes faith, hope, and love in personal freedom on the part of those people who respond positively to God.

5. Unconditional Love for the Neighbor as the Universal Criterion and Standard Measure of True Christianity or Redemptive Religion

As part of the central thesis of this book, it will be strongly argued that the true criterion for true Christianity, whether explicit or anonymous, is the human practice of the unconditional love for our concrete neighbors and other persons we happen to encounter during the course of the ordinary routine of day-to-day living.[90]

This is held as the essence and grounding of true Christianity and evidence of our love for God. This is the case since by virtue of the incarnation God has become a human being. Therefore, by virtue of the Incarnation God has united with humanity, and thereby symbolically become our concrete temporal neighbor. This is because through Christ, God has also correlatively and coextensively become symbolically incarnate, and has also thereby, become fully present in every person in the world.[91]

Consequently, the question of "Who is my neighbor?" has been only settled for explicit Christians, and it still remains to be fully answered for anonymous Christianity. This requires an explicit Christian missionary activity, evangelization and Christian explicit teaching regarding God's commandment of unconditional love for the neighbor, where the neighbor is defined as every human being in the world.

There is still a need for Christian missionary activity among the non-Christians including the "anonymous Christians."[92] There is no doubt that "anonymous Christianity," though efficaciously salvific, is still a deficient modality of Christianity and human existence, as it is usually lacking in the fullness of unconditional love, explicit knowledge, confession of faith in Christ, fellowship and nurture of the historical Church and Sacraments.

Therefore, the humble task of the Church's missionary activity is to remedy these deficiencies wherever and whenever it is possible.[93] Since the historical Apostolic Church is not to be erroneously, literally regarded as the equivalent of the mythological Noah's Ark of divine salvation in this world,[94] it is therefore, the Apostolic Church, is both more correctly, theologically viewed as a divine symbolic historical presence of Christ as the eternal Logos, which has become inculturated, or incarnate in historical process.

Nevertheless, this local inculturation and historicization of the incarnate Christ, as the Word of God or the Logos, who has become part of our own local human and cultural images, has to be successfully accomplished without losing universality.

In the case of the central Christian doctrine of God's incarnation in history, society, culture and humanity through the divine Logos or the Christ, the doctrine has to become theologically formulated in local meaningful appropriate contexts and cultural traditions. This is what inculturation or incarnation of God, Christ and the gospel is about. God or Christ must be heard speaking to the hearers of the Word, and the Word of God or the Logos must be heard speaking to them in their own local language, historical and societal context. This is the ultimate meaning and essence of God's incarnation in the world of history and culture, in the Logos or Christ.

This inculturation or theological incarnation and historicization of God's revelation, should be positively carried, out and achieved without either the rejection or negation of the prior nature of its cosmic transcendental dimension of God and his eternal Logos. It is the same eternal cosmic Logos that is also locally incarnate as part of God's ongoing universal work in the whole cosmos, namely, gratuitous agapic creative and redemptive processes. As such, it is the same God working universally through the cosmic Logos, that both creates and redeems all human beings everywhere, regardless of era or religious tradition.

Ultimately, God works universally in the world incognito, through the Logos in order to effect free, unmerited and unconditional works of creation and salvation everywhere in the cosmos. To this end, it is God's unmerited and free God's gift of the power of grace or the Holy Spirit, that quietly works within each human being, incognito in order to effect God's universal salvific will. By God grace the human being is persuaded to actualize himself or herself more positively and most fully. He or she is also lured toward a voluntary advance to greater heights for more creative, and exciting self-actualization, positive fulfillment, personal maturity in creative growth, and positive transformation, in divinely guided personal freedom.[95]

NOTES

1. This is, as far as we can tell, the main distinguishing mark of a human being as opposed to other animals, especially the higher primates such as chimpanzees and other apes. For instance, the latter are considered to be lacking in the necessary capabilities that would lead them to ask such ultimate questions as: Who am I? Where did I come from? And where is my existence heading? If or whenever these ordinary animals ask these kinds of profound ultimate questions of life and meaning, then they will cease to be mere animals. According to Rahner, they will have become extraordinary animals like us. They will have become supernatural (*imago Dei*) and human no matter what else they might look like! For a human being is a creature that possesses the capacity to ask these self-transcending questions (cf. Gen. 1:26-31).

2. Cf. Karl Rahner, *Foundations of Christian Faith* (New York: Seabury Press, 1978), 44 ff, 85-89; *Spirit in the World* (New York: Herder and Herder, 1968), 406-408; *Grace in Freedom* (New York: Herder and Herder, 1969), 183-196, 203-207 and 229 ff. Rahner argues that the proper name or term given to the Infinite Mystery is not considered important. What is considered important is our attitude and response to this Mystery. That is why the rejection of the term "God" does not necessarily lead to atheism as long as the person remains open to life, the world and its mystery. Cf. Rahner, "Atheism and Implicit Christianity," *Theological Investigations* 9:145-164.

3. This theological method of correlation is the chief means by which relevant theology addresses questions and problems raised by being a human being in the world. Karl Rahner uses it but the most famous utilizer and expounder of this method remains Paul Tillich; cf. *Systematic Theology* (Chicago: University of Chicago Press, 1967) 1:59-66, where Tillich summarizes his method of correlation in theology. For Africa, this method means that

Christian theology should address the questions of polygamy, spirits, ancestors and evil, most especially as it manifests itself in poverty, witchcraft, tribalism, corruption and political irresponsibility.

4. The God of human worship has to be not only Creator, Mystery, Ground of Being and Knowledge, but he also has to be personal and responsive to human prayer and needs. See: *Prayers and Meditations* (New York: Seabury Press, 1980), 5-14; and *Foundations of Christian Faith*, 42-89.

This kind of approach avoids the kind of religious problem that arises with Tillich's conception of God as the Ground of Being with the implied impersonality of this Ground. Worship tends to reject or ignore a philosophically conceived God lacking in personal warmth toward the human worshippers. This is the dilemma of Christian theology as meaningful "God-talk" that seeks to be theologically and philosophically acceptable without losing the religious personal appeal for the ordinary worshippers. Maybe this is why some people find anthropomorphic religious language very appealing, especially in liturgical worship.

5. According to Karl Rahner, the quest for God is a result of self-transcendence and the "supernatural existential." This is God's prior gratuitous orientation of the human being in creation toward the supernatural destiny in the beatific vision; cf. Rahner, *Foundations of Christian Faith*, 75-80; "The Experience of Self and the Experience of God," *Theological Investigations* 13: 122-132; *Hearers of the Word* (New York: Seabury Press, 1960), Chs. 5 and 11; "The Existential," *Sacramentum Mundi: An Encyclopedia of Theology*, ed. Karl Rahner et al. (New York: Seabury Press, 1968-1970) 2:304-307. Rahner argues that the human being is a Spirit because of personal freedom and self-transcendence. This Spirit as a human being is historical because it is emergent in history. In light of evolution, it can be said that "the ape" became human when "it spoke," if language is considered as the evidence and unique tool of human abstract thought, self-transcendence and communication.

6. It can be argued that evil is, particularly felt by human beings because of this superior structure for abstract thought, self-transcendence and self-evaluation. The human being is usually aware of personal moral responsibility, unlike most animals. The human being is also able to ponder and speculate about such evils as war, famine, disease, poverty, slavery, injustice, political repression, corruption, pain and death. This capability tends to make the human being feel more vulnerable and overwhelmed with evil, the result being usually the kind of despair (*angst*) which Soren Kierkegaard very ably and vividly described in his works, particularly in *The Concept of Dread* and *The Sickness unto Death*. The animals have a natural instinct for survival. Therefore, they are radically sensitive to danger.

However, they feel no dread or despair as Kierkegaard describes it, as a general pervasive dread which is not a specific fear of this or that object that one could, therefore, remedy by the removal of those specific objects that are the effective cause of fear. Therefore, it appears that dread (*angst*) is a constitutive element of being in the world.

7. It is perhaps due to this sense of dread and vulnerability that the human being lives in the perpetual quest for salvation as well-being and security *vis-a-vis* evil with its tragedy and destruction that seem to abound in the world. It was Feuerbach's contention that if the human being was not aware of evil and his or her finitude and vulnerability in this world, there would not be any need for religion, which he saw as the conscious quest for salvation by an illusory immortal God from the threat of evil, pain and death; cf. *The Essence of Religion* (New York: Harper & Row, 1967), 16 ff.; *Essence of Christianity* (New York: Harper & Row Publishers, 1957), 13 ff.

8. Humankind and life in general, both zoological and botanical, exist only on this planet, earth. So far, scientific explorations of extraterrestrial space and the cosmos have not yet been able to detect the existence of any other kind of life in this wide cosmos apart from the terrestrial one. However, the search will continues for other intelligent beings in the cosmos if these beings do not discover us first!

9. Contrary to the teaching of the Balokole of Uganda, and other Evangelical or fundamentalist Christian groups like them, who teach that for salvation, only the spirit matters and nothing else, salvation in its broad or wholistic understanding includes the totality of the human being, as the individual is always a unity and not a loose collection of parts. Therefore, divine salvation should be viewed more broadly to include better health of both body and mind, personal freedom, and general well-being. That is, one should not be threatened by extreme poverty, starvation or lack of basic freedoms. Jesus' ministry was basically oriented to the poor and the ignorant. He healed the sick, taught the ignorant crowds, and fed the hungry. Similarly, we too who are his followers are called upon to imitate his example as we try to follow his teaching and to keep his commandments; cf. Matt. 25:31-46; Karl Rahner, "Anonymous Christians," *Theological Investigations* 6:231-249.

10. Karl Rahner argues that it is not the label for oneself that matters; that what really matters is our attitude and response to the Mystery and the life given to us, and how we live it in this world. Our own actions definitely speak louder than our words. Therefore, whether a person calls himself or herself a Christian or an atheist, it is of little importance. What really counts is what a person is and the quality of the life he or she is living as a result of personal free choice to become that person; cf. Rahner, "The Theology of Freedom," *Theological Investigations* 6:178-196; "On the Dignity and Freedom of Man," *Theological Investigations* 2:235-263; and "Atheism and Implicit Christianity," *Theological Investigations* 9:145-164.

The major problem of labels, or terms such as "Evangelical," "Marxist," "Communist," "Mulokole" and the like, is that they are already stereotyped in such a way that the individual so labeled tends to lose his or her unique individuality. For the debate of salvation within the Anglican Church of Uganda on the position of labels such as Balokole and "Sinners" in regard to this divine salvation, see the following articles and Letters to the Editor in *New Day*, a bi-weekly newspaper published by the Church of Uganda, Kampala: The Rev. E.M.K. Baluku, "A Challenge to the Balokole" *New Day* 4 January 1968; J.T.H. Deborrah, "One-Sided Challenge," *New Day* 1 February 1968; the Rev. Canon A. J. Binaisa's Letter to the Editor, *New Day* 1 February 1968; the Rev. Enos T. Bagona, "The Devil's Sermon," *New Day* 15 February 1968; C. C. Galiwango, "Canon in Darkness," *New Day* 25 April 1968; the Rev. E. Wamala, "Clergy are not necessarily called by God," *New Day* 9 May 1968 (front page headline in thick black print); Willis B. Shalita, "Their Acts Differ from Their Words," *New Day* 9 May 1968.

See also Joseph Kisubika's argument that "Jesus was a Mulokole" in "The Saved Are Sinners Too," *New Day* 6 June 1968; Dan Lukwago, "Roman Catholics are not God's Chosen People," *New Day* 4 July 1968; Keith Kanyogonya's interview of Bishop Festo Kivengere as the leader of the Balokole revivalists in Uganda, *New Day* 18 July 1968 (front page with a continuation on page 6); M. Y. Musoke. "There are Two Types of Sinners," *New Day* 1 August 1968; and an editorial on 1 August 1968 that summed up this debate and closed it formally with a theological explanation of salvation which is inclusive and embraces even non-Balokole. See also the Rev. Kauma, "Salvation," *New Day* 4 December 1969.

11. Within a Rahnerian understanding, salvation in this context is human life that is lived in the world in divine grace and harmony with one's *a priori* destiny. This life has to be characterized by the awareness of one's dependency on God for one's being, origin and destiny. Life lived in movement toward one's true destiny is the life of salvation, and salvation is realized in this finite life. That is life faithfully oriented and moving in hope towards fulfillment in the ultimate divine destiny that still lies in the Mystery of the Future; cf. Wolfhart Pannenberg, *What Is Man? Contemporary Anthropology in Theological Perspective* (Philadelphia: Fortress Press, 1970), 54-67.

12. For instance, "Islam" is an Arabic word which means "total surrender" or "submission," and in this case, it means total submission to God. Therefore, those Christians who sing the popular revival hymn, "All to Jesus I surrender... I surrender all," can be termed Muslims, that is, people who have surrendered all to God! The Qur'an (Koran) and the "*Shari'a*," which constitute the Islamic scriptures and the Islamic law, respectively, do reveal a close similarity to the Old Testament and the Mosaic law. Under Rahner's theory, the same God inspired the emergence of both types, inasmuch as both types do contain a degree of divine revelation and answers to human existential questions.

13. In African traditional religion there is no division between sacred and mundane. God created everything, and though God is transcendent, he is also present everywhere in creation directly or indirectly, by means of mediation through nature or human ancestral spirits and phenomena; cf. John Mbiti, *African Religions and Philosophy* (London: Heinemann, 1969), 1-3, 88-100; *Introduction to African Religion*, 65 ff.; and Newell S. Booth, ed., *African Religions: A Symposium* (New York: NOK Publishers, Ltd., 1977), 7.

For the African, the ordinary is the conveyor of the extra-ordinary for those willing to see with their inner eyes of faith and having willing ears to hear the silent divine Word of the Invisible, Transcendent Mystery, locally known as "Ruhanga" in Kigezi, Ankole, Bunyoro and Toro, and "Katonda" in Buganda and Busoga. Ruhanga or Katonda literally means and translates "The Creator." It has to be noted that in this part of Africa God is God only if he is "The Creator" creating *ex nihilo*. However, this Creator-God is not a static "Pure Act" of St. Thomas. He is too transcendent to act in the world directly most of the time, so he acts through a chain of mediators and delegates like a mighty Celestial King.

14. See, e.g., John Mbiti, *African Religion and Philosophy*, 1-3, 6, 20 and 343. However, Western missionary Christianity is beginning to change this picture, as it has attacked and still continues to attack traditional religion and its values in order to westernize the African as evidence of successful Christian conversion. This mistaken evangelical missionary method has been destructive to African values. As expected, the reactionary voices of skepticism and even atheism are beginning to be heard at the universities and among the educated youth. Therefore, in this respect, Christianity has brought damnation and destruction to Africa.

Consequently, the main effective remedy and preventive measure against this impending calamity is to contextualize Christianity in African religious milieu rather than seek to destroy it, as the C.M.S. missionaries tried to do in Uganda; cf. F.B. Welbourn, *East African Rebels: A Study of Some Independent Churches* (London: C.M.S. Press, 1961), 3-14 and Chs. 2-5, 9. Chapter 9 is particularly important, as it deals with the "Missionary Culture and the African response," and in this case revolt and schism as the African response to this apparent cultural imperialism of the Western Christian missionaries in East Africa.

15. See Mbiti, *African Religion and Philosophy*, 13, for a detailed discussion of these Western ethnocentric derogatory descriptions of the African people and their religion. He

points out that terms such as "ancestor worship," "primitive," "totemism," "savage," "fetish," "magic," "pagan," "Satanic," "hellish," "superstition," "animism" and the like, previously used to describe African religion by Western writers, are inaccurate, racist, derogatory and unacceptable both academically and to the African people as such.

16. Ibid. Animism as a belief that everything has *anima* (soul) in it is probably a close description of most African people, since they view the world as pervaded by divine energy or powerful spirit that can be accessible to people, especially kings, priests, elders, medicine men and women, mediums and diviners. It is also believed that evil people, such as witches and evil magicians, can gain access to it too, and use it to do harm to people and their property. Nevertheless, the belief in a "world-soul" pervading the universe cannot constitute a religion, as it is just one of the numerous major beliefs in African religion.

This energy pervading the universe has been called "vital force" by Placide Tempels in *Bantu Philosophy* (Paris: Presence Africaine, 1959). However, Mbiti rejects Tempels' "vital force" as the center of African philosophy. Instead of "*NTU*," Mbiti claims that the concept of time is the center; *African Religion and Philosophy*, 14-15. However, both points of view should be treated together as mutually correlative, since together they explain much of African metaphysics better than does either one of these views in isolation. Janheinz Jahn, *Muntu: An Outline of the New African Culture* (New York: Grove Press, 1961) and Alexis Kagame (Fr.), *La Philosophie Bantu-Rwandaise de l'Etre* (Brussels: Academie Royale des Sciences Coloniales, 1956) follow Tempels in their analysis of African philosophies, as Mbiti's theory of time as the basis for African metaphysics and ontology had not yet been put forward.

17. For East Africans God is considered to be omnipotent, but whether he is also omnispatial is not clearly thought out. Consequently, it is thought that, although divine presence is pervasive in the world, it only manifests itself occasionally in a specific place such as a high mountain, big river, huge rock, even in an animal such as a huge snake. Wherever this divine presence reveals itself in its varied mystery, it is always for the same benefit of human beings, i.e. to awe or amaze them and motivate them to worship Ruhanga as the Creator of this wonderful mystery. See Mbiti, *Concepts of God in Africa* (New York: Praeger, 1970), *passim*.

18. For instance, all human beings experience dread (*Angst*) and usually have a religion and generally fear to die.

19. Fuller life (as in John 10:10) and its quest can be considered to amount to the quest for salvation whether it is carried out by religious or by secular means such as "Marxism" or "Secular Humanism;" see Jurgen Moltmann, *What is Man? Christian Anthropology in the Conflicts of the Present* (Philadelphia: Fortress Press, 1971), 46-96. See also note 11 above.

20. Cf., e.g., W.K.C. Guthrie, *The Greek Philosophers: from Thales to Aristotle* (New York: Harper & Row, Publishers, 1960), 6-12 and 153 ff.; Bertrand Russell, *A History of Western Philosophy* (New York: Simon Schuster, 1945), 178-189. Happiness is the general goal of authentic human activity unless there is something wrong in the doer to obscure in his or her mind the ultimate good. In this sense, then, sin can be termed free human self-actualization in the world in such a way that happiness is made impossible most of the time for oneself and others around him or her.

21. Ibid. Good fruits are borne of a good tree while a bad tree yields bad fruits (see Matt. 7:16-20). This argument is important in the debate on salvation and grace, as it can

be used to support Karl Rahner's view that Divine salvation is freely given to human beings everywhere in grace prior to their actions of faith, love and virtue, as these spring from the already present state of grace, which is prior to any human activity. See Rahner, "Reflections on the Experience of Grace," *Theological Investigations* 3:86-90; "Concerning the Relationship of Nature and Grace," *Theological Investigations* 4:165-188; "Some Concepts on Uncreated Grace," *Theological Investigations* 1:319-346; and his articles on "Existential," " Supernatural," "Grace," and "Potentia Oboedientialis" in *Sacramentum Mundi: A Theological Dictionary,* 5 vols. edited by Karl Rahner and Herbert Vorgimeler.

22. *Summum bonum,* variously identified with God or as God. Plato's God as seen in the *Timaeus* was a mere architect, such as a carpenter or potter fashioning an item from pre-existent materials. The idea of the good transcended Plato's God as it was all perfection and all-inclusive. The good, according to Plato, was mediated by beauty as its immanence in this transitory world of constant becoming and change; see *Phaedrus* 250e. However, Plato's followers such as Plotinus modified his concept of God by combining the Idea of the Good with Plato's Architect God. The result was a good Creator-God taught in Neoplatonism, the kind that St. Augustine learned from Porphyry. See St. Augustine's *City of God,* Book VIII, particularly Chapter 8, which deals with the *summum bonum* in the context of Platonism.

23. For Socrates and Plato, philosophy and the knowledge gained, were considered as ground for practical moral theology or applied ethics. Knowledge was pursued, not as an end in itself, but as a means to virtue, a good life and happiness; see note 20 above. Even today, education is positive if the knowledge and skills it confers on the young lead to a positive mode of life.

24. The *"rudes"* or the ignorant masses were left to perish in ignorance, as not everyone could become a philosopher. It is not surprising, therefore, that both Socrates and Jesus were alike in that both saw their missions as teachers of divine salvific moral truths to all who those cared to listen and follow their ethical and moral teachings. It is ironic that both of them were accused of impiety and subsequently put to death, and that both went to their deaths willingly and calmly. See Plato's *Crito* for the execution of Socrates, and Matt. 25-27 or Luke 22-23 for the passion story of Jesus.

25. This is the main grounding of Platonic and Christian mysticism. In this mysticism there are usually three stages of theosis. The first stage is self-purgation from base or bodily desires that distract the mind from concentration. The second stage is a disciplined contemplation of God until the thinker is finally lost in the object of his or her thought. This is the climactic unitive stage and it is very much like Hegel's "Absolute Knowledge," in which there is the abrogation of the distinction between object and subject, thought and thinker. See Hegel's *Phenomenology of Spirit,* the section on the "Absolute Knowledge;" St. John of the Cross, *The Ascent of Mount Carmel*; and *The Cloud of Unknowing.*

26. It can be argued that Plato was right. The current troubled politics and economies of the Third World could be largely attributed to a lack of Philosopher-Kings! The military tyrants heading most of these nations are the very opposite of the Philosopher-King. For instance, the notorious Idi Amin of Uganda was a bare elementary school dropout. He proved that without good education he could not rule the country insightfully, despite his supposed great military power. President Nyerere of Tanzania, his opponent, on the other hand, has a Master of Arts degree. Could it be mere coincidence, then, that even in actual battle, Nyerere was able to defeat the semi-literate Idi Amin and drive him out of Uganda in 1979?

Probably not. The excesses of Idi Amin could be attributed mainly to ignorance, tribalism, greed, sin, and personal sadism.

27. In East Africa political order and religion were very much part of each other. They were both thought to have been given to humanity and sanctioned by God, as the myth of *Kairu, Kahima and Kakama* in Western and Southern Uganda illustrates. Therefore, to these people Plato's king, who is also a kind of high priest by virtue of his divine knowledge and exemplary virtue, would probably be most welcome. For concepts of theocracy and divine kingship held in this area, see: A. G. Katate and L. Kamugungunu, *Abagabe b'Ankole* (Kampala: E.A.P.B., 1955); S. M. Kiwanuka, *Kings of Buganda* and A History of Buganda; M. Beattie, *Bunyoro*; Nyakatura, *Bunyoro-Kitara*; Paul Ngorogoza, *Kigezi n'Abantu Bayo*; and Apollo Kagwa, *Ba Ssekabaka Be Buganda*.

28. See Gen. 12:1-4, 15:7-18; Exod. 6:4 ff., 19:5 ff; Isa. 42-55. The election of Israel by God was purely out of God's free grace and universal will to save the world and not just those special elect people who were to be his main historical symbol of grace and salvation in the world (cf. Rom. 1-4). For this divine unconditional salvation of Israel, and other people too; see Gerhard von Rad, *Old Testament Theology* (New York: Harper & Row, 1957) 1:121-135; Ps. 104:20-32.

29. See Ezekiel 18, where individuals are to be punished for their personal transgressions of the divine statutes. As regards universal salvation beyond the covenant, it can be said that in general, the Jewish prophets and priests had little interest, as Israel's credo in Deut. 25:5-9 very clearly proves. Israel became too preoccupied with the covenant, election and its demands of holiness to be concerned with the possible conversion and salvation of Gentiles. Election, the covenant and salvation were considered Jewish birthrights, and Judaism was synonymous with both Jewish and divine election to salvation or the *ecclesium*. As a result, foreign mission to the Gentiles in this case was thought either as unnecessary, since it meant Jewish imperialism, or as a matter to be left to God; cf. Isa. 55:5.

30. As they were excluded from the covenant, the Torah and its guidance; see Psalms 9, 10; Isa. 16:8, 10:25; and Joel 3:12. However, there were exceptions to this Jewish exclusiveness regarding salvation. For instance, Cyrus a gentile is mentioned in Isaiah 44 as one who helped to rebuild Jerusalem and the temple, is portrayed as God's "Messiah" for the Jews now in exile. People like Jethrow and Cyrus are used as illustrative examples of how God's work of gratuitous universal grace and salvation transcends the covenant people and their Jewish borders. Similarly, it can be argued that today, God's salvific work in gratuitous grace transcends the baptismal covenant and its narrow borders of the historical Church.

31. Yet, God's mercy and salvation are, nevertheless, to be mediated to these Gentiles; cf. Gen. 12:1-4; Zech. 8:7-23; and most of all the dramatic story of prophet Jonah, the reluctant missionary to Nineveh. The book of Jonah can be viewed as a symbolic commissioning of Israel to foreign mission among the Gentiles, to convert them to God's mercy and by so doing humanize them more, thus sensitizing them against inhumane acts of injustice and cruelty. This is why Christian missionary activity to the world is a must, if it remains true to God's commission as the divine historical means of humanization of the world by means of unconditional neighborly and brotherly love.

32. Cf. Matt. 5:17: "Think not that I come to destroy the law or the prophets; I am not come to destroy but to fulfill..." (KJV). See also the kind of reforms Jesus is concerned with

as recorded in Matt. 5-7, such as the rejection of the Mosaic law of *"lex talionis"* (Matt. 5:38) as seen in "an eye for an eye and a tooth for a tooth" (Exod. 21:24). However, Jesus inaugurated a new era when he commanded his followers to love one another without counting the cost (Mark 12:30-31, 33; John 15:12, 17), because it is this very commandment that has led to the Christian transformation and revolution in the world, both directly and indirectly, to enhance human freedom and dignity.

33. Paul himself was compelled to argue that Jesus' commandment to love God and one's neighbor is not only the summary of the law but is its very essence and energizing power. Therefore, in agreement with both Paul and John, one can say, like Rahner, that whoever loves unconditionally, whether he/she is a self-labeled "atheist," "Muslim," or "Humanist," he or she has fulfilled the requirements of God's law in grace and is an heir to supernatural salvation and eternal life (cf. I John 4:7-21), since without God's grace no one can either fulfill the demands of the law or express love without conditions attached to it for personal ends. See Paul's insightful analysis of the nature of this unconditional love (agape) in I Cor. 13; see also Anders Nygren, *Agape and Eros* (London: MacMillan, 1939), which deals in great detail with the subject of love and its role in the Christian faith.

34. This is one of the reasons why Jesus should be considered a reformer rather than a religious revolutionary. If Jesus had included a woman within this inner circle of the twelve Apostles, the current heated debates on the ordination of women within the Anglican and Catholic Churches would have been entirely out of place! However, since the Apostolic ministry was opened to Gentiles who were originally not included among the twelve Apostles, why should it not be open to women too? After all, women have a valid claim to the Eucharistic ministry if it is the confection of the elements into the body and blood of Jesus Christ and to distribute them to "the worshippers of the Son of Mary"!

It could be argued that Mary brought Jesus into the world and through this act of chastity, faith and obedience to the *Theotokos*, all women have been symbolically cleansed and elevated in grace and status, in both religious and secular affairs. But the Church has been slow in realizing this in the same way that it has been slow in seeing God's salvific activity among non-Christians. See: Mary Daly, *Beyond God the Father: Toward a Philosophy of Women's Liberation* (New York: Beacon Press, 1973); Rose Mary Radford Ruether, *The Feminine Face of the Church* and *New Woman, New Earth: Sexist Ideologies and Human Liberation* (New York: Seabury Press, 1975).

35. It seems that Jesus understood his ministry to be primarily the fulfillment of Judaism; c.f., e.g., Matt. 5:17, 27; 15:21-28; Mark 7:24-30. It could also be pointed out that the incident at Gerasa (Gadara) recorded in the Synoptic Gospels (Matt. 8:24-34; Luke 8:26-39; Mark 5:1-20) further illustrates that, though Jesus cared and healed the demoniac, he did not care enough for the local non-Jewish populace, their culture and their property, since he allegedly killed about 2,000 of their herd of pigs!

36. These can be understood as the words of the risen Christ as he is known and experienced by the Church in his abiding presence through the Holy Spirit. In this sense the words and the commissioning of the Church to the venture of world mission stem from the Church's own nature, self-consciousness and self-understanding. The Church had began to see itself as the visible and historical embodiment of the risen Christ in the temporal world. As such, the Church began to understand her message and mission in new universal dimensions. As a result of the resurrection experience, and positive affirmation of God's original universal salvific will (cf. John 3:16), the Church also began to shape her theology and mission in the world in those universal terms.

Pannenberg, in reference to this great commission of the Church to world mission, skeptically asks: "Do we really have to baptize everybody?" See *Human Nature, Election and History* (Philadelphia: The Westminster Press, 1977), 36. The answer to this question is the concern of this book. But in short, the answer of Karl Rahner is "No." Despite thousand years of Christianity, there are still many people who are not Christians. According to David Barrett's recent statistical study, all baptized Christians constitute just a bare 33 percent of the world's total population, which in 1986 was estimated to be about 5 billion people; see *The World Christian Encyclopedia: A Comparative Survey of Churches and Religions in the Modern World, A.D. 1900-2000* (London: Oxford University Press, 1982).

37. See Acts 9:1-23, 15:1-35; Galatians; and Rom. 2-4. Paul, a self-styled Apostle to the Gentiles, successfully transformed the nature of Christianity and its theology from a narrow Jewish base and adapted it for a universal (Catholic) creative advance into the whole world.

38. Such as the vanished Essenes of Qumran Community. Judaism at the time of Jesus was already divided into doctrinal parties or sects, such as the Sadducees and the rigorist Pharisees who, contrary to the Sadducees, believed in the resurrection, the real existence of spirits, angels and a spiritual kingdom of God; see Acts 23:6-9.

39. Because our present Christianity is basically Pauline, especially in the Protestant churches, which adopted Paul's principle of *sola gratia,* particularly as taught in both his letters to the Romans and the Galatians, and Martin Luther being the most keen and famous exponent of this Pauline doctrine. However, modern Roman Catholic theologians like Kung and Karl Rahner agree with this doctrine; cf. Rahner, *Grace in Freedom* (New York: Herder & Herder, 1969), 101-111; *Foundations of Christian Faith,* 116-170; see also note 21 above.

40. For example, see Rom. 1-4; 1 Cor. 5-10; Galatians; Hebrews; and the Johannine epistles which deal with heresies originating from Greek and Oriental dualistic philosophies. If Christianity had remained Jewish, such problems as those that these epistles were written to address, would probably not have arisen, and consequently, the Epistles as we have them in the New Testament today would not have existed!

41. This claim is based on the fact that Orthodox Judaism was becoming increasingly strictly monotheistic. Consequently, Jesus would have been understood, not as God become incarnate, as John puts it (John 1:1-4, 14), but rather as a "divine-man" (*theos-aner*), or the "Son of Man" as Mark puts it (cf. Mark 2:10). The God-Man or divine-man was supposed to possess the power to effect God's redemptive or supernatural liberationist and messianic mission to Israel and beyond. This was considered to be the case, since this divine messianic agent was also considered to be God's eschatological gift of grace and salvation to all nations (Luke 2:30-32) for the glory of Israel, which would become the new central focus (Zion) for the world as the terrestrial symbol of divine light and salvation in the world (cf. Gen. 12:1-4; Isa. 51:1-16, 52:9, 53:12, 55:5 and 59:16-61:3).

Main-line Christianity insists that such a bringer of divine salvation should be God himself, as orthodox Christology and soteriology teach. It is mainly, therefore, on the question of the divinity of Christ that other universal religions such as Islam part company with Christianity; see the Qur'an (Koran), "*Suras*" (or chapters) entitled "Mary," "Christians," "Infidels," "God," "Jesus," "People of the Book," and "Judgment Day." For Israel's requirement for a monotheistic conception of God, see the "*Schema*"; "Hear O Israel... I am the Lord your God... You shall not have other gods besides me..." (Deut. 5:1-21, Exod. 20:1-17). The oneness (*monos*) of God is the core of the "*Schema*" or the decalogue; see

Bernhard W. Anderson, *Understanding the Old Testament* (Englewood Cliffs: Prentice-Hall, Inc., 1975), 356-357; von Rad, *Old Testament Theology*, 239 ff,.

43. See Acts 15:1-35; Paul's letters to the Galatians and the Romans.

44. Ibid. Peter had a big problem of indecision (cf. Gal. 2:11-21). But he must have overcome it adequately for him to be able to undertake a foreign missionary venture in the cosmopolitan city of Rome. It is in Rome where St. Peter was reported to have perished in Nero's Christian persecution and holocaust of 64 C.E. It was widely believed that he was crucified upside down at his request, according to popular, but unvalidated Christian tradition; Eusebius, *The History of the Church from Christ to Constantine*, trans. G.A. Williamson (Minneapolis: Augsburg Publishing House, 1965) 25:1, 104 ff.

45. A doctrine taught by Jesus but without any further elaboration as it is recorded in the New Testament; see Matt. 9:17; Mark 2:22; Luke 5:37-38. Stephen's address and martyrdom (Acts 6-7) played a role in Paul's conversion and theological formation. In this sense Stephen was a forerunner of St. Paul almost in the same way that John the Baptist was a forerunner of Jesus (cf. Mark 1:1-15 and compare it with Acts 6:1-9:31).

46. See Rom. 3-11; cf. Heb. 1-5. St. Augustine, like Justin Martyr, could say that what was unique in Christianity was the incarnation of the Logos in a particular individual man, Jesus. See *The City of God*, Book VIII; *Confessions*, Book VIII; and Justin Martyr's *Dialogues* and *I Apol.*

47. Cf. II Cor. 5:16-20; I Cor. 13; John 10:10, 15:12-17; and 1 John 4:7-21.

48. With the exception of Paul (cf. Rom. 2-4), statements such as "I am the Way, and the truth and the life; and no one comes to the Father but by me" (John 14:6) and the claims in John 6:35-40 and 10:1-18 were possibly meant by the evangelist to exclude non-Christians or unbelievers from Christ's benefits and God's eternal life. But it is also possible that such exclusiveness had an apologetic and evangelistic purpose, namely, to frighten non-believers into faith, and not to deny them divine salvation that John has previously announced to be universal in scope (John 3:16). After all, Christ as the creative Logos of God mentioned in the prologue was also the Life-Giver to all the world, to whom he was now adding even more life to make it fully abundant (John 10:10). In the final analysis, John does not intend to deny anybody God's salvation in Christ. It is precisely because Christ as the eternal Logos of God is the only "way, and the truth and the life" and no one ever goes to God except through Christ, that we can be sure that all God's salvation is through Christ both as the pre-Incarnate Logos or the Incarnate Christ (cf. Jn. 1:1-18; 14:6).

It is for lack of a better inclusive Christian term, we can therefore, positively affirm that all those who have known the truth in the Logos of God and have lived according to this truth in agape, are from a Christocentric and Christian perspective, correctly termed "Christians" whether they know it explicitly and were baptized in the Church or did not know it and were Muslims, Jews, atheists, Buddhists, Hindus, African or American Traditionalists. To this latter category Carl Rahner has attached the term "anonymous Christians," even when they might themselves object to being called Christians! They could be called "Muslims" if we were writing from an Islamic perspective, since the "Muslim" can be inclusive enough to mean all those people who have surrendered themselves to God, including Adam, Moses, David, Jesus and all the prophets.

49. See, e.g., Luke 23:1-5. However, for the Christians this failure of justice and the apparent triumph of evil and death was overcome by the resurrection, which proved that the power of God is stronger than that of evil. Similarly, the power of God to save is stronger than the power of evil and destruction.

50. Cf. "I believed in Him so strongly that I wanted to take an army and destroy the Jews who crucified Him, if I had not been prevented by the imperial power of Rome from doing so." This is an extract quoted from King Abgar's letter (inauthentic) cited by Eusebius, *The History of the Church*, 68. Josephus' *Book of Antiquities* is strongly anti-Semitic. For instance, he is happy that Christ's murder was vindicated by severe famine and a prolonged Roman siege of the City of Jerusalem that destroyed the city and the temple, in 70 A.D.

51. I have myself heard an anti-Semitic sermon preached on this text. The preacher claimed that the current Jewish diaspora and persecution, especially by Hitler, is God's punishment on them for having murdered the innocent Jesus as a criminal and having spared Barabbas the murderer, saying, "Let his blood be upon us and our children."

52. See "The Declaration on the Relationship of the Church to Non-Christian Religions," *The Documents of Vatican II*, trans. and ed. Walter M. Abbott and Joseph Gallagher (Chicago: Follett Publishing Co., 1966), 660-668. Anti-Semitism is condemned in strong terms: "The Church repudiates all persecutions...mindful of her common patrimony with the Jews, and motivated by the gospel's spiritual love...she deplores the hatred, persecutions and displays of anti-Semitism directed against the Jews at any time from any source" (665-667). See also notes 19-30 above for the vital information regarding previous Christian persecutions of the Jews based on the charge that the Jews were Christ's murderers to be punished by both God and man.

53. Ibid. This is to my mind the greatest decree of the Council, as it did away with the Tridentine adaptation of Cyprianic Church exclusiveness and bigotry of *extra ecclesiam nulla salus*, which was the grounding of the Roman Catholic non-ecumenical dogmatic theology. St. Thomas also expounded a strict form of this dogma of *extra ecclesiam nulla salus;* cf. *Summa Theologiae* III, qq. 1 ff., especially 8 and 60-65. He excludes heretics, schismatics and non-Christians (non-believers). For St. Thomas Aquinas, predestination to salvation includes predestination to these sacraments that were considered essential for salvation (cf. *Summa Theologiae* III, qq. 60 ff.). However, Thomas complicates the issue when he says that the faithful Old Testament community belongs to this same redemptive church (cf. *Summa Theologiae* III, q. 3).

54. Cf. Rom.1-5. Paul considers God as "One," "the Creator" and source of all revelation, salvation and judgment. There is no partiality with God. God's love and salvation are unconditional (Rom. 5:6-8) and salvific for all human beings (cf. Mark 12:29-31; 1 Cor. 13). Since no person is ever excluded by God from the kingdom and his free universal gifts of sufficient redemptive grace, agape, and the possibility of salvation, nor should we deny these divine free gifts to any one. God has freely given people the choice to respond to his invitation to salvation and be saved.

55.Ibid. See also Karl Rahner's writings mentioned in note 21. In addition, see Karl Rahner and Joseph Ratzinger, *Revelation and Tradition*; Karl Rahner, *Kerygma and Dogma* (New York: Herder and Herder, 1969); "The Order of Redemption within the Order of Creation," *The Christian Commitment* (New York: Sheed and Ward, 1963), 38-74; "Nature and Grace," in *Nature and Grace* (New York: Sheed and Ward, 1964), 114-149.

56. For a fuller treatment of this controversy, see: Henry Chadwick, *Early Christian Thought and Classical Tradition* (New York: Oxford University Press, 1966), 1 ff.; Tertullian, *de Praescr.* 7; Justin Martyr, *Apol.* 46.

57. This controversy over philosophy and its role in Christian theology still rages on, especially among Protestant theologians. For instance, Karl Barth rejected the alliance between theology and philosophy and attacked both Emil Brunner and Paul Tillich on this matter and the question of "natural theology," to which philosophical theology gives basis and logical validation. See: Karl Barth, *Church Dogmatics I* for this debate; Brunner, *The Christian Doctrine of Creation and Redemption, Dogmatics II* (Philadelphia: The Westminster Press, 1952); *Revelation and Reason* (Philadelphia: The Westminster Press, 1946); *Natural Theology*, comprising "Nature and Grace" by Emil Brunner and the emphatic "No" in reply by Karl Barth (London: Geoffrey Bles, 1946). For Paul Tillich's basic position, see his collected essays on the subject in *What Is Religion?*, trans. James Luther Adams (New York: Harper and Row Publishers, 1969) and *Systematic Theology* 2:71-162. Tillich's position is that philosophy is a tool and resource for doing theology without being held captive by it.

Hegel's attempt to turn theology into philosophy (cf. *Phenomenology of Spirit*, section on Absolute Knowledge; *Christian Religion: Lectures on the Philosophy of Religion, Part III; The Revelatory, Consummate, Absolute Religion,* trans. and ed. Peter C. Hodgson (AAR: Scholars Press, 1979) represents another extreme example which is cautiously approached by most theologians.

If we adopt the helpful Aristotelian axiom that virtue lies in the middle, it will then follow that in the debate above, Brunner and Tillich have a more moderate stand and therefore a better position than Barth and his followers. Karl Rahner, whose thought underlies most of this book, is very much like Tillich as regards this debate; cf., e.g., "Theology and Anthropology," *The Word in History*, ed. Patrick T. Burke (New York: Sheed and Ward, 1968); "Philosophy and Theology," *Theological Investigations* 6:77-81; "Philosophy and Philosophizing in Theology," *Theological Investigations* 9:46-63; "Christian Humanism," ibid., 187-204.

As Christian theologians, philosophers and other kinds of social moral thinkers, we can also employ them as valuable indispensable tools for local Africanization and theological contextualization of Christianity in African life. Like Justin Martyr, Origen and Augustine found Platonism a useful tool in explaining their new Christian faith to their contemporaries; St. Thomas found Aristotelianism handy for his theological task in the Middle Ages; and presently theologians like John Cobb and Norman Pittenger have found a modern theological tool in Whitehead's Process Philosophy. The African Christian thinkers need the right philosophical tools in order to accomplish their own theological task of contextualization and inculturation of the Christian faith that has been received from the foreign Western missionaries and former colonialists, into the local indigenous cultural context, in order to render this Christian faith essentially meaningful.

It is hoped that this process will unmask the potent power of the Gospel and thus enable it to transform us as Africans more effectively into the very authentic human beings that God intends us to be as Africans, and not poor imitations of our former Western imperialists, colonialists and/or the white foreign Western missionaries. God created us Africans to be Africans and not something else. Therefore, the task of the Gospel should ideally be to enable us to become the true Africans God wants us to be. This is, indeed the very essence of the good news of God's incarnation in Christ for us and nothing else.

58. The West was characterized by Rome's political and administrative centrality and pride of being the capital of the Roman Empire, and therefore, the pivot of the known civilized world. Lacking in the Eastern Greek tradition of speculative philosophy, the Church

in the West began to imitate the administrative structure of the civil Roman Empire and to pattern the Church hierarchy, authority and structure. It is not surprising, therefore, that the institution of the Papacy developed in Rome. This was developed in competition with the Roman Emperor! Finally, the Pope triumphed and became the new global divine-Emperor, on God's behalf, ruling the world from holy Vatican City in Rome! The Petrine texts (Matt. 16:17-20; John 21:15-17) were used later on to prove the validity of the Papal position and not prior to this institutional development; cf. Philip Schaff, *History of the Christian Church* 2:121-193, 228-619.

It has been suggested by African historians that, because of this Latin authoritarian ecclesiology and Roman imperial repression, North Africans welcomed the conquering Arab Muslims in the seventh century in order to free themselves from Roman imperialism that had become synonymous with Christianity. There is no evidence that local Christians put up a fight to resist conquest or the subsequent Islamization. This in part accounts for the disappearance of Christianity in Latin North Africa, whereas it survived in Egypt and Ethiopia. In Egypt and Ethiopia, the Coptic (native) Christianity survived as evidence to the validity of this phenomenon.

59. Consequently, whereas the Eastern Church was generally not threatened by schism and rebellion as the Latin Church in the West, it was threatened by heresy. See, e.g., J.N.D. Kelly, *Early Christian Doctrines* (New York: Harper & Row, 1960), 223-400.

60. See Justin Martyr, *Apologies* and *Dialogue with Tripho*, which develop an acceptable divine universal salvation based on the universal efficacy of divine truth available in God's cosmic Logos. However, Origen developed this position further to an unacceptable conclusion in his teaching on "*Apocatastasis*," he affirmed that all free moral creatures, that is all human beings, angels, evil spirits and even the devil, will *all* finally repent, and share in the supernatural gratuitous grace and divine salvation (cf. Hom. in Lev. VII:2, de Princ. IV, 4:9). Clement of Alexandria and Gregory of Nyssa taught (to some extent) this kind of universalism, whereas St. Augustine and St. Thomas repudiated and negated it in their own teaching and affirmation of predestination; see, e.g., Augustine, *De diversis quaestionibus ad Simplicianum* I, q.2; *De spiritu littera*, 52-66; *De natura et gratia*; *De gratia Christi*, 13-27; *De gratia et libero arbitrio*; *De corruptione et gratia* 11:26 ff.; *De praedestinatione sanctorum;* St. Thomas, *Contra Gentiles* III, Chs. 147-163; *Summa Theologiae* I-II, qq. 110-113, I q. 23.

61. See also Eusebius, *Hist. Eccl.* I, 4, where "pre-Christian" men such as Abraham, Moses, etc., are said to be "Christians."

62. Cf. Cyprian's harsh administrative and episcopal treatment of his opponents in schism: "The spouse of Christ...preserves us for God...enrolls into the Kingdom the sons she has borne. Whoso stands aloof from the Church...is cut off from the promises of the Church; and he that leaves the Church of Christ attains not to Christ's rewards. He is an alien, an outcast, and an enemy. He cannot have God for his father who has not the Church for his mother. If any one was able to escape outside Noah's ark, then he also escapes who is outside the doors of the Church" (*De Catholicae Unitate*, 6). See also Epistle LXVI:7, in which he claims that the bishop is the symbol of the Church and 35, therefore, all Christians desiring salvation should obey their bishop, for "the bishop is the Church!"

The doctrine of *extra ecclesiam nulla salus* was formulated in this ecclesiastical internal strife, schism and rivalry. It is seen by many as a negative, bitter, revengeful castigation of rivals by denying them salvation, and as the most unchristian attitude toward an enemy, as it ignores Christ's commandment to love our neighbors and even our enemies, too (cf. Matt.

5:43-48; Mk. 12:29-31; Jn. 15:12-17; 1 Cor. 13; 1 Jn. 4:13-21). See also notes 52, 53 and 58.

63.Ibid. See also Vatican "Decree on Ecumenism," *Documents of Vatican II* (ed. Abbott), 336-371, and "Declaration on the Relationship of the Church to Non-Christian Religions," *Doc. Vat. II*, 656-672.

64. See, e.g., front page, *The Tennessean* and *The Banner*, Aug. 31, 1980; *Time*, Sept. 29, 1980, p. 85 (among other publications and television news headlines).

65. See Reinhold Niebuhr, *The Nature and Destiny of Man* .Jurgen Moltman, *Man: Christian Anthropology in the Conflicts of the Present*, 47-96; Paul Tillich, *Systematic Theology* 3:382 ff.; Karl Rahner, "Atheism and Implicit Christianity," *Theological Investigations* 9:145-164.

66. Failure to love the neighbor is perhaps the primary cause of some major political and economic problems in the world today. For instance, the division of West-East ideological conflicts, nuclear arms race, and the division of rich and poor nations, imperialist and dominated nations in the world, tribalism, most *coups d'etat*, and repressive governments can all be attributed mainly to this failure in unconditional love for the neighbor.

67. As an example, the United States of America's motto is "In God We Trust." And Uganda's motto is "For God and My Country," despite the kind of ungodly and unpatriotic state of affairs that has prevailed there for a long time!

68. See notes 32 and 33 above. Christian unconditional love can be said to be the origin, essence, grounding, uniqueness and objective of Christianity. It is possibly this emphasis on unconditional love that makes Christianity the "Absolute Religion," as it enables reconciliation between an individual and his neighbor in free love and unmerited forgiveness, and in so doing gains fellowship with God (cf. 1 John 4:13-21; Mark 12:29-31; Rom. 13:8; 1 Cor. 13; Gal. 5:14, and Jam. 2:8).

69. This acceptance would possibly help to neutralize political, religious, cultural and racial prejudice and our unwillingness to treat those who are different from us as human beings. Love is believed to transcend most barriers to human relationships if given an opportunity to function well.

70. The problems of Uganda, such as the religious wars exclusive tribalism in the Church, employment and politics, and Catholic-Anglican rivalry and hostility, are clear evidence of failure in Christian unconditional love (Agape). Idi Amin's ascendance to power in a *coup d'etat* of January 25, 1971, and his consequent repressive regime and ruthless mass murder of rivals and the Christian elite (including the Most Rev. Jenani Luwum, the Anglican Archbishop of Uganda) that left the world aghast, is a clear illustration of this point. If the Ugandan Christians (80 percent of the Ugandan population), had loved one another, irrespective of tribe, party and religious affiliations and had also loved their Muslim neighbors (who are just about seven percent), Idi Amin, an evil, illiterate Muslim, would probably not have risen to power in Uganda.

For more details of the history of religious and political conflicts in Uganda, see Henry Kyemba, *The State of Blood: The Inside Story of Idi Amin's Reign of Terror* (London: Paddington Press, Ltd., 1977); see also *AF Press Clips*, Bureau of African Affairs, U.S. Dept. of State, Washington, D.C., May 25, 1982, XVII No. 21, and June 4, 1982, XVII

No. 22; articles on Uganda by Charles T. Powers for an update on the Ugandan situation. It is not surprising, therefore, that Powers himself was arrested, imprisoned and beaten during his journalistic assignment to Uganda in May, 1982.

Therefore, in Uganda, it is only unconditional love (agape) that can reconcile even these two neighbors, who should know better, but rather choose exclusiveness, as they both individually claim to be the only authentic Church of Christ and faithful custodian of the Gospel. (See, e.g., Tom Tuma and Phares Mutibwa, eds., *A Century of Christianity in Uganda, 1877-1977*, published by the Church of Uganda, 1978; F. B. Welbourn, *Politics and Religion in Uganda* (Nairobi: East African Publishing Co., 1965); J. F. Taylor, *Christianity and Politics in Africa* (London: Harmondsworth, 1957); J. J. Taylor, *The Growth of the Church in Buganda* (London: S.C.M. Press, 1958); and Roland Oliver, *The Missionary Factor in East Africa.*

71. Despite God's benevolent goodness, it is self-evident that evil is present in the world is the main problem. Plato himself speculated that since there is evil in the world, God must be either Good and less powerful to get rid of it or Omnipotent but lacking in goodness! For this discussion, see John Hick, *Evil and the God of Love* (New York: Harper and Row, 1978), 25-27, 32 ff., 72-75. The whole book should be read for its treatment of evil in the world while the Christian claim is that it was created and is controlled by the same God who is Good and Omnipotent.

For other views on this topic, see St. Thomas, *Summa Theologiae* I, qq. 2-3, 9-10, 47-49; *De Malo* I. 1; *Contra Gentiles* III, Chs. 7-9, 18; *Summa Theologiae* II q. 42; *Sent.* 44:1, 2, 6; and Whitehead, *Process and Reality*, ed. David Griffin and Donald W. Sherburne (New York: MacMillan, 1978), 340-351. See Whitehead's treatment of evil in his other works such as the *Adventures of Ideas* (New York: MacMillan Publishing Co., Inc., 1967), 284 ff. His doctrine on the "Divine Lure" helps me to see how God can offer gratuitous salvific grace to human beings and enable them to move towards positive, maximum self-actualization of themselves in complete personal freedom and self-determination (cf. 25, 184-189, 224, 259, 263-277, and 334).

72. There was generally mass murder of natives during the last century by Western imperialist nations in many parts of Africa during the conquest of Africa and the establishment of the colonial governments. In East Africa, the Germans used brutal force to overcome African resistance in the southern part of Tanzania (then known as Tanganyika) and later on to put down the *Maji Maji* rebellion. In Uganda, King Kabalega's nationalist resistance was crushed by the British, who enlisted the help of their Buganda allies. This was also generally true in Kigezi. But perhaps the most injustice was done to the Kikuyu, who were conquered and deprived of their fertile land by the British settlers. This injustice led to the well-known *Mau Mau* nationalist liberation movement and prolonged war in Kenya, in which thousands of innocent Africans perished; cf. Rosberg Nottingham and Karaari Njama, *Mau Mau from Within* (London/Nairobi: Oxford University Press, 1968). For a complete history of East Africa in its socio-economic and political context, see R. Oliver's *History of East Africa*, 2 vols. They are a standard reference text for this area.

73. Ibid. Most of the forced African labor was required by the British settlers in Kenya and the Germans in Tanzania before World War I, when they lost their territorial possessions in Africa following their defeat in the war.

74. The Portuguese Roman Catholics undertook missionary activity in Africa in the 17th century without much success, as they demanded that baptized African kings and individuals should swear allegiance to the King of Portugal; see Stephen Neill, *A History of Christian*

Missions (New York: Penguin Books, 1977), 197-200. It is also known that some Portuguese missionaries involved themselves in African slave trade in order to support their mission, and as a result they were resented and finally rejected together with their religion by the Africans in the Kongo Kingdom and Angola where they were working.

Effective African missionary activity in the interior of Africa did not take place until the second half of the 19th century. Unfortunately, it coincided with European imperialistic and colonial invasion and conquest of Africa. The fact that missionaries were soon followed by the imperialists in Africa has given rise to the dictum: "The Cross before the Flag!" See Stephen Neill, *History of Christian Missions*, 368-389; C. P. Groves, *The Planting of Christianity in Africa*, 4 vols. (London: Lutterworth Press, 1948-1958), vol. 1 and first half of vol. 2; Kenneth Scott Latourette, *A History of Christianity* (New York: Harper & Row, 1975) 2:1302-1333.

75. Uganda is possibly the most Christian and Anglican country in Africa; cf. Stephen Neill, *op. cit.*, 368-389; Adrian Hastings, *African Christianity* (New York: The Seabury Press, 1976), 29-32. It was no coincidence that the first Papal visit ever to an African nation was a visit to Uganda by Pope Paul VI in 1969. The Ugandan martyrs were also canonized by the Pope at this visit. He also consecrated the African Saints' and Uganda Martyrs' Shrine at Namugongo, which has become an African Holy Christian Center for Christian pilgrimage.

With the exception of the nomadic cattle-keeping Karamojong of Northeastern Uganda, there are almost no more "pagans" in Uganda. Nevertheless, the traditional religion is not yet dead. Ironically, it has become the very grounding for Christianity; cf. J. Mbiti, *African Religion and Philosophy*, 219 ff., 360 ff. Most of all, the African world view, metaphysics and ontology are still deeply grounded in African traditional religious culture, and whereas Christianity tends to divide the Africans, the Traditional Religion tends to reunite them.

76. See notes 4 and 21 above.

77. *Omuntu* is the local Ugandan Bantu word for the people of Kigezi, Ankole, Bunyoro, Toro, Buganda and others, meaning "a human being." It is neutral as regards gender. Here, the claim is that salvation consists in our full acceptance to be what we were created to be, namely, human beings *qua* human beings and not some other super beings such as angels or any other immortal spirits (if there be any). See notes 11 and 58 above.

78. In Uganda and Rwanda, "*Obuntu*" is regarded as the essence of "*Omuntu*". The "*Obuntu*" are abstract human qualities that make a person humane. Such qualities include love, understanding, being considerate, kindness, generosity, wisdom, politeness, bravery and the like. "*Omuntu*" without "*Obuntu*" is the kind termed "wicked," "savage," "cruel," "witch," "anti-social," "mean," "hater of people" and the like.

79. Logos is used here in the sense of John 1:1 1, 9 10, 14. That is the Word that was in the beginning with God, the medium of creation, life, light, illumination and truth (John 14:6) that became enfleshed (Incarnate) in Jesus of Nazareth (John 1:14).

80. This statement suggests that Jesus should be viewed as the archetypal human being to whom humanity should look for what true humanity should be like in its essential quality. The qualities of humanness (Obuntu) mentioned in note 78 were definitely manifested in their fullness in his life. Hence the example and origin of the commandment to love the neighbor and even the enemy (Mark 5:43-48). Jesus vividly epitomized the fullness of this unconditional love and humane quality when he asked God his Father to forgive his executioners as they mocked him and nailed him to the cross (Luke 23:34). This view is in

full harmony with Emil Brunner, Karl Barth, Rahner and others who say that Christian anthropology presupposes Christology (cf. Brunner, *Man in Revolt*, 98 ff.; Barth, *Church Dogmatics* III:II; Rahner, *Foundations of Christian Faith*, 178-219. See also Eph. 4:13, which states that Christ is the measure of our humanity).

81. See notes 11, 33, 36 and 48. See also Karl Rahner, "Anonymous Christians," *Theological Investigations* 9:145-164; "Reflections on the Unity of Neighbour and the Love of God," *Theological Investigations* 6:231-249; *Foundations of Christian Faith*, 311-321; "Observations Concerning Anonymous Christianity," *Theological Investigations,* 12:163 ff.; *Grace in Freedom*, 81-86; Anita Roper, *The Anonymous Christian*, with an afterward, "The Anonymous Christian According to Karl Rahner" by Klaus Riesenhuber, S.J. (New York: Sheed and Ward, 1966); Donald Maloney, "Rahner and the Anonymous Christian," *America* 23 (1970), 348-350.

82. Ibid. See also notes 10 and 81 above.

83. See notes 10, 11, 36, 48 and 81 above.

84. See notes 7, 11 and 37. See also John 3:16-17, 10:10; Rom. 5-6; and 2 Cor. 5:17. Divine salvation is here viewed as a present reality, though it remains future oriented in anticipation of fulfillment and perfection. Rahner suggests that if salvation is not present now, neither will it be present in the future, namely, after death, for death is the final and irrevocable eternal ratification of our personal free historical life by God. This is also the final divine judgment of our personal lives as they acquire eternal divine approval or disapproval and hence enter the state of eternal blessedness for those whose lives are deemed worthy, or eternal isolation and remorse for those who were unloving, uncaring, the foolish and the wicked; cf. Matt. 25; Karl Rahner, *Foundations of Christian Faith*, 311 ff.

85. Modern theologians emphasize that God is ceaselessly active, creating something new, saving and transforming the old (2 Cor. 5:17). God is the ground of all creativity, transformation, novelty and advancement in improvement; cf. Alfred North Whitehead, *Process and Reality*, Part I, Chs. 2, 3; Part II, Chs. 2, 8, 10; Part III, Ch. 1; Part IV, Chs. 1, 4; and Part V, Chs. 1, 2; Lewis S. Ford, *The Lure of God: A Biblical Background for Process Theism* (Philadelphia: Fortress Press, 1978), Chs. 1, 2, 3; Whitehead, *Adventures in Ideas,* Parts II and III; *Science and the Modern World* (New York: MacMillan Publishing Co., 1925), Chs. 7-13; and *Religion in the Making.*

86. Cf., e.g., John 1:1-4, 14; 3:16-21; Rom. 1-5. As creation is entirely the work of God, so is supernatural salvation. St. Augustine saw no room for Pelagianism in supernatural salvation; cf. *De Gratia Cristi.* See also notes 21, 31, 36, 48, 53-56 and 81 above. The human being can just respond in freedom and grace to God's prior proffer of salvation in grace with either a "Yes" and acceptance, or rejection and therefore with a "No" to this divine gratuitous proffer of God's free redemptive grace and salvation.

87. As it tends to be the case! See notes 10, 12 and 82 above.

88. Ibid. See also notes 81, 82 and 86 above.

89. See note 8 above. The love of neighbor is towards a concrete person and not a mere abstraction (Cf. Matt. 25:31-46).

90. See, e.g., Matt. 5:43-48; Mark 12:29-31; and especially, Luke 10:25-37. The Good Samaritan here can be a Muslim or even a Communist as regards our own modern global context.

91. Ibid., and see also notes 10-12, 81 and 85 above. The missionary task of the Church is the announcing of the Good News that, by virtue of the incarnation, all human beings have become friends and "blood brothers and sisters" in Christ, and that we are therefore, to love all human beings as we love ourselves and members of our immediate families. This approach makes sense in Africa, where the family and kinship ties are still strong and obligatory for each family or community member.

92. Cf., e.g., Karl Rahner, "Anonymous Christianity and the Missionary Task of the Church," *Theological Investigations* 12:161-178; "Observations on the Problem of the 'Anonymous Christians'," *Theological Investigations* 14:280-294; "The Commandment of Love in Relation to the Other Commandments," *Theological Investigations* 5:439-467; and "Reflections on the Unity of the Love of Neighbor and the Love of God," *Theological Investigations* 6:231-249; *Grace in Freedom*, 81-86, 183-264.

93. See notes 53, 59 and 62 above.

94. Cf. John 1:1-4, 9-14; Isa. 55:11; and note 84 above. See also, e.g., Karl Rahner, "Nature and Grace," *Nature and Grace* (New York: Sheed and Ward, 1964), 114-149; *Grace in Freedom*, 203-265; "The Order of Redemption within the Order of Creation," *The Christian Commitment* (New York: Sheed and Ward, 1963), 38-74; "The Theology of Freedom," *Theological Investigations* 6:178-196; "On the Dignity and Freedom of Man," *Theological Investigations* 2:235-263; *Hearers of the Word*, Chs. 5-11; Alfred North Whitehead, *Adventures of Ideas* (London: MacMillan, 1933), IV-V, VI-X; *Process and Reality*, Part V; *Religion in the Making* (New York: MacMillan, 1926), II-IV, 47-160.

95. Despite the redemptive value of "anonymous Christianity," it remains a deficient mode of spirituality. It lacks a community of self-conscious Christians who meet to celebrate God's activities of agape, grace and salvation. The community serves as the Church. Coextensively, the rituals of the community become the correlative sacraments of this community. Ultimately, Christian missionaries and Christocentric apostles of Agape, non-violence and peace are still greatly needed in this hate and conflict filled and violent world.

V

KARL RAHNER'S CHRISTIAN ANTHROPOLOGICAL AND PHILOSOPHICAL FRAMEWORK AS BASIS FOR A BROAD CHRISTIAN REFLECTION ON AUTHENTIC HUMAN EXISTENCE AND SOTERIOLOGY

Having outlined the history and development of some of the familiar narrow and exclusive soteriological doctrines in the previous two chapters of this book, we now turn to the problem of salvation itself. Since Karl Rahner has been the greatest expounder of the more academically acceptable post-colonialist "agapic" inclusive Catholic Christian doctrine of God's gratuitous universal salvation including non-Christians,[1] subsequently, he has been positively presented, critically examined, and normatively accepted as one of the greatest Western Christian philosophical-theologians of our era.

In this work, Rahner has been adopted as the primary and normative philosophical-theological spokesman, expounder and defender of the modern Christian inclusive doctrine of supernatural salvation, particularly as it finds its logical expression and climax in his extensive teachings on universally free efficacious and redemptive cosmic grace of God. For Rahner, this divine universal free redemptive grace and salvation are correlative with the universal "implicit" or "anonymous Christianity"[2] through God's universal creative and redemptive Word as the Logos-Christ (cf. Gen. 1:1-3; John 1:1-18). Correspondingly, on the African scene, John Mbiti will also be employed as the primary spokesman for the African Religion.

1. The Human Being as God's Temporal Mirror and Mystery in the World

The Judeo-Christian traditional central theological positive affirmation, is that the finite, historical and evolutionary human being, is actually a unique creature who has been created in God's own image (*imago Dei*). As "*imago*

Dei" the human being is complex moral agent in the world. The human being is an intelligent, creative moral being, self-transcending spirit, mind, and infinite mystery, just like God, in whose image or likeness, the human being has been created. As such, the human being both reveals and represents God, in the cosmos, nature or creation, by virtue of his or her special intrinsic divine nature as mind, spirit and moral agent.

Understandably, Rahner's theology is grounded in this kind of fundamental philosophical-theological anthropology.[3] This anthropological starting point is very advantageous for his theological task, which is the interpretation of human existence as it is lived daily before God and fellow human beings in the community.

This anthropological method enables Rahner to discern better and explain more constructively God's universal gratuitous self-communication in grace to all human beings he has created, in order to draw them to the self-realization in a more complete manner and towards the ultimate destiny of their being and fulfillment of life in his mystery.[4] By doing so, Rahner is again both enabled to discern more meaningfully and insightfully both the co-extensive nature and correlation between the divine act of creation and that of salvation as two moments of the same divine creative process and not two separate events in time and space.[5]

Consequently, Rahner is able to perceive more clearly that creation requires salvation as its guidance to positive self-actualization, maturity, wholeness, health, wholesome self-enjoyment, joy, and happiness as fulfillment. This is why he insists that salvation must be a present reality for those to be saved, since divine salvation is not to be regarded as just the fulfillment in the distant future, but rather that it is chiefly the radical divine humanization of the individuals here and now in this temporal world.[6]

Since according to Rahner's theological methodology, anthropology is the logical primary starting point for Christian theology, philosophy and ethics, including basic theological dogmas, such as those of revelation and soteriology, then it is both logical and fundamental for this work that we should carefully study his anthropological framework in order to appreciate his inclusive or universalist Christian theology, and philosophy. In this case, we have to study his concepts of universal divine revelation, gratuitous grace and salvation, which are the three basic concepts underlying his great Christian inclusive teaching on God's gratuitous universal salvation and "anonymous Christianity."

Karl Rahner affirms that the human being, is a great mystery almost akin to God his or her creator, in whose image and mystery, the human being has been created.[7] Consequently, the human being is a mystery to himself or herself and to those around him or her. Rahner contends that, because the human being is a mystery, he or she asks infinite questions of his or her origin, destiny and about his or her being as a person.

Similarly, the human being asks questions of humanity in general. But in the end, no definitive answers are found because, like God, the infinite cosmic creative Mystery, the human being is, likewise, a mystery. Rahner puts this point simply in the following terms: *"Man is a mystery...What do we mean by man? My reply, stripped to its essentials, is simple: Man is the question to which there is no answer."*[8]

For Rahner, therefore, human knowledge and self-investigation cannot exhaust this human mystery, as it is infinite. In this respect it could also be argued that the writer of Genesis, who declared that "God created man in his own image, in the image of God he created him; male and female he created them..." (Gen. 1:27), was also in a sense trying to say the same thing, but in his own way.[9]

Rahner conveys this same message of Genesis in a more contemporary language, utilizing modern philosophical anthropology, in order to make this divine Word relevant and revelatory for the modern man and contemporary theology, which seeks to address the contemporary human existential questions in a meaningful manner that will enable God's Word of invitation to a fuller life to be heard.

Rahner, like the writer of the book of Genesis, sees human uniqueness as divine and purposeful. This human uniqueness points back to the majesty, skill and power of God the Creator as well as pointing to the affinity between God as the Creator and the human being as the creature, the very affinity that enables meaningful, effective communication and fellowship between God and the human being to take place. Rahner explicates this affinity between God and the human being as follows:

> Man is a mystery. He is more than this. He is the mystery, not because he is open to the mystery of the incomprehensible fullness of God, but also because God has expressed this mystery as his own. Assuming that God wanted to express himself in the empty void and that he wanted to call his Word into that void, how could he do anything other than create in man an inner hearing of the Word and express his Word in such a way that the self-expression of that Word and its being heard become one?[10]

For Karl Rahner, then, the human being is God's unique creature that mirrors God in the created world. He or she is able to "hear God's Word," and respond accordingly. In other words, the human being is a creature that is radically oriented to God as its main constitutive characteristic elements.[11] This prior divine ontological atonement of the human being to its origin and destiny in the Infinite Mystery, is for Rahner, the distinguishing mark of human beings from the rest of animality of which the human being is part.[12]

This free divine election and ordination of the human being by God to be a special creature in creation and to be God's temporal representative in the world is symbolized by the special human features which participate in divine qualities to which they have affinity, the chief one being human self-transcendence to an Infinite Horizon which Rahner calls God.[13] The other unique features of the human being include the capacity for unrestricted creative love, which is, according to the Bible, the main definitive quality or fundamental quintessence of God.[14]

As "*homo sapiens*" and "*imago Dei,*" the special divine features of the human being include supernatural gifts which are bestowed on the human being in the human process of evolution and development. The human being acquires these distinctive unique human features and divine gifts in the seemingly ordinary and natural process of evolution and growth. This divine-human process includes the growth from an infant into a responsible and mature human being in the historical process, or participant and citizen of the local community and thereby, a citizen of God's world and the kingdom.

In the historical process the divine-human special features of the human being as both a "*homo sapiens*" and "*imago Dei*" manifest themselves in the human being, the community and the world in the form of a highly evolved and developed intellect,[15] spirit, mind, critical thinking, choice, responsibility, creativity, insight, judgement, self-awareness, self-transcendence, agape, freedom, language, a refined neurological system, a well-developed, and well-coordinated body.

However, since the human being is a historical being and has evolved like and along with the rest of the creatures, there is also some human sharing in animal qualities. The human being, despite his/her being akin to God in respect to the transcendental qualities, biologically still remains akin to the animals. For instance, the human being has physical needs just as the other animals do, such as the need for food, shelter, security, sex, reproduction, and the nurture and protection of the offspring.

Similarly, the human being sometimes gets angry, irrational and brutal. Perhaps, even worse than the other animals, the human being is capable of being deliberately, calculatingly, and maliciously mean, sadistic, cruel and destructive. This survival of some malignant animality in the human being, and the human failure or misuse of his/her higher faculties, is called evil because the human being has already been elevated by God to a higher level where love, humaneness and moral responsibility are expected as the universal characteristics of the authentic mode of human behavior.[16]

At this level, humanity is faced with either the acceptance of this gratuitous divine election and elevation in grace to be human beings who are loving, free, moral, responsible creatures accountable to each other, and to God, or to sink back into the animality whence humanity has emerged by way of evolution, thereby rejecting God's salvific love and personal freedom, and thereby also rejecting personal moral responsibility as the accountability that is correlative to this exercise of freedom which is constitutive of authentic humanity.[17]

Human beings find themselves in a dilemma of choosing in accordance with their higher ideals, because the human being still has within him/her an irrational animality that is usually stronger in its impulsive drive towards mere physical satisfaction, which is most often in sharp contradiction to the perceived divine ideals. Consequently, the human being is racked by guilt when he or she becomes aware that the animality has taken control instead of the divine. St. Paul expressed vividly this very human problem when he wrote of his inner tormenting conflicts and moral struggle as follows:

> So I find it to be a law that when I want to do right, evil lies close at hand. For I delight in the law of God, in my innermost self, but I see in my members another law at war with the law of my mind and making me captive to the law of sin which dwells in my members. Wretched man that I am! Who will deliver me from this body of death? Thanks be to God through Jesus Christ our Lord! So then, I of myself serve the law of God with my mind, but with my flesh I serve the law of sin (Rom. 7:21-25).[18]

Dualistic philosophical and religious conceptions of humanity which teach that the human being as consisting of spirit and matter that were mutually opposed to each other, is similar to Platonism,[19] were trying to provide a logical solution to this problematic nature of humanity, which is aware of its own noble and divine ideals and goals, yet does not achieve them because of the hindrance that is experienced by the human being to be a constitutive element of human nature itself.

The popular Platonic idealistic solution to this human existential paradox was that the human soul is divine, eternal and good, but it finds itself trapped in the human body, which is oriented to insatiable pleasure and the satisfaction of physical needs, particularly of food and sex.[20] Therefore, the soul should seek to be freed from this degradation of embodiment in matter that was perceived to be evil. Consequently, for the Platonists, death was to be regarded as a welcome event for a philosopher, as it led to the totality of knowledge, freedom and the beatific vision.[21]

However, for Karl Rahner this Platonic solution is unacceptable to orthodox Christianity. He says that there is no possible division of humanity into constitutive elements such as spirit and matter (that can be joined together or separated) without destroying the unity of the human being. For Rahner, the human being is an indivisible unity, and that applies to him or her as these dualities of both matter and spirit; animal and divine; sinner and redeemed saint; human and divinized creature into the adopted son or daughter of God, and heir of God's world and kingdom.[22]

Rahner rejects all attempts to simplify the question of the nature of the human being into a narrow, comprehensive, final statement such as the popular Aristotelian definition of *"animal rationale"* or *"animal politicus."* Rahner insists that the human being is more than that being which can be described or defined. For instance, the human being is not just rational (as in any case many people are irrational) but, is also, intuitive and emotional creature. A rational person without any kind of intuition or emotion, would be more or less a living version of a computer or a robot, and not a real human being.

Therefore, to be an authentic human being means more than being a creature which possesses an intellectual or cognitive ability. That is where Descartes' *"cogito ergo sum"* fails, too.[23] For instance, what happens when Descartes falls asleep? Does he cease to be since *"cogito"* has ceased? What about those who are either too young or are mentally handicapped and unable to cogitate; do they possess being or are they even considered to be human beings?

Since human beings are aware of themselves apart from "cogito," therefore, intellect in "cogito" cannot be the definitive, inclusive definition of a human being. Moreover, that definition would exclude children, the senile, those in sleep or mentally retarded from the category of humanity. Ideally, therefore, we need a definition of the human being that keeps the beasts out, but yet is inclusive enough to permit the inclusion of those individuals who are for some reason unable to cogitate.[24]

Modern depth psychology and psychiatry, especially the Freudian school, has claimed to have uncovered evidence to support the fact that much of the human behavior and activity is controlled by the unconscious mind.[25] This subconscious control is supposedly done in the same way that bodily coordination and involuntary activity are carried out by the involuntary nervous system.

In this respect, it is clearly inaccurate to claim that the human being is primarily characterized by intellect alone, as great Western thinkers such as Hegel, Descartes, St. Thomas, Aristotle and Plato have positively affirmed. Like Emil Brunner and Reinhold Niebuhr, Rahner positively affirms that the main uniqueness of the human being is not the intellect, but rather human self-transcendence.[26] This human self-transcendence includes intellect, intuition, imagination, emotions, self-awareness and personal freedom.

However, Rahner goes on to affirm that the human being, as God's image, still remains an infinite mystery to himself or herself and to scholars (be it philosophical or theological anthropologists, social and natural scientists such as physicians, biologists, psychologists and psychiatrists). Consequently, Rahner counsels us that the human mystery is an inconceivable complexity and, being such, we should not try to over-simplify it in order to understand it. This is because such a move would amount to a falsification of humanity in order to make it comprehensible to ourselves. Sometimes, this is done by a dishonest intellectual rejection and amputation of those human complex dimensions that appear either transcendental and non-verifiable by an empirical experiment and inquiry or because they appear to be mere religious formulations claiming divine supernatural revelation as their undemonstrable basis. Rahner sums up his insightful observations on this question as follows:

> Man as we know him today, man of metaphysics, of abstract thought, the creator of his own environment, the space-traveller, the molder of himself, the man of God and of grace and of the promise of eternal life, precisely this man who is radically distinct from any animal and who at the moment of man's origin...very slowly, took a path that led him so far away from all that is merely animal, yet in such a fashion that he carried with him the whole inheritance of his biological pre-history into these realms of his existence remote from the animals, was there when man began to exist.

Then Rahner goes on to link together creation and biological evolution as one moment of God's creative activity in the following manner:

> what now is historically and externally manifest, was then present as a task and as an active potentiality. Because how his biological, spiritual and divine elements are present in him, they are also plainly and simply to be affirmed of the beginning...Today there are plenty of theories which consider that they must amputate

man of one of these dimensions of his existence, in order to understand him...However, ...only a very complex answer...can be a correct one and that any simplification of the problem can lead to error.[27]

Consequently, Rahner affirms the infinite mystery of the human being, origin, development, and ultimate destiny in the infinite Mystery that he calls God. Again, this implies that the human being is by essential nature a mystery from the very beginning to the end, and that we should not be so presumptuous to claim the complete knowability of humanity, nor to disclaim as illusion the mystery surrounding humanity. This applies to the transcendental human dimensions, such as intelligence, mind, consciousness, conscience, soul and freedom which are mystical and elusive to the mind. Some materialists may tend to think that these are mere illusions.[28]

The human question, which is well stated by the Psalmist, "What is man, that thou art mindful of him?" (Ps. 8:4, K.J.V.), is therefore, a puzzling question to which there is no definitive answer yet. However, the kind of tentative answer given to this question can be definitive for human existence. For instance, if the human being is understood to be essentially a laborer, as both capitalism and marxism tend to present him or her, then it follows that the authentic life of a human being is also considered to consist in work.

Within this context, the human worth is measured by the value of one's labor or profit of the product, if sold. In this understanding, the human being is just a biological machine for work. The human value corresponds to the capacity to produce profit. Therefore, human beings are expendable labor forces or commodities. They can be replaced by more efficient workers or more sophisticated forms of workers in the form of robots and other machines.

In contrast, when the human being is understood to be "a child of God" as in Christianity, then all human beings gain incalculable value and infinite worth as "God's children," fellow brothers and sisters whose chief objective as an authentic life is the contemplation of God and to seek to live in unrestricted love, fellowship and harmony with all human beings.

Furthermore, the human being ideally has to live in respect and in thoughtful preservation of the rest of God's creation and the world on which human life is contingent for life-support, and divine revelation through self-awareness, knowledge, beauty, wonder and mystery which result from the human encounter with this wonder-filled world and God's mystifying cosmic creation in general. This leads us then to the inevitable affirmation that the human being cannot be known nor can he or she know himself or herself as a unique mystery in isolation. Consequently, the human being is only known as such, only within this total background of interrelations in the total context of the world and the totality of God's creation.

2. The Human Being as the Creature That Asks
the Ultimate Questions of Origin and Destiny

Karl Rahner puts great emphasis on the fact that all normal human beings ask endless metaphysical questions or as Paul Tillich put it, human beings ask the questions of ultimate concern and destiny.

These ultimate human questions of concern for fundamental values, meaning, origins and ultimate destiny include the following: Who am I? Where did I come from? Why am I here? Does human existence have any meaning or purpose? Is death the ultimate end of human life? Is there personal life beyond the grave, and if not, how is a good or virtuous person who suffers in this life for the sake of truth vindicated? These questions, and the like, are unique to the human being and Rahner attributes them to human self-transcendence and human mystery.[29]

The fact that the human being is a mystery to himself or herself leads to the endless self-quest and self-investigation in order to understand one's own existence. Self-understanding is sought so that the human being can become his or her own responsible master, in terms of informed and deliberate self-determinative, self-actualization in personal freedom and positive choice. Consequently, it could be said that most of the human knowledge, particularly in the sciences, is concerned with the human self-investigation, such as the investigation of the human structure and its processes, human existence and its interpretation, or the investigation of the world for better human masterly control and exploitation.[30]

In other words, the human being is engaged in the process of self-discovery, self-understanding, self-improvement and even self-deification into a god. This is the universal human condition because "the primal human temptation of eating the forbidden fruit of knowledge," self-deification, self-determination, and rebellion are endemic in every normal human being. These traits are part of the human nature due to freedom and the uncertainties and ambiguities which are encountered in finite human existence. This is the human condition, in which God is, sometimes deistically experienced as being radically distant, or even as some kind of disinterested absentee land-lord or monarch.

However, despite this self-investigation the human being never gets any definitive answers, and subsequently, he or she remains in the perpetual quest for the full definitive truth. Consequently, since God is the definitive eternal truth and the source of life and its fulfillment, the human being finds himself or herself dealing with the questions of God as the Ultimate human Origin, and Destiny. God is both of these by virtue of being the Creator and the Savior and the Ultimate Source of human self-fulfillment.

Rahner insists that the human questions of origin or destiny may be silent and non-verbal, but they are always there. Whenever human beings are faced with danger, pain, loss of property or friends, and perhaps most of all, when they are confronted with death face to face; what they experience or express is this universal ultimate human concern. This is the implicit and explicit universal human quest for the ultimate answers to give them ultimate meaning of life, particularly that of human existence and its final destiny.[31]

For Rahner this ultimate concern lies at the core of human existence and it cannot be ignored. It is so important that it marks off humanity from animality. For instance, no other animal ever asks: What am I? Where did I come from? or, Is death the end of my life? If ever any animal, whether ape, dog or dolphin, asks such questions, it will have become human no matter what else it looks like, as this is the chief characteristic uniqueness of humanity *vis-a-vis* animality. For Rahner these metaphysical questions arise only in the human being because it is only the human being that possesses the divine gratuitous gift of self-transcendence and abstract thought.

However, Rahner does not offer any evidence for this assertion. Nevertheless, in support of Rahner one could probably argue that, since such an abstract thought requires the use of language, whether verbal, sign, or another system of conventional coding and decoding of thought, information, and messages or the instruction of others, we should expect to notice such an advanced activity among the animals should it ever occur. For instance, cultural anthropologists have been able to study cultures of the so-called "primitive peoples" and it has been almost always observed that, in these underdeveloped or non-technological societies, the most important cultural dimension is religion.[32]

Archaeology, too, testifies that all pre-historical *homo sapiens* were real human beings like us, since they had some form of religion. This is because religion is the major reliable indication of the existence of authentic humanity and the correlative essential human mental or spiritual faculties, and the great capability for abstract thought, self-transcendence, awareness of their human existential predicament, and quest for supernatural salvation.[33] The ancient Egyptian pyramids and mummies are probably a good illustration of this characteristic human orientation to some form of supernatural salvation as the fulfillment of this earthly life.

It can also be said that the Christian fundamentalists, who reject all forms of the theory of human biological evolution from a lower form of animal life slowly to the present sophisticated state of human neurological structure and human existence, do so not just because the book of Genesis contradicts this evolutionary theory, but also because they feel threatened by the realization that their Destiny is inevitably and essentially correlatively bound up with their Origin. They correctly reason that, unless God is their Creator and Origin, he cannot be their Destiny either.[34]

However, what is often forgotten in this argument is that God does not have to directly create each individual human being in order to be each individual's Ultimate Origin and Destiny. God can choose to work through secondary agents and causes to create or effect his will in the world. These secondary vehicles of God's activities in the world include natural laws, history, and the human beings as free moral agents, in order to modify and transform an already existing thing or to bring into being another individual human being into the world.

God cannot be limited in his mystery or infinite mode of activity in the world by human restricted and stereotyped concepts or expectations. For instance, most of the Jews who heard the message of Jesus were skeptical mainly because of their own stereotyped conceptions of what an eschatological Jewish Messiah should be. Consequently, they rejected the transcendent Creator and Redeemer God as their very own Destiny and fulfillment, precisely because of their lack of faith in God's mystery and activity that did not seem majestic and impressive enough in correspondence with their own beliefs and expectations. Jesus was mocked and rejected because of his humble origins as the son of Joseph, the local carpenter, and his wife Mary, the potter.[35]

Similarly, it can be argued that today some people make the mistake of seeing only the human being's humble origins from the lower forms of life, and stumble in their own faith because they fail to see that this humble human origin is itself rooted and ultimately originated in God himself as the very creative Mystery that grounds all life as its origin, sustenance, fulfillment, perfecter and ultimate Destiny.

The human questions of both ultimate Origin and Destiny are of paramount importance for the human being, as they determine and orient the human being's total existence in accordance with and towards the perceived destiny, in order to realize this perceived destiny for self-fulfillment and the definitive, irrevocable, climactic crowning of one's life or the attainment of salvation.

Since the perceived destiny determines the nature and course of one's total existence, it is therefore, important for the human being to ask these vital questions, as they constitute the meaning, direction, and fulfillment of human existence in the ultimate Destiny, which Rahner identifies with the beatific vision and union with God.[36]

However, some confessed destinies of the human life are sometimes explicitly different from this Rahnerian ideal and even appear to be in complete contradiction to it. For instance, Marxists try to visualize their own destiny in a "utopian" communist classless society, whereas the Christians and Muslims anticipate their own destiny as being in heaven with God (if they are found worthy, and in hell if they are judged to be unfaithful!).

Therefore, one's perceived destiny and the attempts to realize it can be considered as vital guides for human action and behavior in the present and the "lure" as final cause for future activity arising out of human free personal choice. It is also the principle of limitation to multiple alternatives that present themselves for choice in every personal free human action. Consequently, the human destiny as perceived by the human being is of fundamental importance as the focus and grounding of human life as it is lived in the present and in the future.

Without this utopian or lure for a vision of a better future, and hope for complete fulfillment in the future, life loses its meaning in the present, especially, when one is confronted with adversity and other life's unpleasant hurdles of life. As such, utopia is essential to keep life meaningful, regardless of whether this "utopian" future is Marxist or religious and theocentric in essence. Utopia in the form of heaven or a better future, is a necessary dimension of human life.

Like myth, utopia empowers and directs human life in all its sophisticated temporal manifestations, particularly in the religious, political and economic realms.[37] This is similar an infinite horizon, utopia or heaven, which is ever before us, and continues calling us to come forward, whereas receding; and yet, still unceasingly beckoning to us to keep coming forward to touch it. But, it is never reached. Nevertheless, we keep going forward to actualize our particular beckoning light of utopia, dream or horizon, and finally die without ever reaching it nor actualizing it.

In other words, it is impossible for a human being to live a fully meaningful life unless life is lived in accordance with hope and toward the realization of this perceived destiny, whether it is a utopian dream of a humanitarian vision of universal brotherhood-sisterhood or life in heaven. There must be something very valuable, meaningful and loved enough for the human being to wish to keep living in order to gain. If there is no ultimate underlying or driving reason or ideal for living, then life becomes purposeless, and a tedious mundane chore. Subsequently, life and living becomes correspondingly aimless, drifting along, and a mere struggle for survival for the day.

In this inauthentic mode of life, human life is debased and degraded to the animal level, to live just like the other less intelligent animals, whose existence seems to consist of merely meeting biological or physical needs to eat, reproduce, and avoid pain or danger. Obviously, these animals lack the necessary intelligence that would lead to self-transcendence or any observable sense of quest for purpose, direction or destiny.

Rahner argues that most people find this definitive ultimate Destiny in the infinite nameless, transcendent Cosmic Creative and Redemptive Mystery, that they just simply refer to as "God." He then, goes on to argue and positively affirm that these are, therefore, "Christians," even when they may not know it, and or may for various historical, religious, cultural and social reasons, reject the term being applied to them.

Nevertheless, for Rahner, these people are "anonymous Christians" and they are truly redeemed by God through Christ. Rahner convincingly argues that this is the case, since they implicitly know God, and do good works of grace and agape, through the cosmic Christ as the universal divine Logos that mediates gratuitously the very divine life, love, truth and hope that make humanity authentic, and human life exciting, worth living, and fulfilling.

Accordingly, within this inclusive Christian theological-philosophical and anthropological context, idolatry and unauthentic human life can be said to derive from an erroneous or false sense and understanding of the cosmic and human Ultimate Origin and Destiny. This is error or falsehood identifies one's Ultimate Origin and Destiny with any other power or explanation, other than the true and real one.

The real or true one is that transcendent, creative and redemptive Ultimate Origin and Destiny, which is the same as the primordial and eternal, cosmic, divine infinite Mystery, the Abyss known as God.[38] Similarly, Rahner argues that the life of salvation means an authentic human life which is lived faithfully in hopeful anticipation, in harmony and movement towards a definitive fulfillment in the ultimate Destiny as Infinite Mystery, Absolute Future, Creator, and redemptive personal God of human adoration and worship.

However, according to Rahner this process is not always conscious or explicit to all human beings and that some people fulfill God's law and then meet the requirement for salvation even in that state of unawareness, and therefore, appropriately belong to the community of salvation as unaware members, or "anonymous Christians." This Rahnerian theocentric inclusive Logos-soteriological theology has serious implications for both the world and for the Christian Church.

Rahner's theology embodies arguments and teachings which effectively support theological and soteriological doctrines and claims for the universal validity of God's universal salvific will. This divine will operates in the cosmos through unmerited free efficacious divine supernatural grace and free salvation for all God's loving, just and obedient people anywhere in the world and in every age, irrespective of their creed or religious affiliation, culture, system of government or economics and level of technological development.

This radical theological position threatens the exclusive unfounded dogmatic claims of traditional Christianity, especially those problematic and erroneous Christian dogmas regarding revelation and the Incarnation. This in itself has the implications for both explicit and implicit relativization for historical Christianity.

As a result, this inclusive Rahnerian theology has been rejected by many conservative theologians as demeaning to the Christian monopoly to God's Christian grace which is claimed to be preferentially mediated by God to the post-Incarnation world exclusively through the Apostolic Church revelation, redemption, the sacraments and Christian missionary activity. However, a close study of Rahner reveals him to be apologetic, biblical and within the patristic tradition of the Apostolic Church both within his inclusive universal Theocentric Logos soteriology and ecclesiology.

3. Human Infinite Self-Transcendence as an *a Priori* Divine Orientation to Ultimate Destiny

According to Rahner, human self-transcendence is infinite in its nature, scope and horizon. He affirms that this infinite human transcendence is by its nature given in creation by God and not satisfied in itself.

Human nature as *imago Dei*, has been uniquely both supernaturally oriented and attuned by God to find its fulfillment in God as the infinite Mystery, which fulfills the lives of moral or intelligent creatures with the fullness of life and lasting happiness. By *a priori* open and incomplete nature, in need of growth and completion, the human mind, and spirit or soul have been programmed in creation by God, to seek their own ultimate completion and fulfillment in God as the Creator-Redeemer.

God appears and reveals himself to the human being, and uses blank screen of thee mind and soul or spirit to disclose himself as YAHWEH or this cosmic redemptive Mystery (Exod. 4:1-10). This the Creator-Redeemer Mystery which is presented to the human being as the ever-inviting and tantalizing, receding Horizon of pure knowledge, happiness, love and self-fulfillment. This inviting, attractive, ever-receding Horizon as human beings come eagerly toward it, this infinite Horizon of human self-transcendence and human existence, yet tantalizingly unobtainable and ever-receding, is God. Rahner identified the as God the infinite incomprehensible Mystery or eternal Horizon, that serves humanity as the "visible" final cause is the lure, energizer and ultimate Destiny of all authentic human existence.[39]

Rahner argues that the structure of human self-transcendence is a complex divine gratuitous gift, as it is the main distinguishing feature between the human being and the lower animals which are close to us. The kind of affinity between us and the apes is one that we both have similar anatomical structure, the same embryonic developmental stages, similar metabolism, and it could be argued also that these apes have a degree of intelligence, as they can learn human sign language, be taught to behave appropriately or even be trained to perform fantastic feats in a circus.[40]

In short, these trained apes have some cognitive ability and they are capable of limited intellectual activity. Nevertheless, they have not become human! To become a human being requires more than mere intellectual or cognitive ability. Otherwise, more sophisticated robots, and "smart" powerful computers would have surpassed men and women in human quality, if intellectual activity was the criterion of humanity. Nonetheless, these "intelligent" robots and computers remain machines, as apes remain apes, despite their programmed fantastic feats.[41]

However, although these apes possess a measure of intelligence, it is so limited that, even if it were fully developed to its maximum capacity by training and instruction, the ape would still fail to achieve self-transcendence. Therefore, the chimpanzee might look impressive in human clothing, eating at a table with a spoon, smoking a cigar, watching television, riding a bicycle or doing some other human-like activity. However, since the chimp's brain is smaller and less developed, correlatively, the chimp's intelligence, mental capacities, technical capabilities, freedom, thinking, choices, moral responsibilities are also correspondingly limited. As a result, the chimp, both individually or collectively with other chimps, apart from coaching or conditioning and training received from human beings, is unable to think critically and analytically like us.

Therefore, unlike human beings, chimps do not ordinarily as part of their nature, reflect upon the meaning and end of these activities of daily routine, or to reflect upon the meaning of life and existence in general and its ultimate Destiny. As a result, despite the fact that the chimp is according to its DNA structure is, both biologically and evolutionary more than 99.8% related to humans, yet still, the chimp is still morally unlike the human beings. Ultimately, the chimp still remains both intellectually, morally, linguistically, socially, and culturally, just a mere simple ape and "a beast."

Accordingly, it can be positively affirmed that as long as this is the real intellectual nature of chimps, naturally then, all chimps will always remain non-self-reflective, non-self-transcending, non-linguistic, dumb and amoral beast, just like other non-human animals in the world. As such, unlike the free human beings, the chimps will continue doing things and living mechanically by both the internal instinct, and external environmental programming, and conditioning, including human attempts to train or "civilize" them. This human mode of life is unlike that of the normal human being who essentially lives by reflective, responsible personal moral free choice, and self-determination, as is the case of human beings, who in contrast can be said to be essentially free, knowing and morally responsible creatures.[42]

Reflection is regarded by Rahner as a unique human quality that constitutes the core component of the general structure of human self-transcendence. The human being is able to transcend his or her bodily limitations, and by an act of the mind he or she can go beyond them to reflect, pray, judge, imagine, dream, fantasize, and even to innovate and invent new things. Consequently, Rahner describes the human being as "a free historical spirit" by virtue of this quality of unlimited self-transcendence.[43]

The human being as a free spirit is, therefore, not bound by space or time. Rahner asserts that these limitations of the categorical world are transcended by the human mind in its act of self-transcendental reflection. In the act of reflection, the human being as free spirit is able to transcend all the categorical limitations of time, space and matter. For instance, he or she is able to traverse space, irrespective of the magnitude of distance involved, and is able to visualize mentally what is taking place in another location as an interested invisible spectator or even a keen participant. In the same way, the human being is able to move forwards in time to peep into the tantalizing mystery of the future and backwards into history to enjoy reliving the joyous experiences of the past, while avoiding and repressing the painful memory and anguish of the unhappy ones.[44]

It is also precisely because of this same human quality of self-transcendence and consequent human capacity to transcend time, that the human being is able to reflect and speculate on one's ultimate future. But this ultimate future lies carefully hidden in the divine encompassing impenetrable Mystery, that is why also the human being is the only creature in the known cosmos that is able to suffer from undifferentiated anxiety and despair (*angst*).[45]

The human being is able to suffer in this way because of his or her logical mind which demands a logical conclusion in connection with the human Ultimate Destiny in the infinite Mystery, yet he or she cannot get one, for any conclusion is enshrined in this very Mystery that is infinitely impenetrable to the human finite mind.

Being aware of his or her finitude, and also being unable to foresee the future, the human being, therefore, worries about his or her mysterious future, and particularly, he or she fears the impending inescapable death, not because of the unpleasant, painful or slow manner it might occur, but chiefly because the human being is frightened to face the unknown final destiny that lies beyond the grave. Feuerbach, too, made this important observation. However, he concluded that human religion and human concepts of the Immortal, Redemptive God were mere illusions and forms of escapism created by the human mind as result of human finitude and the fear of death. In this respect, Feuerbach was the forerunner of Karl Marx, Frederick Nietzsche and Sigmund Freud.

The result was the human quest for salvation and immortality in a benevolent, omnipotent and immortal God, and in Feuerbach's view, human beings created such an ideal God in their own imaginative minds and projected him externally into the sky by the same process of self-redemptive objectification, and hypostasization of the projected human being's ideals and expectations into their God, as the object of worship, imitation, norms, and most of all, salvation.[46]

This is the kind of false God that Feuerbach and his followers, such as Karl Marx and Sigmund Freud, correctly saw as an illusion to be exorcised from the human minds and human mode of existence.[47] Any gods that were created by the human being, either by careful artistic work in clay, concrete or wood, or by the act of the mind and projection, are all equally repugnant idols and false gods to be destroyed.

The real God who is the Creator of the cosmos, is always the infinite Mystery that underlies all mystery in the world, and even the very human quest that leads to the misguided fashioning and creation of a concrete image as a god is itself prompted by the human awareness of the cosmic infinite Mystery and the desire to make it more accessible by concretizing it into a visible and tangible god.

The maker and worshipper of the idol, however, soon realizes that the transcendent Mystery is greater than his or her idol. As a result, he or she makes more and more idols to gain power. However, these idols prove incapable of providing protection and salvation from evil. This process goes until idol maker is overcome by despair at the inability of these (false) gods to offer him or her the desired security and salvation. This is followed by the inevitable realization that only the transcendent Mystery or God can save him or her from the existential vulnerability, the threats of evil and chaos, loneliness, disease, pain and death.[48]

Rahner argues further that human self-transcendence, is the capacity for human self-possession as self-consciousness and total self-awareness as a historical, material and spiritual being, which is self-aware as a finite and transitory historical material being, rooted in this historical or categorical world of flux. He also affirms that the human being as a historical spirit transcends the historical world, simultaneously as spirit, and just like God his or her maker and heavenly Parent.

The human being's self-transcendence enables him or her to the rare creaturely opportunity to investigate the origins in the past and to survey the future as hidden Destiny in infinite Divine Mystery. However, this human special structure of self-transcendence and quest for God, is not the ground or driving human force to invent God as the human being's Creator, Savior and Destiny as Feuerback, Marx, Nietzsche, Durkheim and Freud erroneously claimed.

On the contrary, this Cosmic Infinite holy Creative Mystery, is the very ground for the redemptive divine self-disclosure to the human being, as God the Creator, Savior and ultimate human Destiny. Rahner affirms that human self-transcendence is God's gratuitous prior orientation of every human being to divine Destiny which is the beatific vision, and sin is the human resistance or personal free contradiction of this Destiny.[49]

Furthermore, Rahner affirms that the human being as a free historical spirit in this categorical world is characterized by personal freedom. This is not just "transcendental" freedom to move forwards and backwards in time and space, by means of the act of the mind in reflection; it is also the "historical" or "categorical" freedom of movement, expression, worship and association.[50] It is because the human being has intellect, personal freedom and knowledge that he or she is able to become a moral agent.

As a moral being, the human being is a free moral agent responsible for one's choice and its attending consequences, whether good or bad.[51] Without this human knowledge, real personal freedom and free choice, there would not be any meaningful human moral responsibility. Similarly, without human moral responsibility there would not be any guilt, since guilt is due to knowledge and the moral awareness involved in the contrast of what is *vis-a-vis* what should have been. Guilt is therefore a product of human knowledge, personal freedom and awareness of moral failure.

Animals, therefore, have no guilt, since they do not have the kind of personal freedom and the knowledge that moral responsibility presupposes. Similarly, the young and the mentally handicapped may have no consciousness of guilt, since they have no moral responsibility. Otherwise human maturity and authenticity can be measured by this personal moral responsibility, as this is the true indication of how well the human being has lived his or her life in personal freedom, harmony and pilgrimage towards the definitive destiny in God, who is the author of human life, knowledge, freedom, self-transcendence, and moral and structural order in the world.[52]

These open and infinite dimensions not only orient the human being to his or her eternal quest and mystical journey to fulfillment in the beatific vision in God, but they also open up the possibility of dialogue with God, since these dimensions themselves are divine qualities and, as such, open media for such a dialogue between God and the human being and channels of self-revelation in grace and gratuitous supernatural salvation for the human being.[53]

4. Human *a Priori* Openness to the Divine Infinite Mystery

The fact that the human being is created by God as a self-transcending creature is an *a priori* human existential. It is the main constitutive feature of the human being *qua* human being. As an *a priori* human structure it leads to permanent human openness and orientation to God as the Infinite Mystery, the Ground and ever-receding Horizon of human knowledge and self-transcendence. Karl Rahner describes the human transcendental experience as an *a priori* human openness to God as the Infinite Mystery and Ground of reality. He puts it as follows:

> We shall call transcendental experience the subjective, unthematic, necessary and unfailing consciousness of the knowing subject that is co-present in every spiritual act of knowledge, and the subject's openness to the unlimited expanse of all possible reality. It is an 'experience' because this knowledge, unthematic but ever-present, is a moment within and a condition of possibility for every concrete experience of any and every object...This transcendental experience, of course, is not merely an experience of pure knowledge, but also of the will and of freedom. The same character of transcendentality belongs to them, so that basically one can ask about the source and the destiny of the subject as a knowing being and as a free being together...There is present in this transcendental experience an unthematic and anonymous, as it were, knowledge of God...Transcendence is always oriented towards the holy mystery.[54]

It is quite clear, therefore, that for Rahner the human being is like Heidegger's *Dasein*, which is by its essential nature oriented and open to Being and Being's luminosity and self-disclosure on *Dasein*'s open receptive region and through *Dasein's a priori* existential structures of language, reflection and mood.[55]

As a moral agent, the human being is essentially God's concrete representative or ambassador, steward and tenant in the world. This world is also God's temporal kingdom and arena of God's cosmic drama and free activities of creation and redemption. God as the creator of the world and the cosmic King is the owner of world and the human being is the beneficiary. As such, the human being is eternally both oriented and attuned to God in creation just as ears are attuned and receptive to sound and eyes to light. The human being was created in God's image to love, worship and contemplate God, the Infinite Mystery, in whom the human being finds authentic happiness, rest, beatitude and fulfillment.[56]

In addition, the human being, as a self-transcendent, free historical spirit oriented to the Infinite Mystery, and as a knowing, moral, responsible agent, is tormented by guilt due to the awareness of moral failure, weakness, sin and its consequent internal and social tension and disharmony. The tension and disharmony are mainly a result of human pride, greed, selfishness and excessive love for material things and wealth at the expense of the neighbor and God.

However, if God as the embodiment of goodness or as the *summum bonum* is ignored, then the human being becomes the miserable creature that is self-immersed and lost in the material world, groping in the dark (tripping on worldly things lying in and around the dim path), but nevertheless striving forward toward the beckoning divine light of God's gratuitous salvation that shines beyond. Through God's unmerited universal redemptive grace and agape, the human being is ever driven forward to God in quest of unconditional love, peace and salvation and the removal of personal and collective sin and guilt. This human guilt is universal and seeks forgiveness, cleansing and restoration to wholeness by the holy, loving and redemptive Creator-God. This kind of guilt cannot be effectively removed by mere counselling. It requires confession, atonement, absolution from sin and guilt.

Since every normal human being experiences love, personal freedom, mystery, choice, responsibility and guilt, then the human being is ever in process of quest for meaningful self-expression and perfection in these dimensions. Subsequently, the human being lives in an implicit or explicit search of ultimate or lasting unconditional acceptance, love, forgiveness and cleansing from personal guilt incurred in the process of living, by failure to realize and to actualize oneself to the maximum possibility.

God effects and assists the human being in this universal salvific process by creating the human being with an *a priori* internal structure of supernatural grace which alerts him or her of God, mystery, agape, goodness and guilt. By this divine gift of indwelling grace of God, the human being is ever oriented in faith, hope and receptive openness to God in Logos-Christ.

The human being's mind and spirit serving as God's antennae implanted in the human being allow the human being to be attuned to God's Word and to hear God's Word or the Logos-Christ as the ultimate and true source and mediation of all genuine forgiveness and cleansing from guilt and sin, and also as the enabler, lure, mover and energizing power of the human being to move ever forwards in growth towards perfect self-realization and the categorical self-actualization of faith, hope, love in personal freedom and responsibility.

Rahner's concept that the human being is a finite categorical being, who as spirit is a mystery like God the Creator and Infinite Mystery, is inseparably bound up with the idea that the human being by *a priori* essential constitutive nature and structure, and ontological receptive openness to this Infinite Mystery to which the human being is oriented and attuned *a priori* in creation.

5. The Human Being as the Hearer of God's Word

Rahner's anthropology has its focal axis, grounding and climax in the notion that the human being who is essentially a self-transcendent being as a free historical spirit (characterized by self-conscious self-presence and reflection, personal freedom, knowledge, choice, moral responsibility and guilt), this finite creature, yet infinite as spirit in virtue of unlimited self-transcendence, and its *a priori* orientation to holy Mystery, and receptive openness to this Mystery, this complex human being is "the Hearer of the Divine Word."[57]

In short, this is the main grounding of Rahner's philosophical anthropology and theology. This is also the main basis for Rahner's theology of God's universal free self-communication in unconditional love and gratuitous grace to all human beings, everywhere and throughout the ages for their gratuitous salvation in as much as they heard and responded positively to God's word. Rahner sums up his argument on "the human being as hearer of the (divine) Word" (Logos) in the following manner:

> We started with the question of what our first metaphysical question about being had to tell us, in its aspect, about the nature of man as the possible subject of a revelation. The answer has been that it belongs to man's fundamental make-up to be the absolute openness for being as such. Through the 'Vorgriff,' which is the condition of the possibility of objective knowledge and of man's self-subsistence, man continually transcends everything towards pure being. Man is the first of these finite knowing subjects that stand open for the absolute fullness of being in such a way that this openness is the condition of the possibility for every single knowledge...capable of freely acting and deciding his own destiny. Man is spirit i.e. he lives his life while reaching unceasingly for the absolute, in openness toward God...Only that makes him into a man: that he is always already on the way to God, whether or not he wills it. He is forever the infinite openness of the finite for God.[58]

Because of *Vorgriff* or human infinite self-transcendence, and also because
the human being is a finite historical spirit oriented to the Infinite Divine
Spirit to which it is irresistibly drawn by virtue or orientation and prior
affinity, as St. Augustine himself realized through this personal experience,
the human being is ever restless and in search of union with God as the
ultimate destiny of human life and its definitive fulfillment. Rahner himself
puts it this way:

> Man is spirit and, as such, he is always already to stand before the infinite God
> who, as infinite, is always more than only the ideal unity of the essentially finite
> powers of human existence and of the world. He does not only acknowledge
> God in fact, but in the daily drift of his existence he is man, self-subsistant,
> capable of judgment and of free activity, only because he continually reaches out
> into a domain that only the fullness of God's absolute being can fill.[59]

The human capability to seek God and apprehend his implicit self-disclosure
or revelation in the world, and to view its wonders, beauty and mystery as
divine revelation, is the human openness to the world and the Cosmic
Mystery. As such, the human insatiable search for knowledge, truth and its
ultimate origin and basis, and the correlative perpetual human quest for a
meaningful life, love, health, comfort, happiness is also quest for God and
salvation. In some cases it is explicit as the quest for God when it is self-
conscious as the quest for deliverance from the threat of evil, chaos, pain
and death. But this is not all.

Karl Rahner, like St. Augustine, further affirms that God made the
human being in such a manner that at the core of his or her being there is
a void of an infinite abyss or a yearning openness towards fulfillment in the
Infinite Mystery and God. Only God's transcendence, infinite Agape and
grace are sufficient to this human void at the center of his or her being. God
designed the human being incomplete at the center and hollow so that this
infinite human void or abyss could only be appropriately filled by the
infinite God as this Infinite Mystery required to complete and fulfill the
human being as the incomplete finite mystery.

This being the case, misguided and misdirected attempts to fill this
infinite void with finite things fail, as our own experiences or those of St.
Paul and St. Augustine clearly demonstrate.[60] As both of these saints
realized, human life is incomplete, restless and ever searching for its
completion and fulfillment, which can only be found in God.

This inner void which is universally experienced by the human being is
for Rahner, God's ontological ordering of the human being by God's grace.

That is God has structured the human being in such a way that the human being remains permanently open and oriented to God and his Word (Logos) of life and salvation. Therefore, God's eternal Word or the Logos is desired at least implicitly by the human being as the source of human fulfillment and happiness.

Rahner explains this complexity in other complex terms. He affirms that in reality God calls his Word into being in this void at the center of the human being. Subsequently, the human being hears this divine Word, not as an alien message coming from outside, the human being himself or herself, but rather, as intimately personal. He argues that this is the case since God and his Word are within the core of the human being, therefore, they are heard as coming from within the center of the human being. Since God is omnipresent, the Word of God or the indwelling Logos as the Christ is heard from within the human being's innermost essence and being, because God and his Word or the Christ are not external objects nor are they alien or inseparable from the human being.

According to Rahner, God is as the cosmic Omnipresent Mystery, is always present in the world and its mundane or temporal processes. God is sometimes presented to the human being as the "Ground" and "Condition" of being, self-transcendence, knowing, personal freedom, moral choice and responsibility. God's knowledge is given to the human being in an undifferentiated, pre-thematic, non-cognitive, unobjective and anonymous manner. In this form it is given to the human being as the ground and horizon of all human knowing, as it is the intelligibility itself and without which nothing is knowable. It is also the luminosity of Being that enables all beings to be seen as they are by and within its light and background.[61]

For Rahner, the human being is both able to hear God's silent word and to see the cosmic divine revelation by looking at the world reflectively and by reflecting upon life and human experience. Furthermore, the human being is able to discern God's Word as the message for human life now and also as being directive and determinative for future action and positive self-realization. For Rahner this personal discerning inner eye and "mystical experience" is the main goal of humanization as divinization in Christ.

Rahner also argues that Jesus and the prophets manifested the nature of this quality to which every human being is called. This is namely, to be able to hear and speak God's Word in and to the world, through human existence and the prevailing state of affairs be it social, economic, medical or political.

However, Jesus and the prophets were more able to discern and see God's invisible hand at work in history, and daily human affairs. Human beings saw God's power creating, directing, saving and judging human choices, actions and the affairs of the world. They were also completely open to God and attuned to hear his silent cosmic Word (Logos), which speaks to them from within. God's Logos speaks to them in their own souls, minds and from the insatiable gaping internal void at the innermost core of each human being. They were able to hear, and see what other people could not hear and see what other people could not see. This is because they were in full orientation, openness and receptive "attunement," to God through the inner mystical antenna or transcendental dimension of the spirit which is by grace able to transcend human finite limitations, and thereby, like Jesus, to ascend to God, in heaven.

According to Rahner, God's Word, which is implicit in every human being as non-cognitive, undifferentiated intuition of the Transcendent Mystery and Ground for knowledge and truth, quietly guides in free grace the human being toward the ultimate Destiny and fulfillment in God as this Mystery. However, sometimes this pre-thematic and uncognitive revelation of God comes to human beings in full consciousness and becomes an objective or explicit knowledge in relationship to the knowing subject. Then the silent, implicit Word of God becomes the explicit, verbal, proclaimed and written Word of God of the Apostolic and historical Church confessional and creeds. Nevertheless, this takes place without exhausting or replacing that portion of the cosmic divine Word that remains for many people implicit, unthematic and anonymous as the pre-Incarnate Christ and the Cosmic Logos.[62]

The Scriptures, creeds and doctrinal dogmatic formulations as systematic cognitive propositional statements of faith have to do with the divine Incarnate Word or the Christ. This Word of God perceived as objectified and thematized by the human being as the hearer of the divine Word. This objectification of the Logos or Christ as the Word of God takes place in the human beings thematic and unthematic *a priori* intrinsic existence in the human being as the condition of human knowing, freedom, self-transcendence, choice and responsibility. In addition, it also exists in the human being as the ground energizer and lure for human beings to reflection, self-examination and self-evaluation in social, moral, and religious dimensions as well as temporal terms and dimensions, such as past, present, and future (cf. John 1:1-18).

However, it is erroneous for anyone to claim that only the thematic divine Word of God or the Incarnate Christ really counts as divine revelation. Therefore, it is erroneous to affirm that there is no divine revelation apart from the Holy Bible, as most reformers seemed to be affirming by their narrow doctrine of *sola scriptura*. This is particularly significant since this dogma or principle of *sola scriptura* did not admit that the Koran, the Hindu and Buddhist holy books were themselves true and valid scriptures revealed by God; and as such, serving as an essential part of this principle of *sola scriptura*.[63]

God's Word is infinite and, therefore, unlimited to certain books whether written by prophets or saints, including the holy Bible, Torah and the holy Qur'an themselves. God's Infinite Word cannot ever be written down in its totality. Therefore, only finite portions or fragments of God's eternal and infinite Word can be heard as addressed to specific finite human beings in their finite, human existential conditions at a specific historical time, and in a given place.[64]

The Word of God is personal to the hearer(s). Since every human being is unique, it should be also logical to assume that each human being hears God speak to him or her personally in his or her own cultural context and language. Therefore, it would seem logical to affirm that God speaks differently to various different people.

This is essential if God is to communicate effectively, relevantly and meaningfully as he seeks to address each individual person as his or her unique beloved child. That means that God has to design his Word and message specifically for the needs and context of the specific individual in full respect of that specific individual's personal uniqueness, freedoms, needs, fears and experiences. In this manner, God will call his Word (Logos) of life and salvation into meaningful existence in the life of that person.

This is the ultimate meaning and essence of the divine Incarnation in the human being and the world. God seeks to speak his Word in the local context of the people and their needs and experiences. In this manner, God is, therefore, able to be meaningful in the filling of the infinite void that exists at the center of the human being as the eternal receptive openness to the divine Mystery, and prior ontological attunement in readiness for the reception of the Divine Word.

The Word of God itself, as understood by the writer of the fourth Gospel, cannot be itself written down. This is because this Word of God is God himself, in the cosmic creative and redemptive action as the medium and instrumentality of both divine processes of creation and redemption. Both creation and redemption are simultaneous intertwined free universal actions of God's grace and agape.

These free cosmic divine activities are ever ongoing, creative and sustaining processes, which are constitutive of this world. In these processes the human being as the self-conscious and intelligent being, that is most akin to God feels himself or herself egocentrically, idolatrously, and anthropomorphically as being the real main center of the world, or focus of life. This is the primordial or original Adamic temptation, and sin, namely, to deify oneself, dethrone God and install oneself as God in his place. Hitler and Idi Amin tried to do this at a political level. However, in the same process, God acted in love actually to divinize the human beings through Agape and divine free and unmerited action of God's grace, love and Incarnation of his Word/Logos into the world.

Therefore, what can be written, then, are words, and our own experiences and objectification of the Word of God as we hear it speaking to us individually and collectively. The scriptures as God's Written Word also include our intuitions of God, interpretations of what we discern, see or perceive in the world to be constitutive of God's interventions in history or the actions of God in the salvation history or process of the world. This includes, our perception of God in humanity or the Incarnation of God in the world through Christ.

However, this is the living Eternal Word which cannot be written down in a dead or static form of a holy book.[65] God speaks his redemptive Word, from within and inside each human being as the true holy temple and the cosmic dwelling place of God. Therefore, all human beings have access to God and his true living, revelatory and redemptive eternal Word. Therefore, human beings are like mobile God's satellites and phones who can hear God's Word of saving grace, love, and forgiveness, anywhere and any time since, the omnipresent God and his creative and redemptive Word, are permanent inhabitants within the spirit of the human being and do not reside or come from the outside of the human being as some alien forces or beings.

However, these sacred writings as Scriptures can be loosely called the Word of God, since they came into being through the inspiration and motivation by the Word of God which was heard by the godly men and women and recorded as they personally heard and understood it themselves in their own uniqueness, time, culture and general prevailing circumstances as background context for this hearing, interpretation, understanding and writing.[66]

Like Karl Barth, Karl Rahner affirms that the written Word becomes the true living Word of God when its readers or hearers hear God speaking to them, addressing them individually or collectively in challenge, direction for the future or in judgment. When this divine speaking and human hearing take place, then, one can truly say that God has spoken his Word and likewise, that these pieces of religious literature are inspired Holy Scriptures and that they are God's word.[67]

Karl Barth himself was very perceptive of the heresy and theological problem of claiming that *sola scriptura* implied that God's salvific Word had been captured and somehow transcribed into the Bible as holy Scripture. His solution for this complex problem was his tripartite doctrine of the Word of God. For Barth God's Word (Logos) had a threefold essential nature: "The Written Word," "the Incarnate Word" and "the Proclaimed Word."[68] Whereas this solution is a noteworthy theological attempt at arriving at a consistent and comprehensive understanding of God's Word, it is too restrictive to answer many contemporary questions.

In Rahner's view God's Word must be recognized as infinite, universal, and omnipresent to everybody as it is co-present with God as the Speaker addressed to every human being as the hearer of this divine Word that calls everything into being and to life, love, happiness, hope, personal freedom and responsibility. This is also the silent Word of God in the inner life of the human being that calls him or her into question and judgment, and similarly, divine forgiveness.

This is the divine creative, sustaining and transforming Word of God that is universally present, silently, anonymously, and ceaselessly at God's work of creation and salvation as guided creative self-actualization in harmony, and movement towards fulfillment in eternal Destiny and Mystery as God. All this is the work of God out of his pure gratuitous, efficacious grace and universal salvific will. His will is that all human beings should live in accordance with his grace, which is given through the inner directive Word, love, faith and hope, and be saved.[69]

Therefore, God's Word cannot be captured and be encapsulated in a book or pamphlet. Otherwise, God would have sent down a holy book into the world, instead of sending his Son or Word/Logos. The Logos as God's eternal Word sent into the world is infinite, yet personal. As personal the Logos as Son of God became a human being in the incarnation. This was necessary in order for God to communicate more effectively and concretely with human beings, who are historical and temporal creatures. Jesus as the

Christ was and is God's Word addressed to human beings in a historical and temporal context.

However, this historical mediation of God's Word in the world cannot be considered to represent the totality of God's Word, since there is still a transcendental, universal dimension of the divine Cosmic Word that transcends these temporal-spatial dimensions.

Therefore, it could also be argued that Jesus, as the Incarnate Word of God in historical process, was no doubt aware of this Infinite dimension of God's Word and that is one of the main reasons why he never wrote a book himself either about God or about his message of God's kingdom. Rather, he challenged his audience "to hear the Word of God by opening their inner, mystical ears and to open their inner eyes. By so doing they would be able to see and hear God's voiceless, silent Word uttered, and to see his invisible, mysterious, protecting and guiding hand at work in the course of the world's history and in the ordinary events of human daily life and/or history."[70]

It follows, therefore, that Rahner's human being, like Heidegger's *Dasein*, is not just an a priori receptive openness and readiness in the world for the reception of God's free-willed self-disclosure as revelation and illumination for himself/herself and on behalf of the whole world. In addition, the human unique structures of language, mind and mood, have also become correlative unique divine revelatory media and channels of God's Word in which language finds its expression in and through the human thought and emotions.

In turn, these then become adapted as God's means of making his voiceless silent Word heard, perceived and loved by the human being to whom it is addressed both universally, as the transcendental Logos in human transcendence, and historically in Jesus Christ and the Church as his temporal embodiment and mediation in this historical and temporal world's processes.

Since the human structure is the revelatory vehicle and medium of the divine Word which is addressed to the human being, and the human condition in the world, Rahner argues that it could also be affirmed that the human being who is the cosmic finite hearer of this divine eternal Word, is also in a sense the co-speaker of the Word with God. He argues that this is the case since without the human being the Word remains unheard and remains without voice, thought, and language for self-expression.

The human being, as this medium of God's Word, and as the creature whose constitutive unique structure is the revelatory instrumentality of God, is then probably deservedly well described by Rahner as "the hearer of the divine Word." According to Rahner, this remains true whether the human being is explicitly aware of it or not. This is because to be a human being is correlatively and coextensively, also to be a hearer of God's Word. This is the Word of God which calls all human beings into existence and then, again invites them to actualize themselves towards a more complete humanity and humaneness.

This self-completion or self-realization takes place according to God's will and plan as made possible by divine grace finding expression in faith, hope and unrestricted love for fellow human beings and God. This is important since by virtue of the incarnation God has become correlative and coextensive with humanity.

Therefore, to love and serve humanity has become a prerequisite as the service and love for God, since humanity and divinity are inseparable and fully co-extensive in Jesus-Christ. Subsequently, love for humanity is love for God, and love for God requires love for humanity (cf. Matt. 25:31-46). According to Rahner, God cannot ever be found nor can he be loved apart from our concrete love (agape) and caring service for humanity. This is because by virtue of God's Incarnation in humanity through Jesus-Christ, all humanity has correlatively and coextensively become the concrete cosmic dwelling temple of God. All human beings have also thereby become God's own historical, and temporal expression, concrete representation and the very Incarnation of God in the historical process, and this temporal world.[71]

According to classical Christian teaching, in the Incarnation, God speaks culturally and historically by means of his Incarnate Word as a human being (Jesus as the Christ). God undertook this mission in the world in order to address himself to humanity, directly and personally, in its temporal and historical forms and unique modalities of existence.

God also "became man" or human being in order to reveal to the world what true humanity, undistorted by sin, is supposed to be like. In this respect, Jesus as the Christ and the "*shekinah*" or *theophany* of God is the authentic archetypal form of the human being. In other words, Jesus as the incarnate Logos of God into humanity, has symbolically become a second Adam. Thus, God concretized his abstract Infinite, eternal Creative and Redemptive Word of God, or the Logos of grace, love (Agape), life, harmony, peace, justice, righteousness, order, and creative transformation in human history through the divine Incarnation.

Since God's Word has become a human being, and since divine revelation is deposited in every human being by God in creation, therefore, to be the hearer of the Word and/or to accept God's revelation, the human being must accept himself or herself in his or her *a priori* mystery and listen to his or her inner voice in order to hear God speak. For God and his Word have become incarnated in the center of humanity and therefore in each human being.

God and his Word as the pre-existent cosmic Logos or Christ and the Holy Spirit as their energizing power are no longer alien to the human being, since they have their dwelling in the inner core of humanity, not as foreign objects, but as the very "Ground" for human life itself, which is constituted by hearing the Word of God, which calls all things into being and quietly guides them to their respective fulfillment in their prior divinely given destinations unless they rebel and choose otherwise.

Consequently, all human existential life is lived in the presence of God's Word of invitation to life in its fullness. Therefore, the human being lives in the daily open possibility of hearing God's Word of invitation to a fuller life as salvation in grace, and to respond in individual, personally accountable and consequential freedom with either "Yes" or "No" to this universal, unconditional divine proffer of gratuitous salvific grace.

Furthermore, since God in his Word and through the power and mystery of his Holy Spirit has become human, Rahner is right to affirm that we can only seek God as we seek humanity, and that we can only find truth about ourselves as we find truth about God, since the Divine and the human essence and natures, have become permanently, and irrevocably co-extensive and inseparable twin correlatives, due to this divine Incarnation. This permanent universal symbolic and historical human-divine union was accomplished by God, in his universal gratuitous creative and redemptive grace, to effect the free universal complete human positive transformation and salvation.

This has been universally achieved by God through the free divinization, humanization and salvation of all obedient human beings in the world. This has been achieved by God, and by virtue of this agapic universal divine Incarnation into humanity, and the consequent negation of the human self-alienation from God.

This previously universalized primordial human alienation from God through the fall or rebellion and guilt, has been universally reversed, neutralized and permanently removed by God in his free universal and unmerited redemptive grace and agape working through the cosmic Logos-Christ. Through the Incarnation of the Logos into the world, God has freely recreated the world and humanity, anew. God has done this by effecting a universal permanent reconciliation with God through the deification of all human beings into God's reconciled children, by virtue of the Divine Incarnation and the "Hypostatic Union."[72]

6. The Supernatural Existential and Gratuitous Divine Universal Salvific Grace

Rahner's anthropology and theology have one basic essential theme, pivot, grounding and destiny, namely, the supernatural gratuitous grace in love as prior to creation and as reason for creation, creation's *raison d'etre* and Ultimate Destiny. In this sense, then creation is good, infused by grace and destined to fulfillment in God both as its free Creator and Destiny. This is especially true of human beings as knowing, transcendent, moral, free, responsible, and loving creatures rendered by the supernatural existential in order to respond to God. And do so willingly and joyfully in personal, responsible freedom to God's proffer of himself in grace.

This Rahnerian starting point renders frivolous the question why the good creation should be in need of God's salvific grace, while at the same time it puts an end to the debate between the extrinsicists and the intrinsicists regarding the supernatural and human nature.[73] Rahner's theory of the supernatural existential as God's free gift of grace to the human being in creation as a permanent ontological divine elevation of the human to supernatural, and as prior ordering and permanent ontological receptive openness, readiness and atonement to God's Word in gratuitous grace for positive self-actualization, and self-determination in personal freedom and in the midst of this divine encompassing efficacious grace, positively affirms that the human being is created with an *"obediential potency."*

This means that the human being is by *"a priori"* divine gratuitous universal creative and salvific grace, a special creature. This is an intelligent free moral creature, who is also both freely divinely oriented and elected by the Creator and Agapic God, to divine destiny in the *beatific vision*. This divinizing *beatific vision* is only found in God's own presence and fulfillment in the perfection of happiness experienced in fellowship of love with God and the saints. However, according to Rahner, this is universally freely done by God and achieved by obedient human beings everywhere, without putting a demand on this supernatural grace as a condition for the human fulfillment in this destiny, or without making grace an alien force that overrides essential human personal freedom.

Since human freedom is real and consequential, therefore, all human beings shape themselves and destiny. This is accomplished through personal choice and the responsibility for one's moral being. Human freedom gives the human being the power of God in God's free creative and redemptive grace to choose one's concrete actions and the correlative consequent destiny, which they shape for the human being in his or her personal consequential moral freedom and the corresponding responsibilities. Nevertheless, even in this exercise of human freedom, God's efficacious grace as the lure towards the good, is always universally efficaciously offered to all human beings, everywhere and in all ages. It is effectively available in creation, religion and conscience (cf. Rom. 1:17-32).

According to Rahner, the human supernatural existential is a universal neutral divine proffer of supernatural grace which allows the human being to exercise his or her personal consequential freedom to either accept it or reject it in this same freedom.[74] In this way the human being determines himself or herself to a fuller meaningful, fulfilling life as it is offered to him or her by God in love and mystery, and therefore to happiness, love, fellowship, community, and salvation or its negation in personal freedom and consequential self-imposed isolation, loneliness, a lesser mode of life, minimum self-actualization, meaningless misery, and damnation. The supernatural existential, therefore, is the impartial divine instrumentality for free actualization of salvation or damnation.

The existence of the supernatural existential is vital for Rahner's works, as it is the grounding for his understanding of God's universal divine self-communication to every normal human being for revelatory and salvific purposes in gratuitous grace. According to Rahner, the supernatural existential allows every reflective human being, in grace and responsible personal freedoms, to respond to the divine immanent revelation and divine Word deposited at the center of his or her inner being, ever calling him or her to a fuller life, love, hope, forgiveness, healing, wholeness, happiness, perfection and definitive fulfillment in the *"visio beatifica"* with either a "Yes" or a "No." Those who answer "Yes" to this invitation to supernatural salvation are Christians, since they do so through the Word which is Christ.

Those who are unaware of this title as descriptive of their surrender to God as the Mystery, source and Destiny of life and salvation, or those who resent this title for past unfortunate associations and misunderstandings, yet completely surrendering themselves to the fullness of life, unrestricted love and Mystery in which these are wrapped up, especially in the future dimension, these people are termed by Rahner "anonymous Christians."[75]

7. Anonymous Christianity

Rahner's theology can be said to be basically an exposition of God's fundamental attributes of Agape and universal activities of supernatural universal gratuitous, creative and salvific grace. This free divine creative and salvific grace finds its logical climactic expression in the concept of "anonymous Christianity." For Rahner "anonymous Christianity" is the term for the obedient and positive condition of human response to this free universal offer of God's free divine salvation and self-communication to the world. This divine salvific grace was not only offered to the world in the Incarnation, but also to the world prior to that historical event.

Therefore, to the pre-Incarnation world, God offered his free efficacious grace and salvation through the Logos as the pre-existent Cosmic Word. As such, God's gratuitous grace for the salvation of all human beings, has been freely and generously bestowed to the world and all the intelligent beings, whatever or wherever they are, irrespective of religion, technology, culture, literacy, education, economy, color, race and time.[76] This "anonymous Christianity" as the free divine proffer of universal efficacious salvific grace, is also revelatory of God's correlative gratuitous grace of humanization, and fulfillment is co-extensive with human history.

Therefore, God has no favorites. God as our free Creator and Redeemer, is an impartial cosmic parent. As such, God loves all people equally and without condition. Therefore, God has no favorite or preferred races, religions, holy books, cultures, languages, system of government, system of economics, ideology, class, color or gender. In this manner, God's concrete grace and salvation in the world are universal and efficacious in the world preceding and transcending the divine historical election of Israel, the giving of the Torah by Moses and the Scriptures, the Incarnation of the Word in historical process, and the emergence of the Apostolic Church, as its visible historical embodiment, and sacramental or ritual mediation in this temporal world.

Consequently, God's salvific activity in his supernatural grace is inseparable from creation. Like cosmic free divine creation, salvation is also universal, unconditional and free. Therefore, God's universal salvific will and efficacious grace to effect it cannot to be restricted and limited either by human sin of selfishness or bigotry. Consequently, any religious leader or theologian who seeks to define God and his transcendent activities in such limited forms of bigotry and exclusive doctrines or dogmas, sins against God's grace, and Agape.

Therefore, we should not let the human sins of religious denominational zeal, arrogance, bigotry, politics, racism, ethnocentrism, jealousy, sadism, religious intolerance and hatred lead into the sinful traps of theological errors of uncharitable exclusiveness by such doctrines as *massa damnata*; *extra ecclesiam nulla salus,* and the narrow double predestinarian dogmas found in hard-line Calvinism, and among some protestant groups, such as the Jehovah's Witnesses.[77]

Ultimately, for Rahner salvation implies the ultimate completion and fulfillment of the human being as such, therefore, it cannot be limited either to the Church or to certain religions. That kind of limitation or doctrine would leave the majority of the human race incomplete and unfulfilled as human beings. This would be contrary to God's essential nature as Agape and *Sola Gratia.* It would also be contrary to reality as observed in the world, namely, that there are people who do not claim to be "saved" nor to be "Christians," yet these same people have already accepted themselves as human beings; and they live a full human life, open to the world, its mystery and the open future.

Perhaps most important of all, these people either implicitly or explicitly, live in unrestricted love for their neighbors, which is the authentic universal explicit concrete or practical expression and evidence of the presence of God's efficacious work of free redemptive grace, which leads to faith as positive orientation to life in its mystery, hope, agape, and supernatural grace salvation. Rahner puts it this way:

> According to the Christian view of things, even though a person is co-condi-
> tioned by original sin in his situation of salvation and sin, he always and
> everywhere has the genuine possibility of encountering God and achieving
> salvation by the acceptance of God's supernatural self-communication in grace,
> a possibility which is forfeited only through his own guilt. There is a serious,
> effective and universal will of God in the sense of that salvation which the
> Christian means by his own Christian salvation. In Catholic dogmatics, God's
> salvific will is characterized as universal in contrast to the pessimism in
> Augustine or in Calvinism; that is, it is promised to every person regardless of
> where or at what time he lives, but this does not just mean that a person in some
> way or other is kept from being lost.[78]

In the same place, Rahner goes on to argue very constructively in the following manner:

Salvation in the proper and Christian sense of God's absolute self-communication in absolute closeness and hence it also means the beatific vision...But this salvation takes place as the salvation of a free person as such, and hence it takes place precisely when this person in fact actualizes himself in freedom, that is, towards his salvation.[79]

Rahner goes on to argue very insightfully that whoever has turned to God as the Infinite Mystery, experienced from within and/or as seen in the world that leads to the human infinite questioning and wonder, whoever has accepted his or her own humanity in its given mystery, contingency, vulnerability and finitude, whoever seeks to live in unrestricted love, peace and harmony with his/her fellow human beings and the world, that person has surrendered himself or herself to God and God's gratuitous salvific grace, whether he or she knows it explicitly, as in the case of a confessing Christian, or is still unaware of it and therefore an "anonymous Christian."[80]

This can be regarded as a good criterion for salvation, since it has to do with the quality of categorical human life and the way it is daily lived before God as the transcendent Holy Mystery in the world and in relation to one's fellow human beings, the community and the world, as the rest of this book will attempt to show, taking the Central and Southern Bantu people of Uganda as the main focus.

Therefore, the main task in the rest of this book will be to try to demonstrate that these Bantu people traditionally live a life that is both oriented and receptive to God, while at the same time seeking to live in neighborly love, and to enhance peace and harmony within the community. The main criterion by which they will be measured, to see if they fulfill God's moral law and holiness, or Rahner's primary criteria of "anonymous Christians." If they fulfill God's criteria, then they thereby, declared to have been qualified to become the true heirs of God's kingdom and supernatural salvation, is that of concrete good and humane social deeds, for the neighbor and the community.

These social and moral good deeds, are the concrete external means of the praxis of agape and correlatively, the practical expression of the redemptive fruits of grace which, are both explicit and implicit, in the exercise of unconditional love for the neighbor (cf. Matt. 7:13-23; 25:31-46). Therefore, contrary to the familiar Protestant dogmatic claims of "sola fide" or salvation by faith alone, faith alone, by itself and without the corresponding necessary good works of grace, and Agape or charity, is impotent, unable to save anyone, and therefore, both religiously and morally worthless. As such, no one can ever be truly, saved by faith alone, if they are devoid of altruistic good deeds.

On the other hand, good deeds deeply rooted in God and his goodness, both in creation and redemption. Accordingly, all good works are rewarded by God and society, for they are expressive of God, goodness and his creative and transforming power redemptive love or agape. These good works, also originate from positive dynamic faith in the intrinsic goodness and high value of life, the self, God, the neighbor and the world as God's good creation, in which they are divinely rooted.

NOTES

1. See Ch. II, notes 9, 10, 21, 36, 39, 54-58.

2. Ibid. Anonymous Christianity can be considered as the logical apex of Rahner's theory of divine gratuitous grace. For Rahner, universal supernatural salvation is dependent on God's universal salvific will, which is correlative to his universal, supernatural, gratuitous, efficaciously salvific grace as the means to achieve God's universal will to save every human being. In this sense, every human being has been elected to supernatural salvation and will only lose it by his or her personal free will to defect and live in contradiction to this divine Destiny. As a result, Rahner affirms that every human being is a potential member of God's kingdom and life in heaven.

This approach seems to make more sense than that of Anita Roper, who declares that everybody is an "anonymous Christian," see, *The Anonymous Christian*, 126, where she writes that: "Every human being is a Christian, and he is one not always expressly but very often anonymously. This statement, which summarizes what we have said so far...All men are Christians in some way, although the ways differ widely. That is a fact." Here, one has to heed Kierkegaard's critique, namely, that "If we are all Christians, the concept is annulled...and so Christianity is *'eo ipso'* abolished." See "Attack upon 'Christendom'" in *A Kierkegaard Anthology*, ed. Robert Bretall (New York: The Modern Library, 1946), 447; see also "What It Is to Become a Christian," which is Kierkegaard's conclusion of the famous *Concluding Unscientific Postscript*, and/or *Training in Christianity*, "The Offence," C, Supplement 2, 108 ff,.

3. The major philosophical anthropological works being *Spirit in the World* and *Hearers of the Word*. Rahner starts with anthropology in order to do theology because the human being is the given and God is the implicit in this given (the human being), which is the only explicit. Rahner affirms that the divine revelation has been deposited in the human being by God in creation, and that the human being is the cipher of God and, as such, revelatory of God, particularly since, by virtue of the Incarnation and Hypostatic Union, God has become irrevocably united and inseparable from the human being; cf. *Foundations of Christian Faith*, 24-70, 212-227. For Rahner, without anthropology, theology is impossible, because theology is a theistic and meaningful study of humanity and a theistic interpretation of human existence in light of the Incarnation; see "Theology and Anthropology," *Theological Investigations* 9:28-45; "Philosophy and Philosophizing in Theology," *Theological Investigations* 9:46-63.

4. For Rahner, and Mbiti, salvation is not a future fulfillment in the beatific vision. For Rahner, salvation is present positive mode of human life now. Salvation now exists as the movement towards the Ultimate divine Destiny or God; cf. Rahner, *Foundations of Christian Faith*, 97-105, 142-170, and Pannenberg, *What Is Man?* 54-67. See also Chapter I, note 11.

5. Contrary to the historicization and the popular literal interpretation of Genesis 1-3, found among some Christian fundamentalists.

6. See note 4 above. Rahner defines salvation as the humanization of the human being. This humanization is making humanity more loving and humane. In this sense, the Incarnation is a complete humanization of humankind, and as such, its divinization, since authentic humanity is impossible to achieve without divine help in the form of the supernatural grace that elevates the mere human nature (which tends to be more inclined to animality from which it previously emerged in evolution) to a supernatural level, where it is oriented to Mystery and to seek fulfillment in God as its ultimate Origin and Destiny.

According to Rahner, these two levels exist simultaneously together in the human being right from the beginning, since he regards grace not as something added to the human being later, as an ornament or an attire, but rather as constitutive of the human being in terms of the supernatural existential that is a permanent divine proffer of grace to the human being. See: *Foundations of Christian Faith*, 39 ff.; "The Order of Redemption within the Order of Creation," *The Christian Commitment* New York: Sheed and Ward, 1963), 38-74; "Nature and Grace," *Nature and Grace* (New York: Sheed and Ward, 1964), 114-149; "Concerning the Relationship between Nature and Grace," *Theological Investigations* 1:297-317; "Some Implications of the Scholastic Concept of Uncreated Grace," ibid., 347-382; "Reflections of the Experience of Grace," *Theological Investigations* 3:86-90; "Nature and Grace," *Theological Investigations* 4:165-188; "The Existential," *Sacramentum Mundi* 2:304-307; "Grace," ibid., 412-427; "Potentia Oboedientialis," *Sacramentum Mundi* 5: 65-67; "Salvation (Universal Salvific Will)," ibid., 405-409.

7. Cf. Karl Rahner, *Prayers and Meditations*, 115-116.

8. Ibid., 17.

9. It is conceivable, therefore, that if Rahner were writing Genesis today, it is most probable that he would say: "God created man in his own mystery," instead of saying that "God created man in his own image." Unlike Barth, Rahner starts with anthropology in order to do theology mainly because he believes that the human mystery points back to its Creator/Origin, which Rahner identifies as the transcendent incomprehensible Infinite Mystery that is known as God in the English language.

10. Karl Rahner, *Prayers and Meditations*, 115.

11. See *Hearers of the Word*, Chs. 5-13; *Spirit in the World*, 65-77, 279-298, 387-408; *The Foundations of Christian Faith*, 24-132.

12. See Ch. II, notes 1, 5 and 6.

13. See note 11 above.
14. Cf. John 3:16; Rom. 5:8; 1 Cor. 13; John 4:7-21. "Beloved, let us love one another; for love is of God; and he who loves is born of God and knows God. He who does not love does not know God for God is love" (1 John 4:7-8).

15. If we characterize God as love, then intellect becomes a secondary quality of God, contrary to St. Thomas and Hegel, who tend to view God as primarily intellect. (Cf. *Summa Theologiae* I:1 qq. 3, 4 and 12; Hegel's *Phenomenology of Spirit*; and *Lectures on Philosophy of Religion: The Christian Religion*.)

16. For instance, all normal human beings are aware of moral norms and all human societies have an ethical code of some kind to regulate moral behavior. This cannot be said to be true of the rest of the animals.

17. Human moral responsibility presupposes human freedom as ground and condition of that responsibility arising out of personal free choice. Without freedom, Rahner argues, the human being is incomplete and cannot be morally accountable as such; cf. Rahner, *Grace in Freedom*, 203-265, and *Prayers and Meditations*, 74; see also Alfred North Whitehead, *Adventures in Ideas*, 43-86.

18. This can be described as St. Paul's dualistic way of describing the conflicts he experienced within himself, between the animality and the divine constitutive elements of his human nature. He correctly identifies animality with the bodily or physical desires but, like the Platonists, wrongly assumes deliverance as salvation to be apart from the troublesome body; hence his cry, "Who will deliver me from this body of death?"
The Incarnation affirms that for Christians, divine salvation does not consist in the abolition of the human body or escape from it; rather, that salvation consists in its healing, and positive orientation and response to God, and to seek to live in unity and harmony with the neighbor and the power of the Holy Spirit.

19. See: Plato's *Crito* and *Phaedo*; W.K.C. Guthrie, *The Greek Philosophers*, 86-121; G. H. Clark, *Thales to Dewey: A History of Philosophy* (Boston: Riverside, 1957), 70-77.

20. Ibid. Need for food, sex and shelter are usually singled out as the primary basic physical needs that govern most of human behavior. Consequently, these physical drives affect the human spirit and moral life. According to Sigmund Freud, in some cases of unmet or repressed needs for food and sex lead to personal and collective trouble, such as criminal behavior. When frustrated, these physical needs can become a great destructive negative force, and the demonic. They can also become a serious hindrance to the person's or the community's moral well-being, health, responsibility, and fundamentally influence both personal and collective spirituality, moral judgement and the general societal well-being.

21. See note 19 above. The body was regarded as the prison and as the tomb for the soul and consequently death as its release from this misery and bondage. This dualistic unchristian anthropological philosophy entered into Christianity through the early Church usage of Greek philosophy to explicate and contextualize the Christian faith to the Hellenized world of their day. However, this does not necessarily make it either any more Christian or acceptable to us. For a corrective, see Karl Rahner, *Hominization*, 32-111.

22. Cf. Karl Rahner, *Spirit in the World*, 135-142, 248-252; *Hearers of the Word*, Chs. 5-13; *Foundations of Christian Faith*, 24-175; *Grace in Freedom*, 113-116; *Opportunities for Faith* (New York: Seabury Press, 1970), 92-122, 194-198.

23. *Cogito ergo sum* perceives the human being to be essentially an intellect. This view of humanity follows from the Thomistic view of God as "Perfect Intellect" or, as Hegel

clearly puts it, "Absolute Intellect" or "Pure Thought thinking itself;" cf. "Absolute Knowledge" which concludes *The Phenomenology of Spirit*.

24. A proper definition of a human being is required in order to solve the ethical debates involved in abortion, euthanasia and genetic engineering. Careless and irresponsible definitions of the human being should be avoided. An example is that of Nietzsche's philosophy, and particularly, the notion of the *Ubermensch*, was used by the Nazi fascists as their blueprint for life and action. Slavery and economic exploitation of some people by another group is based on and justified by some crude definition of humanity.

25. S. Freud's studies and discoveries have opened up the unconscious mind and have made it accessible to scientific investigation. He divided the mind into three sections. The biggest section of these three he called "Id;" this is the unconscious region in which the basic animal (physical) instincts of human nature jostle together with no pattern of determined order or sense of value. The others are "Ego" and "Superego;" these determine which of the Id's demands is satisfied and which one is rejected if its satisfaction would lead to social disapproval and ostracizing of the individual. Freud found that the rejected drives did not vanish entirely, but rather they vanished out of sight into the unconscious mind, and showed up now and again in the acceptable guise of dreams and fantasies, or even manifested themselves destructively in pathological ways such as neuroses. Cf. Freud, *New Introductory Lectures on Psychoanalysis, An Outline of Psychoanalysis*, 5-45.

26. See Emil Brunner, "The Christian Understanding of Man," in *The Christian Understanding of Man*, 141-178; Reinhold Niebuhr, *The Nature and Destiny of Man* 1:1-92. See also notes 22 and 23 above.

27. Karl Rahner, *Hominization: The Evolutionary Origin of Man as a Theological Problem* (New York: Herder and Herder, 1965), 108-109.

28. Ibid. See also Rahner, *Prayers and Meditations*, 17, 115-116.

29. See Ch. II, notes 1, 5 and 6.

30. See Karl Rahner, "The Problem of Genetic Manipulation," *Theological Investigations* 9:225-252, and "The Experiment with Man," ibid., 205-224. This human knowledge and self-mastery creates ethical problems arising from potential abuses, such as those involved in abortions, sex changes, genetic engineering, and the prior determination of the sex of the fetus even before conception. As Socrates, positively affirmed, correct knowledge is by itself intrinsically good and to be acquired by all human beings. However, the evil person who has access to unlimited knowledge is far more dangerous to society, since he or she has more capability for greater evil and destruction, than the evil person who is ignorant

31. The questions of Destiny and those of Origin are usually inseparable in the human mind as they are by nature correlative. This is to say that human beings tend to think that the Destiny is determined by the Origin; cf. Chapter 1, notes 1, 4, 6 and 7. God is acts as the cosmic Creator, sustainer, transformer and ultimate fulfiller or completor. Consequently, Rahner argues that unless God is at the beginning of the process, such as the philosophical proofs for God's existence, that he cannot be at the end; cf. Rahner, *Foundations of Christian Faith*, 44-80; *Spirit in the World*, 67-77; *Hearers of the Word*, Chs. 5-13; Soren Kierkegaard, *Philosophical Fragments*, Ch. III (46-60).

32. Cf. E. E. Evans-Pritchard, *Theories of Primitive Religion* (Oxford: Oxford University Press, 1965), 1-9.

33. Ibid. See also Chapter I, notes 4-6.

34. See note 31 above.

35. See: Mark 6:2-3; John 6:35-66)

See also Kierkegaard's teaching on Jesus's lowliness as God incognito in humanity. Faith in God disguised as a "servant" who suffers in order to win the trust and love of his own beloved people, is a source of intellectual offence, and spiritual stumbling block. Faith is irrational according to the laws of logic, and the empirical sciences. This is the kind of Christianity's intellectual absurdity which can only be transcended by an active "leap of faith." See the *Philosophical Fragments*, translated by Howard V. Hong (Princeton: Princeton University Press, 1974), 37-45; *Training in Christianity*, translated by Walter Lowrie (Princeton: Princeton University Press, 1972) 25-26, 79-144.

36. For example, see Rahner, *Foundations of Christian Faith*, 430.

37. In this African ontological system, time reckoning, and metaphysics, tomorrow was supposed to resemble the past and only a few days or months were projected into the future, and planned for accordingly, instead of years and decades. Generally, life was lived in the present time (*Sasa*), which embodies the remembered past (*Zamani*) and the immediate or foreseeable future; cf. John Mbiti, *African Religion and Philosophy*, 21-36. Since there was no extended future dimension and the primary focus was on the golden past (*Zamani*) rather than the unknown future, Africans tended to live a static life oriented to the past. Consequently, there was no technological advancement. As a result, there were no permanent buildings built except in Egypt and the Zimbabwe stone city walls.

The Western linear concept of time has advantages. It leads to a future-oriented modality of life, open to change, innovation and a conscious process towards the realization of the projected or perceived goals, dreams utopias, hence leading to a forward movement in civilization or a creative advance, innovation and technological development in the West.

38. Cf. Karl Rahner, "The Concept of Mystery in Catholic Theology," *Theological Investigations* 4:37-73; *Hearers of the Word*, Chs. 5-13; *Foundations of Christian Faith*, 44-89; *Grace in Freedom*, 183-196. See also Chapter I, note 4.

39. Ibid.

40. Some of chimps are even trained to perform for television commercials and to star in a variety of movies, such as "Born Free," "Lassie Come Home," "Tarzan of the Apes," "Grizzle Ben," and "The Wild and the Free."

41. The human socialization of the young cannot be compared to the programming of the computer or the training of a chimpanzee. Human instruction of the young leads to both conditioning and understanding, whereas the training of the chimpanzee is mainly conditioning it to behave or react in a specific way in a given specific situation. On the contrary, for human beings, education is, on the contrary, supposed to cultivate responsible and imaginative behavior or activity and originality.

42. Ibid. Human beings possess personal freedom, knowledge, intellect, language, religion and moral responsibility, in contrast to animals, who generally lack them or posses them at a very low level that is not significant enough to affect their way of life as animals.

43. See Ch. II, notes 1, 5 and 7.

44. See note 25 above. These repressed unhappy experiences end up causing mental diseases unless they are given positive release or another acceptable outlet.

45. Kierkegaard has most vividly described this statement of *Angst* in his books, *Fear and Trembling* and *The Sickness Unto Death*. This is basically a human condition in which the subject is aware of his or her vulnerability and finitude. Kierkegaard's solution is the human acceptance of God as the Infinite Ground of finitude. This submission to God is not just a total surrender in worship, but also a "leap of faith" into this Mystery he perceives to be God and Savior; cf. *Philosophical Fragments*, Ch. II; *Training in Christianity*, 122 ff., 144; *The Unscientific Postscript*, 186 ff. This human surrender to God in the "leap of faith" is what Schleiermacher describes as the human awareness of "absolute dependence;" see *The Christian Faith*, ed. H.R. Mackintosh (Philadelphia: Fortress, 1977), 12-19, 34, 40 and 125.

46. Cf. Ludwig Feuerbach, *The Essence of Christianity,* trans. George Elliot (New York: Harper and Row, 1957), xxxvi, 50, 120-134, 270-336; *The Essence of Religion*, 17-25, 140-285. Freud followed Feuerbach in his interpretation of religion as an illusion.

47. Both Feuerbach and Freud are probably right in affirming that human needs, ideals and human projection are worked into most people's theology as crude idols, as anthropomorphism clearly illustrates. Rahner would argue that this human failure to represent God adequately in both thought and language should be expected, since God is by definition incomprehensible, creative, transforming, infinitely Transcendent holy Mystery.

48. It is necessary that the God of worship who must be the Creator should also be capable of loving his creation and powerful enough to save his people from evil and the threat of chaos and premature death. The Hebrew *"Schema"* (Deut. 6:4-5) is placed in the context of divine salvation history (Exod. 1-20). Israel's concrete historical experience of God's free grace, and redemption in the exodus event from bondage in Egypt, is the concrete, moral, mythical and theological background, context and historical grounding for Judaism and the Ten Commandments which are its center. We hear the following religious affirmation, "and God spoke all these words saying, "I am the Lord the God, who have brought thee out of the land of Egypt, out of the house of bondage. Thou shalt have no other gods before me." (Exod. 20:1-3, K.J.V.).

49. Sin is the human state of free resistance against God, or defection from his or her ultimate Destiny. Cf. Karl Rahner,*Foundations of Christian Faith*, 44-137; *Opportunities for Faith*, 79-108; Pannenberg, *What is Man?*, 54-67; Paul Tillich, *Dynamics of Faith*(New York: Harper & Row, 1957), 1-29; *Systematic Theology* 3:11-110; Jurgen Moltman, *Man*, 16-45, 105-119; Reinhold Niebuhr, *The Nature and Destiny of Man* 1:54 ff., 296 ff.

50. E.g., see Karl Rahner, *Grace in Freedom*, 203-264; "The Theology of Freedom," *Theological Investigations* 6:178-196; "On the Dignity and Freedom of Man," ibid. 2:235-263. Rahner asserts that the Christian should be the divine ambassador and harbinger of freedom in the world so as to enhance human rights and to enhance human rights and to encourage a more positive process of humanization of humankind and the world in which we

live. He emphasizes that agape for neighbor is the guiding principle and the basis of Christian community, freedom and socio-political activity in the world. Accordingly, Whitehead is insightful when he attributes Western civilization to be a growth in freedom due to Christianity, which teaches that love and persuasion are preferable to the use of force; cf. *Adventures in Ideas*, 26-86. Similarly, Whitehead views slavery as the worst social evil and case of inhumanity, as it deprives other people of their rights and freedoms which constitute them as human beings. See: Whitehead, *Process and Reality*, Part II, Chs.VII-X; Part III.

51. Rahner argues that inasmuch as human beings are free, moral and knowing creatures, they must also accept the concomitant consequences and responsibility for their freedom, knowledge and inevitable choice in their daily lives. Therefore, it is not responsible to drift through life in order either to avoid choosing for fear of consequences or to shrink back from responsibility for one's choice, be it good or bad.

52. Cf. Anita Roper, *The Anonymous Christian*, 126-137. See also Kierkegaard's pointed book, *Either/Or*, especially the last section; Karl Rahner, *Faith Today* (London: Sheed and Ward, Order of Creation and the Order of Redemption," *The Christian Commitment* (London: Sheed and Ward, Ltd., 1963), 44-55.

53. See *Hearers of the Word*, entire book, with special attention to Chs. 5-13; *Foundation of Christian Faith*, 24-115; *Hominization*, 62-110; Ch. I, notes 6 and 7, above.

54. Karl Rahner, *Foundation of Christian Faith*, 20-21.

55. Cf. Martin Heidegger, "Being and Time," *Martin Heidegger: Basic Writings*, ed. David Farrell Krell (New York: Harper & Row, 1977), 41-89; "The End of philosophy and the Task of Thinking," ibid., 373-392. See also Karl Rahner, *Foundations of Christian Faith*, 24-115; *Hearers of the Word*, entire book; *Spirit in the World*, 57-230, 279-308, 387-408.

56. Ibid. There must be some kind of affinity between God and the human being that enables meaningful communication between them, love, fellowship and community. The writer of Genesis affirms this same basic truth when he states that God created man both male and female in his own image (Gen. 1:26-27). The Pentateuch affirms that God made a covenant between himself and Israel (cf. Exod. 6;4, 19:5, etc.), whereas the New Testament says that "God (Logos) became man" (John 1: 1-14, 3:16, etc.). Due to the Incarnation and by virtue of this "Hypostatic Union," it can be affirmed that "God became man" and likewise, "man has become God!" See Athanasius, *On the Incarnation*, 54: "Immortality has reached to all, and that by the Word becoming man, the universal providence has been known, and its giver and artificer the very Word of God. For he was made man that we might be made God." (Cited in *Christology of the Later Fathers*,ed. Edward R. Hardy (Philadelphia: The Westminster Press, 1954), 107).

57. See notes 50, 51, 55 and 56 above.

58. Karl Rahner, *Hearers of the Word*, ending of Ch. 5; *A Rahner Reader*, ed. Gerald A. McCool (New York: The Seabury Press, 1957), 20-21.

59. Ibid.

60. See St. Augustine's *Confessions*, I-X; Phil. 3:7-9; Romans 7:15-25. Things such as pleasure, romance, sex, food, drugs, wealth and success will probably not fill this emptiness

or void felt at the very center of the human being. This kind of escapism eventually proves futile as this emptiness can become even more accentuated, sometimes leading to drug addiction and despair.

61. See Karl Rahner, *Hearers of the Word*, Ch. 3; *Spirit in the World*, 379-408; *Foundation of Christian Faith*, 51-70.

62. Cf. Karl Rahner,*Foundations of Christian Faith*, 14-175; 311-321. See also Chapter I, notes 21, 22, 81 and 91.

63. The question of what constitutes "Holy Scripture" as the definitive and authentic normative Word of God, as opposed to other forms of religious of literature, such as hymns, poetry, drama and fiction like John Banyan's book, the books of Job and Jonah, is a central issue here. Accordingly, Martin Luther did not just regard all the Old Testament and the New Testament as the holy scripture, he excluded the Apocrypha and also questioned the canonical value of some New Testament books, particularly the Epistle of James which he derogatorily referred to as the "Epistle of Straw."
Luther's special canon included the Gospels, Romans, Galatians. He preferred the New Testament to the Old Testament and in matters of doctrine the New Testament, especially, the gospels and Romans had the greatest weight. See: John Dillenberger and Claude Welch, *Protestant Christianity: Interpreted Through its Development* (New York: Charles Scribener's Sons, 1954), 45-56; Gerhard Ebeling, *Luther: An introduction to His thought* (Philadelphia: Fortress Press, 1980), 110-124; Paul Althaus, *The Theology of Martin Luther*, trans. Robert C. Schultz (Philadelphia: Fortress Press, 1979), 72-104; Paul Tillich, *A History of Christian Thought: From Its Judaic and Hellenistic Origins to Existentialism*, ed. Carl R. Braaten (New York: Simon and Schuster, 1967), 242 ff.; Rahner, *Grace in Freedom*, 95-112, and *Revelation and Tradition*, 9-49. Given this complex background, it should not be surprising, therefore, that for many Christians the Koran or Hindu and Buddhist scriptures cannot be accepted as part of the genre of literature termed God's Word or "Scripture," and respected as part of God's Word addressed to all humanity.

64. Each book in the Bible was written from a specific point of view, and from a specific historical or social context. The epistles contain valuable evidence of the issues they were written to deal with, namely, divisions, heresy and discipline (cf. 1 Cor. 1:10-17, 5:1, 15:1-3 and 12-20; Gal. 1:6-9, 3:1-5; 2 Thess. 1:5-12, 3:6-15; 1 John 1:9-10, 2:18-27, etc.).

65. See previous note above.

66. See notes 56, 63 and 64 above.

67. Ibid.

68. Karl Barth, *Church Dogmatics* 1:1, especially p. 136. See also Klaas Runia, Karl Barth's Doctrine of Holy Scripture (Grand Rapids: Eerdman's Publishing Co., 1962), 4 ff.

69. See notes 1, 3, 6, 31, 50 and 64 above.

70. See Karl Rahner, *Foundations of Christian Faith*, 24-175; *Grace in Freedom*, 69-94; *Opportunities for Faith*, 7-122; *Faith Today* (entire book); *Hearers of the Word*, Chs. 5-13; *Christian at the Crossroads*, 45-81; *Prayers and meditations* 111 ff. The stage of life both human and supernatural, the life of both salvation or perdition, is the everyday life. The

ordinary human life and existence is the stage and the means of human encounter with the divine or the extraordinary. This is the encounter with God who exists in dynamic energy or process as both in self-communication in continuing creation and salvation. This is a universal phenomenon which accounts for religion wherever people have existed.

71. See Leo J. O'Donovan, ed., *A World of Grace*, viii; notes 3, 6, 26, 55, 63 and 64 above. See also Chapter 1, notes 4, 5 and 58.

72. Ibid. See also Karl Rahner, *Foundation of Christian Faith*, 212-228; *Christology Today?*; "Jesus Christ in the Question about Man," *Theological Investigations* 17:24-70; Emil Brunner, *Man in Revolt*, 98 ff.; Karl Barth, *Church Dogmatics*, 3:2; Pannenberg, *Human Nature, Election and History*, 13-61; Moltmann, *Man*, 1-45, 105-119. However, this is not a concept that is unique to christianity. For instance, Mahatma Gandhi, the famous Hindu mystic who successfully mobilized the Indian peaceful mass nationalist (Satygraha) protest against the British colonial occupation of India, affirmed that he experienced God in the midst of social and political as well as religious action, and that he saw God wherever his fellow human beings were and in whatever activities they were engaged as such. For instance, Gandhi wrote the following in his *Harijan* periodical:

Man's ultimate goal is the realization of God, and all his activities, social, political and religious have to be guided by the ultimate aim of the vision of God. The immediate service of all human beings becomes a necessary part of the endeavor simply because *the only way to find God is to see him in his creation and to be one with it* [emphasis his own]. This can only be done by service to all. I am part and parcel of the whole and I cannot find him apart from the rest of humanity. My countrymen are my nearest neighbors. They have become helpless, so inert that I must concentrate on serving them...*I know I can not find him* [God] *apart from humanity*. (Cited in William Johnson, *The Inner Eye of Love* (New York: Harper & Row, Publishers, 1978), 26.

73. E.g, see William C Sherpard, *Man's Condition: God and the World Process* (New York: Herder and Herder, 1969, 31-96, 229-264; Karl Rahner, "The Order of Redemption within the Order of Creation," *The Christian Commitment*, 38-74; "Nature and Grace," *Nature and Grace*, 114-149; "Concerning the Relationship between Nature and Grace," *Theological Investigations* 1:297-317; "Some Implications of the Scholastic concept of Uncreated Grace, ibid., 319-346; "The Theological Concept of Concupiscentia," ibid., 347-382; "Reflections on the Experience of Grace," *Theological Investigations* 3:86-90; "Nature and Grace," *Theological Investigations* 4:165-188; "The 'Existential'," *Sacramentum Mundi* 2:304-307; "Grace," ibid., 412-427; "Potentia Oboedientials," *Sacramentum Mundi* 5:65-67; "Salvation (Universal Salvific Will)," ibid., 405-409. See also Regina Bechtle, "Rahner's Supernatural Existential," *Thought* 48 (1973), 61-77; Kenneth D. Eberhard, "Karl Rahner and the Supernatural Existential," *Thought* 46 (1971), 537-561; J. P. Kenny, "Reflections on Human Nature and the Supernatural," *Theological Studies* 14 (1953), 280-287; Thomas Motherway, "Supernatural Existential," *Chicago Studies* 4 (1965), 79-103; Carl J. Peter, The Position of Karl Rahner Regarding the Supernatural: A Comparative Study of Nature and Grace," *Proceedings of the Catholic Theological Society of America* 20 (1965), 81-84.

74. Ibid. See notes 17 and 50 above.

75. See notes 1, 2, 63, and 72 above.

76. See Ch. II, notes 9, 21, 36, 80, and 91. See also note 73 above.

77. Cf. John Calvin, *Institutes*, 111; Karl Rahner, *Foundations of Christian Faith*, 146 ff.; see also note 73 above.

78. Karl Rahner, *Foundations of Christian Faith*, 146-147.

79. Ibid.

80. See notes 63, 64, 73 and 76 above; K. Rahner, *Foundations of Christian Faith*, 228:

In this understanding, God and the grace of Christ are present as the secret essence of every reality we can choose...it is not so easy to opt for something without having to do with God and Christ either by believing or nor believing...anyone who accepts his existence in patient silence (or, better, in faith, hope and love), accepts it as the mystery of eternal love and which bears life in the womb of death, is saying "yes" to Christ even if he does not know it.

VI

THE AFRICAN CONCEPT OF GOD AS BASIS FOR UNDERSTANDING CREATION, HUMAN AUTHENTIC EXISTENCE AND SALVATION: AGAPE, WELL-BEING, HARMONY AND PEACE (*SHALOM/MIREMBE* AND *MAGARA*)

Human beings or "*homo sapiens*" are God's unique, intelligent, free, thinking, moral agents and special creative creatures in the world. All human beings are unique two-natured beings. They simultaneously belong to both the biological animal (natural) kingdom, just like any other bodied creatures, and as divine historical spirits, and unlike any other species of animals, human beings as "*homo sapiens*" and "*imago Dei*," are also akin to God. They are supernatural. And they belong to God's spiritual or moral kingdom. Subsequently, all human beings are by special quintessential divine nature free, thinking, knowing, self-transcending spirits, social moral agents.

These "*homo sapiens*" have been created through God's processes of creation through the slow processes of biological evolution of animal life into mind as the "*homo sapiens*." However, this evolutionary process is essentially also both correlatively and coextensively, both a natural and a supernatural process of evolution and divinization. In other words, this is an interrelated natural-supernatural or twin divine process in which there is an intrinsic correlative evolution of the animal into a self-transcendent spirit, mind, "*imago Dei*" and the adopted child of God in the world.

As "*imago Dei*," all human beings everywhere in the cosmos are by an essential intrinsic "*a priori*" fundamental divine-human nature intelligent, social, linguistic, communicative, story-telling, relational, religious, free, moral and responsible loving beings.

Human beings are theocentric, cultural, moral, celebrative, social and community based religious creatures. This is, particularly, true of traditional Africans. The individual's creation, growth, continuing meaningful existence, and fulfillment were completely social and rooted in the local existence of the human community and its well-being. That is, for the African, the local human community and its general well-being are central God's arena, sacrament and instrument of supernatural creation, socialization or humanization, redemption, deification and immortality of the individual human being, as a humane and constitutive primary member of the community.

In this understanding, the human community is organically analogous to the human body. Subsequently, the body's respective constitutive individual cells are also analogous to various individual human beings and their different roles as constitutive members of the respective community. There is a mutual interdependence between the body and the various constitutive parts or members. For instance, the respective individual body cells derive their own existence, life and nurture from the body.

However, it is only when functioning collectively as a group or total sum of body's cells working together in harmonious relationships that the visible body emerges within the world. The body is actually a complex single society or community of these collective cells. Like in all stable societies and communities, there is a requirement for peace and well-being in the body as the organic community of cells, is the strict observance of law and order and the promotion of good communication, equitable sharing, justice and harmony among the various competing members of the community.

In human communities love, justice, equitable sharing of resources and hard work are some of the prerequisites for a well organized system or healthy society. Otherwise, without this kind of harmonious relationship in the community, there maybe a raise of moral or societal evil in the form of rebellion, crime, conflict and mutual destruction. For instance, lack of good communication among the body cells may result in cancer. This form of organic evil occurs in the body and the total body dies, unless the contaminated cell and the original or secondary offenders are immediately removed from the body.

In turn, the body gets existence from its well ordered, healthy specialized cells, and their timely death and replacement by some fresh and healthy ones. As such, like God, in essence the community prior to the creation, existence and well-being of the individual. Creation, redemption, and the kingdom of God are for the African inseparable from the harmonious life and well-being of the temporal human community. In this context, the human community is analogous to the redemptive microcosmic "Ark of

Noah." Therefore, God must redeem the human community in order to redeem its individual constitutive members.

The loving and harmonious human community is God's concrete arena for creation, redemption, salvation, peace and happiness. As such, the human community is also the universal divine "locus" for all God's supernatural creative, and redemptive activities in relation to the human being. Therefore, God is concretely experienced in creation, preservation, punishment, redemption, and blessings as part of the local harmonious human, ancestral or spiritual community, and the concrete natural world. The world itself is a community of beings and sub-communities of its creatures, such as, the animals, trees, mountains, rivers, lakes, and space along with its billions of inhabitants in the form of the sun, the moon, the planets and the innumerable stars.

Nevertheless, Africans put a great emphasis on the local human community as opposed to the sky and its extraterrestrial beings. Human beings are culturally and linguistically diverse. Despite, the apparent superficial physical, cultural, religious, linguistic, gender and color differences, all human beings are essentially members of a single race of God's people. However, many people tend to get confused because the human race is divided into exclusive different skin colors or races, nations, tribes pr ethnic groups, and local linguistic or cultural groups.

Each culturally distinct group of human beings anywhere and everywhere, in the cosmos has it's own stories or myths of creation or the genesis of the cosmos and an explanation of how they came to be a special elect people of God the Creator. The stories of creation have a correlative secondary unpleasant part on the subject of human disobedience to the Creator's commandments or moral law or will, and the entry of imperfection, evil and death into God's perfect creation.

For the ancient monotheistic Hebrews, the myths of creation and the fall include God's creation of Adam and Eve. In this patriarchal creation and fall myth, naturally, evil as sin and disobedience against the primordial Patriarch God, is blamed on women. This is theologically achieved by blaming Eve as the scapegoat for the cosmic, and all human, moral and intellectual weakness, including temptation and disobedience against God's will and commandments.

Similarly, the monotheistic and patriarchal Ugandan stories of primordial creation and fall include Kintu (Adam) and Nnambi (Eve). Nnambi, just like Eve disobeys God's moral law. This is similar to the book of Genesis. Evil, suffering, pain and death enter God's originally perfect world as a result of human (woman's) disobedience against God through the original primordial rebellious woman! Original sin in both patriarchal Africa and the Bible is associated a woman.

These myths and stories of creation and the fall in Genesis and outside the Bible, are all the same, in social and religious purpose, function and effects. They are all theologically and culturally legitimate and valid vehicles for God's revelation. They are religiously definitive for the people who believe in them. They are guide for those who live by their moral guidance, and directives. They contain guidance for social interaction within society as children of God, who fear God, respect one another, and the environment as God's sacred creation. These creation and fall stories are neither historical nor scientific. They are mere societal myths, and spiritual maps for a moral and godly life.

These stories are timeless religious and ultimate cultural explanations of why the human being, the community and world exist by virtue of unmerited free grace in creation. At the same time, they also, simultaneously, explain why creation, life and humanity, now universally exist in a state of imperfection, dislocation and discord. As such, all human stories and myths of creation and the fall point to the existence of a good God who is a Cosmic creative holy Mystery, from whom creation is alienated due to the misuse of freedom and sin, and to whom all creation and particularly, the human beings yearns for return in fellowship of love (agape) through God's own acts of grace in recreation or redemption and supernatural salvation.

1. The General Conception of God

Ultimately, God is a nameless, omnidimensional, multimedia, absolutely Transcendent Creative-Redemptive Cosmic Mystery, whose existence has remained the universal, holy Infinite Mystery (Amen/Amun or Yahweh).

This nameless holy, Cosmic, Creative-Redemptive and Transcendent Mystery is the very Creator-Redeemer God who is praised and worshipped in African Religion, Mosaic Judaism, Islam, Native American Religions, Buddhism, and Hinduism. Even Christianity which claims to possess the definitive revelation of God in the Incarnation through Jesus as the Christ, does not posses any more insights into God's basic nature, any more than any other revealed religions, apart from its special emphasis of God's essence as forgiving and redemptive Agape and "*Sola Gratia*" (cf. Rom. 1-7; John 1-3; 1 John 3:7-21).

In a more crude theological analysis and the literal meaning of the Incarnation, it could also be the affirmation that the authentic and Agapic human being is more than just *"imago Dei."* For instance, it could be affirmed that the human being is, in fact, the very essential permanent Incarnation of God himself in the material world! After all, Jesus as both the man of Nazareth, the carpenter and Rabbi is also traditionally affirmed by orthodox Western Christianity to have been the historical Incarnation of God in the world (John 1:1-18).

Indeed, it is theologically and morally incontrovertible, that Jesus as the Christ and moral teacher of unconditional love and free forgiveness for the neighbor, was the theophany (*Shekinah*) and moral Incarnation of God in human society, and its co-extensive existential condition, moral values, religions and history. As such, to seek Jesus and follow his teachings was, indeed, both to find and to see God the Father or the Creator. This was the meaning behind Jesus' saying that "My Father and I are one;" and "whoever has seen me has also seen my Father who is in heaven;" "I am in the Father and the Father is in me;" and "my Father does his works through me" (John 14:7-13).

The pre-Christian Africans were more like Jesus as the Christ who was in direct mystical union with God as both the cosmic Creator and also his transcendent holy redemptive Father in heaven. Unlike many Western secular humanists, agnostics and atheists, the pre-Christian theocentric and intrinsically religious traditional Africans, intimately knew God through observing the cosmos or creation and its amazing governing laws.

In addition, these African people also knew God personally and collectively through their own revelatory history, God's Word as spoken through the mediums, prophets, elders, kings and the priests. Furthermore, they also knew God through special experiences of the encounters with the divine transcendence, and the Ultimate Cosmic Mystery. Subsequently, through these channels of God's natural and special revelation, most traditional Africans came to know God, and accordingly, they taught their own offspring that God was essentially the Cosmic Creative-Redemptive Mystery and the Primordial Ancestor of human beings as his children.

However, unlike the Africans and other non-Western people, many Western intellectuals have a problem with a God who cannot be seen with a naked eye or special electronic instruments. The Western intellectuals with their secular finite minds tend to reject the traditional claims of the existence of infinite and the invisible reality, including God; unless the alleged invisible reality or spiritual existence can be definitively proved through experimentation in their own human-made laboratories. Therefore, for these people and their Western trained African disciples, any adequate, post-modernist, globally relevant and meaningful theological and philosophical ideas, doctrines and understanding of God, must be convincingly formulated within the post-modernist academic scientific context.

Accordingly, the ideas and concepts of God have to be formulated within the contemporary context of the available data, and information about human biological evolution, astrophysics, world history, world-religions, cultural anthropology, and archeology. To do otherwise, is to distort God's work in history. It is also a sinful denial or rejection of God's truth, therefore, in the name of God the cosmic Creator, to seek to perpetuate myths for history and facts. This is because, such a sinful human being dislikes the truth about God's essence, and his evolutionary method for creating the universe.

Biological and cosmic evolution is misunderstood and rejected by such religious, and theological fundamentalists, to be merely an ordinary and non-miraculous impersonal and mindless process. Instead of the appreciation of God's miraculous cosmic creativity by this slow evolution, they prefer a more instant show of God's power, by *creatio ex nihilo*.

These kinds of religious people also subscribe to the Genesis stories of creation of the universe in six literal calendar days as history of God's miraculous creation of the cosmos. Absurdly, many process theologians and philosophers, disturbingly and almost naively, also believe that like a tired human carpenter or farmer, God required some rest after his long labors of creation, and therefore, rested on the seventh day.

Thus, these religious and theological fundamentalists fail to see that this a story which originally created by the priests in order to validate or theologically justify and sanctify the already existing traditional Jewish observances of the Sabbath day as both a day of rest and worship (cf. Gen. 1-3). This crude anthropomorphism is not an acceptable viable theological or scientific option, except by people who are ignorant of modern science, biology, history and archeology.

Therefore, the absurd literalist reading of the mythical theories of creationism, and the uncritical or non-academic literal interpretation of the myths of creation as found in the biblical book of Genesis, are not academically acceptable, nor theologically sound or necessary. Here, the culprits are those theologically naive Protestant fundamentalists, and poorly theologically educated evangelicals, such as, the American Southern Baptists, the

"Balokole of East Africa," and other African fundamentalist groups and the extreme evangelical Protestants.

However, one can understand the tenacity of these evangelicals in holding on to such outdated and erroneous views and theological doctrines. This is understandable, when one realizes that these people also erroneously believe that the acceptance of evolution as God's method for the creation of the universe, correlatively amounts to the denial of God's existence and salvation. Nevertheless, acceptance of evolution and other scientific data regarding the origins and functioning of the cosmos is not to be rejected as some kind of evil or atheism, as the Church erroneously did in the infamous theological era of inquisition and Galileo. As the "Process theologians" and philosophers, such as Pierre Teilhard de Chardin, North Whitehead, John Cobb, David Griffin, Ewert Cousins, Donald Sherbourne, Charles Hartshorne and others have clearly shown in their various respective theologies and philosophies, the acceptance of evolution does not in any way nullify belief in God as creator and primordial initiator of the process of evolution.

On the contrary, the evolution of the human being, mind and moral agency among creatures, is proof of God's benevolent primordial creative existence. God's cosmic redemption of the creatures, the divine Incarnation, human salvation, God's kingdom of love, harmony and peace are correlative with both faith in God, and reason as the tool for science, knowledge and truth. Therefore, there is no theological need to avoid or reject the scientific evidence which supports evolution in order to believe in God or protect him from the evolutionists. Such a finite god is a mere idol. Therefore, this idol should be rejected by Christian theologians and great thinkers of other enlightened or intellectually sophisticated religious traditions.

A defenseless god who needs to be defended from destruction by the truth, is a mere idol. Truly, this kind of idol is what Freud rejects as a mental illusion. The this mental creation and illusion is not the primordial cosmic creator, constant preserver and redeemer. Only the Creator-Redeemer God is the true God. And only this cosmic agapic Creator and Redeemer-God, deserves human worship. This is fitting since worship is human praise for his wonder-filled work, and personal and collective thanksgiving and worship in gratefulness of this undeserved divine gift of life, beauty and mind to contemplate and appreciate it.

Scientifically, it has already been conclusively proven and irrevocably established as the truth, that East Africa is actually the origin of the *homo sapiens*, and as such, the origin of humankind.[2]

Africa as the cradle of humanity and all the human civilization; the home of Aken-Aton the Pharaoh of Egypt who invented the monotheistic doctrine, which Moses refined and gave to the Hebrews and the rest of the World, in the name of Yahweh, the "Hebraicized" version of the Egyptian Mystery God who was variously known as *"Amun," "Amen," "Amon"* and *"Ra."* These African secret mystery religious teachings which Moses (Mose) had learned as a privileged African price, and the future Egyptian Priest-King to be were later modified by Moses, and then, in the name of God (Yahweh) taught and revealed to the Hebrews as new commandments and teachings.

In essence, God's special revelation in Moses consists of these ancient African and Mediterranean region mystery religions. However, these sacred African or Egyptian secret holy mysteries were further monotheistically refined and redefined in the Ten Commandments and the Torah as the foundations of Israel's new relationship with God, the community and the neighboring people, who were despised as idolatrous polytheists. This new Hebrew special relationship with God is metaphorically referred to as "the new covenant" or "election" as a special group of people whose common religious and societal moral, political and liturgical bond will be the Law of Moses and the common religious tradition as worshippers of Yahweh as the redefined Amun. However, unlike Amun or Amen-Ra, Yahweh was affirmed to be the one Creator-Redeemer God, who had no other associate gods, as the Egyptians and other Africans had taught.

In much of Africa, particularly, Egypt, the sun was his heavenly symbol of God. And the Pharaoh as the supreme emperor of the earth was considered to be God's earthly symbol, concrete Supreme Pontiff or Priest-King, visible temporal representative and ultimate "Vicar of God" on earth. This was the theological and political context of education of Moses as Prince and future African high Priest-King, rebelled, and instead turned into the great prophet and lawgiver of Israel.[3] Because of its theological centrality, Africa is mythologically portrayed as the refuge of the infant Jesus and his parents, from where God was supposed to call his son.[4]

In addition, Africa is the great patron and producer of great philosophers and Christian theologian bishops. These great African theologians and philosophers have been documented in Western theology and philosophy as the foundations of western thought. These world intellectual giants from Africa, include the Church Fathers, such as Bishop Cyprian and St. Augustine, and famous laymen such as Tertullian, Novatus and Donatus, has been given little attention by Western scholars in the past, largely because of racism and color-prejudice. Consequently, for many of these prejudiced Western White scholars, Africa has remained the "Dark Continent."[5]

This is especially true of Africa south of the Sahara, which became isolated by the almost insurmountable harsh barrier of the Sahara desert which stretches hundreds of miles between North Africa and the rest of Africa south of this huge the desert. However, North Africa was always in trade and religious contacts with the region south of the Sahara.

As we now know, there were well-established trade caravan routes between these two regions of Africa, going back before the time of the Roman empire, which included North Africa. Moreover, the Sahara desert itself was never so wide as it is now. Hannibal's African elephants as tropical animals indicates this ancient African trade, military and religious sub-Saharan connections.

Furthermore, the rock drawings and archaeological findings in the Sahara desert yield plenty of irrefutable evidence that the present desert itself was once a fertile land with rivers, and lakes greatly populated with aquatic creatures, such as fish and hippos.[6] Consequently, the Western popular rigid and exclusive division of Africa between North Africa and the rest of Africa can be said to be rather superficial and, as such, untenable.[7]

However, whereas North Africa became internationally linked with the Mediterranean civilization, and subsequently became Christian during the Apostolic era, and later became Muslim in the seventh century as a result of Arab conquest and the African desire to be independent of the Roman imperialism, Africa south of the Sahara remained largely traditionalist until the last two decades of the nineteenth century. Nevertheless, prior to the arrival of *Dini*[8] (foreign religions), Africans were very religious, loving, virtuous and God fearing people. They had their own effectively functional religion, with a system of beliefs and practices or rituals, both individual/private and collective/public, that regulated life, both secular and religious.[9]

The pre-Christian and pre-Islamic Africans had a sound, noble and deep religious understanding of humanity, God and community. Human finitude, existence and vulnerability were attributed to the omnipresent threat of evil forces in the guise of malevolent evil spirits, witchcraft, misfortune, illness, disasters, such as droughts, famines, accidents, floods, fires, injury, wars, etc., and the need for supernatural intervention to avert the evil and save the human beings from pain, harm and destruction.[10]

Therefore, the African Traditional Religion is the context for African philosophy, anthropology, and soteriology. The African metaphysics, world-view and ontology are contextually grounded in and determined by this all-pervasive African Traditional Religion. Unlike Western dualistic Christianity, and like monistic Islam, African Religion permeates all the departments of African life and orients traditional Africans to the divine presence of the Incomprehensible Mystery in whatever place and situation the person happens to find himself or herself.

Tragically, many Western observers and analysts viewed Africa from a Darwinist and White-supremacist ethnocentric perspectives. As a result, they characteristically misinterpreted and misrepresented this African religiosity, and understanding of God's cosmic omnipresence and immanence as manifested in the doctrines, life and values as "animism," "superstition" and "paganism." Consequently, much of the redemptively practical and moral aspects of African Religion were rejected for being "all-God-pervasive (or Spirit-pervasive).

The intrinsic African theocentric cultural world-view or religious orientation was rejected by Western secularists and Darwinists. Subsequently, it was caricatured and misrepresented in Western literature as "primitive superstition," and "heathenism" to be saved from by the Western Christian missionaries. Nevertheless, the positive and redemptive intrinsic grace and reality of the African Religion or positive aspects of its cultural or moral nature and significance, could not thereby be removed by these people. It is God who both creates and redeems all his people in the world.

Therefore, it is remarkable that even when the traditional African Religion was persecuted and tarnished in reputation, nevertheless, it survived and still remains one of God's chosen viable instruments for temporal mediation of his supernatural redemptive grace, and salvation in the world. This is still the case, today, despite these Christian missionary attempts to eliminate or degrade it by this kind of colonialist and Western ethnocentric misrepresentation of non-Western institutions due to ignorance, and racism or White-supremacy. Western missionaries launched a cultural and religious assault against the African Religion and world-view by denigrating it in derogatory terms, such as "pagan," "superstition," "primitive," "magic," "ancestor worship," "devilish," or animism."[11]

Unfortunately, due to this kind of destructive Western Christianity and colonialism in the world, particularly, Africa, non-Christian religions came to be viewed as inferior and non-redemptive religions to be superseded by both Christianity and European culture. Western missionary work, education and colonialism were often intertwined and presented to the colonized people as God's will and means for civilization and salvation. This model worked well among Africans and the surviving American Native Americans. It was tragic because many African and Native American converts to Christianity believed these destructive, White-supremacist negative teachings and hated themselves and their own cultures; and then in vain tried hard to become "White" or European-like, in order to be acceptable to God, "obtain salvation through Jesus-Christ" and become civilized!

2. The Non-Explicit and Flexible Nature of
the African Traditional Religion

The African Religion, unlike Judaism, Christianity, Islam, Hinduism, and Buddhism, does no have any fixed canon in the form of sacred books in the form of written Scriptures. It's scriptures exist a flexible oral and an open canon. This African open canon is oriented to God's continuing supernatural activities of revelation in both cosmic creation and redemption. Secondly, the African Religion has no individual founder nor reformers (with the exception of individual cults).[12] Thirdly, unlike dogmatic Christianity, Judaism, and Islam, African Religion does have any definitive creeds or dogmas governing or limiting African beliefs or practice. As a result, there is no uniformity or orthodoxy, and heresy in African Religion.

There is great flexibility and tolerance for pluralism in beliefs, practices and rituals, as there is no one dogmatic way of doing things. In African Traditional Religion there is great inclusiveness for diverse beliefs and even apparent contradictory practices, since there is neither orthodoxy nor heresy. Whatever ritual or belief functions best in at a given time, in any given local community, and if it is meaningful or convenient, it is adopted. This may be the case even if it may mean that other rituals, and beliefs may have to be ignored, until they are required to meet a specific need.

As a result, the main distinguishing feature of the African traditional religion is that there is an absence of heretics and atheists.[13] For Africans, all human beings are considered religious creatures, regardless of whether those people know they are religious or not; and whether they practice any religion or not. For most traditional Africans, authentic human life and harmonious human existence were inseparable from God as their true source and grounding. Subsequently, these divine gifts were also considered religious dimensions or modes of being in the world.

Traditionally, African people generally believed, that being religious was co-extensive with being human, and for that matter, they did not attempt any missionary activity among other people they came in contact with, whether African or foreigners, since they believed that each human being has some kind of religion. Nevertheless, there was the mutual borrowing and exchange of religious ideas and the abandonment of the old dysfunctional and ineffective cults and the spreading of new ones such as the Nyabingi cult in Kigezi, Ankole and Rwanda at the turn of this century.

However, the traditional African people never converted from their own traditional religion to another form of African traditional religion because religion was inseparable from their own culture and probably because they realized that all the African traditional religious cults and practices were basically different aspects of the same religion in its complex diversity and pluralism both in beliefs and practices. This phenomenon and complexity of the African religion is described by Aylward Shorter in reference to the debate among African scholars on the subject. He writes:

> More common, perhaps, is a third approach, followed by writers who explicitly declare their faith in the basic unity and comparability of African religious traditions. Their hypothesis is based usually upon impressions gained from wide reading, travel or discussion, but it is not systematically elaborated or tested out. For Professor Abraham there is a basic 'paradigm' which justifies his study of the Akan religious system as representative of all other African religions. For Professor Mbiti African religions are many, but they all derive from, and subscribe to, a basic religious philosophy. For Canon Taylor there is, in Africa south of the Sahara, 'a basic world-view which fundamentally is everywhere the same,' while for Professor Idowu there is a 'common factor' or 'common Africanness' behind African religion. Faith in, or intuition of, this common unity then allows these authors to enumerate instances on grounds of similarity.[14]

In support of Idowu, it can be pointed out, for instance, that the Africans consider the African traditional religion an *a priori* in one's given community and ethnic group. Mbiti, also realizes this fact that, for instance, one is born a Mukiga or a Munyankole and is, subsequently, brought up as such. In short, one is born and nurtured in the religious tradition of the society into which he or she is born or adopted. This theocentric and intrinsic inclusive religious training is simultaneously carried out through the usual normal process of socialization and humanization of the young into morally responsible human beings (*Abantu*).

Like Judaism or Hinduism, one has to be an African in order to belong to the African Traditional Religion, as it is by nature the main element for the grounding of Africanness as such. It does not only determine and orient us to the omnipresence of the awe-inspiring Supernatural, Holy Infinite,

Incomprehensible Mystery that encompasses us as the ocean water encompasses the fish; but it also acts as the effective epistemological filter for our knowledge, being the main grounding principle of the African world view and metaphysics, since for the African, God's universe is basically a religious universe.[15]

Consequently, Africans, regardless of whether they are well educated, Muslim or Christian, tend to fear evil spirits, witchcraft and sorcery. They also tend to attribute natural disasters such as lightning, drought and floods to these malignant evil spirits, hatred and witchcraft, mainly due to the implicit conditioning received from the African Traditional Religion. As a result, many well-educated Christians consciously or unconsciously still live in two worlds, one western and Christian or Islamic and the other African, determined and regulated by African Traditional Religion.[16]

Subsequently, many African Christians go to Church on Sunday morning, and African Muslims go to the mosque on friday afternoons, and the rest of the week's six days and a half are lived in the guidance and practice of the African Traditional Religion! Christians still visit the diviners and the "*Bafumu*" ("medicine-men" and "witch-doctors") for the purpose of divination, diagnosis and healing or obtaining protective medicine against witchcraft and misfortune.[17]

This means that the African Traditional Religion, which has been identified as the grounding of our Africanness, has withstood the pressure of foreign invading religions from turning the African into either a "Black European" or a "Black Arab." Therefore, it can be said that the African Traditional Religion has in some cases accommodated both Christianity and Islam without being overwhelmed or abandoned by the apparent African conversion to these foreign religions.

However, with time and the gradual Westernization of Africa and the current rapid change due to secular education, modern economy and international politics, one is bound to predict an eventual extinction of the African Traditional Religion in its traditional form, but it would probably survive in the "respectable guise" of an African version of Christianity and an Africanized Islam.[18]

It has been pointed out that the African Traditional Religion was so much all-pervasive and so identical to African life itself that it was hardly conscious of itself as a religion! The term or word "*Dini*" which is an Arab-Swahili word adopted in East Africa for religion. Characteristically, the term "*Dini*" or religion denotes only the foreign religions (Islam and Christianity), mainly because the Africans in this area never referred to their own traditional religious practices as constituting a separate social or religious institution called "religion."

In African traditional society and its modes of daily life, God or religion was the central component of life and society. God and the sacred realm were inseparable from life in the same way heat and fire are inseparable. In the African ontological and philosophical understanding and functional theocentric world-view, the human being existed in God's sacred realm or "kingdom." Subsequently, all of life was regarded as sacred and therefore, to be daily hallowed and sanctified.

As a result of this theocentric world-view, religion was regarded as a God-given way (*yoga*) of authentic daily life, culture, rituals (ordinances), harmonious collective life in the community, humane values (buntu or agape) and divine commandments (laws) that enhanced the vitality, general human and societal well-being, happiness and the enrichment of the goodness of life.[19] However, there were several additional religious cults which individuals could elect to belong to, in addition to their own basic African Traditional Religion which was usually co-extensive and sometimes identical with the tribal way of life.[20]

These cults were given names such as Emandwa, Nyabingi, Kasente and Ryangombe in Ankole and Kigezi. As these cults were optional, no one was ever forced to be initiated into them although the Ryangombe cult probably tried to coerce people indirectly to join it by preaching that those who were not initiated into it by the time of their death would be judged, when they died. It was strongly affirmed that the non-initiates would be posthumously judged on God' behalf by Ryangombe as his eschatological agent (or the Christ). Those found to be unrepentant disobedient sinners and as rebels against him, would be thrown into the fires of the Birunga Volcanic Mountains, while the initiates enjoyed bliss in fellowship with the Imaana (God) and Ryangombe as Lord in the more beautiful and cooler ranges of the Birunga Mountains.[21]

It is also these very same religious people who even believe in Ruhanga or Katonda as the omniscient and omnipotent creator *ex nihilo* and who are also described by Professor Mbiti as "incurably religious," who if asked the question, "What is your religion?" then reply, "I have no religion," unless they have been converted to either Islam or Christianity.[22] Others will even claim that they are "*Bakafiri" (Kaffir)*, an Arabic derogatory word meaning an infidel (or *pagan*) because they have been made to believe that is what their religious state is![23]

This kind of imperialistic missionary attitude and the denigration of the African traditional religion was sometimes also prompted by the fact that these "African people had no religion" that the foreigners could readily recognize as a religion, since it was on the whole unorganized, with no imposing features such as temples, books, creeds, hierarchy, and regular worship meetings. Whereas the travelers and explorers often wrote about the bizarre religious practices of the "primitive peoples" they encountered on their adventures in Africa, Professor E. E. Evans-Pritchard cautions us:

> What travelers liked to put on paper was what struck them as curious, crude, and sensational. Magic, barbaric religious rites, superstitious beliefs, took precedence over daily empirical, humdrum routines which comprise nine-tenths of the life of the primitive man and his chief interest and concern...[24]

Having discredited these sources as ethnocentric, prejudiced and unreliable, Evans-Pritchard goes on to evaluate western missionary literature on African religion in the same way, though he admits that this category of literature is more reliable and less distorted in favor of the sensational than the first category. However, he makes the following apt remark concerning all the literature on the African Traditional Religion:

> Statements about a people's religious beliefs must always be treated with the greatest caution, for we are then dealing with what neither European nor native can directly observe, with conceptions, images, words, which require for understanding a thorough knowledge of a people's language and also an awareness of the entire system of ideas of which any particular belief is part, for it may be meaningless when divorced from the set of beliefs and practices to which they belong.[25]

Professor Evans-Pritchard's evaluation and critique of the western religious anthropological literature and *Theories of Primitive Religion* have been a positive influence on the study of African Traditional Religion, as it happens to be one of the major types of the so-called "primitive religion," being without sacred books, creeds, literature and dogmas to be studied by scholars, and also being the religion of a non-technological people who still live a simple rural life in their natural "habitat!"

Evans-Pritchard rejects the theories of religion that degrade "primitive religion" as either totemism, magic, or the psychological theories that try to discredit it as superstition. Or to explain it away as an illusion, or as a form of escapism and coping mechanism created by human beings as a result of fear of the unpredictable environment and vulnerability. As such, Freud and his followers dismissed religion as a mental aberration or an illusion.[26]

Evans-Pritchard's main argument against these views is that the source of the "higher religions," the universal religions such as Christianity, is the same source for other religions, be it Judaism, Islam, Buddhism, Hinduism, and so-called primitive religions, such as the African Traditional Religion. If one is attributed to mental aberration and, as such, an illusion, then all of them could be explained away in the same fashion. And if one of them is to be attributed to divine revelation, then, all of them are similarly, to be attributed to the same divine revelatory source (to some degree). Professor Evans-Pritchard puts it very vividly as follows:

> I am of course aware that theologians, classical historians, Semitic scholars, and other students of religion often ignore primitive religions as being of little account, but I take comfort in the reflection that less than a hundred years ago Max Muller was battling against the same complacently entrenched forces for the recognition of the languages and religions of India and China as important for an understanding of language and religion in general, a fight which it is true has yet to be won... but in which some advance has been made.

He goes on to elaborate the point more emphatically:

> Indeed I would go further and say that, to understand fully the nature of so-called natural religion, for nothing could have been revealed about anything if men had not already had an idea about that thing... The dichotomy between natural and revealed is false and makes for obscurity, for there is a good sense in which it may be said that all religions are religions of revelation: the world around them and their reason have everywhere revealed to men something of the divine and of their own nature and destiny. We might ponder the words of St. Augustine: 'What is now called Christian religion, has existed among the ancients, and was not absent from the beginning of the human race, until Christ came in flesh: from which time the true religion, which existed already, began to be called Christian.'[27]

3. The Hierarchy and Chain of Being

The interlacustrine Bantu people of Uganda are famous in pre-colonial history of East Africa and African history in general for their well organized successive kingdoms, the best known being Bunyoro-Kitara Empire, which is supposed at one time to have covered most of Uganda, Rwanda and Burundi, parts of Tanzania, Kenya and Ethiopia, followed by Buganda, which by Bunyoro-Bito tradition is said to be an offshoot dynasty from

Bunyoro in the same way Ankole, Rwanda, Burundi, Mpororo, Igara, Koki and Toro kingdoms, were all supposed to have had their origin directly or indirectly from the Babito Empire of Bunyoro Kitara.[28]

The historical significance of the Bunyoro-Kitara empire in much of East and Central Africa, is that all these various groups of people were in direct political, religious and cultural contact with Bunyoro. And since Bunyoro had advanced religious ideas, such as those of the One Supreme God (Kazoba-Ruhanga), whose divine qualities included, omniscience, omnipotence, creation *ex nihilo,* along with the concept of divine kingship, these religious ideas must have also spread to these areas, along with Bunyoro imperialism. This was inevitable, unless these ideas existed there before the arrival of the Banyoro imperialists. Subsequently, the various African people of Burundi, Rwanda, northern Tanzania, Western Zaire, central and western Kenya, share a common basic theology or an underlying understanding of God.

Since many people tend to correlate their political concepts with their main religious views, in as much as they aspire to become like the God they worship. However, these people also tend to conceive God anthropomorphically as King or the chief "Ancestral spirit," depending on the cultural ideals of a given society. As a result, it would therefore, be self-evident that the people of Bunyoro, Buganda, Toro, Ankole, Kigezi and Rwanda, anthropomorphically understood God or Ruhanga/Katonda to be like their great kings except in matters of magnitude, perfection, power and benevolence. As a result, in these areas God is also known a Great King of Heaven (and earth). Possibly, this is the origin of the local conception of God as a king who often opts to conduct business with mundane creatures through a chain of mediators such as kings, priests, diviners, healers and elders, except in some desperate cases of emergency, such as: despair, disaster or conflict within the society or within the chain of mediation itself, when the individual is considered free to approach God directly.

On the top of the African "chain of being," such as in the Bakiga-Banyankole (Bantu) metaphysical hierarchy, is God (Ruhanga) as the transcendent, infinite creative Mystery, followed by spiritual beings such as divinities and the good ancestral spirits (or other good spirits). Thirdly, come the Bantu (human beings); next are evil spirits (rejected by God and the good spirits because of their wicked lives while on earth); then animals, followed by the plants, then inanimate objects, and finally at the bottom of the hierarchy comes the category of space and time. This hierarchy has an implicit valuation of these categories. For instance, time being put as the least important of these categories would tend to support Professor Mbiti's observations regarding the African understanding of life.

This African conception of time would probably also explain why most Africans and the people of African descent living abroad in the African diaspora, tend to be late or appear not to be mindful of time. Obviously, these Africans are mindful of the right time or *"kairos"* as opposed to the Western linear or chronological time. In addition, Mbiti also convincingly argues that for traditional Africans future or potential time is not real or an actuality. The future has not yet attained existence or reality. This is because future time only possesses potentiality for being or probability to be realized and actualized in the present or history. Therefore, only the past and present real. The present is the only reality in which the future becomes a concrete reality in the active present or moves on to become part of the sedimentary experience, historical reality or *Zamani* period.[29]

This relative concept of time and hierarchical chain of being correlatively indicate the intrinsic value placed on each category of being by the *"Muntu"* (human being), who regards himself/herself as "the creaturely center of God's created universe."[30] Nevertheless, both relative and absolute forms of value are relatively measured against good and powerful people, such as heros, ancestors, kings and priests. However, God is the real standard and absolute measure of all things and values.

God as the Creator as embodiment of all positive values, such as goodness, love, mercy, knowledge, wisdom, reality and pure perfection is the absolute, and perfect cosmic measure of all these values. Therefore, the further away from God, the person, or thing exists, the less value it has. This is because value is derived from God, who is the Absolute Reality, origin (as creator *ex nihilo*), sustainer and perfecter of everything.[31] God is Creator-King and reigns supreme at the top of reality and Being. From the throne of God, life and being or reality comes down through the Logos, emanating down and creating a hierarchy or chain of being, followed by spiritual beings, then human beings, animals, plants, animate beings (*ebintu* or "things") and at the bottom, comes the categories of time and space.

It is also widely believed that these categories of being and modalities of existence, inasmuch as they have being (*NTU/Ozovehe*) in themselves, to some varying degree, they correspondingly participate in the universal divine *"NTU"* (BEING), which is the source and ground of all forms of being or existence.[32] Those beings that are most close to God are consequently thought to have more perfection in "*-NTU.*" This perfection is thought to manifest itself in terms of greater access to the divine infinite knowledge, a "spiritual body" that transcends the limitations of both time and space, wealth, power, beauty, great strengths, ability to heal, and greater capacity for unconditional love and uprightness.

"*Omuntu,*" inasmuch as he or she acquired human perfection by practicing "*Buntu*" (humaneness/humanness), he/she can be regarded as the categorical self-revelatory expression of divine being itself "*NTU*" in this concrete world of things (*bi-ntu*) and of space (*ha-ntu*). In this sense, "*NTU*" is not the equivalent of Aristotle's substance that constitutes actuality, but rather it is more like Heidegger's "Being" that expresses itself in beings and *Dasein* (the human being) in particular.[33]

However, "*NTU/Ozovehe*" as being or essence, is to be distinguished from becoming, which is denoted by the Runyankole-Rukiga verb "*Ku-ba*" (to be). The "*Ku-ba*" indicates a process of becoming and implies improvement or an increase in essence, perfection and value. In addition, "*Ku-ba*" can also mean that an event is coming into being or taking place, whereas "*NTU*" generally indicates a static form of being. Consequently, God as both the source and this "*NTU*" (Being or Reality) itself, is also generally thought of by these people in a static manner. For instance, Ruhanga is generally conceived of in a Thomistic kind of understanding, being omniscient, benevolent, perfect, and omnipotent.[34]

4. God as the Cosmic Creator and Transcendent Infinite Mystery

The people of Kigezi, Ankole, Toro, Bunyoro and Buganda, among other African people, are monotheistic, inasmuch as they recognize only Ruhanga or Katonda in Buganda as God the Creator (creating *ex nihilo*) and Sustainer of everything that has being or existence.[35] The term or name Ruhanga/-Katonda literally means "Creator." It is derived from the verb "*kuhanga/-kutonda*" which means "to create." In the case of God the term means that God can create *ex nihilo* or can create from pre-existing matter.

Therefore, this Bantu idea of the Cosmic Creator being God and creation as God's essence, is similar to that found in Judaism, particularly in the book of Genesis. In the book of Genesis, God calls or brings into existence the world and its various categories of beings that had no prior existence. This affirmation of creation by the Logos *ex nihilo* is unlike Plato's account of creation in the *Timaeus* where the Demiurge creates or fashions the world from pre-existent matter, following the *a priori* eternal "ideas" or "forms" as patterns like a carpenter or architect.[36]

For the Bakiga, Banyankole, Baganda, Banyoro, Batoro, and Banyarwanda and other Bantu people in this area, God is only God in as he/she or it is the primordial Cosmic Creator *ex nihilo*, and the Sustainer or continuing Creator and Redeemer of the world. In other words, whatever Being, Mystery, Spirit, Force or Power that is the Primordial cosmic Creator (Ruhanga/Katonda), is according to this African Religion, theology and philosophy, what they refer to as God.[37]

The Africans pray and worship this Creator-Sustainer and Redeemer God, in order to be sustained, preserved, delivered from evil or redeemed and blessed with good health, plenty of children, food, cattle, loving relatives, friends, peace and harmony both within the community, and the world. God is supposed to accomplish all this in the mystery of his power, love, benevolence and mercy. To this end, in this mystery of God's activities and processes, human beings, spirits, ancestors (saints and angels), priests, kings and other supernatural phenomena play an important role as God's special agents, advocates, mediators or intermediaries.

Since most Bantus use titles or nicknames for the people they respect, such as kings, priests, parents, and ancestors, instead of their real names which would be considered rude, God is treated the same way. Consequently, among the Bantu people of Africa, God is fundamentally conceived of as being an the essentially nameless, incomprehensible, creative, sustaining and redemptive Cosmic Mystery.

In Africa, God is generally referred to by his attributes, such as, Creator or "Katonda" and "Ruhanga." Unlike ordinary beings, God is the great Cosmic Ruler or King who is respectfully referred to by his titles and great works. As such, God being the transcendent Cosmic Mystery and King of the universe, has no proper names. In addition, God has no name, since a name is considered to be expressive of the essential inner nature of its bearer.[38] Therefore, the so-called names for God in this area should be more appropriately termed divine attributes and descriptions rather than God's names.[39]   For instance, in Southern and Western Uganda God is most reverently referred to ın the following in the following honorific terms:

Ruhanga: The Omnipotent Creator (i.e. capable to create *ex nihilo).*

Omuhangi/Nyamuhanga: The Creator; Ultimate Origin of everything.

Kazoba: Light/Sun and Seer of everything on earth; the Omniscient; He who makes the sun to rise or set; the Eternal One. The cause of sunrises.

Rugaba: The Great Giver of everything on earth (and similarly, the one who takes it away); the Supernatural Provider.

Mukama (we) Iguru: The Heavenly King; Lord of the heavens/sky.

Nyine Iguru: The Owner/Lord of Heaven/Sky. Sky-God.

Biheeko: The Great Being that carries everything and everyone on its back, i.e. the Omnipotent,and unconditional Sustainer of everything that has existence. An analogy is that of a ship on the sea with its assorted cargo on board, or the planet earth which carries everything on its "back."

Mukama: Cosmic King; Master, Lord and Chief.

As a characteristic example of African concepts and names of God, is that of Buganda. God is known to be an incomprehensible, transcendent Cosmic Mystery, who is the ever all-seeing cosmic Creator, Sustainer and Redeemer. Accordingly, God is variously referred to in many different honorific descriptive terms or glorification metaphors and titles, such to as:

Katonda/Ruhanga: The Creator of all visible and invisible things.

Kigingo: Creator, Master and Giver of life.

Mukama: Master/Lord; God; Owner of all things (living and non-living).

Ddunda: Supernatural Shepherd or Divine Pastor.

Lugaba: The Ultimate Divine Giver of all things. The Provider.

Ssebintu: The Owner and Master/Lord of all things. The Provider.

Lisoddene: The Great Eye that sees all things; the Omniscient one.

Nyinigguru: Owner or Lord of heaven, the sky and space. Sky-God.

Namuginga: The One who shapes or creates; the Great Architect/Designer.

Ssewannaku: The Everlasting; He who has pity on the poor, the destitute and the suffering. The Eternal One. The Primordial Cosmic Ancestor.

Gguluddene: The Great One; the One who fills the sky/heaven.

Namugereka: He who creates or arranges things and distributes them, freely according to his free will and discretion.

This African sample of the catalogue of terms, titles and "names" or attributes of God indicates a profound understanding of God as primarily being an Omniscient and Omnipotent Creator who creates *ex nihilo* (Ruhanga/Katonda), the Transcendent King/Lord, the Giver/Provider and the Protector of the weak, the needy and the poor; i.e., Ssewannaku. Nevertheless, this list shows consistently that according to these African people God is essentially an intelligent, Supreme, Eternal, Omnipotent, Infinite, Creator, Holy, Primordial Ancestor, Giver/Provider, Creative Transcendence and Incomprehensible Mystery.

Most of these people (both Christian and non-Christian) generally agree that God is an infinite and transcendent mystery. And that apart from God's own revelation or works as manifested in the historical processes of the world, particularly in creation and it's wonders and mysteries, God remains an incomprehensible transcendent mystery to be worshipped in awe, reverence and faith rather than the subject of impersonal study or detached scientific analysis and speculation alone.[40] In additions, both traditions affirm that such a mere philosophical or theological inquiry would end up in human moral frustration, skepticism, "*anomie*" and self-destructive atheism.[41]

5. Some Pre-Christian Understanding of God in Southern and Western Uganda

On my recent research trip to Uganda, during an interview with Mr. Antyeri Bintukwanga, an outstanding old man in Ankole, who is more than a hundred years old, I became aware for the first time that in the traditional speculation about God (Ruhanga) there existed a trinitarian understanding of God that is almost similar to the Christian one. However, it existed in both Ankole and Kigezi before the arrival of Christianity in these areas, and therefore, could not have borrowed from it, since this local trinitarian understanding of God predates the arrival of Christianity itself. Mr. Bintukwanga testified that:

> Before the Europeans came to Uganda and before the white Christian missionaries came to our land of Ankole or to your homeland of Kigezi, we had our own religion and we knew God well. We knew God so well that the missionaries added to us little...worship of the Blessed Mary the Virgin Mother of Jesus...We even knew God to be some kind of externally existing triplets: *Nyamuhanga* being the first one and being also the creator of everything, *Kazooba Nyamuhanga* being his second brother who gives light to all human beings so that they should not stumble either on the path or even in their own lives. Kazooba sees what good or evil is hidden in the hearts of men, since he is *Nyamuhanga* (the Creator). Then either rewards them with the blessings of much cattle many good wives, many healthy children and a happy life. But *Kazooba* punishes the wicked with misfortune, diseases, enemies, poverty, pain and a lonely miserable death, with few to mourn and remember him.

Mr. Bintukwanga went on to describe Kazooba in terms usually associated with the Logos in Western religious and philosophical thought:

> *Kazooba's* light penetrates the hearts of people and God sees the contents of the human hearts by *Kazooba's* eternal light...The third brother in the group is *Rugaba Rwa Nyamuhanga*, who takes what *Nyamuhanga* has created and gives it to people as he wishes...You see! We had it all before the white missionaries came, and all they could teach us was that *Nyamuhanga* is God the Father, *Kazooba* Jesus Christ his son and not his brother as we thought, and that *Rugaba* as the divine giver is the Holy Spirit.[42]

Since this was the first time that I had ever come across this claim, namely, that the Banyankole and the Bakiga people had a trinitarian concept of God prior to the arrival of Christianity, and it had been so well and clearly stated and compared to the Christian trinitarian doctrine, I decided to check it out for authenticity. Surprisingly, I found reliable written evidence recorded by Fr. F. Geraud, a Roman Catholic pioneer missionary priest in Kigezi and an amateur historian and ethnographer, to support it. Father F. Geraud writes concerning the "Idea of God" among the pre-colonial and pre-Christian Bantu of Kigezi in Southern Uganda, East Africa as follows:

> To analyze the idea of God, here is a testimony about an ancient cult which provides a clue about the understanding of the divinity: They [the Bakiga] were offering sacrifices, and after roasting the meat they would gather some of it, put it on leaves (kiko) and bring it to the hut dedicated to the Mandwa. Then they would say: 'eat, be satisfied, give to the one who gives to you, and recognize the one who gives to you, and recognize the one who refuses you. Come to me, your ears and eyes, and return to your dwelling; open my eyes to see you and the mysteries...

Then Father Geraud goes on to describe the African sacramental ritual in the following graphic terms:

> 'They would then gather some meat, not offered to the Mandwa and divide it into three parts. A man would throw up one piece saying: "This is for you 'Ruhanga/Nyamuhanga' (God Creator) who created me." Then he would take another piece and say: "This is for 'Rugaba' (the Giver) who gives me life." With the third piece of meat he would say "This is for 'Kazooba'" (Sun/Light) who shows me the way." Sometimes they would take the three pieces of meat together and throw them up [all at once] saying: "These are yours...Banyinabu-taka (Landlords) 'Nyamuhanga,' 'Kazooba,' and 'Rugaba' (Creator, Light/Sun, Giver)." Then after the meal they would say: "Landlords eat from there, make me see, travel and return, take away from me all my enemies."[43]

It is very clear from Father Geraud's account that the Bakiga and the Banyankole worshipped God (Ruhanga) as One God who is who he is by essential nature of creativity (Kuhanga) an "Eternal Tribune of Divine Brothers": Nyamuhanga being their senior as Creator of everything, followed by Kazooba who, being the Divine Light, illumines the world and enlightens the lives, minds and hearts of human beings,[44] and Rugaba, who is the Giver of life to all living things and the free Distributor of talents, wealth and all the other things according to free personal discretion. As in

Christian theology, this trinity is always inseparably bound together working jointly as a team (Ruhanga/Godhead) complementing each other's work, and it could also be misunderstood in a "Sabellian modalistic" manner.

6. Extreme Divine Transcendence and the Human Need for Mediation

God is quintessentially, the unnameable, infinitely, Incomprehensible Cosmic Transcendent, Ultimate Creative and Redemptive Reality and Infinite Mystery. The explicit for this Cosmic Creative Force or Spirit that is God is variously referred to as God, Yahweh, Allah, Mungu, Deus, Theos and the like, is the concrete existence of the world as his creation or work in the form of dream, thought, drama or self-embodiment. As long as the cosmos exists, this creative power and sustaining force that maintains and nurtures it, so as to bring about order, mind, self-consciousness and thought, is what we mean by God.

Accordingly, there are very many different locally culturally conditioned terms, "names," and titles for the Cosmic Creator or God as found among the African people of Uganda and Rwanda, under discussion, focus on the essence of God as a Cosmic Creative Power that is Completely a Transcendent Infinite Mystery. God is not a personal God. God is conceived of the Cosmic feudal King who has delegated his effective temporal powers or mundane duties to his agents in the form of the provincial and departmental subordinate gods, spirits and human ancestors.

Because of this African concept of the ontological radical transcendence of God as the wholly other, distinct and independent of all human beings, who being unlike finite contingent creation, is self-subsisting and requires no human beings to be who he is, then human beings find it necessary, to entreat him to continue being merciful and compassionate to them, and not to destroy them because of their evils and sins, against him, their neighbors and his creation.

In this African understanding, humanity and creation simply exists by God's will and mercy and self-entertainment. Both humanity and creation as his unmerited free creation are utterly dependent upon him for all their existence and sustenance or redemption from the threat of chaos, despair, anxiety and threat of death and annihilation or turning into "*busha*" or total "nothingness."

However, although human beings are aware of their own dependence on God, nevertheless, they sometimes feel that their own lives radically threatened by the over present negative and evil forces of chaos and "non-being" or annihilation. This is partly due to human intellect, thinking, self-transcendence and acute awareness of personal finitude, utter-dependence on God for existence and the complete vulnerability of any mortal life.

Unlike other animals, human life is generally lived in personal causal freedom. It is lived both self-consciously and reflectively. It is self-willed, planned and experienced with either festive joy or apathy and guilt. It is within this complex process of self-conscious human causal freedom, moral agency in the world, self-reflection, self-examination and self-determination, both individually and collectively as a community, that human uniqueness, joy, greatness, as well as limitations and frustrations are all experienced.

For instance, the human being discovers his/her own finitude and powerlessness in the presence of evil in the world as it manifests itself, particularly, in disease, pain, evil spirits, poverty, ignorance, wars, human irresponsibility, malice, wickedness, envy, witchcraft, hatred, murder, and natural evils and disasters such as floods, lightning, drought, famine, misfortune and accidents. According to Tempels, it is when the Bantu are faced with this predicament that they are meaningfully oriented to God the Creator as the source of life, strength, well-being, protection, guidance and safe-keeping, and divine salvation.[45]

However, the theological problem of divine radical transcendence presents the problem of intimate communication and personal dialogue between God and the *Abantu* (human beings). This presents a problem for both meaningful personal prayer and contemplation. Consequently, in African theology and spirituality, there is an essential need for a chain of intermediaries between to bridge the gulf between holy transcendent God or Cosmic King in heaven and the sinful human beings as his finite subjects on earth.

This African religious need for a interconnected "great chain" of intermediaries was, subsequently, modelled according to the prevailing social and religious culturally established procedures of observing the hierarchical chain of seniority in the local community. As a result, the African religious "*chain of being*," life, and well-being depends on reliable and saintly of holy intermediaries between finite and sinful human beings or the imperfect human community on earth and the holy and perfect God (the Holy Creative and Redemptive Transcendent Spirit/Force) in heaven (God's abode). Intermediaries are required to bridge the gap between the Infinite holy God and finite sinful human beings.

As protocol the human priestly and spiritual intermediaries to the Ultimate Cosmic King were expected to follow the well established local traditional socio-political hierarchical chain of communication and relationships between people (subjects) and their rulers or divine kings. The divine king is "God's Vicar" or representative on earth. This akin to the role of the Pharaoh in ancient Egypt or that of the Pope, in today's society.

In traditional Africa, the chain of mediation to God began with the worshipper or member of the community, then went through the father, elders, chiefs, priest, king, ancestors (spirits and gods) who connected the living and the dead to God, in heaven. This system of religious intermediaries was developed in order to bridge the great gap between the transcendent God "*Omwiguru*" (in heaven or up in the sky) and the human beings below "*Omunsi*" (here on earth). The venerated virtuous ancestors as the departed saints or agapic, holy and benevolent guardian or spirits angels and regional gods are supposed to provide the spiritual linkage between God in heaven and the people on earth.

Therefore, the Mandwa, the Chwezi, Nyabingi, Kasente, Mukasa, and Ryangombe cults were either "invented" or it evolved to serve this religious need for human mediation.[46] The ancestral spirits, being concerned for the well-being of their offspring, were instituted as the category in this chain of mediators, as they were considered to be the most concerned and capable of understanding, since they had previously lived exemplary lives themselves and were now in direct communication with God, unlike the Abantu, who still need mediation.

This chain of mediators was initially developed by the finite human beings as a means of reaching the transcendent God in heaven in order to be heard. Consequently, most of the traditional African prayers and petitions for protection from threats of evil and chaos, pain and a premature death, and for blessings in the form of material wealth, many children, peace, good health and general well-being, are usually relayed to God through these intermediaries.[47]

The intermediaries between the human beings and God are usually very many, and vary depending on occasion, time and place. Nevertheless, in Kigezi, Ankole, Buganda, Bunyoro and Toro, the intermediaries will often include an elder or the head of the household, a medium or a diviner, a priest, an ancestral spirit and a deity (such as Nyabingi, Kasente, and deified heroes like Mukasa or Kibuka in the case of Buganda).[48]

Nevertheless, if this mediation did not produce the desired results, then the worshippers and petitioners often petition God directly themselves, pleading their own case as best they can in order to persuade him to hear their pleas and petitions, and to respond favorably. For these people, God is free to act as he wills and even to change his own mind and reverse his earlier decrees, the same way that their own earthly kings did.[49]

The fact that the African peoples have been found to have many gods and a host of religious intermediaries has led to some denunciations of the African religion as pagan, polytheist and devilish.[50] However, none of these same writers would probably describe Roman Catholicism in the same way, even when it also has a comparable system of intermediaries in the form of Jesus, "the ascended Blessed Virgin Mary," angels and a whole host of saints and priests.

Therefore, the African long chain of intermediaries and the deification of the departed heroes and the ancestral spirits is to be viewed positively as they are agents or human representatives, priestly advocates or mediators and ambassadors to the transcendent God, who is thought to dwell in celestial remoteness. This essential and efficacious divine presence is thought to express itself in healing, good health, general prosperity, fertility of people, farm animals and of the fields; peace and harmony within the individual and the community.[51]

7. Radical Divine Transcendence and Anthropocentricity

According to the African people under discussion, God is conceived to be an extremely holy transcendent, remote, yet immanent Creative and Redemptive Cosmic Spirit.

This transcendent holy God, who is also anthropomorphically and culturally considered to be the Cosmic King, who was virtue of his holiness and position as Cosmic King, also radically removed from the ordinary sinful life of his subjects. As such, he was not considered to be in direct charge of the human freedom, choices, actions or the human history as composed of the detailed affairs of existence of daily life. Like an earthly king, emperor or pharaoh, God is supposed to delegate to his subordinates as ambassadors, including priests, kings, ancestors and the elders, and given them varying hierarchical powers, according to rank and status, for running the world and its mundane events.

Nevertheless, the human being finds himself or herself internally and physically free, to do as he or she likes, but with terrible consequences. This human consequential freedom frightens him or her, since it also bears responsibility for one's decision, actions and their consequences, before God and the community. This seemingly unlimited human freedom is attributed by these Bantu Africans to the apparent "absence of God" brought about by the divine radical transcendence. Subsequently, the Africans like any other people, have in the holy name of God created religion, commandments, societal regulations, laws and taboos to curb this seemingly human infinite freedom.

Unlimited human freedom tends to threaten the human being and the society, largely due to the uncertainty and unpredictable results, and consequences of such unlimited human causal and definitive freedom. Consequently, the African society has taken steps to limit this human freedom in order to ensure social stability, harmony and peace between individuals, families, clans, and tribes, hence safeguarding peace and general well-being within the whole community.

This is normally done within the context of culture and the "socialization" of the young to observe appropriate customs, norms, taboos, and religious laws and prohibitions. By the end of this process, human freedom in these African traditional societies is so cropped that usually there is a kind of conformity to be observed about the various ethnic groups in their behavior and general mode of life.

Therefore, deviation from the communal consensus or culturally established ways of doing things is generally strongly discouraged, as it is considered a possible source of tension or disruption within the community, and therefore, a potential threat to communal harmony and as such, to be crushed at its earliest manifestation.[52]

This is mainly because it is believed that the greatest societal value is order, peace and harmony within the community. Subsequently, whatever enhances this peaceful harmony is esteemed as good and encouraged, whereas whatever creates tension, disharmony and disruption within the community, especially at the family level, which constitutes the primary unit of the society, is considered to be evil (or sin) and to be resisted or uprooted altogether.[53] Consequently, among these Bantu people the society and the ancestors are regarded as the main custodians of moral law, its police and magistrates, rather than God, who is considered too remote to be bothered with the details of human daily life far away on earth. Exceptions are the very serious cases of moral failure or breach in divine law, such as committing murder, incest or bestiality.

Subsequently, the human being is regarded as the center of the world (*Ensi*), since God is centered in heaven (*Eiguru*) far away "above" the world.[54] For instance, according to the Kiganda tradition of both creation and "The Fall," Kintu [Adam], the first human being, was created by God in heaven and then dropped down on the lonely earth with a cow, which supplied him with milk but failed to give him a satisfying companionship. Then God saw the misery and loneliness of Kintu and had compassion on him and gave him Nnambi [Eve] for a wife.

Nnambi came down to Kintu on earth from heaven bringing some chickens along with her for food. But she had to return to heaven to get the chicken feed, which she had forgotten, thus disobeying God's command that, once she left heaven for her new home on earth, she should never return to heaven if she wanted to live in eternal peace and happiness with Kintu, her husband, and the children that would be born to them. When Nnambi returned to heaven in disobedience to God's advice, "*Walumbe*" (Death) followed her back to earth, subsequently, causing death on earth, to Nnambi herself, her husband Kintu, their descendants, and all the other living things.[55]

This myth or tradition illustrates the African anthropocentric religious ontology, as it indicates that Kintu and Nnambi were created in heaven and put on the earth (or world/*Omunsi*) to be its masters and to try to make it as comfortable as possible for themselves as their eternal home. It is made very clear that everything on earth is created for the sake of the human being (either as food, as the case of Kintu's cow and Nnambi's chickens[56] clearly illustrates, or as a companion and sexual partner, as in the case of Nnambi in relation to Kintu, the first man). In other words, the human being becomes the center of the world and its terrestrial things in the same way God is the center of heaven and everything in it.

For these African people, therefore, the human being becomes the measure of all things on earth.[57] Whatever is of use to the "Abantu" becomes valuable and its worth becomes equivalent to its potential utility for the human being. This African utility principle is applicable to everything, including the value of the divinities, and religious cults which are themselves measured by their functional utility.[58] For instance, if a given divinity delivers to these people the needed security and protection against evil in the form of disease, witchcraft, theft and misfortune, it is esteemed and retained, whereas it is usually abandoned if it fails to deliver these services and is replaced with another that will at least appear to be rendering this desperately needed supernatural salvific activity.

As a result, in Buganda, Ankole, Kigezi, Toro and Bunyoro there is a constant heavy traffic in religious sales of new religious objects and the acquisition or adaptations of new gods to replace the old ones that have either malfunctioned or have become completely dysfunctional.

This religious cultural trend, partly explains why a great number of Africans have recently become converted to either Christianity or Islam without abandoning a large portion of the African Traditional Religion, which they know from experience to function well.

Very often, there is deliberate syncretism and synergism. This is done in order to produce a what is perceived to be an ideal, culturally better or more relevant and more efficient functioning religion. This is desirable in order to meet the challenges and stresses of this modern age, which the African Traditional Religion alone is unable to meet most effectively, due to its being largely tribal, culturally bound, static and rural community oriented in nature, whereas modern times are characterized by rapid social change, urbanization, technological development, westernization and globalization or "universalization."

8. The African Concept of Time as Ground for African Metaphysics and Ontology

Having done a detailed study in Africa, particularly in East Africa, Professor John Mbiti correctly came to a strong belief that the African concept of time is the key to the understanding of African metaphysics, ontology and interpretation of African religion and philosophy. Certainly, the African concept of time is fundamental for the understanding of African culture, values and luxury modes of life. Accordingly, Mbiti writes:

> The concept of time may help to explain beliefs, attitudes, practices and general way of life of African peoples not only in the traditional set up but also in the modern situation (whether political, economic, educational or Church life). On this subject there is, unfortunately, no literature... The question of time is of little or of no academic concern to African peoples in their traditional life.

In the same place, Mbiti goes on to make the following fundamental statement which underlies most of his understanding of African metaphysics and ontology:

> For them [Africans] time is simply a composition of events which have occurred, those which are taking place now and those which are immediately to occur. What has not taken place or what has no likelihood of an immediate occurrence falls in the category of "no time." What is certain to occur, or what falls within the rhythm of natural phenomena, is in the category of inevitable or *potential time*. The most significant consequence of this is that, according to traditional concepts, time is a two dimensional phenomenon, with a long *past*, a *present* and virtually *no future*.

> The linear concept of time in Western thought, with an indefinite past, present and infinite future, is practically foreign to African thinking.[59]

Mbiti's insightful exposition of the African concept of time helps us to understand and explain the constant conflict and tension between the Western missionaries and expatriates working in Africa and their African colleagues and subordinates. Some Westerners have accused East Africans of being "rather lazy," not time-conscious and ever coming late to the office, meetings and appointments.[60] This conflict is mainly rooted in the difference between the African circular concept of time and the Western linear concept of time.

The African concept of time is both people and event-centered. People make time and they are not slaves of the god "*chronos*" as in the Western world. For instance, African festivals begin when important guests arrival, such wedding parties, kings and chiefs. People eat when food is ready, and not because, it is "time to eat!"

Characteristically, the African concept of time is meaning, value, and human-centered (*kairos*) and ever stands in opposition to the Western linear concept of time (*chronos*), and "keeping time" or "being on time." As a result of this clashing of operational concepts of time and world-view, Westerners or Whites often accuse Africans or Blacks of being habitually late for events and lazy or "wasting time." Obviously, for Africans, time was not a commodity which could not be wasted, since people made time by their own presence, actions and events.

For the traditional African, as Professor Mbiti correctly observes, time is made by the human being and other happenings or events. These events as value-loaded or meaningful events as markers and measures of time as the process of human conceptual finitization or periodization of infinity and divine creativity (*NTU*), include God and creatures as the expressions, embodiments, measures and measurers of time. As a result, time is accumulated in the past or "*Zamani*" period. That is where the world was created by God, and that is where the primordial fellowship with God (or Garden of Eden) existed prior to human disobedience and fall from heaven as a state of pure perfection and fellowship with God.

Consequently, according to the Africans, time begins with God as part of God's essence and substance which creatures are allowed to share by God. Therefore, creation of the world, the existence of free intelligent and moral creatures, not governed by biological needs and clocks for all their activities, choices and behavior is part of this process of time. As such, time is the arena of God's cosmic drama of creation, sustenance and redemption of creatures from self-destructive moral evil in the form of malice, ignorance, hate, violence, greed, selfishness and materialism. In general, traditional Africans reckoned time in events and happenings such as the falling down of a big tree near or on the house, morning, noon, evening, night, rain, drought, planting or harvesting, and the like. Cattle keepers reckoned time in terms of cattle.

These examples are taken from Southern and Western Uganda cattle keepers, including the Bahima. Milking time of *"kukama ente"* (6:30-7:40 a.m.); *"kusetura ente"* or to take the cattle out of the kraal to feed (about 8:00-9:00 a.m.); *"kweshera ente"* or to take cows to the well to drink (2:00-3:30 p.m.); *"ente zeinuka"* or cattle to come from the well (3:30-4:30 p.m.), *"ente zazagira"* (4:30-6:30 p.m.); *"ente zataaha"* or the cattle is going home (6:00-7:30); *"kukama omu mwebazo"* or evening milking of cattle (7:00-8:00); *"kukingira ente"* or close the gate after the cattle is inside the kraal for the night (7:40-8:30 p.m.); *"abarisa banyaama"* (night: people are asleep or *Abantu bagonoka*).

Obviously, in the absence of clocks, time is relative and non-absolute for any event. Events both make and mark time. Without events, time an abyss of creativity and medium for creation, with nothing created. Unlike the West where people are slaves of time, in Africa, people create and govern time, and chronological time as measured by the clock is of little value until God or people give it value and meaning by creating something new or important.

In this understanding, time is relative, and flexible. For the Africans, time is not "lord over human beings." And human beings are not slaves of time! In Africa, "people make time!" Time is God's gift which is reckoned and measured in terms of cattle routine, days and nights according to sunrise, noon, afternoon, sunset and night.

Time is also measured in lunar months, seasons, years and generations extending backwards in time. Biological time was recognized by growth of babies into girls or boys, puberty changes which were celebrated by initiation rites, such as circumcision and marriage. Women's regular monthly menstrual cycles were also used to measure and track time in terms of months and years.

In traditional African life, daily routine is eternally self-repetitive. Life tended to be the same for each day, depending on the seasonal changes, except in Kigezi, where the Kasente cult demanded that one day in a week, namely, Thursday, should be set aside as a religious holy rest day dedicated for the worship of God and Kasente as the intermediary. Where the people had no cattle, this daily routine was adapted and based on an agricultural routine, such as going to the garden (8:00 a.m.), resting for lunch (12:00 noon), "*okuhinguuka*" (returning from the garden, 5:00 p.m.), and chickens or goats coming home (7:00 p.m.), and the rest being the same.[61]

The daily routine of the cattle-keepers tended to remain exactly the same from one day to the next, whereas it varied for those people engaged in agriculture, depending on the seasons. For instance, in the rainy months the people planted their seeds in the previously prepared fields, then later weeded their crops and harvested them when they were ready.

Then, there followed a dry season in which these people, having now plenty of newly harvested food, which they often used for collective feasting. A family would usually invite neighbors and relatives to join in communal festivities, eating, drinking, dancing and making merry. This season would also be the annual time when the people of the community would gather together for communal activities such as games, hunting, feasting, weddings, and probably most important of all, communal religious cultic worship activities, such as "*Kubandwa*" ceremonies. The other rituals and ceremonies include the initiations of the young people into the mystery and secrecy of the Mandwa cult and "*Kubandwa*."

The training of the young adults and their initiation process into the "Mandwa" cult in both Kigezi and Ankole was usually carried out in such a ceremonial manner in order to impress the initiates, and to convey to them through awe, ritual and mystery, the fact that the human being exists in a state of finitude, and mystery. And that as such, he or she is limited in strength and knowledge and that he/she is vulnerable, subject to evil, pain and death; and that human beings require God's intervention and the community in order to live more meaningful and satisfying lives.

Consequently, the candidates for initiation were, generally, subjected to difficult tasks which needed collective work, and painful experiences in order to impress on them the need for cooperation and working together in society, bravery, and endurance, since being alive and life involved acceptance of suffering.

An African traditional pragmatic existential truth, which was akin to Buddha's noble truth, namely that life is *"Dukkha"* or suffering and needed to be accepted as such in order to live it fully, was at the heart of these African initiation rites. Therefore, these were some of the valued societal skills needed in the community, since singularly and collectively, they faced the uncertainties of life in its unforeseen future.[62] The priests and elders strongly impressed upon the initiates that life in its capricious nature can be faced courageously together with their fellow human beings, particularly their kinsfolk and their neighbors, in the community.

What this training process teaches, then, is that the future is unpredictable, consequently requiring collective solidarity and mutual support in case of any eventualities such as misfortune, accidents, hard times, and most of all, death. Humanity and harmonious, reliable, supportive human relationships are considered to be the highest value in the community[63] and as such, they are valued more than time, whose value is in turn measured by its potential utility for enhancing these human relationships.

For instance, a full traditional greeting in Buganda lasts for about twenty minutes! Should a Muganda office worker meet his visiting mother-in-law or father-in-law on his way to the office, he will be understandably late on that day, and his fellow Baganda colleagues in the office would probably understand and excuse him. But, what about his Western colleagues? Will they too do the same? They might have a different impression, and might even take serious offense at him if they had an appointment with him for that morning. Nevertheless, for the African, he or she would rather be late or even not go to work at all rather than cause a breach in this close relationship.[64]

Furthermore, for the African, what is important is this humane treatment of one's relatives, since this is regarded as the quintessence of a good life (as far as the African traditional society is concerned). For instance, an individual is known as good or bad for his/her manner of treating other human beings. If he or she is kind, patient, considerate and generous, he or she is considered good, whereas if he or she is hurried or plans in such a way that he or she becomes too orderly to allow casualness and flexibility, the individual is usually disliked as proud, anti-social and inconsiderate. This is because in the African traditional society people generally make no appointments to see or to visit others. They just go and may even expect more hospitality due to the added element of surprise and the joy it is supposed to create![65]

For traditional Africans, the time to enjoy oneself or to be kind, generous and loving is the present. According to Professor Mbiti, for the African, the future has no existence, as it has not yet acquired any actuality or concreteness as reality, which it can only acquire by becoming part of human history. He argues that for the African the future dimension has such a short span that it only covers the immediate predictable future.

It is the "extended present" into the realm of "potential being" which is still in the process of becoming "actual time." That is, time as an eternal Spirit or dimension, becomes historical and concrete as the present (*Sasa/Hati*), as it gradually passes on into the realm of the "accumulated sedimenting or current and sedimentary past" (*Zamani/Ebya-Ira*). Mbiti elaborates on this African orientation to both the present (*Sasa*), and to the past (*Zamani*), as the only reality and actuality that counts. He writes:

> The future is virtually absent because events which lie in it have not taken place, they have not been realized and cannot, therefore, constitute time. If, however, future events are certain to occur, or if they fall within the inevitable rhythm of nature, they at best constitute only *potential time*. What is taking place now no doubt unfolds the future, but once an event has taken place, it is no longer in the future but in the present and the past. *Actual time* is therefore what is present and what is past. It moves "backward" rather than "forward;" and people set their minds not on future things, but chiefly on what has taken place.[66]

As a result of this African orientation to *Zamani* (past), which is regarded in creation traditions (or myths) as the golden time of direct human interaction with God, the beatific vision and eternal life are consequently located in this *Zamani* period before human disobedience to God and the consequent entry of death into the world,[67] according to the "Creation and Fall Myths" (accounts or traditions) found in Buganda, Ankole, Kigezi and Rwanda.[68] Because of this disobedience (in all cases by the woman) against God, death is said to have come into the world as punishment for this human sin. Consequently, death had become an irrevocable constitutive part of the natural order, causing the familiar conditions of pain, loss, chaos and decay in the world.[69]

According to the Bakiga and the Banyankole traditions, in the beginning human beings had the supernatural gifts of resurrection and rejuvenation freely given to them by God, but these gifts had become lost because of human social discord and hatred. This loss is symbolized by the Musingo Woman tradition, which states that a Musingo woman hated her mother-in-law so much that when her mother-in-law died the Musingo woman was determined to stop her from resurrecting. Consequently, she waited by the grave-side and when the grave began to heave, trying to let out the newly resurrected and rejuvenated mother-in-law, she pounded it with a big stick (*omuhini*) saying, "*Abafa tibazooka*" (those who die should never resurrect to life again).

It is said that as a result of this incident, the mother-in-law died again, and subsequently, no human being ever resurrects, because God punished all humanity due to this woman's hatred and cruelty to her mother-in-law. For these people, therefore, both creation, resurrection or eternal life lie in the golden past (*Zamani*); consequently, as far as they are concerned, there is nothing to look for (or to hope for) in the distant future (eschaton) apart from posterity, old age and death, which for them marks the end of all meaningful human existence as "*Abantu*" (human beings) *vis-a-vis* "*Bafu*" (the dead).[70]

Unlike Christianity, in African Traditional Religion there is no concept of future fulfillment in heaven or punishment in hell after one's death. The Africans generally believe that the best and most fulfilling life for human beings is to be found here on earth and not anywhere else. Consequently, the present is the arena of life in its fullness and, as such, to be celebrated now. Self-enjoyment, generous living and loving are to be expressed here and now in the course of day-to-day ordinary living and not to be deferred to the unknown and unforeseeable future.

This emphasis on the celebration of life *now* very often leads to the hedonistic philosophy of "Eat, drink and be merry now, for tomorrow we die."[71] It also accounts for much of Africa's poverty, mismanagement, corruption and poor planning both in Church and State, and subsequently, the serious prevailing unrest in much of Africa today.

Since for the African, the fullness of life lies on earth in the present, (despite the threat of evil, disease, pain, chaos and death), society, acting on behalf of God, is expected to reward the good people (with approval, praises them as "good") and expects God, too, to reward them here on earth (with prosperity, good health and general well-being). Conversely, the evil people are castigated as "wicked," ostracized and occasionally beaten, mutilated or even sentenced to humiliating public execution as a deterrent and warning to others.

The community generally deals harshly with serious crimes, such as murder, witchcraft, disobedience to the elders, and sex-related offenses, particularly incest. Punishment for this kind of wickedness was usually very severe because it was believed that there was no other punishment to be meted out by God in the distant future for these crimes and offenses.

Nevertheless, it is speculated that when the wicked people die, their spirits turn into malignant evil spirits or ghosts (*emizimu*), the very evil beings ostracized by God and feared by the living, who would ordinarily honor them as the "living dead."[72] Conversely, the spirits of the good people are thought to be acceptable in the "sight of God" and to the community. It is these good spirits that are generally categorized as "the ancestors" (*Ba-ishe-nkuru-itwe*),[73] despite the fact that they include the spirits of those people who were not progenitors themselves.

The spirits of non-genitors are elevated and honored as those of genitors (ancestors) because of their good social service by their good acts and general good behavior while alive on earth. They are also esteemed as exemplary parents and hence ancestors. In this sense, God would qualify to be called the "Chief Ancestor," both literally as the ultimate origin of humanity, and also, as the example of perfection.[74] People, like God, are measured, known and categorized by their actions, whether good or bad. People are thought to be what they do, as action is thought to be the personal self-expression and self-externalization of the hidden inner being of the doer.

In African traditional philosophical and theological thought the world created by the eternal God, and is eternal. The creation and redemption or sustaining the world, and its delicate processes and systems constitute a single ongoing eternal multi-dimensional activity of the eternal Creator-Redeemer God. Accordingly, just like God its eternal Creator or Originator, the world is also correlatively, eternal. God is God because he creates the world.

Therefore, if God would cease to create, sustain and redeem the world, he would cease to be God. Correlatively, the contingent world as cosmic creation would also necessarily cease to exist, since God as its centrifical force, gravity, creative energy, mind, direction, ground for being and constitutive reality, would have dissolved and ceased "to be." Ultimately, God is the only absolute and Ultimate Reality in the cosmos which both creates and grounds all other contingent beings as finite created realities in the temporal world or the cosmos. God is the positive cosmic force that creates, redeems or sustains being and beings by providing general resistance to entropy or constant threat of creation by death, chaos, nothingness and meaninglessness.

As God's eternal world and the kingdom, existing in eternity, the wheels of finite time keep on rotating endlessly, into God's eternity where all events are equally present now in the present moment, regardless of whether, they are past events or potential events in the future, which are not yet actualized in cosmic history. Days, months and seasons come and go with their correlated events and activities.

These typical events include, seasonal events, such as planting and harvesting; birth, growth, aging and death. Events appear to come and go, as if they were rotating endlessly in self-repeating cycles. Furthermore, the geographical area being tropical, provides no sharp break in the life cycle (such as winter in the temperate climates, which creates an impression of death and spring, a return of new life analogous to a resurrection, so as to bring to the African mind the possibility of an overall human, definitive, eschatological resurrection).

Consequently, these African people, being *Zamani*-oriented and having no "mythical utopias" in their religious tradition to be actualized in the future nor a concept and hope of a "kingdom to come" or messianic expectations, and being primarily oriented to God's activities in *Zamani* or the past, as a result have no interest either in speculative eschatology.

Nevertheless, they have great interest in the personal and collective continuity of life in their own offspring as the kind of immortality that matters *vis-a-vis* the change into a free spiritual being at death. The disembodied life as a spirit is generally distasteful to these people, even if one had to be elevated as an ancestral spirit or even to be deified, as in the cases of Ryangombe, Mukasa, Kibuka and Khabengu.[75]

However, whereas for these Bantu people the human being lives only in the present (*Sasa*) as the real arena of human life and meaningful existence, being in reference and continuity with the past (*Zamani*), and whereas the indefinite future is so meaningless that there is no word to denote it,[76] God or Ruhanga or Katonda is thought to transcend the dimensions of time, space and matter or extension, since he is their creator, master and controller.

In this philosophical and religious ontology or metaphysics, God is also thought of in terms which sound both Greek and Hebraic. For instance, God is affirmed to be One, holy, creator, redeemer, compassionate, remote transcendent, or requiring a chain of intermediaries, and omnipresent, therefore equally present now in us, trees, mountains, rocks, water and other creatures. For some Western prejudiced observer this is called "animism."

However, this phenomenon is what we mean by God's omnipresence or what Paul Till called "The Ground of Being" and Heideggar called "Being" and Jaspers referred to as the "All-encompassing." Therefore, within this context, God is simultaneously, eternal, transcendent and omnipresent in all these three dimensions of time as past, present and future. This is what the Bible also refers to as God being "the Alpha and the Omega." Accordingly, for the Africans, God is eternal and omnipresent in dimensions of being including that of time which to him all the three dimensions of time and cosmic being, including the processes of both creation and redemption, form a single process and a single eternal present moment in the "NOW."[77]

As such, God's kingdom and those obedient saints who constitute it are enabled by God's election in free redemptive grace, praxis of agape and positive faith for self-transcendence to join God's fellowship of agape, and to share in God's eternity to live for ever, in as much as they are incorporated into God's nature through the Logos or the Christ and the cosmic agapic transforming presence.

Therefore, those who are in the Logos of God or in Christ have also been given God's special divinizing free gift to share in the full benefits of an irrevocable citizenship and full membership in the kingdom and eternity of God. Moreover, God's kingdom and eternal life as a present reality in the cosmos can be inherited and experienced in the present moment by all those people who live by and exercise agape and live in obedience to God's will and commandments.

These saints of God can truly experience both God and eternal life in his kingdom of unconditional love and transcendental peace as they mutually exercise their gifts of agape and forgive their neighbors without condition (cf. Mk. 1:14-15; Matt. 5-7; 25:31-46; 1 John 4:7-22). There is a universal divine requirement for obedience to God moral law, and the implicit or explicit requirement for observation of the commandment of the unconditional love. Therefore, anyone who by God's universal free grace obeys God and observes this moral, then he or she has fulfilled the essential universal pre-requisites for the entry into the kingdom of God, and also the means by which human beings participate and experience salvation and eternal life in God's kingdom.

The highly cherished traditional Christian sacraments of baptism and the eucharist are worthless and meaningless to God and the world, unless they are also accompanied by the necessary fruits of God's supernatural salvific grace and agape for the neighbor (cf. Matt. 7:13-23; 25:31-46; Jam. 2:8-26; 1 Cor. 13; Rom. 13:8-12; 1 John 4:7-22). As such, God's supernatural salvation does not depend on baptism and the eucharist. On the contrary, God's salvation depends on God's grace and agape alone, since it is a free gift of God which has been freely bestowed on the whole cosmos, and all its free, obedient and intelligent inhabitants.

NOTES

1. The main focus being on the central, western and southern Bantu ethnic groups of East Africa, particularly, the Baganda, Banyankole, Banyoro, Batoro and the Banya-Kigezi (Bakiga, Bahororo, and Banyarwanda). The Bantu people form a great percentage of the total population of Africa. Professor John S. Mbiti, being the main authority in East Africa on African Traditional Religion, will be tentatively regarded as its main authoritative exponent.

2. In September 1982, Dr. Leakey, the famous archaeologist, discovered yet another proto-human fossil at the Oldvern George Valley in Tanzania. With this new discovery, Dr. Leakey is convinced that at last he has now discovered the so-called missing link in the evolutionary ascent between us as the *homo sapiens* and "our distant cousins, the apes." The University of Oxford in a BBC Science Magazine aired in April 1986; and research in genetics in 1993, and 1995 provided further evidence and proof of this African origin of all humanity. Racial differences are biologically superficial, but cultural significant!

3. Cf. Exod. 2; Egypt and the rest of North Africa is regarded as African. In this respect, therefore, Egyptian and North African civilizations and Christianity will be claimed as African. See: John S. Mbiti, *African Religions and Philosophy*, 300 ff.; Richard A. Wright, ed., *African Philosophy: An Introduction* (Washington, D.C.: University of America, 1980), 55-70, 201 ff.

4. Cf. Matt. 2:13-23.

5. And supposedly remained so until the 19th century colonial conquest and occupation of Africa, when written records were made by the various groups interested and working in Africa, particularly, the explorers and the missionaries. Until recently most universities rarely offered courses in African pre-colonial history, traditional religion and philosophy, because it was generally believed that where there are no written sources for analysis, there was no objective knowledge. It is more difficult to get objective sources without written texts, but even written texts themselves, like oral tradition, are often lacking in objectivity due to the personal biases and idiosyncrasies of their authors.

6. See Henri Lhote, "The Fertile Sahara: Men, Animals and Art of a Lost World," *Vanished Civilizations of the Ancient World*, ed. Edward Bacon (New York: McGraw-Hill Book Co., Inc., 1963), 11-32, 55-78.

7. The fact that the Organization of African Unity (O.A.U.) includes these African states north of the Sahara, such as Egypt, Libya and Morocco, is another form of evidence to indicate the essential unity of these two regions despite the apparent differences of color, language and history. The fact that Egypt and the Sudan are currently working on a merger plan illustrates this point even further.

8. Like Judaism, Islam, Hinduism, and Buddhism, the African Religion is a wholistic inclusive African theocentric mode of life. Technically, the African Religion is not self-conscious as a religion. Accordingly, it membership would not identify itself as being members of the African Religion or "*Dini.*" The Western concept of religion as a distinct mode of life apart from the every day life in the community, is foreign to traditional Africa.

In traditional Africa life was not divided into the secular and the sacred realms. All of life and its events were theocentric and sacred.

"*Dini*" is a foreign Arab-Swahili word which was adopted in East Africa to mean religion. This was necessitated by the fact that there was generally an absence of the word "religion" or its equivalent in the local languages. Due to foreign missionary influence, the word "*Dini*" was then locally understood to mean only the foreign religions. In Uganda these missionary or foreign "religions" ("*ama-dini*") are generally known to be three religions. They are as the following: a. "*Aba-Kurisito*" (the elitist Protestants/Anglicans, about 41% of the population); b. "*Aba-Kirisito*" (Roman Catholics, about 44% of the population); and c. "*Aba-Salaamu*" (Muslims, about 7% and the least educated).

Tragically, the Anglican and Catholic pioneer missionaries in Africa, especially, Uganda were so violently opposed to each other that their local converts were led to misconstrue Anglicanism and Catholicism as two religions rather than two denominations or branches of the same religion, namely, Christianity. These kinds of original Western missionary religious hostilities and intolerance still pervade and disrupt the religious and political life in modern Africa, including Uganda that is currently divided and ravaged by war, hatred and repression, which are mainly attributed to these religious misconceptions, bigotry and intolerance in personal ambition and excessive tribalism.

9. Cf. John S. Mbiti, *African Religions and Philosophy,* page one claims that "Africans are notoriously religious, and each people has its own religious system with a set of beliefs and practices. Religion permeates into all the departments of life so fully, that it is not easy or possible to isolate it." This total religious permeation into the spheres of life probably explains why in these African languages there is no single word for religion, because there is no such thing as religion in traditional African life, as the whole entire sphere of life itself is by nature essentially religious. In other words, the entire life of an African is conceived to be lived in a religious arena before God (*Ruhanga*) *as Kazooba* (Light or Sun), who sees and reviews every human act in light of humanity and the context of the community. See also N. S. Booth, ed., *African Religions: A Symposium* (New York: NOK, 1977), 3-10, 22-68.

10. God (Ruhanga) as Nyamuhanga is Creator, but as *Kazooba* (Light/Guide) and as *Rugaba* (Giver/Provider) he is also considered Redeemer or Savior. He saves people in each given moment of human existence, since every moment is regarded as lived by divine protection and sustenance against the equally pervasive forces of evil in terms of threats of disease, poverty, witchcraft, misfortune, distorted relationships, pain and most of all death, and the irrevocable loss and heartbreaking agony it brings to those left behind. Cf. Noel King, *Religions of Africa* (New York/London: Harper & Row, 1970), 32-61; Placide Tempels *Bantu Philosophy* (Paris: Presence Africaine, 1969), 17-114, 167-189.

11. Cf. John S. Mbiti, *African Religions and Philosophy,* 11-12, and E. Bolaji Idowu, *African Traditional Religion: A Definition* (New York: Maryknoll, and London: SCM Press, 1973), 108-135; P. Tempels, *Bantu Philosophy,* 10-15, 167-189. See also note 9 above.

12. Such as Nyabingi, Ryangombe and Bachwezi in Ankole and Kigezi, Mukasa and Kibuka in Buganda, Khabengu among the Sonjo of Tanzania. These cults are founded by people and get reformed while the African traditional religion in itself generally remains static and the same or unaffected; cf. Aylward Shorter, "Symbolism, Ritual and History: An Examination of the Work of Victor Turner," ed. Ranger and Kimambo, *The Historical Study of the African Religion* (Berkeley: University of California Press, 1972), 137-150.

13. Both concepts of "heresy" and "atheism" are foreign to traditional Africa and they were introduced by foreign religions. It can also be said that missionary Christianity has done harm in Africa by rejecting and repudiating the African culture as "pagan" and introducing Western secularism that is responsible for turning some educated Africans into agnostics and even atheists! When these Christian missionaries rejected the well-entrenched African traditional religion as a viable religion, they created ground in the African mind for doubting the truth and validity of all other religions, including Christianity itself.

Consequently, at first, many Africans adopted Christianity or Islam as long as there were demonstrated material advantages to be realized. The Africans also tended to view Western superior technological development and Western Christianity as correlatives, in the same way African traditional religion and the African modality of human existence were so intertwined that it was impossible to separate them. Cf. note 9 above; Mbiti, *Africans Religion and Philosophy*, 302 ff. "There is no Roman Catholic priest and a European are both the same!" (p. 302). See also Asavia Wandira, *Early Missionary Education in Uganda* (Kampala: Makerere University, 1972), 2 ff.; Ranger and Kimambo, ed., *The Historical Study of African Religion*, 219-276.

14. Aylward Shorter, *Prayer in the Religious Traditions of Africa* (New York/Nairobi: Oxford University Press, 1975), 6; see also P. Tempels, *Bantu Philosophy*, 38 and note 1.

15. See Mbiti, *African Religions and Philosophy*, 1-7, 19-21, 341 ff. He writes: "In their traditional life African peoples are deeply religious. It is religion, more than anything else, which colors their understanding of the universe, and their empirical participation in that universe making life a profoundly religious phenomenon. To be is to be religious in a religious universe. This is the fundamental philosophical understanding behind African myths, customs, traditions, morals, actions, and social relationships." (Mbiti, *African Religions*, 341). See also Newell S. Booth, ed., *African Religions: A Symposium*, 1-10, 32-62; Noel King, *Religions of Africa*, 20 ff., P. Tempels, *Bantu Philosophy*, 17-70, 167-189.

16. This is confirmed by my own professional personal experience and research. See also Mbiti, *African Religions and Philosophy*, 342 ff.; Fred Welbourn, *The East African Christian* (Nairobi: Oxford Uni., 1960); Placide Tempels, *Bantu Philosophy*, 18-69, 95-166.

17. Cf. Noel King, *Religions of Africa*, 32-61.

18. See: Mbiti, *African Religions and Philosophy*, 299-363. African Christianity and Islam are extensions of the African Religion. Therefore, they allow the practice of basic African traditional elements such as polygamy, spirit possession, divination or prophecy, and an emphasis on charismatic healing by prayer, ritual ointment and laying on of the hands. See, Adrian Hastings, *African Christianity* (New York: The Seabury Press, 1976), 60-76; David Barrett, *Schism and Renewal in Africa; African Initiatives in Religion* (Nairobi: APH, 1971); J. S. Trimmingham, *Islam in East Africa* (London: Cambridge Uni., 1964).

19. See Tempels, *Bantu Philosophy*, 55-57.

20. See notes 8 and 16 above.

21. See Anthony Munyazangabo, "The Function of Religion in Bufumbira History," in *A History of Kigezi*, ed. Donald Denoon, 258-263. The presence of an active volcano in these mountain ranges, that some time back erupted disastrously, burning the people around, probably gave the local people a unique concept of future punishment in this volcano for the

disobedient non-believers, i.e. non-initiates. This concept is almost similar to that of "hell/Gehenna" in the New Testament. However, this concept and that of the Sonjo of Tanzania and Shilluk of Sudan, which expect future judgement and punishment of the evildoers and the rewarding of those found good and faithful, is unique in traditional Africa. Generally, there is an absence of such eschatological concepts in the African traditional religion. Cf. Mbiti, *African Religions and Philosophy*, 6: "There is neither paradise to be hoped for nor hell to be feared in the hereafter. The soul of man does not long for spiritual redemption, or for close contact with God in the next world. This is an important element in traditional religions, and which will help us to understand the concentration of African religiosity on earthly matters, with man at the centre of this religiosity."

22. And for that matter, the Portuguese voyagers and explorers reported that they had found people in Africa who were atheists, i.e. having no religion; cf. Newell S. Booth, *African Religions*, 1, 10.

23. Christian missionaries and Muslims rejected the African Traditional Religion as a valid religion. This was also probably missionary strategy to scare the people into conversion. As a missionary strategy, it was ineffective, since conversion out of fear is neither meaningful nor as endearing for the convert as conversion out of conviction and love. Conversion out of conviction and love endures, as the Ugandan martyrs clearly illustrated.

24. E. E. Evans-Pritchard, *The Theories of Primitive Religion* (London: Oxford University Press, 1965), 8.

25. Pritchard, *Theories of Primitive Religion*, 7; see also Placide Tempels, *Bantu Philosophy*, 17-38, 167-189; Emmanuel K. Twesigye, (ed.) God, *Race, Myth and Power: An Africanist Research Corrective Analysis* (New York: Peter Lang, 1991), 1-11.

26. Evans-Pritchard, *Theories of Primitive Religion*, 20-47; Twesigye, *God, Race, Myth and Power*, 1-49.

27. Ibid., 2 ff. Evans-Pritchard makes a lot of sense. The main reason for that is that unless we already had God's preparatory grace, we could not have responded to the missionary preaching of the Gospel in Africa. The Incarnation meant that God could now as a fellow human being in Jesus-Christ be able to persuade them more effectively by presenting to them a concrete personal moral life and praxis of agape as an ideal example to follow. Cf. 1 John 4:7-21. See also Tempels, *Bantu Philosophy*, 17-84, 115-189; Kwasi Wiredu, *Philosophy and African Culture* (New York: Cambridge Uni. Press, 1980), 6-23.

28. E.g. see M. S. Kiwanuka, *The Empire of Bunyoro Kitara: Myth or Reality?*, Makerere History Paper No 1. (Kampala: Longman, 1968); A. R. Dunbar, *History of Bunyoro-Kitara* (Nairobi: Oxford University Press, 1969); *The Bakitara* (London: Cambridge University Press, 1923); J. W. Nyakatura, *Abakama ba Bunyoro-Kitara* (Quebec: St. Justin, 1947); K. W., "Abakama ba Bunyoro-Kitara, the Kings of Bunyoro-Kitara," *Uganda Journal* 3(1935) 149-160, 4 (1936-1937): 65-83, 5 (1937): 53-84; M. C. Fallers, *The Eastern Lacustrine Bantu* (London: Oxford University Press, 1960); John Roscoe, *The Baganda* (London: Cambridge University Press, 1911); John Roscoe, *The Banyankole* (London: Cambridge University Press, 1923); Apollo Kagwa, *Basekabaka be Buganda* (London: Cambridge University Press, 1953); S. M. Kiwanuka, *The Kingdom of Buganda: From Foundation to 1900* (Nairobi/Kampala: Longmans Publishing House, 1970); H. F. Morris, *A History of Ankole* (Kampala: EALB, 1962); Donald Denoon, ed., *The History of Kigezi*.

29. Cf. John S. Mbiti, *New Testament Eschatology in African Background,* 24-62; *African Religions and Philosophy,* 15-27; Tempels, *Bantu Philosophy,* 61 ff.

30. Tempels, *Bantu Philosophy,* 61-64; Mbiti, *African Religions and Philosophy,* 6.

31. Cf. Placide Tempels, *Bantu Philosophy,* 18-70, 95-114.

32. For a full discussion of this subject, see: Alexis Kagame's good treatment in the second half of his book, *La Philosophie Bantu-Rwandaise de l'Etre,* and Janheinz Jahn, *Muntu: An Outline of the New African Culture* (New York: Grove Press, 1961), chapter on African philosophy; Placide Tempels, *Bantu Philosophy,* 39-114. Jahn, like Tempels, sees NTU as a divine universal "vital force" underlying all things, whereas Kagame views it primarily in Aristotelian terms. Subsequently, like Aristotle, he views it as the primary substance that grounds and constitutes all actualities including God and the Soul.

These actualities are grouped together with all the cosmic intelligent beings in the one category of *"Muntu."* This is the first and most important category. Because "Muntu" possesses the unique divine property of mind and intelligence, is therefore, akin to God. Consequently, *"Muntu"* presides over the second category of *"Kintu"* as a "thing" or another non-intelligent force. The third category is that of *"Hantu,"* which covers the dimensions of space and time. Finally, Kagame invents the word *"Kuntu"* as the fourth category, which he describes simply as "mode." This category covers human moods as well as general aesthetics. However, the trouble with this grouping is that God becomes hypostatized into another being besides other beings as a kind of *primus inter pares*! This is therefore, unacceptable as a method of categorization of Being *(NTU)* and beings *(Bintu).* Furthermore, it would seem that if God *(Ruhanga/Imaana/Katonda)* is categorized together with human beings as MUNTU, sharing in the universal Ultimate Force or Reality which is *"NTU/Ozovehe."* In its african implicit understanding *"NTU"* is the correctly understood as the cosmic actuality and transcendent cosmic creative Mystery or God. *NTU* is the Ultimate Creative Reality.

NTU is the all-encompassing Ultimate Reality or God's creative essence is the "Ground of Being. Therefore, *NTU* is the most inclusive Ultimate Reality, Creative Cosmic Force and the Ultimate Origin of everything. Therefore, *"NTU"* serves in the same manner as "Being" serves in both the works of Paul Tillich and Martin Heidegger. *"Omuntu"* can also mean native to or an insider to *"NTU,"* i.e., being more expressive of being, whereas "Eki-ntu" can also mean on the external or the periphery of *NTU,* and as such having less *"NTU"* than the *"Omuntu"* who, being more on the inside *(Omu-NTU),* has more *"NTU"* and is the most akin to *"NTU"* as God in the whole of creation, and therefore, *"NTU's"* image and temporal expression in all creation; cf. Tempels, *Bantu Philosophy,* 49-55.

33. Cf. Martin Heidegger, *Being and Time,* trans. John Macquarrie & Edward Robinson (London: SCM Press, Ltd., 1962), H. 15, H. 41-126, H. 212-246, H. 334-392; see also Tempels, *Bantu Philosophy,* 44-114; Kagame, *Philosophie Bantu-Rwandaise,* 109-123.

34. Cf.Thomas Aquinas, *Summa Theologiae,* I:qq. 1-13. However, the African philosophical understanding of God in this area has not yet been well researched into. Nevertheless, Kagame's work in Rwanda, can be cited to support this claim; cf. *La Philosophie Bantu-Rwandaise de l'Etre,* 240 ff.; Tempels, *Bantu Philosophy,* 44-114; Richard A. Wright, ed., *African Philosophy: An Introduction* (Washington, D.C.: Uni. of America, 1979), 149-156; Kwasi Wiredu, *Philosophy and African Culture,* 37-50.

35. Cf. Tempels, *Bantu Philosophy,* 39-114; Noel King, *Religions of Africa,* 32-61.

36. See Plato's *Timaeus.*

37. Cf. Tempels, *Bantu Philosophy*, 44-94.

38. The exception being the Banyarwanda, who call God "*Imaana.*" They also have additional usual descriptive terms for God, which in this case hinge around the name "*Imaana,*" e.g. "*Hategikimana*" (Imaana/God reigns); "*Bizimana*" (God knows all things), "*Hashakimana*" (only God plans/knows). These divine attributes also form names of people to express total human dependency on God and their humble acknowledgment and gratitude. Cf. Alex Kagame, *La Philosophie Bantu-Rwandaise de l'Etre*, 280-300.

39. For a comprehensive catalogue of these divine terminologies and names, see John Mbiti, *Concepts of God in Africa,* 327-336.

40. Most people that I interviewed in the villages who were not enlightened by Christian teaching did not know much about Ruhanga, whereas they were very familiar with individual religious cults and knew a great deal more about them. Are these cults to be treated, then, as representative of divine immanence in the African traditional world? See, Noel King, *Religions of Africa,* 47-61.

41. In 1941 eight Balokole leading students were expelled from Bishop Tucker Theological College because they refused to go to theological classes, regarding them as "modernist" and "unchristian."

42. Mr. Antyeri Bintukwanga was 105 years old when he was interviewed. He was interviewed at his home in Kakoba, in Mbarara, Southern Uganda. He was still incredibly intellectually alert and strong for his age. Although his sight was failing, his mental powers were still undiminished. I interviewed Mr. Bintukwanga on March 27 and 29, 1982; and May 13-17, 1992. He lived in the pre-colonial, the colonial and post-colonial eras! Mr. Bintukwanga testified that he was 27 years old when the first Christian missionaries came to Ankole. He was a devout Roman Catholic.

43. F. Geraud, "The Idea of God," in Donald Denoon, ed., *A History of Kigezi,* 163.

44. Kazooba is Amen-Ra in the ancient Egyptian religion and the Word of God (Logos) as described in John 1:1-2, 4-5: "In the beginning was the Word, and the Word was with God, and the Word was God. He was in the beginning with God. In him was life and the life was the light of men. The light shines in the darkness...darkness has not overcome it."

45. See Tempels, *Bantu Philosophy*, 17 ff., 44-69.

46. Whereas West Africa is generally rich in divinities, it is generally the reverse in East Africa; Idowu, *African Traditional Religion,* 165-173; Tempels, *Bantu Philosophy,* 44-70.

47. E.g., see A. Shorter, *Prayer in the Religious Traditions of Africa,* 10 ff.

48. See, e.g., Y. K. Bamunooba, "Diviners for the Abagabe," *Uganda Journal,* XXIX:1 (1965), 95-97; Y.K. Bamunooba and F. B. Welbourn, "Emandwa Initiation in Ankole," *Uganda Journal,* XXIX:1 (1965), 13-25; Welbourn, "Some Aspects of Kiganda Religion," *Uganda Journal,* XXVI (September, 1962), 171-182; Noel King, *Religions of Africa,* 32-48.

49. Because of Ugandan political complication by regionalism, tribalism and the military conflict between Buganda Kingdom and the Ugandan central government in 1966, all four kingdoms in Uganda (Buganda, Ankole, Bunyoro and Toro) were abolished by Milton Obote. But, in 1993 they were restored as non-political cutural institutions by Yoweri Museveni.

50. Cf. E. Bolaji Idowu, *African Traditional Religion: A Definition*, 108-189, and John S. Mbiti, *African Religions and Philosophy*, 8-18; also Tempels, *Bantu Philosophy*, 167-186.

51. Cf. Tempels, op. cit., 18-70, 95-114; Newell S. Booth, ed. *African Religions: A Symposium*, 32-68; Mbiti, *African Religions and Philosophy*, 75-100, 166-193; Noel King, *Religions of Africa*, 47-61.

52. Deviants are usually persecuted in the guise of witches and taboo violators. For instance, most of the people accused of witchcraft in this area are usually anti-social, unfriendly or very ugly individuals! See *Africa*, VIII:4 (1935) (whole number is devoted to "witchcraft"); J. Middleton and E. H. Winter, eds., *Witchcraft and Sorcery in East Africa* (London: Cambridge University Press, 1963).

53. Evil is considered to be what disrupts or destroys individual and communal peace and harmony (*Obusingye/Busingye* or *Mirembe*), as this is the *summum bonum* in African thinking. Consequently, whatever enhances this perceived *summum bonum* as peace and harmony is, similarly, considered to be good. Therefore, God is not the measure of ethics and morality; but rather, the human being in the context of the community who is the measure. This is the reverse of the traditional Judeo-Christian approach to ethics and morality. Cf. Tempels, *Bantu Philosophy*, 18-69, 95-166; Mbiti, *African Religions and Philosophy*, 194-215; Newell S. Booth, *African Religions*, 4-10, 32-68.

54. Tempels, *Bantu Philosophy*, 61-69; Mbiti, *African Religions and Philosophy*, 6.

55. This Ugandan creation and fall myth or story sounds like Genesis Chs. 1-3. The myth tells of the original perfect creation by God, the creation of man (Kintu) first and woman (Nnambi) to keep him company, and to reproduce and populate the earth. There is a divine commandment not to return to heaven, the woman (Nnambi) breaks it. As a result of this primordial act of human rebellion and sin against God, death (Walumbe) (as the ultimate evil) comes into the world. This because the human being is the cosmic high priest, advocate and mediator to God their creator. The human being is thought to be more akin to God and the finite child of God and concrete ambassador of God on earth and cosmic creation. This being the case, then humanity and the rest of God's creation inseparably bound in their cosmic fate and destiny. What happens to creation happens to humanity and what happens to humanity also happens to creation. This is the theological essence of the biblical stories of Adam and Eve (Gen. 2-3), and the story of Noah and the flood (Gen. 5-10).

56. Just like among the Black Americans, chicken is considered a great delicacy in Buganda. In this context, it can be said that chicken is for Nnambi what the fruit is for Eve in the Genesis "story of The Fall"; cf. Gen. 3:1-6. Both of them are desired for food, and lead to each woman's temptation and finally to the fateful disobedience and the violation of God's commandment that ushers death into the world.

57. Reminiscent of the *Homo Mensura* theory of the Sophist School of Philosophy, whose main exponents were Protagoras and Heraclitus; cf. e.g., Gordin H. Clark, *Thales to Dewey: A History of Philosophy*, 61-70

58. Cf. John S. Mbiti, *African Religions and Philosophy*, 2, 20, 92; Mbiti, *Introduction to African Religion*, 39 ff.; Okot p'Bitek, *African Religions in African Scholarship* (Kampala: East African Literature Bureau, 1970), 109.

59. John S. Mbiti, *African Religions and Philosophy*, 21. See also *New Testament Eschatology in African Background*, 24-62. However, some scholars like Tempels, Jahn and Kagame, whose words on Bantu philosophy predate that of Mbiti, tended to emphasize the Bantu concept of cosmic pervasive dynamism, creativity, or "vital force" (*UNTU/Ozovehe*) as the only key for understanding African philosophy and traditional religions. *NTU* is basic for understanding the African thought and religion. See Newell S. Booth, Jr., "An Approach to African Religions," *African Religions: A Symposium*, 1-10, or Mbiti, *African Religions and Philosophy*, 15-27; *New Testament Eschatology in African Background*, 24-62; Tempels, *Bantu Philosophy*, 17-114.

60. Cf. e.g. J. V. Taylor, *The Growth of the Church in Buganda* (London: S.P.K. Press, 1958), 28 ff., F. B. Welbourn, *East African Rebels: A Study of Some Independent Churches* (London: C.M.S. Press, 1961), 3 ff.

61. Cf. Welbourn, *East African Rebels*, 25 ff., for a slightly different version of this reckoning of time in Ankole.

62. Cf., e.g., Y. K. Bamunooba and F. B. Welbourn, "'Emandwa' Initiation in Ankole," *Uganda Journal*, XXIX:1 (1965), 13-25; Noel King, *Religions of Africa*, 43-46.

63. Cf. Newell S. Booth, ed., *African Religions: A Symposium*, 4-10, 15, 32-62; P. Tempels, *Bantu Philosophy*, 44-64, 95-114; R. A. Wright, ed., *African Philosophy: An Introduction*, 157-168.

64. Ibid. For the African, personal relationships which constitute the harmony and wholeness of the community have priority over everything else. This is because the individual is authentically constituted as "*Omuntu*" (a human being) by the living network of these interpersonal relationships of "I-Thou," in the context of the community (very much reminiscent of Martin Buber's book, *I-Thou).*

65. In Africa it is generally considered unfriendly, and rude for anyone to ask someone coming to visit, "What can I do for you?" That is considered very rude!

66. Mbiti, *African Religions and Philosophy*, 22-23. Mbiti's work on time is generally recognized as a fairly accurate observation and interpretation of the traditional concept of time in East Africa.

67. Cf. Tempels, *Bantu Philosophy*, 61 ff. Tempels and Mbiti are in agreement here that Africans are oriented to creation or genesis in the Zamani period as the glorious human era of the "archipatriarchs" and direct human communication and socializing with God!

68. Examples are the stories of Kintu, Nnambi and Walumbe in Buganda and the Bakiga-Banyankore story of the Musingo woman whose excessive hatred for her mother-in-law led to the general loss of the divine gifts of the resurrection and rejuvenation.

69. It is almost similar to the traditional Catholic doctrine of the Original Sin as it finds its key expression in St. Augustine; e.g., see *On Free Will*, XVI-XX; Rom. 5:12: "Therefore

as sin came into the world through one man and death through sin, and so death spread to all men." See also Tempels, *Bantu Philosophy*, 18-69, 95-114; Mbiti, *African Religions and Philosophy*, 92-100, 194-215.

70. It is thought that the enjoyable state of being "*Omuntu*" (a human being) ends with death. But, some human elements survive death in their new spiritual embodiment. This new state of existence is thought to be less meaningful and less enjoyable than that of being "*Omuntu.*" Consequently, death is thought of as an irrevocable great loss. Cf. Mbiti, *African Religions and Philosophy*, 31-34, 107-118, 195-218; Noel King, *Religions of Africa*, 62-82; Tempels, *Bantu Philosophy*, 18-64, 95-114, 187-189.

71. Cf. Eccl. 2:24, 4:11. This kind of attitude manifests a lack of a future dimension and probably helps to explain the general absence of permanent buildings in Africa South of the Sahara. An exception to this observation is the Zimbabwe stone walls. These walls were built for protection from the surrounding "warlike," "savage" and even presumably cannibal tribes; cf. Roger Summers, "City of Black Gold: The Riddle of Zimbabwe," in Edward Becon, ed., *Vanished Civilizations of the Ancient World*, 33-54.

72. "Living-dead" is Mbiti's term used to refer to the spirits of the recently departed, who are still regarded as part of the daily affairs of the community. For Mbiti, this is the stage of personal immortality, since the remembrance of the dead is still fully vivid and personal. See Mbiti, *African Religions and Philosophy*, 107-118.

73. "*Ba-ishenkuru-itwe*" should ideally be used to refer to ancestral spirits and others that are good. The term "*emizimu*," if used appropriately, should refer to the malignant or evil spirits as the ghosts of the departed. There are no "good *emizimu.*" See Noel King, *Religions of Africa*, 32-46; P. Tempels, *Bantu Philosophy*, 44-70, 115-165.

74. Cf. Tempels, *Bantu Philosophy*, 55, 61 ff.

75. The story of Khabengu as the expected eschatological Messiah of the Sonjo, that reads like the story of Jesus, is unique in Africa. See R. F. Gray, *The Sonjo of Tanganyika* (London: Oxford U Press, 1963); Mbiti, *African Religions and Philosophy*, 30, 250. The Khabengu story or myth illustrates clearly the nature of divine revelation in African Religion.

76. Most African languages there is no single word for "future." There is the word "*Kesho*," which means tomorrow, and beyond that one has to describe the future time in terms of days, weeks, months or years. This is also true for other nine African languages of which I speak. See also Mbiti, *New Testament Eschatology in African Background*, 24-61, and *African Religions and Philosophy*, 19-35; Rechenbach's *Swahili-English Dictionary* (Washington, D.C.: Foreign Service Institute, 1967); H. F. Morris and B. E. R. Kirwan, *A Runyankole Grammar* (Kampala: EALB, 1957); C. Taylor's *Simplified Runyankole-Rukiga English Dictionary* (Kampala: EALB, 1959).

77. This is akin to the traditional Christian conception of God and time as found in St. Thomas; cf. *Summa Theologiae*, I:I q. 10. This is in contradiction to the Whiteheadian Process Philosophy. See Alfred North Whitehead, *Process and Reality*, Parts III and V:II. See also Alex Kagame, *La Philosophie Bantu-Rwandaise de l'Etre*, 332 ff; Tempels, *Bantu Philosophy*, 49-70; R. A. Wright, ed., *African Philosophy: An Introduction*, 149-156.

VII

AFRICAN CONCEPTS OF THE HUMAN BEING
AS A UNIQUE SOCIAL DIVINE-SPIRITUAL
BEING AND GOD'S HIGH-PRIEST
IN THE WORLD

According to the prevailing traditional African Religion, philosophy, and theocentric ontological world-view, God is the multimedia Transcendent, omnipresent creative, animating and redemptive "Cosmic Force." The human being or "*Omuntu/Muntu*" as commonly locally referred to among most Bantu ethnic groups of Africa, is an intelligent and self-conscious embodiment of this divine creative and redemptive force in the world.

Therefore, by virtue of this unique universal human nature which is naturally attuned to God by an *a priori* possession of God-consciousness, the human being is God's concrete revelation of God in the cosmos, the chosen temporal representative and high-priest of God in the cosmos. As a result, the human being is a divine being that belongs with God at the center of the world events, and its affairs. For most Africans the human being is God's freely chosen and elect mediator between the transcendent Mystery and matter; mind and body; spirit and matter; God and creatures, and heaven and earth. This is more so for the elders, kings and those elected and ordained by the community to serve as their specialized priests and mediums to the spiritual world of mind, spirits, departed ancestors or patriarchs, matriarchs, gods, God and eternal life.

Accordingly, human beings are religious and priestly creatures by God's special gift in creation as fragments of his embodied mind, spirit, creativity, and divinity. They were created in order to serve God as his ambassadors in the world of matter. As such, human beings everywhere and in every age have engaged in liturgical and intercessional activities. These sacred or religious activities, include rituals and sacrifices to God and the ancestors are regarded as the center of the human community and the social or human-spirit world (*Ensi*). The main concern of the Creator (Ruhanga) is all creation and not just the world of human beings.[1]

The "*Muntu*" is not only the servant, voice or medium, high-priest or vicar and representative of God in creation, but also shares in divine being (*NTU*) as God's essence of life and spiritual force of existence. This special kinship between "*Omuntu*" and Ruhanga (God/Creator) is demonstrated in the fact that "*Omuntu*" participates in Ruhanga's or Katonda's divine creative intelligence and primordial divine essence as the skill of creativity (*Kuhanga-hanga or Kutonda*).[2]

Consequently, the human being is universally both inwardly and outwardly uniquely marked as God's special creature. This is universally the case by virtue of the human being's possession of these distinctive, unique divine qualities and charismatic gifts. These special divine-human attributes are primarily characterized by a higher level of intelligence, critical or analytical thinking, language, agape, religion or God-consciousness, self-consciousness, self-transcendence, freedom, moral responsibility, knowledge and creativity. These are also the very divine and supernatural attributes, which are generally attributed to God and his nature and quintessence as Ruhanga or Katonda (the Transcendent Cosmic Creator).

God or Ruhanga/Katonda is affirmed to have created human beings, and mercifully or gratuitously given his own divine attributes, and nature and moral qualities as his free gifts to the human beings (*Bantu*). These divine gifts were freely bestowed on human beings by God their creator and Father/Primordial Ancestor, so that they, too, would become like their Father-God, their creator, and have eternal fellowship with him as his children.

Therefore, human beings were originally created in order to participate in God's own divine nature, and to become his intelligent creative assistants, adopted children, temporal heirs, and responsible representatives in the world (*Ensi*) which depends on the human being for brains, mind, intellect, thought and priestly intercession to God for rain and fertility.[3] In return, the human being (*Omuntu*) depends on the earth for livelihood, specifically for food, shelter, possessions, wealth and recreation. Furthermore, the human being is also dependent on the world for the mediation of divine mystery and revelation.

Subsequently, "*Omuntu*" is by essential constitution unique and God's (Ruhanga's) special creature in creation. Although "*Omuntu*" shares in divine qualities of spirit, intelligence, creativity and loving, he simultaneously also shares in the animal characteristics, such as the possession of a body and its physical needs for food, shelter, security and reproduction. In addition, the human being sometimes participates in animality itself by expressions of aggressiveness, selfishness and brutality.

According to the Bantu people under discussion, "*Omuntu*" (the human being) *qua* unique human being (*Omuntu*) is composed of the following essential elements:

1. "*Omubiri*" (body, form, flesh and matter).

2. "*Omwisyo/Amagara*" (breath, air, life, soul and spirit).

3. "*Ekicucu*" (shadow, spirit, soul or the double).

4. "*Amaani*" (vitality, strength, force, energy and power).

5. "*Omutima*" (heart as the seat of emotions and values, such as vice, goodness, virtue, compassion and agape).

6. "*Omutwe/Obwengye*" (head or brain/intellect, mind, and wisdom. It is the universal characteristic human intellectual capacity for abstract thought, or critical and analytical thinking). This is the fundamental universal human quintessence. Mind (*Omutwe*) distinguishes human beings from animals. Its existence enables other unique human characteristics to evolve and function. A person without "*Omutwe*" is "*Omufu*" (dead or a fool). This means that without *Omutwe* (intellect), one cannot speak (*Ororimi*), possess a spirit or shadow (*Ekicucu*), possess strength (*Amaani*) or have a heart (*Omutima*).

7. "*Ororimi*" (language or tongue, speaking and the capacity or skill to speak. The Africans understand human beings to be essentially linguistic and story telling and myth creating animals. Oral expression is more esteemed than the writing. Consequently, according the Africans God is ever speaking his Word. And there is no need for God to write down his eternal Word, since the Word of God, like the human word and story needs to be constantly adjusted to the present audience and its uniqueness. The characteristic nature and needs of the audience and the changing times demand that God and his Word remain current, and therefore, constantly speaking God's Word of love and redemption to human beings, everywhere in the cosmos.

This unique divine-human capacity to hear God's Word and speak, is revelatory of other unique divine qualities which are found in all human beings, such as mind, intelligence and thinking. As a result, speaking transforms a biological animal or evolutionary creature into real human being or "*omuntu*" vis-a-vis "*ekintu*" or thing.)

8. "*Obuntu*" (virtue and agape; "*imago Dei*," humaneness, peace-seeking, humanness or *huminitus vis-a-vis humanitus*).[4]

The first four elements, "*Omubiri*" (body), "*Ekicucu*" (shadow or soul), the "*Amagara/Omwisyo*" (life, breath), and "*Amaani*" (force, strength or energy), are shared in common by all living things as basic ingredients for biological life on earth. The remaining four elements, "*Omutima*" (heart, humane emotions), "*Omutwe*" (intellect, head or thinking), "*Orurimi*" (speaking/language) and "*Obuntu*" (humaneness/humanness), are specific qualities that make "*Omuntu*" qua "*Omuntu*" (the authentic human being), the very special creature of God in the world who is the essential gravitational cosmic center of life and all creation.[5]

It is therefore, only God who can most appropriately and satisfactorily serve as the cosmic pivotal cohesive and sustaining force of life, meaningful creaturely freedoms and self-fulfillment. That is, God is both the natural and supernatural cosmic center of all being, life, creation, human beings and their ultimate meaning, self-fulfillment, peace, love, redemption or salvation, happiness and destiny. Because of these unique human-divine qualities, the human being is the only creature that is self-conscious as a contingent finite being that is completely dependent on God for both its origin, sustenance or redemption and destiny.

Furthermore, the above four special human-divine abstract elements are supposed to survive death. It is generally believed that at the time of death the primary human qualities separate from the material body which then dies. Subsequently, these abstract qualities are supposed to be embodied in the "*ekicucu*" (shadow/spirit) as their own new spiritual embodiment. This new phenomenon is the human phase of existence commonly known as a the "living-dead," "ghost," "*mizimu*" and the "ancestors."

After death or transition from a material-physical body to a non-material and non-physical or spiritual body, the good benevolent spirits being the spirits of good and loving people who are now deceased are immortalized, deified and venerated as the benevolent "ancestors." This divinization and canonization process of good ancestral spirits into guardian saints and angels of God, is co-extensive with God's judgement and reward of just, good and loving people with eternal life in God's kingdom (cf. Matt. 25:31-40).

Although the ancestors are venerated, at the same time, the spirits of the evil people who are now deceased are feared and ostracized as being malicious evil agents who are referred to as ghosts, "evil spirits" or "*mizimu*." As a result, priests are sometimes hired to catch and destroy them before they can do harm to the living relatives and the community. In other words, they are judged and sentenced to hell for eternal destruction (cf. Matt. 25:41-46).

Nevertheless, for the traditional Africans, life on earth is still more preferred to a life either in hell or heaven with God as the ancestors. In this respect, life on earth is for the Africans more akin to God's kingdom than the utopian life after death, when as a good person or hero, one becomes an ancestor, spirit, saint or god. As a result, for the African, death is always considered a great tragedy. Premature death is to be avoided and to be protected from by God.

Through his chain of intermediaries, God intervenes in daily life, and human history in order to offer and mediate his grace, power, mercy and protection from evil, misfortunes and untimely death. These mediators between God and human beings include parents, elders, priests, the ancestors, medicine-men/women, magicians, and divine-kings. Whatever, works to ward off death is deemed as God's divine gift of life and immortality. As such, it is not inconsistent for African Christians to worship both in church and traditional African temples, or to seek advice from mediums, priests and magicians regarding the protection of their own lives or that of their friends, relatives or how to protect their property from harm, especially from witchcraft and other disasters.

Accordingly, many African Christians are, indeed, also the zealous adherents of the African Religion. African Christianity is also in this respect an extension or expansion of the African Religion in quest of modernity. As such, the African Religion has indeed adopted Christianity in Africa, instead of being converted or negated by it.

Inculturation in Africa is, therefore, a process contextualization of Christianity within the African traditional religious world-view. Conversely, Christian inculturation is the process by which African Religion has finally triumphed in adapting and adopting Christianity, the way in which Greek philosophy adopted Christianity as a new religion and created a new hellenic Western Civilization.

Ultimately, within the African ontology, anthropology and philosophy the above eight primary human attributes and special qualities have to be fully present for the creature or being in which they manifest themselves to be recognized as a human being (*Omuntu) vis-a-vis "Ekintu"* (a thing/it). The "*Kintu*" (thing or "an it") category, in contrast to the "*Muntu*" (human) category, is composed of all other objects, creatures and beings in the world which are neither divine nor human.

However, the "*Muntu*" category only includes people who are *whole* in respect to these eight constitutive elements; otherwise they get categorized as "*Kintu.*" For instance, most Bakiga and Banyankole of Southern Uganda categorize the seriously physically or mentally handicapped people as "*Ekintu*" (a thing or "the-it") and as "*Birema*" (the defective or deformed).

These "*Birema*" (deformed/handicapped people) are not recognized as "fully *Bantu*" (human beings). They are regarded as incomplete, and therefore, categorized as "*Kintu*" (things). This also applies to those people who are sexually impotent. They are completely rejected and dehumanized by society. They are derogatorily referred to as "*Ebifeera*" meaning those who are socially, intellectually, morally and genetically/sexually dead.[6] Although they are physically alive, they are regarded as socially and religiously dead, mainly because life, its continuity and personal immortality, according to these people, depend on the stability, viability and continuity of the family through the offspring.

Consequently, the traditional African society valued the ability of each individual member of the society to marry and have a big family. The ideal African traditional family was supposed to be composed of many wives and many children. This was practice was societally highly valued and economically desirable in order to be able to work the agricultural fields more easily with this large free labor force.

Perhaps, most important of all, the large and extended African family was also greatly desired and valued for political and religious reasons. It was considered necessary in order to strengthen the "clan" or ethnic group, and to immortalize the departed ancestors. The larger the family, the more regular and effective were the rituals performed in order to preserve more effectively the memory and names of the departed ancestors and relatives, since it was generally believed that with more numbers there is a "corresponding increase" in the ability and potential for immortality of family members through their posterity.[7]

The African society is strongly oriented to practical communal action, and requires participation by all its members, including even children at their own level. Therefore, anybody who is too handicapped to participate will also be unable to maintain relationships and the required obligations to join in these family and communal activities.

These activities are considered essential, since they are believed to constitute the authentic life of "*Omuntu*." To be a true or an authentic "*Omuntu*" is basically to become both correlatively and coextensively a human being who is essentially humane, considerate, loving, social, able-bodied and a willing participatory member of the respective human community. Consequently, the term "*Omuntu*" only refers to the normal people and not to the "*Birema*" (deformed people), "*Empumi*" (the physically blind), "*Biteeta*" (the dumb or those unable to speak) and the like, because these handicapped individuals are regarded as incomplete, and even more important, perhaps, they are unable to participate fully in the activities of the community. For that matter, those who were born abnormal (*Ebihiindi*) were usually secretly and quietly killed at birth.[8]

In West Africa, particularly Ghana, some of these abnormal children were left by the river banks for the water spirit to take them away. In parts of East and central Africa, these kinds of children were also sometimes left at the junctions of the paths. More often, these abnormal children were also taken and abandoned in remote or lonely places such as rivers, swamps, forests, wooded valleys, mountains or other isolated places, where diseases and evil spirits connected with such abnormalities and malice would be harmlessly confined.

For these Bantu people of East and Central Africa, language or speaking is considered to be a uniquely human characteristic. To be human means to speak and to speak is both to be divine and human or *"Bantu."* Language and speaking are definitive of essential humanity to the extent that whatever speaks would be regarded as a form of *"Omuntu."* Furthermore, all people are ethnically identified with their own language. For instance, you are French if you speak French as your mother or native language, regardless of whether you are White, Black or Brown! Therefore, for a person to be unable to speak or dumb or to be deaf, was regarded as a terrible misfortune. It was pessimistically viewed as God's punishment for the sins of the ancestors and the community.

Nevertheless, not being able to speak is negatively regarded as a great tragedy and an existential evil. In the understanding of the African philosophy and ontology, this physical or natural evil deprives the individual of the opportunity of ever becoming fully human, since to be human is to be linguistic. Within this African religious ontology, philosophical metaphysics and world-view, the inability to speak or communicate fully limits the human potential for full personhood and divinization as a social child of God in the community which is characterized by language and oral communication.

In any oral society anywhere in the world, language or speech is the essential fundamental medium for the verbal expressive of the unique personal or collective story, which is the fundamental essence of being a human being. This is particularly true in ancient Africa, Native America, Arabia, Polynesia, Palestine, India, China, Japan, New Zealand, and Australia.

The human being as a social, story-telling animal is also a self-transcending divine spirit or finite mystery which exists in "the never ending great cycle of life" or "perpetual humanization process" of self-actualization, self-completion, self-discovery, and joyful self-revelation to the neighbor and the community. This is affirmed to be the case since to be fully human is not only to be humane (to possess the of *Obuntu*), but also to be fully revelatory of God and these noble virtues and humanizing qualities to the community. This requires that an authentic human being should be essentially humane, linguistic, communicative and dialogical.

Subsequently, among these predominantly illiterate African people, language in its story, flowery, poetic and memorable verbal form is greatly esteemed as indicative of "*Omutwe*" (mind, intellect and wisdom), "*Orurimi*" (tongue or language, capacity for speaking) and being expressive of the "*Omutima*" (the heart, emotion, compassion and mind or person-hood). Perhaps most important of all, language is the primary medium for "*Omuntu's*" or human being's self-consciousness, explicit self-communication or self-revelation and the essential expression to the self, the neighbor and the community.

Therefore, both verbal and non-verbal or symbolic language is the essential medium for humanization. It is the essential vehicle for active human self-understanding, basic social self-expression of both the implicit and explicit forms of "*Obuntu*" or the human essence. This expression of authentic humanity or *Obuntu* is expressed through nonverbal and effective symbolic language which is composed of concrete benevolent and altruistic acts of love or agape and compassion, which is considered to constitute authentic human existence and "*Bantu*" (human) *raison d'etre*.[9]

In this respect, the Africans universally affirm that the nonverbal body and symbolic language of works, ritual, attitudes, behavior and both unintentional and intentional or explicit deeds and actions speak louder than words alone. Therefore, for the African a person is truly what he or she does in life and not what he or she consciously confesses.

The wicked people are wicked because they do evil things and not because they confess to be evil. Conversely, the good, just and righteous holy saints of God, are good and holy because they both implicitly or explicitly obey God's commandments; and also in faith by appropriating the power of God's universal redemptive grace, are enabled by God to live in concrete humane paths of justice, goodness, holiness, love and peace with themselves and their neighbors.

Therefore, the saints of God in traditional Africa, India and native America, are externally known by their own concrete and explicit manner of life as judged by the nature and quality and quantity of good and charitable deeds and the just or holy ways or habits of personal life as lived with one's neighbors in the social context of the total human community and the rest of God's creation. As such, the African traditional religion is in full harmony with the basic ethical, social and religious teachings of Jesus Christ as regards the real state of virtue, agape, justice, godliness, sainthood and eternal salvation (cf. Matt. 7:13-23; 25:31-46).

1. "*Buntu*" as the Quintessence of Authentic Humanity (*Muntu*) Expressing Itself in Altruism as the Unconditional Love for the Neighbor

Among the "Bantu people" of Central and Southern Africa, Zaire, Rwanda, Burundi, parts of Tanzania, Ankole, Kigezi, Toro, Bunyoro, Buganda, Busoga, Bugisu, Bugwere and parts of Kenya the "*Buntu*" is considered to be the most important quality of "*Omuntu.*" This is because Obuntu constitute the basic human essential ethical, moral, spiritual, social and religious fundamental synergistic quintessence of authentic human existence. The person possessing the greater degree of "*Buntu*" is greatly praised as good, humane, thoughtful, caring, considerate, kind, wise, godly (religious), loving, generous, polite, hospitable, mature, virtuous and blessed."

Obuntu" indicates an inner state of complete humanization and diviniza- tion or transformation into the fullness of God's own image (*imago Dei*) and concrete representative on earth. "*Obuntu*" as this ideal state of divine salvation and heaven on earth, is externally manifested to the world and exercised in society by the diligent praxis of the noble godly moral and societal qualities and divinizing virtues of love or agape as in the case of altruism, peace-making (*Busingye/Mirembe*), contentedness, joyfulness, generosity, humanness, humility, wisdom (*amagezi*) and understanding.

Since "*Obuntu*" is regarded as the quintessence of authentic humanity and being, the essence of the "*Omuntu*," it is possible then to be a good person or an authentic "*Muntu*" without the "*Buntu*" as the main element that constitutes the human being, as such.[10]

"*Obuntu*" is then a free divine gift as well as positive training and regular practicing of virtue by doing good deeds and treating other people appropriately and treating them with respect and dignity as "*Abantu*" (human beings) *vis-a-vis* "*Ebintu*" (things/"its") or treating them impersonally as the nameless and faceless in the form of the undifferentiated crowd. This also includes those people who are depersonalized and impersonally referred to "*en mass*" simply as "they."

Therefore, society tries to train the young in virtue in order to condition them into a permanent state of virtue that is grounded in the "*Obuntu*." In the final analysis, it is this state of virtue as free human existential personal condition of the degree of humanization, that is self-expressed externally in free personal deeds or acts and attitudes that reveal the state of the inner quality at the core of one's humanity. The positive expression of humanity in humane acts of love is what is generally termed "*Obuntu*" and applauded as human perfection, whereas its absence is condemned as evil, wickedness and animality. The underlying philosophical and moral or ethical normative basis of value judgement being the fundamental hypothesis and ontological affirmation that "*HUMAN BEINGS ARE WHAT THEY CHOOSE AND DO!*" Ultimately, human beings are inseparable from their choices and deeds.

This means that in order to tell what kind of human being the respective person is, you simply look at their moral explicit choices, nature and quality deeds or actions and the manifested external behavior. As Jesus also correctly put it, you know them by their fruits (cf. Matt. 7:13-14). Those people who are good are known by their good deeds or "*Obuntu*" and are judged by God and society and rewarded accordingly as such. Conversely, those people who are evil are also known by their wickedness. This wickedness is externally manifested in evil deeds ("*kibi/bubi/ebibi*" or "*mbaya*"). Consequently, these evil-doers are also accordingly sanctioned and punished by both God and their own society (cf. Matt. 7:13-21; 25:31-46). To put it differently, "*Obuntu*" is the divine means for the humanization of the "*Abantu*" and as such, God's gratuitous proffer of salvation and perfection. The person with full "*Obuntu*" is consequently esteemed as the ideal, authentic, complete, blessed, good, loving, godly and "perfect human being." Like Jesus the Christ, the traditional Africans, being a God, community, Agape and good social action oriented, also tend to think that a person is what he/she does in the community in relation to the neighbor.

For both Jesus and the Africans, a good person or God's saint is analogous to a good fruit tree, which is only known, and practically judged to be good merely on the basis of the nature of the good quality and abundance of the good fruits. Therefore, for both Jesus and the Africans, a person's worth, goodness, godliness, and moral character, are also correspondingly definitively societally expressed, revealed, known, and measured by the practical concrete scales in terms of social actions of agape, and good deeds in the community and the world (cf. Matt. 5:13-27; James 2:1-26).

These good theocentric deeds are essential to a good personal and collective life in the community and God's kingdom. They are also considered not only to come from a good person, but also to be actually the means for positive transformation of the respective doer of the good into a correlatively loving, good, benevolent, and obedient saint both before God and the human community (cf. Matt. 25:31-46).

Conversely, wicked deeds come from a wicked person as the concrete visible fruits an inward evil disposition. Moreover, evil deeds also make the evil-doer visibly evil so that the public could also see what kind of moral agent the respective person really is. As a result, the greatest compliment a person or the society can pay to an individual is to call him or her "GOOD" (*Omuntu Murungi vs. Omuntu Mubi*). This is the kind of person usually thought to possess a greater degree of the actualized "*Obuntu*" in one's life and actions, particularly, the capability to love and share one's home, food, wealth and goods with the concrete neighbor and relatives.

Consequently, human wickedness and moral evil are mainly attributed to failure in unconditional love (*Rukundo/Kwagara kwa Katonda*) for the relatives, neighbors and other members of the community and the consequent deficiency in "*Obuntu*" or humanity.[11] For instance, most of those people accused of witchcraft are usually those people who are antisocial or those who express hatred for their neighbors and relatives! Therefore, the "*Obuntu*" (Agape) and "*Amagezi*" (correct knowledge and wisdom) are essential foundations for necessary skills in the building and maintenance of good and peaceful interpersonal and societal relationships. They also lead to the respect of human life, dignity and trust, and the enhancement of societal harmony, cohesion, contentedness and peace.

Conversely, its absence leads to tension, conflicts, frustration and the disintegration of these basic human relationships and the community, since "*Buntu bulamu*"[12] is not just human positive qualities, but also the very human essence itself, which "lures" and enables human beings to become "Abantu" or humanized beings, living in daily self-expressive works of love and attempts to create harmonious interpersonal relationships in their community and the world beyond.

2. The Community as the Context for God's Creation, Humanization ("*Muntu*" and "*Buntu*") and Salvation as Harmony and Peace ("*Obusingye/Mirembe*" and "*Magara*")

In African thinking and cultural practices, the collective group as the local human community is the fundamental social, cultural, religious, moral and ontological context and central focus of life.

Accordingly, African life is both essentially social and societal in its primary practical orientation, ideal manifestation, and celebration. All the important human activities are social and collective. Therefore, the community is considered to be the arena of God's twin activities of creation and redemption of the individual as well as the collective group. Correlatively, the social group as the community is also the essential primary grounding of all positive and meaningful or satisfying human existence, particularly at the family level in its indefinitely extended broad scope.[13]

This as true for the living as it is for the departed ancestors or the living dead. Therefore, God through the community provides life and immortality for the individual people, the community and its collective members, either the living or the departed living dead. All the people that ever lived and who are still remembered are considered real social members of the community. The ancestral spirits are part of the living community and act as guardian angels and mediators between the living relatives and their transcendent God in heaven.

In this African social and cultural context, the family in its extended form is not just the primary social arena of the community, it is also the primary economic, political and religious viable social segment of the local community and the rest of society. In this respect, the family is the primary religious community analogous to the local Church parish within the Roman Catholic Church. The African traditional family head served as the mediator, high priest and sacerdotal sacrificial religious leader of the household and the extended family.

This function was analogous and the same with that of the traditional medieval sacerdotal parish priest, that is in as much as he served as the sacrificial priest at mass and high priest or mediator between God, the saints or the ancestors and the people within the life of the parish Church family. Within the African family religious and social context, each major family meal and gathering was a sacred gathering before God, the saints as the departed ancestors of whom libation was poured out by the family head as the family high priest.

The family meal was ritually blessed by the elder, and then reverently distributed and served as the family eucharist and "Agape meal." The eucharistic celebrant was the family head as the elder and official mediator between the family, the ancestors and God. The family home constituted the sacred temple of the omnipresent God, and small alters were elected in the house or in special miniatures temples which were elected outside in the compound or in the privacy of banana plantation or trees near the house.

Temples and shrines varied in shape and size. Nevertheless, most of them were designed to mere miniatures or micro-representations of God's special holy temple of which the macro-representation was the entire cosmos. As such, large rocks, mountains (Kenya, Rwenzori, Kilimanjaro, Birunga), fire, rivers (Congo, Nile, Niger, Zambezi), lakes (Albert, Nyanza (Victoria), Nyasa or Malawi), the sun (Kazooba, Ra), the moon and the like could serve as concrete visible symbols for God's immanent powerful presence in creation and redemption or sustenance. These sacred African symbols for God's own creative power and holy transcendence are analogous to the Hebrew symbols of God in the cloud and fire on Mt. Sinai (cf. Ex. 3:1-6; 19:19-20:26), and the baptismal holy Jordan in the Bible.

Accordingly, Moses encountered God's holy presence and received the Ten Commandments on Mt. Sinai. Moses saw God in the form of the burning bush, and Jesus encountered God's holy divinizing power in the baptismal waters of the holy river of Jordan (cf. Mk. 1:8-11). In this baptism Jesus came to hear God's voice of affirmation that he was, indeed, God's beloved son.

These kinds of human holy encounters of God and experiences of God's power in nature were in harmony with the African traditional religious cultures and historical religious experiences. The only major difference was that the African religious tradition and history of salvation was oral whereas that of Israel and Christianity had been written down and canonized by the respective religious communities as God's Word.

Nevertheless, the African oral scriptures and history of God's special activities of salvation were still meaningful, divinizing and morally edifying to the Africans, who heard them and obeyed God's Word as taught to them through the local religious tradition, the moral guidance of the wise men, the counsel of the elders, the warnings of the priests and prophets.

As a result of this profound African religious tradition, when the historical Apostolic Christianity was introduced in Africa, they did not see it as an alien religion. They saw it as it as a natural completion of their own religious traditions. Roman Catholicism was viewed to be akin to the African traditional religion and local cultural practices.

Therefore, it was almost natural that most Africans who were converted to Christianity, would convert to Roman Catholicism. They did not feel that they were converting to a completely alien new religion. On the contrary, most of them saw Catholicism as a new inclusive global European centered version of the African Traditional Religion.

Catholicism as the new religion was centered in Rome, and had more educated priests, and more complicated mystical system of ancestor-veneration (worship), sacrificial rituals, and ceremonies of sacrifice at mass. For African Catholics, the new religion was a completion and fulfillment of the African Religion. As such, for many less well educated African masses, the Roman Catholicism was positively viewed, and welcomed as a more expanded global form of the African Religion.

Apart from the discouraging restriction of polygamy, in inclusive Catholicism, many traditionalist Africans found meaningful fulfillment and completion of the African Religion. For these Africans, Roman Catholicism presented a larger and more efficacious global system of the elaborate cult and ritualistic veneration of saints or the ancestors, and a global network of cultic and sacrificial priests, who paid allegiance to an ultimate single global presiding Divine-Priest-King in the form of the Pope in Rome. Thus, for many African Catholics, to see the Pope is to see God on earth, and to touch the Pope is to touch the God with us (Emmanuel). In this African philosophical-theological understanding, the Pope is analogous to the Pharaoh in ancient Egypt, the Ashantehene in the ancient kingdom of Ghana, and the Emperor in pre-Marxist Ethiopia.

The Pope in Rome was viewed in the African theocentric feudal terms and cosmic chain of mediation between the radically transcendent and distant holy God in heaven and the sinful, finite human beings who dwelled in a state of anxiety due to the primordial human sin and subsequent alienation from God and estrangement on earth. Therefore, as the "Vicar of Christ" on earth or as the divinely elect, and chosen visible temporal Mediator of God and humanity on earth, the Pope was very highly esteemed.

Within the African cosmology, the Pope was naturally adopted and added to the existing chain of mediators between human beings and God, but was regarded as being next to God, since he was also perceived as the concrete temporal and spiritual God's Cosmic Chief High Priest and Chief Mediator between God and all humanity.

In this respect, for the majority of the rural and less educated African Catholicism, the Pope took over much of the function that the Protestants attribute to Jesus as the Christ in his role as cosmic High Priest and Mediator between God and humanity. In addition, for most uneducated African Catholics the dogma of the "Papal Infallibility" was positively viewed as the evidence of this special divine mediatorial and redemptive role that the Pope was supposed to play efficaciously between human beings on earth and the transcendent holy God in heaven.

Again, Roman Catholicism has greatly succeeded in Africa more than the elitist, anti-Africa culture, and individualistic Protestantism. Catholicism's great success in Africa is largely due to its theological similarity and affinity to the African Religion and the operative theocentric world-view. This is particularly, more visible in the Catholic ritualistic liturgical insight and capacity to plug into the pre-existing African religious ideas, structures of saints, the ancestors, sacerdotal priesthood, sacrifices and the centrality of the family social gathering for the ritual celebration of the family meal as a necessary and essential social and religious social eucharistic feast.

Like the regular family meal is required for nurture and good health, analogously, the regular attendance at mass, and the eucharist, were likewise, required for the continued for a good, and healthy life. This good life is synonymous with a harmonious life in the community, in fellowship with the neighbor, God and ancestors or the saints. This harmonious fellowship mediated the necessary divine Agapic blessings of God and the ancestors, thus, leading to social harmony, peace and the spiritual well-being of the people, community, the ancestors, nature and the rest of God's creation. It is therefore, self-evident, that within the Judeo-Christian tradition, this state of affairs, is what constitutes or is meant by God's kingdom and heaven.

This African fundamental theocentric social principle of the primacy of the community over the individual is probably best summed up in Professor Mbiti's words, "I am, because we are: and since we are, therefore, I am."[14] As such, the African human social principle negates the Western individualistic principle as rationally, stated by Rene Descartes as *"cogito ergo sum"* (I think, therefore, I am).

Contrary to the Western dualistic and individualistic thinkers, like Descartes, the Africans are usually wholistic in their thinking, and for them, the community is more important. The human community is prior to the existence of the individuals as the fundamental prerequisite for that individual occurrence and existence as both an authentic human being, and responsible, social moral agent both in the local community and the world.

For the traditional Africans, the human social community is prior to the individual, because without the prior existence of the community, no individuals would be born. Individuals are born, out of and into the human community. It is also through the medium of the human community, that human beings are brought into being by God, and then, humanized and finally divinized. The young people are born into respective families, and as new members of the human community, they are initiated into the membership of global humanity (*Abantu*), simultaneously, as they are initiated into the local community, and socialized or "processed" into becoming responsible human(e) beings (*Abantu*), who are endowed with *Obuntu* (humanness), which exists prior to the individual, as an *a priori* within the human community in which the individuals are born.

Therefore, the community, on behalf of the wider human society, undertakes the duty of turning the infant into a viable, responsible, well-humanized individual (*Omuntu*) member of the community and the human race (*Abantu*) in general.[15] This means the acquisition of the art of speaking and language (*Orurimi*), the mental development and the acquisition of basic skills (*Omutwe/Obwengye*), the sound grounding in the culture and history of the family and the community (tribe and nation). It also means the acquisition of humane normative principles for responsible decision-making and action (*Obuntu*) in the context of the felt common good and the total community (without disrupting the harmony and communal cohesion and well-being. The ideal condition is that of seeking to enhance these noble and ideal societal virtues.

This is effectively achieved by learning to know, master and effectively control one's emotions ("*okwetonda*" or "*kwetwara mpora*") and not letting the emotions and bodily urges or needs dominate and control him/her so that he/she fails to manifest responsible mature choices or proper reactions (*Omutima*) during situations of stress or danger. This includes social situations which require appropriate behavior and socially acceptable positive responses, such as showing compassion, pity and grief during bereavement, regardless of who has died, whereas manifesting the virtues of courage and bravery in the case of trouble or danger, rather than the despised vice of cowardice.

These elements were generally covered in the training and initiation into the "*Emandwa*" cult in both Kigezi and Ankole. To dramatize it, all the initiation candidates were stripped naked before the community, to impress on them that they were born naked and open to the community, and therefore, the need for them to remain humble, open and receptive to the guidance and customs of the community that seeks to clothe, nurture, nourish and enlighten them as members into the hidden mysteries of God and the community that are required for authentic existence and happiness.[16]

In addition, the community being primary over the individual, imposes over the individual a system of norms, codes of behavior and obligations. Kinship is one of these systems that is central to the life of the community. Mbiti describes vividly the central role kinship plays in the life of the community as follows:

> The deep sense of kinship, with all it implies, has one of the strongest forces in traditional African life. Kinship is reckoned through blood and betrothal (engagement and marriage). It is kinship which controls social relationships between people in a given community: it governs marital customs and regulations, it determines the behaviour of one individual towards another. Indeed, this sense of kinship binds together the entire life of the "tribe," and is even extended to cover animals, plants, and non-living objects through the "totemic" system.[17]

John Mbiti goes on very insightfully to write as follows:

> Almost all the concepts of connected human relationship can be understood and interpreted through the kinship system. This it is which largely governs the behaviour, thinking and whole life of the individual in the society of which he is a member.[18]

Mbiti is probably justified to stress that kinship governs and regulates African life, but he is wrong in claiming that it governs the *whole* life of an individual, because being regarded as a moral creature cannot be entirely regulated by custom. This is where the importance of the "*Obuntu*" as the permanent conditioned or habitual state of human moral goodness, uprightness and humaneness comes into the picture to explain why some individuals fulfill their expected roles, whereas others rebel. The community acts as the divinely appointed custodian, police and court for human holiness, moral law or theocentric ethics and morality.

Therefore, the community regulates human behavior and punishes evil because it believes that it has the divine approval and the mandate of God to do so. The community in a sense thinks of itself as the proper divine representative on earth, rather than any individual finite component member of this human community, which is generally thought to be itself infinite, and the immortal embodiment and source of humanity and as its definitive guardian and source of history, culture and civilization, norms, humanness (*Obuntu*), religion, language, and personal identity.[19]

However, the limitations of kinship were realized and corrective measures were made within the same context of kinship, in the manner of the establishments of "*Omukago*" (blood-brother-hoods) that adopted people of different "tribes," "races" and "colors" as conventional brothers and sisters deserving humane treatment, love and protection under the kinship system as real consanguineous brothers and sisters. This was an extension of kinship and universalization of "brotherhood" under the "*Omukago*" procedure, the customary practice of polygamy and the imperative even more meaningful, for it made intermarriage necessary, thus creating an actual natural kinship and political alliances which were valued for the stability of the African neighboring "tribes" or other people who otherwise would have constituted a threat and danger of war.

Furthermore, the African common practice of polygamy was valued by both men and women. This was mainly because of the positive social, economic and political advantages and prestige it conferred on large and more powerful households. Larger families were richer, more powerful, secure and prestigious. Larger families had more capacity to create more wealth by virtue of larger numbers of people who formed a natural greater work force. Capacity to create more wealth also meant a capability for becoming a powerful political or economic force in the community. In turn, this meant powerful alliances through intermarriages, or other forms of exercise of both direct and indirect power and influence. Nevertheless, many modern African individualistic women and feminists, currently negatively view polygamy as demeaning and degrading to women.

However, for most traditional Africans, polygamy was generally positively viewed as a good practice for those who were wealthy enough to afford supporting several wives and many children. Polygamy gave the African men more prestige as owners of large households, indicating greater capacity for collective cheap labor, greater production, wealth and more prosperity. There were more hands to work in the fields within a polygamous extended family than in a monogamous family, which was equated with youth and poverty. For that matter, a man's wealth was measured both in terms of cattle and number of wives and children. The higher the number, the greater the wealth!

In addition, in a patriarchal society, there was an emphasis on having many children, particularly, the male ones. This was because one's own survival of death and that of the lineage depended on it. Males were the inheritors of property and served as the high priests of the families, the community and the world. Furthermore, there were more children born in a polygamous family, which was thought to be indicative of more divine blessing and better prospects for the future personal immortality of the progenitors through their offspring and their descendants. Wives and children also, generally, felt more secure and proud to be members of a large household overflowing with prosperity, fame and honor in the local community. As such, unlike the Western affinity for small nuclear families, in traditional it was more honorable, preferable to belong to a larger, richer, powerful, polygamous household and extended families than a poor, powerless, single household or nuclear family.

Therefore, in the final analysis, for the traditional African people, such as, the Bantu groups of Zaire, Rwanda, Uganda, Kenya, and Tanzania, the human community is the ultimate divine arena of God's special agapic activities of creation, and redemption. It is the divine and holy context for God's supernatural acts of creation of human beings, and correlatively, their socialization, education, humanization and completion and divinization into the humane and loving "*Abantu*" (human being), with "*Obuntu*" (Agape). In this respect, the local community functions as the local congregation of the cosmic Church of God. In addition, also the context for interpersonal dynamic human relationships ("I-thou" *vis-a-vis* "I-it"). It is also the context for personal identity as a human being (*Omuntu/Muntu*).

In this respect, the harmonious human community is in essence the primordial Garden of Eden. Likewise, the redemptive Church of God in the world, is the kingdom of God for all those with faith and courage to accept God's *a priori* good world as such, and to live in it joyfully and thankfulness as God's kingdom. Subsequently, in faith and agape to be empowered by God's power of grace to do the good works of God and unconditional love for the neighbor. As a result of faith, agape and theocentric good works to make it such a special place of God's unique cosmic activities of life, freedom, mind, love, peace, self-fulfillment, happiness and the cosmos. In short, a good life on earth is life with God in his cosmic redemptive Church of love, heaven and his kingdom.

In addition, God's kingdom being universal, and inclusive of all God's obedient people or the loving saints. It includes all obedient human beings, regardless of race, color, nationality, class, ideology, religious affiliation and creed, era, level of technological development and political or economic system. God is the God of diversity, justice, and true equal opportunity for all his people. God has created all human beings, irrespective of condition, he treats them as his beloved children. Being just and impartial, God attaches equal value and worth on all his people and their respective communities and societal systems, including religion and politics.

However, the imperfect human community as the inclusive Church of God, includes both saints and sinners. As such, the human community is also inevitably the arena for serious personal and group challenges, tension, conflicts and sin. This being the case, the community is also the context for the human quest for forgiveness and the expiation of the torment of guilt and broken relationships. Since this divine and social gift and state of forgiveness is obtained through priestly mediators, it is also correspondingly the temporal, historical context for divine mercy (grace), forgiveness and gratuitous supernatural salvation. This divine gift of supernatural salvation universally efficaciously exists anonymously in all peace-loving human societies, and communities in the cosmos.

Therefore, both correlative and co-extensive with the transcendent Cosmic Creator-Redeemer God, likewise, God's universal implicit redemptive Church or "anonymous Christianity" and supernatural salvation and God's kingdom or heaven, are efficaciously and universally present, everywhere in God's cosmos. This is necessarily the case since these holy universal activities of God are rooted in God's own quintessential nature. essence. Therefore, these free eternal divine twin cosmic activities of creation and redemption are inseparable from the omnipresent cosmic Creator and Redeemer God, who is effectively present everywhere, in God's cosmos to effect his eternal will, and perform his ever ongoing gratuitous work of unmerited grace and unconditional love, both in creation and redemption.

Ultimately, all human societies have their own culturally relevant and divinely revealed religious teachings. These institutions attempt to define, apprehend and mediate to their members God's redemptive truths, and teach them how to gain access, fellowship or union with God. Salvation is social. It consists in both personal and societal experience of positive mutual appreciation and celebration of the God-given free supernatural gifts of life, love, human companionship, forgiveness, fellowship, joy, well-being, wholeness,[20] harmony, and peace (*Shalom/Mirembe* or *Obusingye* and *Magara*).[21] These universal divine or supernatural gifts effectively transform ordinary human creatures into God's adopted children and moral agents in the world. Coextensively, these gifts of God's grace and agape also act as spiritual yeast in the world to transform it into God's temporal kingdom.

NOTES

1. See P. Tempels, *Bantu Philosophy*, 64.

2. Tempels, *Bantu Philosophy*, 18-70, 95-114. This material is a basic key for understanding Bantu ontology or metaphysics. This is where Mbiti's claim that time is the key to understanding African religion and philosophy falls short. By itself, the African concept of time cannot explain Bantu anthropology or philosophy.

3. See John S. Mbiti, *Introduction to African Religion*, 54-76. The human being through prayer to God and worship provides harmony and divine blessings to the world, and by human sin the world loses this harmony and divine blessing; cf. Booth, *African Religion*, 8-9, 32-68; Tempels, *Bantu Philosophy*, 18-64, 95-114.

4. Cf. Newell S. Booth, *African Religions: A Symposium*, 31-68. Booth's detailed analysis of *Muntu* is applicable to the Bantu people under discussion (with just a few minor modifications).

5. See Tempels, *Bantu Philosophy*, 64-66.

6. Cf. Booth, *African Religion*, 36: "'*Muntu*' properly refers only to one who is both alive and healthy. A sexually impotent person is not '*Muntu*' but rather '*mufu*'." This is also both true for an impotent man as well as a barren woman. They are both reproductively and socially dead, even when they are obviously physically alive.

7. Almost functions like Whitehead's objective immortality" except that in African thinking the living people immortalize their departed rather than God; cf. Alfred North Whitehead, *Process and Reality*, Part III:I-IV, PART V:V-VII.

8. Booth, *African Religion*, 7-10, 33-51. It is probable that killings of abnormal children still go quietly in the villages; cf. Emmanuel K. Twesigye, *Death among the Bakiga of Uganda* (Kampala: Makerere University Dept. of Religious Studies and Philosophy, 1971).

9. Cf. Booth, *African Religion*, 7-10, 14-15, 33-51; Tempels, *Bantu Philosophy*, 18-70, 95-114; Kagame, *Philosophie Bantu-Rwandaise*, 53.

10. Cf. Tempels, *Bantu Philosophy*, 18-25, 39-61, 95-114; Booth, *African Religion*, 13-16, 32-46.

11. Cf. Tempels, *Bantu Philosophy*, 18-21, 25, 54-62, 167-182; Kagame, *Philosophie Bantu-Rwandaise*, 53 ff.

12. Booth, *African Religions*, 1-10; King, *Religions of Africa*, 62-82; Tempels, *Bantu Philosophy*, 18-64, 95-165; Wright, *African Philosophy: An Introduction*, 157-168; Mbiti, *African Religions and Philosophy*, 100-110.

13. The African extended family includes several wives and children in a polygamous family, and their own relatives such as brothers, sisters, uncles, aunts, and several degrees of cousins! See also Mbiti, *African Religions and Philosophy*, 104-109, 142-144; Mary Edel, *The Chigga of Western Uganda* (London: Oxford Uni., 1957), 20.

14. Mbiti, *African Religions and Philosophy*, 141.

15. Cf. Tempels, *Bantu Philosophy*, 44-66, 95-114.

16. See note 65 above.

17. Mbiti, *African Religions and Philosophy*, 135. Based on this understanding, it should be easy to understand why tribalism and nepotism seem to be the major problems which account for a great deal of instability in Africa today. As an example see Colin Legum, "After the Amin Nightmare," *Africa Report*, January-February, 1983, 15-22.

18. Mbiti, *African Religions and Philosophy*, 135.

19. "Divine kings" in Uganda were still subject to the community and so were the religious leaders, i.e. priests and diviners; cf. Noel King, *Religions of Africa,* 32-61. As these cultural, religious, sacred persons and pivotal societal and community figureheads, the traditional kingdoms of Uganda were re-established in 1994. Significantly, the title of "*Ssebbataka*" for the *Kabaka* (Baganda King) is also one of the Baganda titles for God. As such, one can justifiably ask to whether the *Kabaka* was symbolically crowned and deified into just a king or and not a god!

If the Baganda King is religiously and culturally venerated as a god, then, one can hardly expect that the Baganda will ever let their kings be subjected to the unitary systems of Ugandan Government, except by political and military coercion.

20. Wholeness is a key concept in African philosophy and religion, as it is the central focus for all African total religious, cultural, moral and political activities as the desired goal and end-result of these activities. It is connected with the "holy," the "moral" and "ideal" state of being in the community.   Wholeness implies peace, harmony and general well-being. It also means good personal relationships between the individual and a. the community (neighbors and relatives); b. the "living-dead" or ancestral spirits; c. God (and the other intermediaries); and d. the physical environment.

Therefore, in African traditional life and society, wholeness was symbolized by traditional round houses, fences, decorations, and cyclical seasons. Wholeness as expressed in harmony is the present expression of divine eternity and human eternal life now in the present. It provides continuity between the past *(Zamani)* and the present *(Sasa)* and the future *(Kesho)*. See also, Booth, *African Religions*, 7-10, 36.

21. This concept of peace, as wholeness and harmony (Obusingye or Mirembe), is considered as a divine temporal gratuitous offer of salvation to human beings right now. This concept is very similar to Whitehead's concept of peace as expressed in the last chapter of his book, *Adventures of Ideas*. See also King, *Religions of Africa*, 47-61.

VIII

CONFRONTATION AND DIALOGUE: CHRISTIANITY, AFRICAN RELIGIONS AND PHILOSOPHY IN COMMON QUEST FOR COMPLETE HUMANIZATION, DIVINIZATION, PEACE OR SALVATION

The doctrines of God, grace, creation (or cosmic genesis and evolution), the fall or "original sin" (disobedience and alienation from the grounding ethos and path or yoga of authentic life) and redemption or soteriology (reconciliation with God or the true source and center of authentic life and Destiny), are both essentially inseparably linked and irrevocably intertwined.

In short, creation anticipates redemption as creation's sustenance, service, repair, "recharging the batteries" of life's internal operating system (soul/spirit or mind) maintenance, redirection and reprogramming itself anticipates creation or re-creation, growth, positive transformation (or salvation), maturation, fulfillment and completion. These are some of the fundamental inseparable aspects and components of God's twin process of both creation and redemption. Inasmuch as there is true consequential freedom bestowed on creation, creation is inseparably linked to redemption as the second moment of creation.

This essential unity of creation and redemption is due to the basic unity and wholistic nature, grace and agape of God, and the gratuitous and agapic basic nature of God's activities. God is by quintessential nature the same Ultimate cosmic Creator, Redeemer and Fulfiller. As such, both cosmic creation and redemption are from beginning to end God's gratuitous inseparable universal twin process of God's universal, free activities of unconditional love, and unmerited supernatural grace. For many people, these divine macrocosmic divine activities of God's creation are impersonal.

However, for other people, particularly, those of the Jewish and Christian traditions, God is a transcendent Person, who cares about his or her human creatures and adopts them as his or her special children, beneficiaries and concrete temporal ambassadors in the realms of matter, time, space, and history. The specific human concept of God as *Abba* or Agape will therefore, yield a more benevolent and personal concept of salvation as opposed to a soteriology based on God who is conceived as primarily a just cosmic Judge who weighs all human sin and punishes them accordingly. This is the case in Islam and some branches of Christianity, such as the extreme forms of Calvinism.

In these theological or religious traditions cases, God's justice is the dominant theme of proclamation as opposed to agape, free universal efficacious grace and the free forgiveness of sins as Jesus clearly taught (Matt. 5-7). As a direct result, hell overshadows heaven as a religious theme in the religious proclamation of God's message of the Gospel. The Gospel of Agape becomes just another Law of God's justice. Jesus becomes another Moses or God's Law-Giver, as opposed to being actually the negation of the Law as the actual and concrete embodiment of God, Agape, free forgiveness of sins and guilt in the world.

However, there is a corruption of religion, particularly Christianity. And as the redemption of Israel from Egypt indicates, salvation is not for saints alone, but rather for all those people who obey God and do his will. In this context, it is not theology or doctrines, such as the creeds that are redemptive, rather it is the doing of God's will, namely, performing the good deeds of agape or altruism. As such, Agape and good deeds of justice, love and forgiveness or peace-making are the true contents of a virtuous life, and indicators of a life of salvation rather than empty rhetoric or excellent sermons and professions of faith in Jesus-Christ alone. The latter is analogous to the tree with green leaves alone which was symbolically cursed by Jesus for lack of the necessary fruits.

Jesus further elaborates on this point in his discourse on the final eschatological cosmic judgement by God. According to Jesus, God's eschatological cosmic judgement is based on the practical universal criteria of good and humane social deeds of compassion and mercy, such as feeding the hungry and providing care for the homeless destitute or seeking peace and justice where there is injustice and strife (cf. Matt. 7:13-29; 25:31-46; John 15:1-17; Jam. 2:1-26).

Since there is only one all-encompassing and constitutive "Cosmic Mother-Father," then all creation, truth, revelation, religion and salvation are intrinsically interrelated and inseparably linked together both in ultimate origin and destiny. Consequently, despite apparent bio-diversity or differences, all creatures and creation are mutually interdependent both in life, being and in the Creator-God as their Ultimate Origin and Ultimate Destiny.

This Creative Cosmic Mystery as the Cosmic Ultimate Reality or Creative-Sustaining Principle or Spirit and Mind, that is variously universally known by different terms, and "names." These include names such as: "Amun," Amen-Ra," "God," "Yahweh," "Allah," "Mungu," "Brahma," "Ngai," "Theos," "Deus," "Ruhanga," "Katonda," "Shango," "Imaana," "Unkulunkulu," and the like. Moreover, since there is only one God and one race of human beings as "*homo sapiens*," the apparent different religions that exist in the world, are bound to have a primary unitive "*common ground*" in this One, transcendent, cosmic Creator-Redeemer-God.

All things find an ultimate *common ground* in the Creator-God. This the case since God is the only Ultimate Reality and cosmic Creative Mystery as the ultimate Source of life and ultimate Destiny of all intelligent, moral and responsible creatures. God as this Ultimate and the Eternal creative and redemptive Cosmic Mind and Consciousness is the source of all human self-consciousness and God-consciousness in which all religions are rooted. This is the universal religious "Common Ground" and Destiny. It is best illustrated by the universal mature spirituality which finds its best and highest universal and transcendental common spiritual expression in mysticism and agape as the universal moral obligation and outward expression of the inner peace which comes from spiritual and ethical condition of harmony with God, the neighbor and the rest of God's creation.

Apart from the mystic experience of God, religion is a mere societal cultural and moral phenomenon. For instance, in the USA, it is generally considered more prestigious and "politically correct" to be a White Protestant elite, such as an Episcopalian, Methodist and Presbyterian than being either a Roman Catholic, a Muslim or a member of Judaism. This is a North American cultural and religious bias which can be traced back to colonialist, and expansionist or imperialist Europe.

Materialism, greed and religious and cultural ethnocentrism were at the heart of European imperialism. In other words, Europe had a desire to recreate the rest of the world in its own religious and cultural image. As a tragic result, this religio-cultural Western imperialism was mistaken for missionary zeal, and Christianity or Christendom was, likewise, also mistakenly identified with God's salvation, and an acceptable form of civilization.

However, because of the complexity and diversity of human experiences, nationalities, technologies, history, environment, languages, values, socio-economic-political structures, and philosophies, each culture has its own appropriate, and most important or meaningful cultural values and taboos which are locally sanctioned in the most authoritative and holy name of God. In order for this sanction to become validated, God is anthropomorphically portrayed as a "Cosmic King," "Law-Giver" and "Judge" or as some kind of cosmic, just Moral Enforcer (omnipresent, omniscient and omnipresent "Cosmic Policeman").

Mysticism transcends this idolatrous anthropomorphism. God is positively viewed as the transcendent and all-encompassing Ultimate reality. This Ultimate reality is variously viewed as the universal mind, truth, consciousness, spirit, knowledge, and Love. As a result, God is found within the innermost core of one's being as spirit, truth, mind, love, reality, peace, life and being.

In this context, to know and love oneself, the neighbor, life or the mystery of cosmic creation or nature is both simultaneously and correlatively, also to know and love God, as both "Emmanuel" or "the God with us" and "God within us" (cf. Matt. 25:31-46). Accordingly St. John affirmed that since God is Love (Agape), therefore, nobody could ever love God and yet still hate his or her brother or fellow human beings (cf. 1 John 4:4-21).

As such, mysticism is the highest, universal, common form of religious mature spiritual expression. In the mystical and personal spiritual encounter and experience of God, there is a voluntary mental union between contemplative subject and the object of his or her desire or contemplation. Materiality and temporal barriers are transcended and the human spirit and divine Spirit or divine Cosmic Consciousness meet and embrace one another in mutual recognition as being the same; and the finite spirit or consciousness as the fragment of the Cosmic divine Spirit or Consciousness find new energy and fulfillment.

This is supernatural divinization of the finite human being or *theosis* is accomplished as the finite or historical spirit or mind immerses itself into the eternal divine Spirit and Consciousness (Mind) from which it had been initially created and then become separated. This universal historical human separation and alienation from God had occurred due to human imperfection, misuse of personal mental freedom, sin and the inherent limitations of temporal immersion of the human mind and spirit into a physical body and the material world.

In this mystical union there is no more distinction or alienation between the finite contemplative subject and the transcendent object of contemplation or prayer. The means as well as the results of this transcendental experience include: a virtuous life, diligent work, practice of agape, and works of justice and mercy. The obedient mystic experiences God in these self-sacrificial benevolent activities (of *karma yoga*) because the boundaries between object and subject have been dissolved. This is the true moment of beatific vision or the experience of the heavenly state which Buddhists seek after as *Nirvana*.

In this self-transcendental divine moment of the union between the creature and the creator, all dualities and boundaries are transcended and dissolved into a single Ultimate Reality. These dualities which are transcended include those of body and the spirit; mind and matter; the finite and the infinite; the lover and the beloved; the *"imago Dei"* and *"Deus"* or the image and the image-Maker or the creature and its Creator. In this moment of ultimate human-divine self-transcendence and union mirrors are removed and the gazer realizes that he or she is a true part of the Creator-God, which is indirectly is both mediated and reflected in the world by finite nature and its imperfect, finite mirrors and distorted images of self and God as the Ultimate Creator, Sustainer and Redeemer of the cosmos and its creatures.

However, even mysticism, where there is no dogma, and the unique individual encounter with God is definitive for that person, human beings have tended to introduce systems and dogmas so as to regulate and impose limits on the intrinsically free and unique human mystical journey and experiences of God. Zen Buddhism and *"Raja yoga"* exercises are some examples of this institutionalization of mysticism.

This analogy of what institutionalized religions world-wide have done with the mystical experience of God-consciousness which is at the heart of any human-made religion. For instance, prophets like Moses, Buddha, Jesus, and Muhammad were all mystics whose "beatific vision" of God or spiritual-moral illumination and the contemplative experience of God got charismatically communicated the faithful disciples, who in turn wrote it down as God's Word, variously known as the "Torah," in the case of Moses and the "Gospels" in the case of Jesus the Christ.

The written or oral testimonies of the mystical experiences or union with God, all scriptures are therefore, God's inspired redemptive Word, regardless of whether this Word of God is found in the Torah, Gospels, the Letters of Paul, the Qur'an, the Veda, the oral texts and traditions of the African Religion or that of the Native Americans.

In this wholistic and inclusive understanding, all religions contain God's redemptive revelation, partial divine truths, efficacious redemptive and divinitive supernatural grace (cf. Rom. 1:1-32). Nevertheless, some religions seem to be functionally better and more open channels and instruments of God's revelation of Agape or unconditional love and free forgiveness for the neighbor (cf. Matt. 5-7).

Christianity being explicitly aware of itself as the embodiment of Agape and free forgiveness of sin and guilt as opposed to the natural tendencies of "*lex talionis*" as the basis of justice and a godly community, as in the case of the Mosaic Law (cf. Exod. 20-23), Apostolic Christianity which is "Agape-centered" as opposed to the corrupt Western cultural Christianity which is merely "faith-in-Jesus-centered," would be a better form of religion in the world, if the world were to become truly transformed into God's temporal peaceful kingdom. That is for God's kingdom to be fully established and experienced on earth as heaven, as Jesus taught his followers to obey God, love and do good for the neighbor; become peace-makers, hope and pray (cf. Matt. 5-7). Unlike the spiritual futility of empty faith without good works (cf. Jam. 2:12-26), the commandment of Agape requires positive moral action and the transformation of the socio-economic structures of the world in order to serve human better as if they were the concrete ambassadors and embodiments of God in the world (cf. Matt. 25:31-46).

In this theological and soteriological context and understanding religion is not essentially a matter of doctrines and dogmas or modes of public or private worship or devotions, as traditional theologians have tended to affirm. On the contrary, true religion deals with the basic God-consciousness, intrinsic human spiritual yearning for meaning, completion, agape, peace, happiness and union with the divine transcendence of which he or she feels to be an alienated fragment in the world. Loving fellowship (*koinonia*) in the religious or moral community (or Church) helps to fill in some of the missing pieces of the life's social puzzle and collective human and God-consciousness.

Therefore, according to the African Religion no one is ever truly saved alone without his or her neighbor, the relatives, the ancestors, and ultimately, the community. Since for the traditional African, it could be affirmed in the same way that life is viewed as being intrinsically or essentially social, similarly, also affirmed to be the case with divine societal peace, well-being, salvation and eternal life or immortality. For instance, the benevolent ancestors and lots of good sons were affirmed to be essential for immortality. For the African, both God's activities for human creation and redemption take place within the social divine arena and context of the community. Both divine activities are inherently social and the community is God's sacred ground or Church to mediate these special divine activities of free and undeserved supernatural, universal creative and redemptive grace and agape of God.

The main constitutive elements of the African[1] Traditional Religion and Philosophy (as already discussed in the preceding chapters), clearly indicate that the African people have both a cognitive or thematic and a pre-thematic knowledge of a triune supreme God ("Ruhanga or Katonda"). This supreme Being or God is conceived of and worshipped as the most transcendent incomprehensible nameless Mystery who is "Nyamuhanga" (the Creator), Kazoba (the Light, Sun, Enlightener, Guide and Savior) and "Rugaba" (the Giver/Provider of everything including life, talents and possessions).

This Rugaba/Ruhanga or "Imaana" is the same God of mystery, the Cosmic Creator whose symbol is the sun or "Kazoba," who was worshipped down the River Nile as "Amen-Ra" or "Amun" by the ancient Egyptians, prior to the time of Moses. As an African divine king to be, Moses as a prince of Egypt, was instructed in the secret mysteries of the Cosmic Creative Mystery or Amun/Amen-Ra as part of the normal training for the divine-king.

Like any other ancient or modern African divine king or emperor, if Prince Moses had been crowned the new Egyptian king or Pharaoh, he would have been both simultaneously and coextensively, installed as king (Pharaoh) and the chief cosmic High-Priest. A High-Priest the Pharaoh is also Mediator between God and humanity. The Pharaoh as both king and High-Priest, is like the Pope, was God's own chosen (elected) concrete temporal and mystical representative or Chief Ambassador of God on planet earth.

Obviously, when Moses was exiled by the Egyptian ruling pharaoh, he no longer felt any moral nor personal obligation to keep secret the sacred African divine mysteries, theologies and moral commandments as guides to the secret path of divine illumination, holy life, societal harmony, happiness, salvation and immortality. In both Africa, and most of the surrounding Mediterranean region, these sacred mysteries were kept secret and were only imparted to those duly initiated and instructed by the authorized priests as their diligent guardians and professors.

As the new founder of Judaism, and the correlative new theocentric or Yahwist nation of Israel, Moses modified and *"Hebraicized"* the same African monotheistic concept of Amun and Amen-Ra, Mystery God of Egyptian or African Religion. Later, Moses reintroduced this modified version of the African Religion to the newly liberated Hebrews from Africa, as the Great Creative Cosmic Mystery or Amun/Amen-Ra, who had delivered them from oppression and who was choosing them to become members of his new nation or Covenant, if they obeyed his new command-ments. Accordingly, this Egyptian God of Moses had a new Hebrew title of "Yahweh" (Exod. 3:4).

This transcendent Cosmic Creative Mystery, as the incomprehensible God was worshipped in most of Africa, including ancient Egypt, as the cause of life, well-being, peace, riches, harmony and the happiness that all human beings (*Abantu*) crave in all they do in hope that God will in his free loving grace be kind enough to bestow blessings on them as reward for their diligent search, godliness, hard work, and for having been considerate, kind, generous and loving to their relatives and neighbors; that is, having prac-ticed the "*Obuntu.*"

Since these people have accepted the divine Mystery and have also accepted their given humanity and that of others they interact with in the community as relatives and neighbors, and they even do respect and provide hospitality for the stranger or traveller without the hope of payment or reward in return except by God (Ruhanga) in heaven, who is attributed with the power of omniscience as the one who sees and knows all human actions even before they happen,[2] they have subsequently, fulfilled the Christian conditions for God's redemption through "anonymous Christianity." Accordingly, Karl Rahner, speaking on behalf of the Catholic Church teaching states this theological phenomenon as follows:

> now God and the grace of Christ are present as the secret essence of every reality we choose. Therefore it is not easy to opt for something without having to do with God and Christ either by accepting them or rejecting them, either by believing or not believing. Consequently, anyone who, though still far from any revelation explicitly formulated in words, accepts his existence in patient silence (or better, in faith, hope and love), accepts it as the mystery which lies hidden in the mystery of love...is saying "yes" to Christ even if one does not know it...Anyone who accepts his humanity... [that] of others, has accepted the Son of Man because in him God has accepted Man...whoever loves his neighbor has fulfilled the law, then this is the ultimate truth because God himself has become this neighbor.[3]

However, as in explicit Christianity, not everyone is an heir to eternal life, similarly, not all "anonymous Christians" are living in accordance with God's will either in its implicit or explicit givenness. As a result, in both kinds of explicit and anonymous Christianity, there are both obedient and disobedient people to God as respective candidates for either heaven or hell as concrete states of existence now in this world, and in the post-resurrection eschatological life still to come.

In other words, the life of salvation and that of damnation are both possible and co-exist with each other, side by side in both explicit Christianity or in the historical Apostolic Church. Likewise, God's free redemption or supernatural salvation are voluntary, just like human rebellion and sin against God's will, commandments, justice, Agape, peace and goodness in life are also free and voluntary.

Subsequently, it is this human free volitional process negative human decision and rejection of God that human beings freely choose a destructive negative path that leads to existential hell on earth. As such, human beings live a life of hell due to self-damnation. God's justice permits such existence of hell as punishment for human rebellion, unrepented sins and guilt.

Nevertheless, God as Agape and Redeemer, does not condemn his people to hell, death and damnation. As such, both salvation and redemption exist as concrete realities and options of human life outside the confines of the Apostolic Church. This is the concrete existential case and human modes of actualizing themselves in life and the world, depending on an individual's freedom, maturity, mind, thinking patterns, decisions, and actions in direct or indirect personal response to God.

However, God may present himself incognito to the person as authentic life, love and the Transcendent Mystery or historically, as the Incarnate Christ. Nevertheless, any positive responses to God and his invitation to a fuller life at any of these levels is fully redemptive.

It is also both simultaneously fully humanizing and mystically divinizing to any human being, who answers affirmatively with "YES," to free universal invitation to salvation, a fuller life and Agapic fellowship with him through the agape and unconditional forgiveness for the neighbor (cf. Matt. 6:8-13). Conversely, the human voluntary rejection of God's cosmic Word or Logos of invitation to a more fulfilling positive and agapic mode life and salvation, leads to self-condemnation to a negative life of self-centeredness, self-deification, idolatry, greed, hate, strife, malice and damnation.

Ironically, this damnation can also take place within the Church. This happens when members of the Church disobey God. And as a result, members, fail to heed the commandment of unconditional love for the neighbor, to obey God, perform good deeds, and practice justice.

Therefore, the kind of damnation that can be experienced by some members of the Church can be even more agonizing, since these individuals have been given a more explicit divine salvific gratuitous revelation which they have consciously and deliberately turned down with a resounding existential life of "No." Since human choice is truly consequential, therefore, it incurs serious guilt due to this rejection of God's universal free proffer of redemptive grace and its correlative divine good life of agape, harmony and peace (*shalom*) as supernatural salvation (Jn. 17:3; 20:21-29).

On the other hand, in traditional Africa, to be human is to belong to God and the community which is itself by nature religious. Subsequently, one had to say "Yes" to God publicly before the corporate community in its collective cultic worship, since deviance would not be tolerated by the community, as the traditional Africans thought that an irreligious member of the community would, invariably, bring divine displeasure, wrath and destruction of that community by God in his righteous retribution for the sacrilege committed by one of its members.

Like the Catholic Church which excommunicates an unrepentant notorious persistent sinner, (and in the past, even executed some of them), the African community also ostracized (*kucwa*) notorious sinners until their repentance, propitiation and expiation of their sins. However, in cases of grave sins such as incest or pre-meditated murder, the individual would be put to death and the entire community would undergo ceremonial purification from the abomination.

In this light, Rahner would probably argue that the African Traditional Religion is a good example of a for God's medium salvation outside the Church, and therefore, as a good example for "anonymous Christianity." He would further elaborate how it is efficaciously endowed by God with unconditional supernatural gratuitous salvific grace, and as such, being efficaciously able to mediate supernatural salvation to its members according to God's unconditional infinite love, and his universal salvific will for all human beings that he has created, and that this is also the case with other world religions, such as Islam, Buddhism, Hinduism and Judaism as the other possible media of this "anonymous Christianity."

According to the African Traditional view of religion and divine salvation, God's salvific activity is thought to be efficaciously universal. Consequently, there is no concept of missionary work in African traditional religion. Traditional Africans believe that all groups of people know God as their Creator and worship him as such.

This African view of God, universal divine revelation and salvation for whoever obeys God and loves the neighbor is very much in line with Rahner's own teaching on universal divine salvific will and the divine universal efficacious self-communication in free salvific grace for the salvation of every human being, regardless of race, color, creed, level of education and technology.

This Rahnerian Catholic inclusive teaching finds its best expression in the concept of "anonymous Christianity." By the Christian affirmation of the doctrine of "anonymous Christianity," Rahner and the Church also positively accept and explicitly affirm that God's salvific self-communication in gratuitous redemptive grace is universal. The purpose of this chapter is to demonstrate that such a divine redemptive revelation existed in the African Traditional Religion, and that it was effectively salvific for the African people who practiced the African Traditional Religion.

The method adopted in this section is to compare and contrast some key concepts in the African Traditional Religion with those of Christianity as taught by the major main-line Church theologians, such as Karl Rahner, who is highly regarded as the exponent of the Christian faith as both grounded and informed by revelation, holy Scriptures, tradition, doctrine (dogma) and Western scholarship.

The underlying fundamental assumption or hypothesis here is that God is inseparable from reality, order, life, truth, meaning, goodness and nature or the cosmos as its source, and embodiment or encompassing as both Creator and Sustainer. As this transcendent and ultimate cosmic Reality, God is one. This God or cosmic Creative Force is the only source of ultimate meaning, which is the realm of religion and philosophy or order and balance, which is the main realm of science and technology.

In the religious realm, God is spiritually apprehended by intuition, faith, intellect, and experience as the Ultimate Source of redemptive revelation and salvific truth or Logos, which manifests itself universally in the world in various forms. God's revelation varies from place to place, and from generation to generation depending on local contexts, such as culture, religion, philosophy, language, world-view, science and technology.

Due to these many differing of religious, cultural, mental, and experiential forms of apprehending God and his self-disclosure in the world, God is therefore, also variously known, and called by different names. Nevertheless, since these are merely different references to the same commonly shared and experienced global Ultimate Reality or God, there is a some basic, universal "common ground" for the fundamental mutual human understanding of this inclusive cosmic Reality or God, humanity, love and global human community. This global basic "common ground" for the experiencing and understanding of God, also exists between Christianity and other religions, including the African Religion. This has been fully explicated by Rahner for Christianity, and I have done the same for the African tradition. However, the African theological paradigm or model, when modified appropriately, also applies to other world religions, including Judaism, Islam, Buddhism, and Hinduism.

It is hoped that by this philosophical, and anthropological-theological wholistic method it will be clearly demonstrated that the traditional Africans were practicing the principles of Christianity long before historical Christianity itself was ever known. However, it is positively affirmed that although "anonymous Christianity" is efficaciously salvific, nevertheless, it still remains a deficient mode of Christianity. The African Religion as an "anonymous Christianity" anticipates the final arrival of an explicit or historical missionary Christianity for its explicit experience and celebration of ultimate fulfillment, and completion.

Through Apostolic or missionary Christianity, the African Religion gains a direct access to salvation and reconciliation or fellowship with God through historical Jesus-Christ as the eternal Son of God, who has voluntarily become our "blood brother" and eternal High-Priest by virtue of the Incarnation. Unlike the long chain of intermediaries of ancestral, priestly and other divine beings of traditional Africa's linkage with God as channels of atonement, prayer, and co-extensively, as the means to receive God's mediation of grace, forgiveness, blessings, and divine salvation, the Incarnate Logos-Christ, has most concretely and efficaciously brought down on earth God's perfect and eternal efficacious atonement for all human sins through Jesus' self-sacrificial innocent vicarious death on the cross.

1. God as the Triune Creative Mystery and Ultimate Origin of Humanity

It is probably a surprise for some people to find a sound understanding of God among the Bantu people of Uganda that is in line with Rahner's main concept of God as the incomprehensible Mystery, which is by nature a self-subsisting intelligent creativity and the ultimate origin of all life and humanity and the Creator of all natural things that exist in the cosmos which have "*NTU/Ozovehe*" or being. God is regarded by both African Religion and Christianity as both the very ground being, and the prerequisite of life, and any form of being or existence, such as the cosmos itself.

For the African Tradition (Culture, Religion and Philosophy), God is such a Mystery that he is the unnameable Creator (Ruhanga). God is unnameable Ultimate Mystery (Amun/Yahweh/Katonda) and Ultimate

Reality. This is because God is considered to be the Incomprehensible, the Transcendent Mystery or "Abyss" who is beyond the grasp of any finite human intellect and understanding (*omutwe n'obwengye/amagezi*). As a result, God being this cosmic Infinite Creative Mystery, is beyond the grasp of human language and thought; and therefore, also beyond naming.

Moreover, for these Africans, just as for the ancient Hebrews, a name is thought to be expressive of the essential identity and inner nature of the named person or thing. This concept is best as expressed in the Bakiga-Banyankole proverb, "*Eiziina niwe muntu*" (the name denotes the person). Accordingly, within this African ontological, theological and epistemological context, God's name would, similarly, be considered both revelatory and expressive of God's hidden inner quintessential nature and mystery. This is impossible, since God is by essential nature an infinitely incomprehensible Mystery, consequently, God as the Ultimate-Creative-Redemptive Mystery has no definitive proper name given to him. As such, God remains the nameless one or "Yahweh/*Mysterium Tremendum*." Subsequently, he is known and called by his various cosmic activities or functions and attributes, such as creating, and therefore, Creator (*Kuhanga-Nyamuhanga/Ruhanga*).

Rahner's primary conception of God as the eternal, Infinite Creative and Redemptive Cosmic Mystery, is in complete harmony with this common African fundamental conception of God. For instance, most traditional concepts of God center focus on God as the Primordial Ancestor-Spirit or the Cosmic Creative Force/Energy or Creator-Spirit.

Likewise, Rahner refers to God in terms such as "the Cosmic Abba," "the Incomprehensible," "the Infinite Mystery," "the Abyss," "the Ground of Being," "the Absolute," "the Transcendent," "the Horizon of human knowledge and human existence," and the like, which are not names of God, but rather, terms that express the transcendence, mystery and the incomprehensibility of God.[4] This Rahnerian Christian inclusive conception of God, would be most appealing to the Bantu of Africa as a better articulation of what they already understood of God, as the holy Transcendent Mystery whose chief activity is creativity and divine salvation or preservation of creation.

This absolute Mystery which both Rahner's Christianity and the members of the African Traditional Religion designate and worship as God, is not the transitory finite mystery that is accounted for by Durkheim's or Freud's atheistic theories of superstition, or limited nature of the finite human mind, lack of knowledge and ignorance.

Western education, knowledge and science have not dislodged this inherent African religious faith and theocentric world-view. That is to affirm that Creator-God is not just a myth, or clever fiction created by human minds in order to fill the gaps in scientific knowledge. Therefore, God is not an illusion or functional lie that will be subsequently dispelled and banished from the human minds by the availability of more and better scientific knowledge.

Faith and belief in God as the Cosmic Creative Energy or Force is not any form of societal or personal evil superstition or ignorance to be cured by anti-religious education and propaganda as the atheists such as Feuerbach, Karl Marx, Nietzsche and Sigmund Freud speculated in their works and vicious attacks on traditional Christianity.[5] On the contrary, God as the Ultimate Cosmic Reality and grounding of being, finite realities, mind, evolution and sustenance or resistance to cosmic principles of entropy, is not an illusion. Any human being who thinks that such a reality is an illusion, is like a fish in the ocean which may speculate that water is an illusion! The name is not the issue, the existence of a cosmic Creative Energy or Force is the issue.

This cosmic creative Force or Spirit is for the African Bantu people referred to in its transcendence and nameless form as the infinite Mystery or NTU/BEING. This is the primordial living eternal, intelligent, all-knowing and all-seeing Cosmic Creative and Sustaining-Redemptive Force which originated and constituted life, and the cosmos. This Creator-God directs the cosmic creative processes through secondary subordinate forces, and agents including the spirits of the ancestors, kings, priests, elders, mothers and fathers.

This is the God who is considered to be both transcendent in heaven, and yet close through his chain of mediators and power of omnipresence. This is also the remote transcendent impersonal God in heaven and in eternity. And yet, through love as a Primordial Ancestor, and by virtue of his cosmic kingly jurisprudence and concern for justice and holiness, he is also still an immanent God that is here with us (Emmanuel) in this world. As the immanent God, he is both personally and indirectly through his mediators, actively involved in human and world affairs.

These divine affairs include hearing, and answering human prayers for supernatural intervention or redemption, meting out judgement and punishment for evil doers, whereas blessing the obedient. As a loving Cosmic Ancestor, God is also considered to be engaged in activities that mediate his (or her) attributes, such those stressing loving, caring, creating and being mindful of each individual's uniqueness, or special needs specific for more appropriate individual forms of self-fulfillment and maximum happiness within the social context of the peaceful and godly community and theocentric world.

However, most of these activities may be delegated to God's own chosen ambassadors and empowered assistants in the world to be accomplished on his behalf. However, in all this process, God's directive is always to lead human beings to greater evolution of larger brains, greater minds and greater capabilities for self-actualization in more meaningful, peace-loving and creative ways. God desires human beings to be his true representatives in creation and to be loving, peaceful and find happiness in life as God's unique gift for the intelligent creatures, particularly, the intelligent and thinking creatures of which the human being as the "*homo sapiens*" is the highest and best example on this planet.

This Mystery-Creative Spirit is the Infinite, Cosmic Creative Mystery at the center of the human self-consciousness or the inner micro-cosmos. This innate human "God-consciousness" or the Ultimate Mystery of which the human being is part as both a self-transcendent finite spirit and a temporal embodiment of the fragment of God's mind and creative Spirit, is what essentially sets apart each human being as "*imago Dei*" in the cosmos. This is also the very Mystery which ever invites all normal human beings to the contemplation of the infinite Mystery and wonders of life, mind, self-consciousness, the complexities and beauties of life processes, which surround him or her.

Religion and finite language are universal attempts to apprehend the divine Infinite Mystery, and process, formulate and express the various human experiences of these wonders and mysteries in finite language with its given local constraints of local cultures, values, world-view and metaphysics. These formulations and records of personal or collective experiences of Mystery and spiritual journeys of quest for meaning, God or Transcendence and redemption are often highly valued by people as God's revelation and canonized as holy Scriptures. Examples are the Torah and the Prophets, the Koran and the Gospels and Epistles of the Apostles in the New Testament. As a result, many of the authors of these materials were not even aware that they were either inspired by God and that they were writing down God revealed Word or the scriptures (cf. Luke 1:1-4).

However, human language is finite and inadequate as a universal definitive vehicle to formulate and express these experiences of unutterable or undescribable phenomena of infinite beauty, wonders of life and Mystery.

Joyful silence and poetry or song may come close to the expression of this experience which cannot be captured by dogmatic definitions. This is probably why Jesus never wrote anything done.

The living Word of God or Logos becomes static and lifeless when it is frozen in time or written down. The human experience of God, as life, mystery, beauty, truth and Agape, goodness, can never be static since it is a dynamic, living and changing process. God as a living reality or experience is the Ultimate source and grounding of reality, life and its dynamic processes. Therefore, all intelligent, self-conscious, knowing and thinking creatures will experience God in a growing evolutionary manner, and a simultaneous revelatory movement towards more truth and perfection as union, maximum fulfillment and self-completion in God.

These mysteries and wonders include the birth of a new healthy baby, the beauty and smell of the flowers, the glow of the stars, the beauty of the moon, the majesty of the sunshine as its modest warmth warms up the human complex body, and the brain, and its functions, particularly, in thought processes and language. Furthermore, the delight of human love and community strike the human being, as elements of that same unnameable impenetrable Creative Mystery that sets the human being indefinitely wondering, and questioning without ever arriving at any definitive final answer that explains it all, most fully and adequately for all time.

This is for Rahner the all-encompassing Absolute Mystery that faces the human being with the inner basic question about one's being itself, how complex it is, and where it ultimately originated, where it is ultimately destined. Human beings are intrinsically unique divine beings as finite intelligent minds, who share in God's infinite Cosmic Mind and the divine activities associated with it.

As finite minds or embodied temporal and evolutionary divine beings, human beings are akin to God from whom they proceed and return. Therefore, all human beings, everywhere and in every age, have been eternally oriented to God as both their own Ultimate Origins and Destiny. In this process, human beings are by intrinsic essential nature as "*homo sapiens*" or "*imago Dei*" inwardly, ever oriented and open to the cosmic and divine Mystery and the mysteries of life, including their own personal and collective existence, as unique intelligent creatures are also by essential human nature, creatures that ever ask profound ultimate questions of being, meaning, ultimate origins, and destiny.

Therefore, all human normal beings are unique divine creatures which are intelligent, free, moral, self-transcendent, and mystical beings and that live in eternal universal quest for God, happiness, salvation, transcendental peace and maximum self-fulfillment in fellowship with God (beatific vision). Consequently, all human beings ask themselves and others universal ultimate existential questions. As an example, all normal human beings ask or wonder whether there is any set purpose or ultimately definitive meaning for one's life or being, and for the cosmic existence in general. Subsequently, ultimate questions are constantly universally asked by worried human beings in their perpetual quest for both Ultimate answers, God as the cosmic Creator, and meaning or ultimate reason for being.

As scholars such as Sam Keen, Joseph Campbell, Paul Tillich and Karl Rahner have indicated, these universal ultimate questions include, questions such as: "Who am I?" "Where did I come from?" "Why am I here?" "What are my special duties?" "Does life have any purpose?" "Why is there evil?" "How should I live?" "What are the reliable guidelines for a good life?" "Who are the heroes/heroines?" "Why is there something rather than nothing?" "Why don't other creatures speak or possess great intelligence like us?" "Why are there different sexes?" "Why are people different or speak different languages?" "Why is there death?" "What happens to people after death?" "Is death the end of life?" "Why should I not do evil?" These ultimate questions may not be always, so explicit and well formulated or articulated, particularly, in the African Tradition. Nevertheless, these the are ultimate and universal human existential questions, and intrinsic universal infinite, human quests for God, which are implicit in human myths, stories, religious questions and answers.

These ultimate questions may be validly posed and asked in any varied forms both implicitly and explicitly. The variation in the nature of questions may be a result of intrinsic factors embedded in local cultures, metaphysics, epistemology, logic, technological level of development, language, historical experience and the correlative unique human encounter with an awareness of the Supernatural, Infinite, Creative Holy Mystery.

Therefore, these questions can be described as the questions of a dilemma, since they usually require the decision of saying "Yes" or "No" to this Transcendent Holy Mystery, as the ground of one's being. The response of "Yes" affirms oneself, life, hope, love and God, whereas "No" leads to self-denial of one's being, one's meaning and the rejection of the *a priori* destiny in God as this Transcendent holy Mystery. However, in so doing the individual chooses separation from God, and subsequently, he/she has a self-imposed sentence to eternal damnation.[6]

This triune Mystery acknowledged by both Rahner and the African tradition is particularly interested in the human being as his special creation and representative on earth. And indeed, in the rest of creation, as both the Rahnerian Christianity and the African Religion clearly positively affirm, the human being is the only intelligent, free, moral or responsible and linguistic creature that is so far known to exist in the whole of the cosmos.

Whereas the African Tradition conceives Kazoba (or Amen-Ra), as the second person of the Trinity, and views him as the eternal Light (Sun), or the Logos that enlightens and guides all human beings from error into truth and from the wrong path into the right one, and protects the individuals from physical and moral or spiritual pitfalls.

Kazoba (Amen-Ra/Amun) as the transcendent, cosmic, omnipresent holy God and Light of the World (cf. John 1:1-6; 3:16-20), also bestows spiritual and moral insight on all obedient and wise people. This special spiritual light or moral guidance and insight enables the righteous person to see through other people's shady motives, and evil schemes. Therefore, by Kazoba's light all obedient human beings everywhere are given God's special power or grace be able to see, and resist evil. With Kazoba's divine light a moral person is enabled to see the clearly the world and its inhabitants as they God sees them, and also enabled to avoid evil company and the harm of enemies posing deceitfully and maliciously as friends, it nowhere claims that Kazoba became a human being in order to enlighten human beings by the way of identification and example, as Rahner teaches in accordance with the traditional Christian (Catholic) Incarnational Christology.[7]

Nevertheless, this absence of the idea of the Incarnation does not in any way nullify the validity of the African Traditional Religion as a divine medium for mediating supernatural salvation. Rather, it should be regarded by the Church as God's own effective preparation of Africa, for the eventual arrival of missionary Apostolic Christianity. In this respect, "anonymous Christianity" is God's universal effective preparation for the most meaningful acceptance of the historical Christianity.

In Africa, wherever, historical Christianity has been effectively and constructively proclaimed through the positive inculturation method of God's positive "Word and deed" or Agape, it has been generally accepted by the local people. Because of the emphasis on God's Agape, free universal unmerited redemptive grace, and effective free forgiveness of sins and guilt, it has also been appropriately welcomed and viewed as the "good news of God's" redemption and the kingdom, which ha finally come, most fully into the world, through God's historical agapic Incarnation into the world.

In Africa, the Roman Catholic Church has fared and theologically performed much better than the rival Protestant brand of "low Church" and conversionist Evangelical Christianity. It was also both self-evident and significant that the Protestant Church in Africa as in the USA, also had the least theologically educated clergy and missionaries.

In the case of East and Central Africa, these revivalist and biblical literalist theologically poorly educated charismatic evangelicals or "Balokole" generally preached the gospel as God's strict moral justice, righteous anger and hell-fire for those not "born again in Christ-Jesus." Nevertheless, the acceptance of this gospel or good news, becomes God's concrete positive fulfillment and completion of this inherently, deficient African "anonymous Christianity," into the explicit and more complete one, in the historical Church.[8]

The historical Apostolic Christianity, is more complete and correspondingly, more satisfying or fulfilling than the anonymous Christianity, as it is deficiently found in various forms, in all the world religions. This advantage is partly, because the historical Christianity and the Apostolic Church, possesses a more explicit revelation of God's essence of infinite, divine *Mysterium tremendum*, Grace and Agape, in the Incarnation. Above all, the superiority of historical Christianity to other revelations of God, in the world can only be morally and theologically established, by virtue of the definitive explicit commandment of the unconditional love for the neighbor.

In addition, this Incarnational process, is the explicit historical means, by which the Logos (Word) of God became an authentic historical human being, thus creating the irrevocable union of the human being with God by the indissoluble bond of the "Hypostatic Union." Therefore, for Christianity, in contrast to the African tradition, God is not only the Ultimate source of humanity as Creator, but he has also become permanently united with humanity, since God has become one with humanity by virtue of the Incarnation.

In the Incarnation of God in the cosmos through humanity, God's Word as God, has become the Ideal Man by uniting itself permanently with Jesus of Nazareth. By this incomprehensible "Hypostatic Union," God symbolically and irrevocably united himself with all human beings and in the same free universal divine act of redemptive free grace, has unconditionally also reconciled all human beings to himself in order to share in his own life of perfection, unconditional love and the cross of Christ by innocent suffering in order to serve or save others.[9]

This is therefore, the "Good News" (Gospel) that Christianity has to bring to Africa, so as to complement and complete the divine salvific self-communication already given to the African via the traditional religion and moral law. Since God and the human being have become one by virtue of the Incarnation, for Christianity, the human being has similarly become like God of whom he/she is the image, and therefore, meaningful cipher in this temporal world, and as such revelatory of God.

The human being is, therefore, the intelligent co-Creator with God, and because God has in Christ become a human being, and therefore, our very close neighbor, being symbolically incarnated in every human being, our search for God and our acceptance and love for God are correlative with our search, acceptance and love for our fellow human beings, for God has become inseparably bound with them through Christ's Incarnation. Hence, Christ's summary of the divine law is to love both God, and our neighbor as we love ourselves.[10] However, it is surprisingly on this crucial point of gratuitous love for the neighbor that both Christianity and the African Religion appear to be in complete agreement. Nevertheless, both of these traditions realize how difficult it is for the human being to love others unconditionally without the hope for either reward or some kind of gain.[11]

2. The Uniqueness and Mystery of Humanity

Both Western Christianity and the African Tradition acknowledge the uniqueness and mystery of the human being as a special creature in the whole of God's creation. Christianity as taught by Rahner, its spokesman, uses terms such as "*imago Dei*," "human self-transcendence," "hearer of the Word," "supernatural existential," "Hypostatic Union," "co-Knower," "co-Creator" and "co-Redeemer" with God in order to express this uniqueness of the human being.[12]

Africans also affirm that humanity is unique in creation. They use terms such as "*Omuntu aine obwengye/amagezi*" (the human being possesses intellect, reason, knowledge and wisdom), "*Omuntu aine Orurimi*" (the human being possesses a tongue/language and is capable of speaking), "*Omuntu aine Omutima*" (the human being possesses a heart, human emotions, understanding and has spirit), and "*Omuntu aine obuntu*" (the human being possesses humanity/humaneness, love, politeness and culture).

All these unique human-divine intrinsic qualities, exist in the human being as "*imago Dei*." As God's special divinizing gifts freely bestowed on the human being in the divine process of evolutionary creation, they stand in contrast to the rest of God's creation. This is particularly, the case when the human being is placed in the rest of the animal kingdom of which, he or she is a biological part.

The human being is through biological evolution a temporal creature which is also biologically related to the other animals. This is especially more visible when one looks at the higher primates, such as chimpanzees, monkeys and gorillas. According to DNA evidence chimpanzees are more than 99% biologically related to human beings. It is clear that Rahner and the African Tradition are complementary to each other on this point. However, the African Tradition can benefit from Rahner's modern Christian understanding of anthropology and biological evolution.

Unique human specialized features such as the large brain and high intellect permit the human being to have a greater capacity for logical thinking processes, or reason, memory, data or information gathering, data analysis, planning, sophisticated means of communication, learning, and progressive creativity as it is seen in poetry, fiction writing, scientific inquiry and technological inventions, which in turn, revolutionize human modes of life and thinking. As a result, human beings have exploited and modified their environment, changing it to fit their ideals, dreams and self-image, whereas animals generally seek to adapt themselves to their environment or migrate to a more favorable one.

This unique human ability to think and create new possibilities for better and improved conditions for human life, whether in the invention and processing of new drugs for treating deadly diseases or in the refinement of new medical diagnostic technology, new efficient surgical instruments and new surgical procedures, demonstrates the uniqueness, complexity and mystery of the human nature itself, which has become inseparably bound up with God's divine nature ever since the time of the Incarnation.

This state of affairs is probably best described by Rahner, who emphasizes the fact that human spirit, mind, intellect, knowledge and human creativity are co-extensive with divine spirit, mind, Logos, knowledge and divine creativity. And as such, these special divine attributes of God which are in a lesser degree found in the finite human being as the historical and temporal *imago Dei*, truly elevate the evolutionary primate into a *homo sapiens* and temporal moral agent or human being who is the special or elected creature that has become the concrete or visible representative of God on earth.

Ultimately, the human being has through evolution and *theosis* or divinization, finally become the true child of God and the heir of God's kingdom. By God's unmerited grace in creation, and redemption, the human being has already become the co-knower, co-Creator, co-Redeemer and co-worker with God in this world as God's kingdom.[13] This Rahnerian understanding can also help us to understand the African view of *"Omuntu"* as being the "insider" of *UNTU*, which is BEING or God.

The mystery of the co-extension and co-existence of such a God-human relationship in knowing, creation and historical process in this temporal world is the very mystery of the Incarnation and "Hypostatic union" in Rahner's Christology. In the African Tradition this mystery is probably to be equated with the mystery of divine-human mediation through a chain of mediators, both human and supernatural, through whom and by which God is supposed to act in the temporal world. In both Rahner and the African Tradition, God and humanity have a special relationship that is wrapped up in mystery.

In the understanding of both traditions, God is the Origin of human beings, although Rahner and the African Tradition differ in their accounts of how the human being came existence. For instance, Rahner espouses the modern biological evolutionary theory as God's historical temporal method of creation. That is evolution is positively viewed as God's gradual process for bringing human beings into existence, whereas in most traditional African Creation Myths are almost similar to those Hebrew stories of Creation and the Fall as recorded in the book of Genesis (1-3).

In these creation and fall myths, God is said to have created the primordial human being in a state of perfection and immortality. Then due to disobedience to God's moral law, both perfection and immortality were lost. For instance, in Uganda, there is Baganda story of creation which is reminiscent of Adam and Eve. "Kintu" was created by God (Katonda). God gave him a cow to provide milk for his nutrition. Since Kintu [Adam] became lonely and the cow [animals] was enable to keep him company, he cried out to God for redemption from this dehumanizing loneliness.

God in heaven heard Kintu's prayers for a more suitable companion, and created a wife for him called "Nnambi" [Eve]. God gave her chickens for food. Unfortunately, Nnambi forgot the chicken feed in heaven, and in tragic disobedience against God's command not to come back, she returned heaven to retrieve it. Nnambi's disobedience against God's commandment, caused death (Walumbe) to come into the world which was previously perfect and free of human moral evil and its consequence of death.

This Ugandan Kintu Creation Myth is characteristic of most African myths or stories of creation, the primordial human rebellion or "the original sin," and "the fall" of God's original perfect creation. This is characteristic of the general positive African religious and ontological affirmation of the original human perfection, prior to the original sin of rebellion and disobedience against God and the subsequent global imperfection, evil, pain, suffering and death. As a result of human disobedience, the world has lost its original order, harmony, lasting happiness, peace and perfection. The entry of death or non-being had, subsequently, caused havoc in the world by pain, suffering, disease and inescapable death to all human beings together with all living beings as they find their central focus, expression, fate, and value in the human being, in whom they have their access to God as the world's high priest.

As a result, in both Christianity and the African Tradition there is agreement on the understanding that the human being is such a special creature in the world to the extent that his/her actions have serious consequences in relation to God and the rest of creation. Both agree that the human action has cosmic consequences (both positive and negative) for the world. For instance, in both the Judeo-Christianity and in the East African Creation and Fall Myths, human disobedience to God not only brought divine retribution and punishment on the offending human beings, but on all creation.

This religio-philosophical presupposition is based on the view that the human being is the head, mediator, and symbol of all the created order. Therefore, this African creation and fall account is in full harmony with that found in the Bible. The one found in Genesis is in no way superior or more definitive on God's activities of creation, human rebellion and the cosmic genesis of moral evil by rebellious free human beings as consequential moral agents in God's essentially good or amoral world.

Subsequently, the African tradition is also in agreement with Rahner and the mainline Christian tradition which affirms that the human being is both the image of God, and the divinely appointed concrete temporal representative in the temporal world and its historical processes. For the Africans this understanding probably is best expressed by the institutions and offices of diviners, mediums, "Bafumu" (healer-priests) and divine kings.

The human being is regarded as the representative of God within the world because of all creatures, he or she of is the only one that both hears and speaks God's Word. The human being is the most intelligent and most equipped by God to fulfill such a role. The human being does not only possess a larger brain, he or she also is a historical spirit that possesses an intellect and greater capacity for abstract thought, knowledge, moral judgement and memory. As a spirit and mind, the human being also possesses self-consciousness and self-transcendence, and therefore, the human being is truly "*imago Dei*" and akin to God, his or her own Creator and heavenly Primordial Ancestor. As a historical spirit and mind, the human being also participates in God's own divinity and divine essence.

Therefore, the human beings also possesses the special divine gifts of freedom, creativity, memory, planning, a movable thumb and an upright posture to enable the hands to do intricate work. Additionally, according to Rahner, the human being is also the essential cosmic finite mind, divine echo and "hearer of God's Word." He affirms the Christian tradition that the human being is permanently ontologically attuned to God's Word and Mystery, *a priori* in creation.

This ontological orientation towards God and permanent ordering of the human being in gratuitous grace by God towards salvation as *visio beatifica* is what Rahner refers to as the "supernatural existential" that enables all human beings, universally, to become aware of God's invitation, and proffer of salvific grace and supernatural salvation, and to be able to respond or react meaningfully to this invitation with either a "yes" or "no" in responsible personal consequential freedom.[14] In this work, the study of the African Traditional Religion has attempted to demonstrate that the Rahnerian explication of Christianity enables us to call traditional Africans, "anonymous Christians," and to accept them honorably, as such members of God's universal interdenominational Church.

3. Human Prior Orientation to Divine Mystery in Creation and Requirement for Faith

The Africans and Rahner believe that God's knowledge is deposited in the human being by God at creation. For instance, in relation to prior human orientation to God, Professor Mbiti points out the African proverb that "No one ever shows the child the moon," in order to illustrate that Africans take it for granted that the young are spontaneously aware of God by the presence of an inner divine illumination which is present *a priori* in the form of the implicit pre-thematic and noncognitive knowledge of God that is spontaneous and co-extensive with humanity.[15]

Even young children are known to ask their parents embarrassing questions of where they came from. These innocent but embarrassing questions are the beginning of asking the more adult religious and scientific unending and insatiable profound questions of meaning and reason for being.

This eternal human quest for meaning and reason for being is both inseparable and the same with the correlative and coextensive human quest for God and divine salvation. This is the same dual quest for both God and salvation, which is both implicitly and explicitly, universally framed terms of the ultimate human questions and quest for the human Ultimate answers in terms of the ultimate human Origin and Destiny in God as the loving Cosmic Creator and its free Redeemer.

Accordingly, it is not uncommon for young children to ask questions such as: "Mummy, where did I come from?" "Where was I before I was born?" "What happens when a person dies?" "Where do dead people go?" "Why do people die?" "Where does God live?" "What is God like?" "Does God love me?" "Does God hate me when I am naughty?" or other similar questions. These kinds of questions may not all be asked at one given time. But, rather may be asked in the course of years as the child grows up and increases in knowledge and curiosity. More complex existential questions are asked later in life due to the increased awareness of the all-encompassing mystery of life and human beings that the child is in daily contact with.

Human beings, apparently, never outgrow this question about the infinite mystery of the human origin, life, meaning and the ultimate destiny. As children grow older and their religious and scientific knowledge expands, these questions, instead of being definitively answered, rather become more complex both philosophically and scientifically more sophisticated in nature, and no definitive answers are ever found that could be empirically supported or permanently intellectually satisfying.

As a result, the human being is faced with the question of the infinitely incomprehensible Transcendent Mystery at the center of humanity and the cosmos that requires the response of faith in order to continue living fully or meaningfully both in face life's uncertainty, and in the presence of the infinite Mystery, that Rahner refers to also as the human Horizon of knowing and living that keeps on beckoning and motivating the human being to advance forward towards it and yet itself remains ever receding.

However, although this Horizon is never near enough to be grasped by the human being, it is nevertheless never too far for the human being to be discouraged in his/her unending desire and attempts to struggle forward to try and get hold of it, in order to complete oneself in it. According to Rahner, the human being's pilgrimage and search for the truth, perfection in knowledge, personal completion, fulfillment and the attainment of happiness are tantalizingly symbolized and reflected by this Horizon as God, which the human being requires for his/her authentic self-actualization and existence.

According to Rahner, this process by which the human being is ever moving forward towards the Mystery or God as the tantalizing ever-receding Horizon is what Rahner refers to as "human self-transcendence" (*Vorgriff*) that is the chief characteristic of all normal human beings. By this human self-transcendence (*Vorgriff*) the human being recognizes human finitude and the infinite beyond that which is enshrined in incomprehensible Mystery, yet recognized and required to give human life its essential true meaning, and direction towards the human fulfillment and destiny that are similarly hidden in this impenetrable Mystery. Consequently, faith is required on the part of the human being as the "courage to be" and to live in the hope that all will be well in this future blind destiny that lies deep in this impenetrable Mystery, the "Abyss" that is God or Imaana or Ruhanga/Katonda.

In this respect, faith is the courage to be a finite human being that is utterly threatened by finitude as non-being, and also being utterly unable to peep into the eventualities of the future that lie hidden in the darkness and incomprehensible Absolute Mystery that is known as God (Ruhanga).

Without this essential faith that is required of human beings, who are aware of their finitude and helplessness due to being utterly dependent on this invisible Absolute Mystery, one can get paralyzed by an all-pervasive and consuming fear, anxiety and despair (*angst*). As a result of this overwhelming human finitude, fear, existential anxiety, and despair, along with evil choices which lead to an evil life, therefore, in reality, many people live in actual state of "hell."

The negative mode of life, especially as characterized by of materialism or greed, chaos, hate, violence, self-centeredness, guilt and torment in this existential hell is by human voluntary choice. This is by virtue of the consequential human freedom, manner of life in relationship to the praxis of agape, justice, and manner of personal or collective volitional use or misuse of personal freedom and their own free will. By their own free will and in personal freedom, they have either through ignorance or malice chosen and done what is evil, and therefore, effected a negation of "the good" and God's will. By so doing, these people have tragically freely or voluntarily rejected God and his will as explicitly revealed his moral laws or implicitly universally revealed in nature (natural law), and therefore, also thereby condemning themselves to a life in hell and damnation.

This hell or damnation consists in an actual negative and destructive mode of life on earth or in the world. This damned mode of life is the opposite alternative and contrast to that of Agape and its peaceful godly community or heaven. The negation of heaven or existential hell is, therefore, negatively characterized by radical alienation from Agape or God, the self, the neighbor, goodness and peace. On the other hand, despite finitude, those people who possess positive faith, and good will, can concretely be positively empowered and enabled to lead a positive and an agapic fuller human life here on earth and in the present.

This is the case despite the felt presence of human vulnerability and uncertainty regarding the unknown future. For those with faith and love for life and their fellow human beings, the unknown future is not threatening. For such a person, the future and its uncertainties are completely entrusted to God. This is reassuring since God is the Cosmic Mystery in whom the future and all its mysteries are hidden as part of his essence as the true and Absolute Cosmic Mystery.

The person with faith believes that since he or she is also a beloved child of the eternal Creator and Redeemer-God, that he or she has nothing to fear about the future, since God is the God of future, and works in the world to bring an evolutionary positive perfection and fulfillment in God as this Ultimate and Absolute Future that is the *a priori* human destiny as *visio beatifica* of every obedient and loving human being who has ever lived in this world.

This Rahnerian exposition is on the whole consistent with the African understanding of God/Ruhanga as the Transcendent Mystery before whom human beings are to live in awe, obedience and trembling. In fact, it is a better articulation of what most Africans generally believe unreflectively. Therefore, both Rahner and the African Tradition recognize that the human being is created by God in such a way that the human being is permanently attuned and oriented to God's mystery as the mystery that ever beckons and guides the human being forward towards positive self-actualization, self-fulfillment, completion and happiness, both now here on earth and in the unknown future that lies hidden in God's mystery.

Subsequently, both traditions agree that the appropriate universal positive free human response to this divine Mystery which is universally operative in the world to effect the unmerited free cosmic creation, supernatural salvation and the well-being of the human being is an active positive faith in God and the corresponding good works of agape or altruism. In addition, there is a common agreement that without this positive and dynamic implicit faith in the Creative Cosmic Mystery and the positive energy and benevolent efficacy of the presence of this pervasive infinite

Absolute Mystery, a positive and loving, meaningful, moral and peaceful human life would be impossible.

Therefore, there is an agreement between Christianity and the African religious traditional religion that God as the unconditional cosmic Creative and Salvific Mystery is also the Transcendent nameless cosmic Creative Force. This is also the same power, energy and Spirit that is ever experienced at the center of humanity and the cosmos. As a result of this immediate universal human apprehension of God, as this Cosmic Transcendence and Creative intelligent Cosmic force, normal human life is enabled to become self-conscious. The human finite consciousness is universally attained in the presence and contrast to the Transcendent Mystery, who is also the Incomprehensible, Infinite holy Creative Cosmic Mind and Ultimate Self-Consciousness or God.

As a result, of this universal Infinite transcendence, and contrast, the human being as a finite mind or spirit becomes universally acutely self-aware and conscious of itself as an utterly finite, imperfect and sinful being. In the presence of the holy transcendence of God, the human being also becomes completely self-conscious as a finite and contingent creature that is completely dependent on God's goodness and unconditional grace in creation, sustenance, redemption and fulfillment.

Nevertheless, as a contingent and vulnerable intelligent moral finite being, the human being feels threatened by finitude, the unknown future, the ever present threat of chaos, other peoples' hatred or malice, disease, pain and death. As a result, human beings everywhere exist in a state of existential anxiety due to this overwhelming nature of the human mind, self-transcendence, self-consciousness, self-reflection, and the awareness of their own condition of finitude and the uncertainties of life.

Accordingly, humanity apart from God's redemptive grace and mystical peace, is utterly crippled by the fear, anxiety and despair that are characteristic of living in hell and damnation, as is well described by both Soren Kierkegaard and Paul Tillich.[16] Hence, it is quite clear that both Rahner and the African tradition, are essentially in agreement that faith in response to the awareness of contingency on this all-encompassing infinitely incomprehensible Transcendent Mystery is the most appropriate human response and attitude, to this Mystery as God, the Holy One, the Creator and Sustainer, who is appropriately worshipped by all thankful intelligent creatures.

This acceptance of God and obedience to God in an implicit faith may also correlatively occur implicitly or anonymously in the course of daily life anywhere and through anyone in the world. For instance, this anonymous self-surrender to God's will and implicit worship may occur simultaneously and correlatively one surrenders to the Mystery that is encountered both at the center of one's being, especially, as symbolized in the insatiable void at the core of the human being and the impenetrable Mystery at the center of the cosmos. It is also explicitly takes place through contemplation or wonder at nature or the cosmic Mystery, adoration, study, research, private or public prayer, and both private and collective (public) formal worship in a church, mosque, temple or any other suitable place.

4. The Supernatural Existential and the "*Obuntu*"

Rahner's view is that human nature as we know it is already infused with the elevating divine gratuitous universal salvific grace, that has elevated the original human nature from "pure human nature," to the one that we know now, which is in this sense "supernature" in that it is open and capable of freely responding to God's universal self-communication in grace for human salvation.[17] This is Rahner's way of explaining how it is possible for supernatural salvation to take place outside the Church, and yet, take place through God's supernatural redemptive grace in the Logos as the cosmic pre-Incarnate Christ.

For Rahner, God's supernatural occurs everywhere, anytime in the cosmos as a direct result of God's own quintessential nature as Agape and *Sola Gratia*; and by virtue of God's unmerited gift of gratuitous universal salvific will. God and his inseparable activities of unmerited grace in creation and salvation take place everywhere, in the world where there are human beings. This is universally assured, since God has in his unmerited universal efficacious grace, freely created within each human being an "*a priori*" intrinsic gift of efficacious grace in the form of a permanent human ontological openness and capacity for apprehending God's universal free salvific self-communication and supernatural salvation.

This divine free efficacious creative and redemptive self-disclosure takes place universally in the form of the implicit, non-cognitive, pre-thematic revelation in nature and inwardly in the mind, conscience and the soul. The particular and historical divine explicit redemptive revelation takes place through the prophets, the Law, and the Scriptures and for the Christians, the Incarnation and Jesus-Christ represent the apex of God's explicit process of self-communication, history of revelation and salvation to the world.

The Rahnerian concept of the universal existence of human *a priori* "supernatural existential" as a unique and free divinizing gift bestowed by God on each human being at creation, helps us to explain the African traditional view that all human beings are freely and personally responsible for the kind of people they finally become both before the holy Cosmic Creator-God as the Primordial Ancestor, the ancestors, and the moral community. That is to affirm that for these Africans, any true or authentic human beings (*Bantu*) *qua* human beings (*Bantu*) must also possess the necessary humane qualities that are constitutive of humanity as "*Abantu.*"

This means that all normal human beings or "*Bantu*" must be endowed or be socialized by society into the acquisition of a significant degree of "*Obuntu*" (humaneness/divine qualities). As such, positive humane qualities are indicative of true humanization, obedience to God's commandments as mediated by the moral society, as God's redemptive community or Church and God's temporal kingdom. Conversely, rebellious and unloving, mean people are in the name of God judged to be bad, evil, sinful and wicked people lacking a sufficient degree of humanization, and therefore, living in hell and "causing hell" to come to their relatives, friends and others with whom they come in social contact.

This is partly, why the traditional society either executed or ostracized such notorious sinful, and rebellious members from the theocentric community. It is therefore, self-evident that the African tradition and the Catholic tradition are in agreement on the essential nature of God's supernatural salvation as a present reality in God now. This is also affirmed by the Rahnerian soteriological system. Accordingly, God's supernatural salvation is for both the African people and Rahner considered to be coextensive and synonymous with complete humanization, which is also correlative to theosis or divinization.[18]

Universally, this process of human creation or evolution, humanization and divinization into God's children is from beginning to end a God's free universal gift of Agape in unconditional love and unmerited grace. It is therefore, freely bestowed on each human being as part of God's "*a priori*" creative-redemptive-divinitive act of grace and unconditional love. This special structure and gift of God's unmerited redemptive and divinizing grace is constitutive of the human being as "*homo sapiens.*"

The Rahnerian Christian concept of the "supernatural existential" enables us to view the whole cosmos as the arena of God's universal creative and salvific activity. If one views supernatural salvation as God's continuing creative activity, then one can also view it as the universal gratuitous divine invitation addressed to all human beings everywhere, to actualize themselves more positively and more fully in unconditional faith, and hope for a more abundant and meaningful life that is still to come in the future.

In addition, the divine invitation calls the human being to practice charity and unconditional love for the concrete temporal neighbor in order to bring the very goodness and happiness to others in the same spirit and measure which we ourselves desire, and seek in both God and our fellow human beings. And in so doing, to experience these same fulfillments ourselves, by the same token, thus experiencing together the eschatological state of divine salvation, both individually and collectively, as a fellowship community of faith, love, brotherhood/sisterhood and righteous action.

For Rahner, the "supernatural existential" does not only enable the individual to be the "hearer of God's Word" of invitation to eternal life, and to respond to it freely and responsibly, with a consequential "yes" or "no" to this proffer of gratuitous supernatural salvific grace, but it also makes the consequences of that "yes" or "no" to this divine invitation to salvation a historical reality. In other words, those who say "yes" to God are led further into the riches and mystery of God's life, of grace and salvation, whereas those who reject him, and the salvation he offers, subsequently, cut themselves off, from the origin and sustenance of life. As a result, they often fall into a kind of paralyzing anxiety and despair (*angst*). This anxiety tends to make living a meaningless hazardous venture full of unnerving fear and uncertainty making life or living unpleasant and hellish.

This is consistent with the African Religion, where one cannot reject God, the neighbor or community, and yet continue to live a meaningful or satisfying life. This because God is regarded as the very ground and condition of human life itself, orientation to the world and action. For that matter, all notorious sinners were usually executed, since they were considered a danger, to the life of the community as they offended God, its source.

Therefore, both the Rahnerian concept of Christianity and the African Tradition essentially agree that the human life and its continued meaningful and positive full existence is entirely dependent on this dynamic human faith in a good creative and redemptive gracious God. The African Traditional Religion is also in harmony with Rahner and the mainline Christian tradition concerning the basic nature of God as free and gracious Transcendent Cosmic Mystery who is the Creator and Redeemer.

This is the Transcendent Holy Mystery, by which this *a priori* concrete sacred life is accepted as both a temporal and supernatural divine free gift which is universally offered by God to all human beings everywhere. Both Western traditional Christianity and the African traditions are also in harmony regarding the central theocentric understanding of human life. Both traditions positively affirm that this life is God's special universal sacred gift to the world, and it is to be always reverently, thankfully and lovingly appropriated by the human being.

Subsequently, both the African tradition and Christianity, condemn murder, abortion, euthanasia and suicide as sins and abominations which are committed against God, humanity and the community. For traditional Africans, these evils, sins and abominations were considered to pollute the evil-doers, and the communities in which these people lived or in which these crimes were committed. Therefore, the respective offending members and their communities had to be ritually cleansed from the pollution and evil of these sins. If confession and cleaning atonement were not carried out, it was believed that God would not only punish the responsible evil-doers, but also the silent community which had acquiesced to the to the presence of evil and the approval of evil-doers.

Ultimately, in both western Christianity and the African Religion there was a spiritual and moral common ground. There was a unitive common understanding and mutual ethical-theological harmony that the human being is invited by God, to respond to this efficacious universal gift of grace in creation and redemption in faith, hope, obedience and love or agape.

Consequently, an obedient godly person anywhere, is that obedient human being who has accepts God's free supernatural gifts of life, love and peace in thanksgiving or worship. And exercises these divine and holy gifts to the maximum in his or her life and for the good of the other people and the community. This also affirms that God's saints everywhere are those people who accept life as God's gift, and live and celebrate it in joy, thanksgiving and positive work. Positive or good works as fruits of God's grace are commanded by God (cf Matt 5-7; 25:31-46). They are necessary to promote justice and improve the quality of this divine gift of life and its positive expression, well-being, goodness, happiness, peace, and the heavenly beatific experience God through the fellowship and love of the members of the theocentric and peaceful community. Such a person, is the true saint of God (cf. John 14-15; 1 John 4:7-22; Jam. 2:14-26).

In short, the true saint of God is any obedient person who does the agapic good works of God's commandments as found both in the scriptures and nature, and loves or unselfishly serves God's his or her neighbors and people anywhere. Such a person is the true saint of God. This the case regardless of religious affiliation or even lack of it. Religious labels in themselves are mere attempts to define this godliness and sainthood. After all, God is neither a Christian nor a Muslim; God is neither a Jew nor Hindu; God is neither a Buddhist nor a Shintoist or a member of any religion or school of theology, since the holy Creator and Redeemer-God is infinite and transcends all these religious traditions, and so are God's unmerited cosmic activities and free gifts of universal redemptive grace, revelation, love and salvation.

The true saints of God are those people anywhere, who live in love, peace, good works, and harmony with their neighbors as fellow members and children of God's community. The saint treats other people as fellow seekers for a meaningful fuller life and fulfillment, in the fellowship of love in the direct transforming and divinizing presence of God.

Therefore, any obedient, humane, morally responsible and loving traditional Africans, native Americans, Buddhists and Hindus, qualify for communion and membership in God's kingdom. They join the Christians in the worship and obedience to God the Father of Jesus-Christ. They worship God the Father through the mediation of the ancestors, saints, Mary the Mother of Jesus, and ultimately through the Christ-Jesus as the Cosmic High-Priest, Mediator between the infinite, holy, transcendent God and finite mundane and sinful human beings. Jesus-Christ as a perfect human being, and risen Primordial-Ancestor is also trusted to become the true and effective Advocate for all human beings. The innocent death of Jesus on the cross is often positively viewed as a sufficient vicarious sacrifice and atonement for all human sins.

However, the most overriding theological soteriological paradigm, metaphor and symbol is that of Jesus-Christ as the incarnate Logos and primordial agent of God's creation, revelation, and therefore, the most effective mediation of God's redemptive Agape, unmerited free grace, free forgiveness of sins, removal of guilt and thus the establishment of the new state of affairs which constitutes salvation and God's kingdom in the world. Thus, the incarnate Logos-Christ is the best temporal cosmic Mediator of this transcendent Cosmic Mystery as the Creator-God, who is also both the Ultimate Redemptive Sustainer and the Ultimate human beatific Fulfillment or the Eternal happy Destiny as our Ultimate primordial Origin and the human Primordial Chief Ancestor (cf. Gen. 1:26-31; Lk. 3:24-38).

5. Human Radical Awareness of Socio-Religio-Moral Responsibility and Intrinsic Guilt

Perhaps more so in the African Tradition than in the Rahnerian type of Catholic Christianity, there is great emphasis placed on human community, fellowship, and socio-religio-moral responsibility as the grounding for the right harmonious human relationships in the ideal human community. This ideal harmonious human community exists on earth as God's Church, kingdom and heaven on earth.

The human community is God's holy arena for human creation or birth, human-divine encounter, supernatural drama, divinization, fellowship of love, re-creation or redemption and ultimate human fulfillment by God. The human community is knitted together by a network of human relationships. It is family-based. An individual member of the family becomes a member of the respective community along with or in close association with other members of his/her immediate family, extended family, neighbors, friends, relatives, general members of the community, and finally total strangers such as foreign travelers.

To be truly human is to belong to a human community. And to be humane or godly, is to be a peaceful, loving, caring, respectful, wise and considerate member of the community. Respect for the ancestors takes the familiar form of pouring out libation, and sacrifice. It also consists in leaving food on altars for the departed or "living-dead" as integral members of the community, who are remembered and fed at major family meal times, and other special occasions, such as religious and social festivals.

This societal moral responsibility and kinship define normative godliness, ethics or social morality and the humane behavior expected of human beings in any given situation. For example, in traditional East Africa it was generally expected that one should give hospitality to a traveler who comes into the village late in the evening. This hospitality usually includes lodging, food, drink, conversation, treatment of any injuries or sickness the traveler might have suffered or contracted on the journey, protection, and helpful information regarding safe travel in the local area and its neighborhoods.

Failure to render a stranger such an needed and essential hospitality in the positive spirit of an unconditional humanitarian loving service, or maliciously causing harm to befall the stranger, such as misleading him or her, so that he or she ends up hurt or traveling on the wrong path, is treated very gravely as a sin before God and an offense against the ancestral spirits. Therefore, it is seriously punished by society and God. It is also a sin to be confessed and atoned for immediately by both the offending member and his/her community.

This is considered essential in order to restore peace, harmony, well being and God's favor. As such, atonement for sin is carried out in order to secure forgiveness by God and the guardian ancestral spirits. It is also mandatory in order to avert the divine wrath and punishment. This divine judgement and punishment for personal and collective sins is said to occur when God allows the negative forces of chaos and destruction to prevail in the form of personal or societal disasters, misfortune, strife, war, loss of property, disease, pain or and death. God and the ancestors are supposed to punish sin by causing holy destruction to occur upon the sinning individual or his or her family and community.

Consequently, in traditional African understanding and cosmology, these manifestations of evil and human suffering, such as disease, epidemics, floods, famines, accidents, misfortunes, disasters and the like, are invariably always attributed to God's righteous anger and punishment due to human sin. In the final analysis, all forms of evil, pain, sufferings and death in the world are attributed to God and the ancestors as supernatural punishment and retribution due to human sin and guilt.

As such, Africans are like the Hebrews who sought to atone for their sins regularly through sacrifice and atonement. Sin was supposed to injure relationships between neighbors in the human community, offend the community of the ancestral spirits or the departed members of the community, and alienate human beings from God in heaven. And result of this alienation from God, the community and its members are deprived of God's blessings of order, plentifulness, wealth, good health, good weather, rain to water the crops, well-being, life, love, harmony, security, safety, peace and happiness.[19]

This is probably the main reason why in the African tradition so much attention and emphasis are placed on the fundamental necessity, societal and religious value of both correctly and diligently observing the customs, laws and taboos or avoidances, as these are supposed to ensure the maintenance of the right harmonious relationships within the community between various members of the community, the departed (ancestral spirits), and God.

Since failure in the observance of these relationships causes a breach within the community that destroys the balance and harmony which are required for the individual and the community to function well at any level, be it socio-political, economic or religious, therefore, the cause and breach of the moral law, have to be diagnosed quickly. This is essential in order to correct and bridge it before any further harm befalls the community.

In this context, it is vital for the well being of humanity and the community, to restore the religio-socio-political social harmony and spiritual balance, that is required for the proper functioning of the African traditional community. The African authentic human existence hinges on the reverence and fear of God, and the departed ancestors. The African religion provides the necessary rituals and context for loving and harmonious relationships within the community to occur.

Coextensively, the African religion also provides moral guidelines, laws and correlative human moral responsibility as *"Obuntu."* The *"Obuntu"* as agape provides the necessary grounding and means for both correct personal and appropriate collective moral conduct to promote societal harmony. When the Obuntu fails, the African religion and society, will then provide the necessary proper social, moral and spiritual mechanisms for punishment, repentance, atonement and reconciliation with the neighbor, the ancestors, God and the community. The African ideal is to maintain harmony, balance, and peace within the context of human, spiritual and theocentric social community.

If the cause of trouble or disharmony was not readily diagnosed by the affected individuals, then a religious expert or consultant was sought and consulted. It was usually a priest or a diviner or both working jointly in order to provide a more effective religious service to the community. The diviner, utilizing his/her special skills and special powers of supernatural vision and by God's grace and permission, was supposed to peep insightfully into the otherwise impenetrable divine mysteries.

Consequently, the diviner was supposed to look into the past of the individuals and the community and be able to see the point and cause of the breach in relationships. He was also supposed to see or correctly diagnose the problem or nature of the moral offense committed, and its magnitude, and therefore, be able to prescribe an effective cure or the necessary atonement. This cure was usually prescribed in terms that would remove and expiate the offense in order to restore general societal well-being, the healing of personal and social relationships, and restoration of religio-social harmony and wholeness within the community. Therefore, it is not an overstatement to claim, as Mbiti does, that the African traditional religious priest, who is usually also a herbalist or a medicine-man, and the diviner are as much God's gift to the people of Africa as the Christian clergy and medical personnel are to the Western world.

In comparison to the African Tradition, Rahner can probably be said to be lacking in emphasis on human sin and its harmful consequences on the human relationships within the context of the general well being of the community. Within the African context, the Rahnerian concept of the "anonymous Christianity" can be said to be inadequate and spiritually deficient. This is necessarily the case, since Rahner presents God's salvation within the context of anonymous Christianity as the an individual matter as opposed to that of the total community, of which the individual is an inseparable member.

Unlike the Western individualistic cultures, where the individual is the focus of society and the center of God's redemptive mission and sacramental activities, for the African the individual member cannot be separated, nurtured and saved outside his or her respective community. Instead of the typical western self-understanding in the Cartesian individualistic familiar dictum of "*Cogito ergo sum*" (I think therefore, I am), for the traditional African is as Mbiti clearly put it, "I am because we are, and since we are, therefore I am).

For the African one cannot be truly be saved or be redeemed by God outside his or her context of the community and no one is ever truly saved or happy without his or her neighbor. Indeed, for the traditional African, such an individualistic type of (Christian) salvation, as zealously proclaimed by Western Evangelicals and revivalists, which would not include the neighbor or the community would be more like hell than heaven! In Rahner, anonymous Christianity, like most of traditional Apostolic Western Christianity there is little stress on being redeemed together with the neighbor.

Therefore, to remedy this inadequacy and correct the implied theological weakness in terms of the absence of the redeemed essential community, and fellowship of the saints, I have stressed the primacy of a practical and existential societal life of agape. This emphasis on agape and the agapic fellowship of all God's obedient people in the world, has been made within the context of the community and positive, harmonious and loving or agapic relationships between individual members of the community, the departed, and ultimately with God.

In this theocentric Community of God, God serves as King or Sovereign, and correlatively, as the veritable Ultimate Guarantor, Ground, Center or locus and pivot for all these essential human networks of relationships and social interactions. These harmonious relationships and the peaceful community which they create are positively affirmed as being essential components of any meaningful state of God's salvation and kingdom on earth. This essential social network of harmonious and agapic relationships can be said to constitute human beings as "*abantu*" or these intelligent creatures who are endowed with "*Obuntu*" (humanity).

The ordinary human community, is also the very supernatural holy community of God's obedient people, the inclusive and God's earthly kingdom. Therefore, the human community is a concrete social arena of God's supernatural activities in the world, which is God's kingdom. These divine activities include the natural and supernatural processes for the creation, humanization, redemption, divinization and fulfillment of the human being. The human family as the core of this human community is the concrete place where human beings are called into being, created and brought into God's world and the kingdom by God.

The morally and economically healthy human family is the essential microcosmic community of God's activities of creation, redemption, worship, immortality and the kingdom. The human family is fundamental nucleus of both the human community and God's cosmic family. Therefore, any good and healthy human family, anywhere, in the world is the primary foundation and the quintessential component of God's cosmic kingdom. The functional or healthy human family is God's concrete historical, socio-economic, special biological and laboratory for supernatural creation of humanity. A healthy human family is the necessary universal prerequisite foundation for any healthy, enduring human community, prosperous nation, and peaceful world.

The human family is also the very sacred and divine starting point, where human beings begin and are also, correlatively, set upon their holy pilgrimage in quest of an authentic existence in the form of a personal meaningful self-actualization, self-enjoyment, and fulfilling process of full humanization and completion as such. For Rahner, the conventional Church is the best form of the community for such a supernatural salvific process to take place.

Nevertheless, like St. Augustine and Thomas Aquinas, Rahner also recognizes that this gratuitous supernatural salvific process can also take place anywhere, including outside the Church (*extra ecclesiam*) or the traditional ecclesial community, with divine approval, validity and a measure of success, as he affirms enthusiastically in his teaching on "anonymous Christianity." However, Rahner tends to view this "anonymous Christianity" from familiar Western and Christian point of view. As a result, he presents anonymous Christianity as a "community-less personal spirituality" consisting of atomic or individual "anonymous Christians" who respond positively to God's inward invitation to salvation. They respond inwardly in response to the inner divine *a priori* salvific revelation deposited at the center of the human being by God at creation. This is done by God in gratuitous universal salvific grace and unconditional love.

This universal gift of salvific grace and the human structure of grace designed to recognize and receive it, as such, manifests itself universally in the human being implicitly as human self-transcendence and ontological orientation to holy Mystery. This is the divine gift of grace and its operative structure which Rahner calls the "supernatural existential."

This supernatural structure of the human being constitutes God's universal salvific grace, and simultaneously, it is also the very intrinsic special divine-human instrument dwelling within each human being. It is God's gift of grace and the Holy Spirit resides within and enables the human being to apprehend God's special activities both in the world and within the soul. This indwelling gift of God's Holy Spirit and the Logos, work together within the mind and soul of the human being and cause the person to seek for God, and to accept the free gift of God's universal redemptive grace, and thereby, to effect the mysteries of God's salvation.

By the free divine gift of God's grace, the obedient person is enabled to do good works as the necessary social fruits of divine salvation within the human being. Good works are acceptable ethical external agapic actions and manifestations of a sound inner spiritual blessings by God, practical faith and moral peaceful life in fulfillment of God's commandments, particularly, the definitive Christocentric moral law of agape. This mode of special divine salvation is universally made possible through the universal redemptive grace operating in each person through the a priori human-divine structure and special divine gift of "supernatural-existential" or Emmanuel (God with and within us).

This structure of grace as the "supernatural existential" structures the human being in a theocentric mode that is like an antenna that is ever positively oriented and attuned to God. This universal free divine gift of the structure of God's grace, and the divine grace that is embedded within this structure effectively enable any obedient human being anywhere, and everywhere, in the cosmos, and in every age, to hear God's Word of Love, forgiveness and salvation. This is because this divine gift of God's supernatural grace through an "*a priori*" human intrinsic or in-built divine structure of grace within each human being which orients the human being to God, goodness, divine grace, salvation, happiness and ultimate human self-fulfillment in God.

The "supernatural existential" is analogous to a television set or satellite antennae and remote control which is permanently turned on attuned to God, who both holds all the remote controls, and yet, also controls the programming. The existence of the inner human special capability to both hear God's Word and obey it through the "supernatural existential" enables each and any obedient human being to become ever open and receptive to God's salvific self-communication in his Word or the Logos and "to be saved" or to obtain God's salvation. This special divine gift of God's Logos and structure of grace is the in-built divine-human modem for communication with God and leads to salvation. It is God's universal gift which has been freely given to all human beings everywhere, in order to bring all human beings, everywhere, and in every age both to the redemptive revelation and true knowledge of God.

Therefore, all human beings everywhere, possess the special supernatural means and the essential power of God's efficacious grace to be able to effectively hear God's redemptive Word (Logos-Christ), and obey. And then, be enabled to practice Agape and experience salvation or even direct union with God by means of this in-built capacity for apprehension of God. Some of the human communications with God take an implicitly non-thematic understanding of God and his divine revelation. However, within the Judeo-Christian tradition, including Islam, there is a clear and explicit content and manner by which human beings are supposed to communicate with God in most reverent manner.

Christians explicitly claim that the existential structure of God's grace and agape was most clearly visible in Jesus as the Logos incarnate in humanity. As such, the Christian claim is that all human beings should be like Jesus is their conception of God, prayer life, practice of Agape, faith in God and forgiveness for all those who sin against them. This is the basic content of the true redemptive Gospel. Therefore, where the Gospel has been constructively and meaningfully preached, there is an acquisition of the clarification of the former implicit revelation has been made explicit and thematic.

Consequently, these "anonymous Christians" are not yet members of any Christian community both explicit and anonymous, according to this Rahnerian conception.[20] Therefore, in this individualistic aspect the Rahnerian concept of "anonymous Christianity" can be attractive to traditional Africans who are basically social and community-oriented in their ideals. However, this problem would be overcome if the African traditional religion itself could be viewed as "anonymous Christianity."

6. The Human Community as the Special Arena of God's Salvific Activities

Rahner recognizes the Church as the special community and arena of God's salvific activity. He also views the whole world as God's general arena of salvific activity for the individuals who as "anonymous Christians" do not belong to a local self-conscious nurturing and an agapic fellowship of other God's pious or obedient loving people in the collective or social form of a Church or other redeemed and theocentric salvific communities. This absence of Church or spiritual community and special fellowship among anonymous Christians as the redeemed children of God is a major weakness in Rahner's concept of "anonymous Christianity."

However, this weakness can be most effectively overcome in the case of non-Western cultures where the human community is the center of religious life. Such communities are both natural and supernatural *ecclesia* or churches of God. They mediate God, grace, absolution, salvation and peace to their respective members. For instance, Native American, Indian, or African traditional community is theocentric and a theocracy. Its religious, and societal activities, are as holy, moral, spiritual, and life enhancing as those found in the Bible. This is particularly, the case when one reads the Old Testament and studies the life in ancient Israel which was also theocentric and centered on temple worship. This was also the case with the Christian Church and the Christian West during the Medieval period.

In the cases of Africa, Native America, China, and Japan by adopting the African concept of the local theocentric human community as God's "*a priori*" redemptive Church and arena of creative and salvific activities, the weaknesses of anonymous christianity are eliminated. I have affirmed this to be the case in traditional Africa inasmuch as it is the locus of human life, meaningful human relationships, sinning and forgiveness, hurting and healing; revelation and worship, cultic religious activity, learning, humanization, love, faith, trust, hope and immortality through posterity and the memorial of the departed members of the community as friends, neighbors, relatives or as ancestors.

The Rahnerian concept of the Church should be appropriately modified. This should be brought in line with his concept of "anonymous Christianity," in order to include the "anonymous Christians" in a kind of "anonymous Christian Community or Church." This is necessary because no human being is able to exist fully and authentically outside the human community, as it is the community that, both grounds and mediates God's activities of the creation and redemption of the individual human being. For instance, the community is God's medium for bringing the individual into being, through the biological birth in any given family. Likewise, the human social and religious loving community, is also correlatively, the divine salvation of that individual being partly constituted in the community's process of humanizing that individual who has been born into it.

In short, there is no humanity if there is no correlative community. Similarly, there cannot be salvation apart from the community, since salvation as authentic human existence and wholeness can only take place within the context of the community. This means that the traditional Catholic dogma of *extra ecclesiam nulla salus* can still be defended as valid and true, inasmuch as the term *ecclesia* is expanded to mean any human community that in some major way serves as the medium for divine self-communication for the humanization or salvation of the individual members of that community.

Therefore, salvation as the complete humanization and human authenticity of both men and women is a historical process that can only take place in a concrete temporal human community, and not outside it nor in total independence or opposition to the community. This is mainly because God works through ordinary human beings and the ordinary human community in order to address the ordinary situations of human beings at their natural or level of sophistication and within their local context. In other words, the ordinary is the bearer of the extra-ordinary and the vehicle for the mediation of the divine. Although this vehicle or medium of divine activity is not always explicitly Christian, nevertheless, it is always explicitly associated with humanity and the human community.

Rahner's anthropology and philosophical-theology should be constructively studied as a whole in order to better understand and insightfully modify his concept of "anonymous Christianity." Accordingly, "anonymous Christianity" being this agapic and inclusive universal Christian soteriological doctrine should be most appropriately theologically developed and meaningfully expanded to include the respective theocentric human community as the "anonymous Christian community," and the necessary inclusive "Universal Redemptive Church" of the pre-Incarnate Cosmic

Christ. In this case, Christianity does not have to be either self-conscious or explicit as in the case of the Apostolic Church and historical Christianity.

Unlike the cosmic "anonymous Christianity" which is essentially informal, non-Western, non-confessional, and non-missionary, Apostolic Christianity is characteristically kerygmatic, confessional and missionary in its essential nature. The explicit central Christian dogma and confession consists of the baptismal covenant faith in the Apostles' and the Nicene creeds, namely, that Jesus is the Christ and the God Incarnate in the world of humanity, matter and cosmic historical processes (cf. John 1:1-18).

Furthermore, with the Incarnation, God has become a human being, and therefore, the extra-ordinary has become ordinary, and consequently, the human being has become the effective mediator and representation of God, and the human community has, likewise become the community of God, the very embodiment and mediation of God in this temporal world. Consequently, it can be affirmed that no one can find God and no one can ever be saved by God apart from humanity and the human community.[21]

Therefore, unless Rahner's concept of "anonymous Christianity" is appropriately modified as suggested above, it may come across to many people as a hollow and deficient Christian postmodernist doctrine of soteriology. Subsequently, in the way it now stands, would be unattractive to those who find meaning and fulfillment in the corporate religious community as opposed to those few who delight in holy solitude, and delight in the direct path of individual quest for God, sought through solitary quiet prayer, meditation and contemplation of God's and his mysteries, in hope for divine illumination, and ultimate spiritual fulfillment in the beatific vision or the spiritual beatitude which come as the results of divine illumination, and human mental-spiritual ecstatic union with God.

7. Unconditional Human Love for the Neighbor as the Concrete Expression and Mediation of Divine Revelation and Salvation

It is perhaps on this topic of Agape and its central societal praxis that we find the most surprising similarity between Rahner and the African Tradition as regards to the fundamental role that love plays in supernatural redemptive revelation and salvation. Perhaps most important of all, in both systems of thought and world-view, God is the Creator and Father of all human beings. And consequently, all human beings are God's beloved children (*Abantu ba Ruhanga*). As God's children, all human beings, are loved by God without any prior conditions. Therefore, God commands all human beings everywhere, also to love one another without any conditions, in order to be just, holy, and perfect like him. Agape or the praxis of altruism as a form of practical societal expression of unconditional love is the Christocentric explicit practical means to love other people as God's children. All human beings as *imago Dei* are also members of his macrocosmic extended family that includes all nations, races, colors, creeds and cultures.

According to the Africans (under study), one cannot love nor say that he/she loves a person whose children he/she hates. On the contrary, it is both positively affirmed and believed that love for a particular parent can be expressed and mediated to that parent by being expressed to his/her children unconditionally. It is believed in Africa that the parents and their children are one and inseparable, as such. This is also considered to be true for God. That is, one cannot truly profess to love God or the Creator (Ruhanga), and to respect him whereas he/she hates, disrespects, and mistreats his creation, particularly the human beings who are usually regarded as the children of God (*Abantu ba Ruhanga*).

This is mainly why traditional Africans in Kigezi and other areas used to pray to God before going out on hunting expeditions, going to war or going to cut down a big tree or clear some virgin land for cultivation. These activities involved an apparent destruction of life, human in the case of war, animal in the case of hunting, and plant life in the case of clearing forests or cutting down trees. These activities were usually done carefully and prayerfully so as not to disturb the divinely given state of balance of nature and the harmony between the human being, the world and God, that is required to ensure this harmony and mutual wholesome contingent existence of both the human being and the world that are both themselves contingent on God as Creator, Sustainer and Protector of his creation.

However, for Western Christianity and the African Religion, although the preservation of the environment and the world are important both to God and to the human being, who is dependent on them, they are nonetheless, secondary to the value and preservation of life and humanity itself. For the African theocentric tradition, it is the human being from whom the rest of creation gains its value and importance, as measured by its degree of utility to sustain human life or provide for human comfort, self-enjoyment, satisfaction and happiness. Therefore, whatever contributes to these human needs is valued, and conversely, what does not is thought to be of less value and importance.

It is generally recognized that the human being has needs that are both spiritual and physical. The physical needs, such as hunger, thirst, sex, shelter and clothing, can easily be satisfied to a reasonable level by providing the required material needs (except in remote African villages, where droughts can cause a severe shortage of both food and water). However, the spiritual needs, such as the need for security, love, recognition, self-worth, identity, freedom, sense of belonging and the like, are usually not easy to fulfill adequately. Nevertheless, through love and the network of relationships, the community tries to meet these human psychological needs.

The African Traditional community, being aware of these two types of needs, took measures to provide an acceptable religio-social context within which these needs could be met. For instance, human sexual drives and needs were recognized and exogamous marriages were devised to make sure that incest and close kin sexual activity did not take place, as it would cause jealousy, rivalry and tension within the family unit itself, probably causing its breakup and consequently the general breakdown and disintegration of the community. The extended family was also generally the context for learning how to express gratuitous love and to practice charity. The idea that charity begins at home was very true here. The extended family, which was usually also polygamous in nature, was also usually full of tension and conflict and thus an ideal arena to train in patience, forgiveness and love.

Furthermore, the African practice of polygamy was encouraged to ensure that all the surplus marriageable girls were married off, in order to give them an acceptable context to meet their sexual needs and to bring up their own offspring within a marriage relationship, hence avoiding "bastardism," which was regarded as a terrible scandal usually punishable by death for both partners and their illegitimate child.[22]

In addition, polygamy was also valued for the new network of kinship relationships and alliances that it made possible, particularly, in pre-colonial tribal Africa, where intertribal fighting broke out very regularly due to the breakdown in alliances or willful and sinful violation of the human rights of one group by another group. These social and moral conflicts, breakdowns in alliances and violations were usually results of failures in the observation and praxis of the basic ideal moral principle unconditional love for other human beings, which was often enough to cause suspicion of strangers and concern to the African communities.[23]

The unconditional love for others, though the ideal, usually failed in the face of a strong sense of kinship ties, extreme ethnocentrism (or tribalism), ethnic pride and arrogance, individualism, greed, selfishness, malice, hatred and brutality. Nevertheless, both Christianity and the African Tradition still insist that this unconditional love for the neighbor, though an apparent failure, is still nonetheless regarded as the authentic mark and full expression, of the inner divine salvific activity in gratuitous grace, as "Obuntu" in the case of Eastern Africa.

In Africa, particularly major parts of East Africa, the unconditional love for the temporal neighbor is treated as divine, a microcosmic expression of the macrocosmic one. This is primarily because to love the neighbor in traditional Africa usually required some degree of unconditional love and forgiveness for the neighbor. This was necessary because the neighbor was usually the very person whose goats or cows ate up and destroyed your gardens, crops and banana plantations. It was also your neighbor's kids that sometimes killed your chickens or dog just for fun or out of malignant rivalry and malice. It was your neighbor that sometimes seduced your wife, spread malicious damaging gossip about you, or dug a portion of your land as his own without your consent.

In modern times it is the neighbor that often refuses you to pass a road, a water pipe, electric poles and wires through his/her land and tells you to get lost when you try to persuade him/her that he/she is being unreasonable and unneighborly. In short, your neighbor is usually the person that "drives you nuts," and yet, it is the very same person that you have to live with as peacefully as you can, even when he/she "is sometimes too much for you" and you would have probably been happier driving a spear or a knife in his/her heart rather than calling him or her to a neighborhood beer party and feasting.

Nevertheless, like Christianity and as expounded by Rahner and the African Tradition, this is the very neighbor that we are taught and called upon to love by our own religion and upbringing as Africans. For instance, in both Ankole and Kigezi, children were required to learn the following poem by heart in the African general context, telling of the necessity of unconditional love for the neighbor as one of the main basic foundations for the African philosophy of human existence:

Mutaahi wangye anshagiza	My neighbor drives me crazy
Tindihemuka.	But I will not lose my composure.
Akanterera omwana	He beat up my son
Owe ndyamushwererera.	But I will help his own son get married.

Akanyokyeza enju	He burned down my house
Nyowe ndyamuha omuganda	But I will give him timber
Nayombeka.	To build his own house.

Akansisira bingi	He destroyed a lot of my
Kwonka Ruhanga we	property and did me great harm
Aryabinyongyera.[24]	But the loving God will reward me.

This Rukiga-Runyankole poem articulates the African version of the unconditional love for the neighbor, whereas at the same time it defines the neighbor that is to be loved. In this teaching context of the poem, the neighbor who is to be loved unconditionally happens to be the very person that beats up your own kids, maliciously burns your own house down, and does many other despicable things to you, "driving you crazy!" This definition of unconditional love for the neighbor is apparently in surprising harmony with the Scriptures and the Christian tradition. For example, James writes: "If you really fulfill the royal law, according to the scripture, 'You shall love your neighbor as yourself, you do well. But if you show partiality, you commit sin" (Jam. 2:8-9a, R.S.V.).

St. John agrees and writes about agape as a basic divine correlative attribute as well as being the basic essence of himself. He also affirms that the praxis of love is the concrete manner and means by which human beings participate in God's own holiness and divine essence. To this end John writes to the Christians and the Church community as follows: "Beloved, let us love one another; for love is of God, and he who loves is born of God and knows God. He who does not love does not know God, and God is love" (1 John 4:7-8, R.S.V.).

The African religious tradition is in full harmony with both Jesus and John in respect to the centrality of agape as the criterion of any true godliness, sound moral and a peaceful and harmonious relationship with the self, God, the neighbor, the community and the rest of creation.

In the African traditional understanding, love or agape is a matter of correct social moral action and conduct. It is concrete in its explicit external expression and direct action in the form of positive attitude, good deeds of altruism, compassion and justice. Therefore, for the traditional African true religion is not a matter of verbal expression, in the form of creeds and dogmas. On the contrary any true religion is a matter of positive action, love, and respect for the self, the neighbor, the elders, the ancestors, the community, nature and God. This positive action and practical agape takes the form of concrete good and compassionate actions and deeds.

Consequently, in a truly African traditional setting, it is very rare to hear a person telling another person that "I love you!" In a social situation where this kind of verbal confession of love is made explicitly, its authenticity and motives will generally be questioned. The individual will also be secretly and carefully scrutinized and investigated to see if he or she is trustworthy. This is because such a verbal confession without the accompanying good deed will be negatively interpreted and construed as mere deceitful flattery, such as that meant to lure the person into evil, such as being conned into an illicit love affair. However, people were always free to sing songs of praises and love for beautiful women. But, for that they were often treated with suspicion and little respect by the African society.

However, if this relationship became serious, positive behavioral transformation in the form of commitment, trust, faithfulness, considerate humane behavior and mutual generous exchange of gifts, and serious intimate personal conversations, and the like, would usually replace mere pious or empty rhetoric of empty cultural polite words alone, as the authentic expressions of genuine love.

In other words, love is lived and acted out rather than being merely talked about as mere noble doctrine. Indeed in this respect, "actions speaker louder than words." And in essence, actions and a virtuous life constitute the true Gospel of Christ as opposed to mere proclamation of the message of God without any good collaborative deeds to validate it.

In this African thinking it is impossible to be a true God-fearing Christian and then trade in slaves, cheat and commit genocide. This is important in Africa where most people, particularly, the Bantu people are on both community-centered and action-oriented. This also applies to matters of love and gratitude, which are generally expressed in terms of concrete action or get acted out rather than being merely verbalized.[25]

Accordingly, for the Africans, religion is a matter of how one lives and behaves rather than professes. Action is the proclamation of God through sound religion which proclaims God's the truths, moral obligation for human mutual expressions of love, forgiveness, respect, acceptance, tolerance and humaneness. This is what God accomplished in the Incarnation.

God has physically and dramatically acted out his unconditional love for the world. He sent a real person, namely his Son or Logos to become incarnate in the world as a morally pure and exemplary historical person for others to emulate. The Christ-event is part of this divine-human drama and effective communication in appropriate cultural context. God did not just speak his Word of love in a cultural vacuum. Jesus as the Christ represents

God's ultimate self-disclosure to the world as God's concrete incarnation of Agape, compassion, grace, forgiveness and peace.

Similarly, in traditional East Africa, love for the neighbor generally means living in positive, humane and loving attitude toward the neighbor, exchanging daily greetings and detailed family and personal news, protecting each other's property, exchanging tools and food-stuffs, eating and drinking together regularly, and helping each other in times of need, disease, disaster or death in the family.

In short, love for the neighbor means open living with the neighbor as if the neighbor were part of the family in its African traditional extended fashion. This kind of love for the neighbor is generally expected to be self-sacrificial, as it usually requires giving generously without counting the cost or expecting anything in return except God's supernatural reward in his mysterious ways. In some cases this appears to be the chief motivation for one's unconditional love, generosity and help for the neighbor.

However, the neighbor is treated as such because he or she happens to be a fellow human being that one is in contact with, in this way being symbolic of the microcosmic human representation of the macrocosmic total humanity and God, who is inseparably bound with the human being as ultimate Origin, Sustainer and absolute Future. Furthermore, according to Rahner's Christocentric theological teaching, God has also become inseparably bound with humanity by virtue of the Incarnation and the "Hypostatic Union," by which process God has become our close neighbor in Christ who as an incarnate human being is inseparable from the temporal neighbor.

Western Christianity and the African Religion and Philosophy, positively affirm that no individual human being can love God and experience God's love or forgiveness apart from other people, the community, and especially apart from the temporal neighbor. Also, in both teachings, God is loved and known by us as we come to know and love the neighbor unconditionally. Similarly, divine forgiveness is experienced as we forgive others, particularly, the neighbor as the person we live closely with and come to know personally and interact with, offend or get offended by, resent and conflict with due to close proximity and constant interaction.

It is in this concrete and imperfect neighbor that God is, still nonetheless, incarnate and categorically present in the world. In this understanding, it can therefore, be affirmed that our unconditional love for the neighbor is the path or ticket to God our true humanity and happiness through our personal acts of unconditional love for him or her. Consequently, our fate as human beings is bound together with that of our neighbor, and as such, to love our neighbor is to love ourselves and to love God. Furthermore, each human being is, consequently, lost without the other. Rahner puts it as follows:

> The act of love of the neighbor is, therefore, the only categorized and original act in which man attains the whole of reality given to us in categories, with regard to which he fulfills himself perfectly correctly and in which he always already makes the transcendental and direct experience of God by grace. The reflected religious act of love of the neighbor, since both acts are necessarily supported by the (experienced by unreflected) reference both to God and to the intramundane Thou and this by grace (of the infused *caritas*) i.e. by that on which the explicit acts both of our relationship to God and of our neighbor 'for God's sake' reflect...

Then Rahner goes on to connect love for God and the love for the neighbor:

> The love of God unreflectedly but really always intends God in supernatural transcendentality in the love of the neighbor as such, and even the explicit love of God is still borne by the openness in trusting love to the whole of reality which takes place in the love of the neighbor. It is radically true, i.e. by ontological and not merely 'moral' of psychological necessity, that whoever does not love the brother whom he 'sees', also cannot love God whom he does not see, and that one can love God whom he does not see only by loving one's brother lovingly.[26]

8. Salvation as the Process of Humanization or the Acquisition of "*Obuntu*"

It can be observed that despite obvious cultural, philosophical and theological differences, both Western Christianity and the African Religion share much in common, and also have an apparent basic unity in their general approach to universal salvation.

Both the African and Western systems of thought are grounded in God's goodness, benevolence and salvation. The basic "common ground" is that whatever else salvation might be, it is first and foremost the process by which God turns "the animal" or primate creature (*ekintu/Kintu*), traditionally referred to in English as "Man," into a person or human being (*Omuntu/-Muntu*) that possesses "*Obuntu*" (essential humanity), and therefore, the capability for moral responsible choice, being kind, humane, tolerant, patient, generous, loving, considerate and forgiving. He/she is also expected to be capable of awe, respect, freedom, responsibility, wonder, worship, awareness of sin and guilt in relation to the Holy Mystery that is God.

The process of the acquisition of these human elements (*Obuntu*), and this state of human self-transcendence is the process of deification which is the same as humanization or movement and transformation from the state of primordial "*Kintu*" or "*ekintu*" to "*Omuntu*." Both Christianity and African Tradition identify this process with the divine salvific historical process. According to the East African Bantu understanding, the acquiring of "*Obuntu*" as those human qualities that make a person a person or turn a primate creature into a human being, the very special creature of God that is described in the Scriptures as "God's image" or "*imago Dei*"[27] is the same correlative divine joint evolutionary temporal process of God's special creation and transformation or salvation of all obedient human beings.

Salvation as the humanization of the human being can be said to begin at conception, and to increase with the level of human growth in virtue such as knowledge, love, self-control, generosity and self-sacrificial giving for the sake of others and for their well-being and happiness. Modern examples include such activities as being a missionary or a voluntary technical worker in the remote rural parts of underdeveloped Africa.

This is necessary in order to bring to these African villagers and others, the good news of the God's Incarnation and salvation. It is necessary to proclaim or tell the story of the divine Incarnation and how God's own beloved Son, Logos or Agape has permanently entered history as a sinless human being in order to provide a godly example for human beings to follow. And also to effect a permanent, and efficacious universal atonement for all human sins, and thereby provide free forgiveness of sins and removal of guilt for all human beings. This is the good news as the human reconciliation to God, and the eschatological freed divine restoration of their primordial paradise which had been lost.

Christianity has the positive message that the basic primordial God-given gift of immortality, eternal life and the resurrection which had been lost due to human rebellion and sin are now restored to humanity by God in Jesus-Christ, and his own innocent death on the cross and resurrection, which destroyed the powers of death and injustice. In addition, western Christian missionaries can also help them in the practical development of the local people from a subsistence agricultural economy to a more efficient, modern, large-scale, and mechanized farming economy.

In these practical matters the missionary role as evangelist should be accompanied with the roles of the Christian missionary as an educator, technical advisor, and medical practitioner. After all, Jesus as the Christ taught the ignorant, fed the hungry, healed the sick and forgive the sins of those who were evil-doers. This is the role-model, paradigm and example of an effective and desirable missionary in Africa, Asia and other places.

Ultimately, the role of the missionary as a religious or a cultural imperialist is not acceptable. Consequently, constructive local and foreign missionary activity can lead to the tangible improvement of life quality and lead to a positive transformation of life and effect God's concrete salvation as societal and human well-being.

Thus, the so called "social gospel" as a gospel of God's moral imperative command to practice agape, and to yield the societal positive fruits of justice, welfare for the neighbor and peace in the world, has been positively reevaluated in light of God's definitive commandment of Agape. And subsequently, the praxis of agape was accepted as the inclusive and universal criterion for true godliness, salvation and entrance into the kingdom of God.

Contrary to the theologically and morally misguided Evangelical and fundamentalist emphasis on "*sola fide*" as the path of salvation, and the exclusion of "*sola gratia*" and its good works of grace in agape, "*sola gratia*" as the effective "praxis of Agape" has been positively affirmed and regarded as a universally valid temporal societal characteristic and concrete existential manifestation of spiritual conversion from greed and self-centeredness. Therefore, altruism and agape of which the "social gospel" proclaim to the world and demand in positive response and obedience to God's commandments is a valid universal evidence or universal criterion for any true obedience to God, and positive human response to God's gratuitous salvific grace, and concrete mediation of supernatural salvation and its blessings in this historical world.

In both the African Tradition and Christianity, as expounded by Rahner and others, such as Karl Barth, Emil Bruner, Teihard de Chardin and Hans Kung, true humanity comes from God alone, and Jesus Christ is the true embodiment of this humanity. What Jesus reveals about this authentic humanity, or what it means is to be an authentic human being the way God created us to be, was manifested in his being and essence as that of an agapic holy life in the community with the neighbor, the ancestors (saints), spirits and God. That is to say that any holy life, including that of Jesus as the Christ, is that which is most open, fully oriented and attuned to God, in being fully open and receptive to God's Word, other people, love, divine grace, humanization and divinization. Consequently, when Jesus said that "My Father and I are one," he meant this harmony of purpose and being between himself and God, his Heavenly Father.[28]

Therefore, inasmuch as it can be said that Jesus is the mediation of authentic humanity, it can be also claimed by African Christians that Christ is the divine medium of authentic humanity, inasmuch as he is both the medium and the embodiment of "*Obuntu*" (authentic humanity or humaneness). As result, despite the explicit absence of the idea of the incarnation in African Traditional teaching, there is an implicit anticipation for the Incarnation, inasmuch as there is this awareness and explicit teaching that "*Obuntu*," which is the human elements that are constitutive of authentic humanity or humaneness, comes from God himself, who is conceived in a trinitarian fashion.

According to this African teaching about God and salvation as the process of supernatural humanization of the "*Abantu*" (humanity), it can be said that it probably anticipates Christ's Incarnation in order to reveal explicitly (in a temporal manner) in this temporal historical process, what it is actually like to be an authentic human being in the world, and also what it means to be complete in humanization, having acquired the fullness of "*Obuntu*" (essential humanity/humaneness).

9. Death as the Eternal Validation of the Human Life for Either Eternal Fellowship With God or Eternal Self-Alienation and Damnation

In the understanding of both Christianity and the African Tradition, death is not the end of the human being. According to Rahner, it is the final definitive culmination of the human process of humanization and growth as a human being. Rahner calls it the climactic zero point that the human passes through to another kind of spiritual life.[29]

Africans refer to it as "departing this life," meaning that the individual has gone into a new kind of life. However, the impenetrable mystery of the future state of existence, the manner of life and usually the kind of pain involved in the dying process and the loss felt by those friends and relatives left behind, make each death seem such a monstrous meaningless evil with no redeeming value. Nevertheless, for both Christianity and the African Religion, it is the climactic divine valuation point of each individual historical being that cannot be indefinitely shirked, not even by pious prayer, intercessions, modern medicine and medical technology, which all have their limits. But, rather, death is to be accepted as a given, very much like one's own life at birth.

In this respect, one can probably justifiably question whether some forms of Christian belief in the literal physical resurrection are not, in fact, some kind of denial of death. That would, indeed, be contrary to the African view of premature death as a great tragedy and an irrevocable loss of humanity (*Obuntu*). However, for the traditional Africans as long as one has lots of well behaved or "good" sons to remember him after his death, that was part of his salvation and immortality. As a result, males were expected and encouraged to marry many wives, and to have many sons if this mode of immortality and salvation was to be maintained and successfully perpetuated.

This extended family and kinship was required as the social and religious foundation for a human immortality and good communication system composed of many intermediaries that was interwoven together to link the living members of the community, the benevolent departed ancestors, gods and God, in heaven. As such, in traditional Africa, polygamy, lot of children and the harmonious community were essential in order to ensure the continuity of the community, the material and spiritual well-being of its members, and finally immortality for the departed benevolent ancestors or "the living-dead."

The traditional African spirituality was balanced and symbiotic in matters between the living and the departed ancestors. The ancestors mediated between God and the living and return they were remembered and feed through the pouring of libation. Most people in traditional Africa, like the Christians in the West, very often live in anticipation of this eventuality. In some cases, this acceptance and preparation for one's eventual death have a profound effect on the type of life the individual actually lives in his/her lifetime, namely, as a preparation for this eventual and unavoidable death.

The Bakiga and the Banyankole believe that God both creates and "kills" by letting death befall the individual. These people express this Job-like idea of God's power to both create life and then, also take it away (or "kill it") whenever he chooses. This African idea is summed up in the Bakiga-Banyankole proverb which states that "*akaguhungire niko kagwata*" (the Creator is also the Destroyer). Therefore, for the African, both creation and its destiny are completely hidden in divine mystery in which the whole process, ultimately, originates and culminates.

However, whereas the individual can do little about his/her origin, he/she is aware that he/she can entreat God to prolong his/her life, thus temporarily keeping back death that is usually perceived as the ultimate enemy of his/her humanity. Consequently, in traditional Africa, death is important in shaping people's lives positively,[30] because, just as in Christianity, it is believed that one's life is definitely evaluated and eternally validated by God for all its total worth, depending on the condition and the state of goodness (*Obuntu*) or wickedness (*Obubi*) in which the individual died. This condition is then ratified as that individual's permanent record and eternal validation of the individual's earthly life by God. For instance, it is believed that if the wicked and angry people die in that wicked state unrepentant, they subsequently, turn into "*Emizimu*" (ghosts and malignant evil spirits) that are eternally rejected by God, the ancestral spirits and the human beings.

It is believed that subsequent to this judgement and rejection they are revengeful and ever plotting evil, harm and mischief against the community, and particularly, against the "good" human beings, whom they envy and seek to destroy or turn into destructive evil people, so as to be like them and eventually join them in their human rejection, consuming hatred, malice and subsequently, eternal damnation.

On the other hand, the good people who possess "*Obuntu*" are said to be transformed into the good or guardian spirits, who serve the same function as the angels within Western context and religious ontology. These African benevolent guardian spirits are ones that are often referred to as "ancestral spirits" in both divine honor and deific elevation to this important status by their own respective communities.

These good ancestors are both religiously canonized, and deified into saints, angels and guardian spirits, as a reward for their good and exemplary life, while they were alive. By bestowing this great social communal recognition, honor and reward on these doers of good deeds and saints, the community keeps the memory of its saints or ancestors alive and thus immortalizes its noble members of the community. By doing so, other members of the community are both recognized and reaffirmed in their own good works, and thereby encouraged to emulate in the same way that some Christians seek to imitate the life of Christ and the Saints.

In this respect, the spirits referred to as "ancestral spirits" are the African equivalent of the Christian "Community of Saints," particularly within the Catholic tradition and devotional practice. For instance, the ancestral spirits are invoked by Africans in prayer in order to act as their guardian angels and to mediate between them and some other people.

However, although in the African Traditional Religion there is a general absence of the concept of hell as "a literal and concrete geographical place" of eternal punishment by God for one's sins not repented and expiated by the time of the individual's death, there is a concept of hell as a real existential condition of hate, social discord, societal rejection, disease, pain, suffering and premature death.

In contrast, heaven, is both a human condition and "place" of eternal blessedness and happiness as the reward for the righteous (as missionary Christianity teaches in Africa). It can be said that the African idea of instant transformation of the human being at the moment of death, the subsequent embodiment in a spiritual body, evaluation, and judgement by God and the ancestral spirits, and the subsequent acceptance by the ancestors and God if judged as good or rejection if judged as unworthy for having lived a life of hatred, malice and lacking in "*Obuntu*," is probably a viable alternative eschatological view to the traditional Christian teaching on death, the resurrection, judgement, hell and heaven.

The African version should be studied further for the promise it holds for a new understanding and a possible reformulation of a new modern version of Christian eschatology that is more consonant with the African Traditional Religion and philosophy,while remaining true to the Scriptures, biological sciences, and modern scientific cosmology. In this way, the African Tradition can be given the full recognition, respect and opportunity to function effectively as the divinely provided African medium for God's revelation and gratuitous salvific activity of humanization (*Bantuzation*) of the human being.

However, since God's revelation and salvific activity have been concretized in the historical process in the Incarnation and therefore, in Jesus Christ, the African tradition, though revelatory of God and mediating his love, grace and salvation, does so in a partial manner in the deficient mode that Rahner terms "anonymous Christianity," which anticipates explicit Christianity for fulfillment and completion.

This partly explains why Christianity is growing in Africa, and why most Christians in Africa are Catholics. Roman Catholicism has meshed in well with the African Religion, Philosophy, and cultural traditions, whereas Protestantism has tented to view these negatively, and consequently has rejected and repudiated them.

Nevertheless, Rahner warns us that this does not mean that all "non-Christians" who qualify for God's salvation as "anonymous Christians," will necessarily be pleased to know that they are some kinds of Christians although they are not baptized nor members of the Christian Church. In fact Muslims, and Jews may probably take offense at such a suggestion that they are "anonymous Christians." Finally, anonymous Christians will not necessarily welcome and convert to historical Christianity itself, if it were presented to them in a culturally and theologically relevant and meaningful manner. If this is the case, then one can most justifiably present serious objections against it, such as: "What is the value of the Anonymous Christianity?" This question and others like it will be dealt with next.

NOTES

1. The term "African" refers to African people that are included in OAU unless specific groups are stated. Remarkably, there is an underlying cultural unity in Black Africa despite ethnic and sub-cultural pluralism. Tribalists focus more on difference than unitive Africanity.

2. God is only God (Ruhanga/Katonda), as far as these people are concerned, if he is also omniscient. This concept is in contrast to the Western Whiteheadian process metaphysics that claims that God like human beings cannot know the contingent events of the future until they have occurred. See *Process and Reality*, Part I, Chs. I:VI, VII-X; Part II and Part V.

3. Karl Rahner, *Foundations of Christian Faith*, 228.

4. Ibid., 14 ff., 84 ff.

5. See: *The Essence of Christianity* (1841) and *The Essence of Religion* (1845).

6. See, Karl Rahner, *Foundations of Christian Faith*, 90 ff.

7. Cf., Karl Rahner, *Foundations of Christian Faith*, 178-321.

8. Ibid., 203-228, 311-321. This might also explain the strength of Christianity in this area of Uganda in contrast to the North.

9. "On the Theology of the Incarnation," *Theological Investigations* 4:107-120; "Christ the Mediator: One Person and Two Natures," *TI* 1:158-182; "Christology within an Evolutionary View of the World," ibid. 5:173-184.

10. Cf. Karl Rahner, "The Commandment of Love in Relation to the Other Commandments," *Theological Investigations* 5:439-467; 6:231-249.

11. There is a strong sense of kinship that is central and regulatory of social life and human existence in general. Kinship might be a good system for regulating life in a small, closely interrelated community in the village. It creates nepotism and corruption in Africa.

12. *Spirit in the World*, 57-202-236, 387-408; *Foundations of Christian Faith*, 24-115.

13. Loc. cit.

14. "Relationship between Nature and Grace: The Supernatural Existential," *Theological Investigations* 1:306-315; "The Order of Creation and the Order of Redemption," *The*

Christian Commitment, 44-53; "Anonymous Christians," *Theological Investigations* 6:390ff.

15. See, Karl Rahner *Foundations of Christian Faith*, 116-175.

16. See, Soren Kierkegaard's *Concept of Dread* and *Sickness unto Death*; Paul Tillich, *New Being* and *The Courage to Be*.

17. Cf. O'Donovan, ed., *A World of Grace*, 64-119. See also note 14 above.

18. In the African understanding "*Obuntu*" as the constitutive essence of an authentic human being is freely given by God to all people, through both heredity, and community or culture, religion, values and the moral guidelines. These values and virtues are either freely accepted or rejected by adult human beings as they grow into moral agents. As free moral agents all mature people are required to become responsible and accountable for their own freedom and moral values since these have serious consequences for society and the world.

19. See John Mbiti, *African Religions and Philosophy*, 50-118.

20. "Anonymous Christians," *Theological Investigations* 6:390-398; "Christianity and the Non-Christian Religions," *TI* 5:115-134; "Atheism and Implicit Christianity," *TI* 9:145-164; "The Appeal to Conscience," *Nature and Grace*, 39-63.

21. See Karl Rahner, "The Commandment of Love in Relationship to the Other Commandments," *Theological Investigations* 5:439-467; "Reflections on the Unity of the Love of Neighbor and the Love of God," ibid. 6:231-249.

22. In pre-colonial Kigezi in southern Uganda, it was usually the unwedded pregnant girl who was killed. But the offending male partner also got killed if found out.

23. Fear of witchcraft, hatred, homicides, tribalism and its implications for the exclusion of other people illustrate this point. It is also experienced by those people engaged in such human negation of their own essence as "*Abantu*" with "*Obuntu*." Hateful and evil people negate humanity and the community whose harmony and stability they destroy.

24. Katiti, *Ninshoma* (Kampala: School Readers, EALB, 1950), 28.

25. Some people may just smile instead of saying "Thank you" and others give gifts or perform another service for the person just to show gratitude and to act out a "Thank you." This custom has led to bribery and corruption in much of Africa.

26 "Union of the Love of Neighbor and God," *Theological Investigations* 6:246-247.

27. Cf. Genesis 1:26-28.

28. See, for example, John 10:30 ff., 17:21-23.

29. See, Karl Rahner, *Foundations of Christian Faith*, 434-443. Death is a transformation rather than a split of a person into a lifeless body and a spirit that departs.

30. See, Placide Tempels, *Bantu Philosophy*, 17-18.

IX

ANONYMOUS CHRISTIANITY
AND ITS SOCIO-THEOLOGICAL IMPLICATIONS
FOR GOD'S KINGDOM OUTSIDE THE CHURCH:
CHRISTIANITY, AFRICAN RELIGIONS
AND PHILOSOPHY

To affirm the efficacious universal reality of God's cosmic unconditional free activities of creation and redemption is to affirm the traditional Christian dogmas of God's universal free and unmerited grace both in creation and redemption (cf. John 1:1-18; Rom. 1:1-31; 5-7; Heb. 1-4). Subsequently, the positive affirmation of the universal efficacy of God's creative, redemptive, transformatory and regenerative grace both inside and outside the confines of the Apostolic Church and its sacraments, is also to positively affirm God's unconditional universal redemptive and creative grace and love (agape) which are constantly at work in the entire cosmos.

Therefore, there is solid ground for intellectual and theological affirmation and social acceptance of all God's people as God's own redeemed children even if they were the very "lost sheep" that Jesus as the Christ came to seek, recover and reconcile back with God (Matt. 18:12-18; Luke 15:3-320). This is the ultimate result of Christian intellectual and moral growth and maturation in obedience to God and his definitive universal commandment of agape. As a result, all saints are essentially mystics.

The doctrine of anonymous Christianity helps us to transcendent the finite barriers of religious dogmas, creeds, discriminatory human-made regulations, social and religious taboos regarding the sacred and the profane. Moses, Buddha, Socrates, Jesus, Paul and Gandhi are such examples. Jesus horrified his followers by breaking the restrictive Sabbath rules, and repudiating the Pharisaic social, religious regulations and food taboos. Jesus was called a blasphemer and a trouble-maker. As a result, he was arrested, falsely charged and executed by crucifixion because he called God his Father, and forgave sinners in God's name (cf. Mk. 2-3; 7:15-23; Matt. 26:59-66).

Ultimately, to affirm universal redemptive value and efficacy of "anonymous Christianity," is thereby, also to affirm the reality of the universal gratuitous divine work of creation, sustenance and persuasive guidance toward meaningful self-actualization and fulfillment. In other words, it is to affirm the following Biblical teaching:

> In the beginning was the Word [Logos] and the Word was with God, and the Word was God. He was in the beginning with God; all things were made through him, and without him was not anything made that was made. In him was life [Zone] and the life was the light of men. The light shines in the darkness, and the darkness has not overcome it...The true light that enlightens every man was coming into the world. He was in the world, and the world was made through him, yet the world knew him not.[1]

Since the "world knew him not" in the text refers to the Logos that was the medium of creation and the Savior as "the life" and "the true light that enlightens every man" and every woman in the world, it is quite explicit that the Gospel text is referring to the Logos as being incognito and anonymously present in the world and active in its temporal processes until the Incarnation, when this divine Logos, the pre-existent Christ, became explicit as a historical human being in Jesus of Nazareth.[2]

This Johannine text illustrates very clearly how God's process of creation in Christ can be coextensive and continuous with the universal elevation in free unmerited grace as "the true light that enlightens every man" in this world. Rahner's insightful and inclusive global categorization of Christianity into the implicit or anonymous and explicit or the confessional traditional Apostolic and historical Christianity, as two different modes of redemptive Christianity constitutes a theological revolution in our time.

This constructive theology was part of the revolutionary thinking behind Vatican II and its radical departure from Vatican I and the Council of Trent in matters of ecclesiology and soteriology. Thus, the previously revered and almost infallible soteriological dogma of "*extra ecclesiam nulla salus*" was critically examined, evaluated and discarded, in favor of ecumenism and the Rahnerian type of approach to interfaith and world-religions as revelatory of God, and efficaciously redemptive, to some varied degrees, depending on the presence of the teaching and practice of agape and free forgiveness of sins for fellow human beings.

First, the Rahnerian concept of the implicit/anonymous Christianity, covers the pre-Incarnation and post-Incarnation period in which Christ's salvific work as the cosmic divine Logos is primarily incognito or anonymous. This theocentric or God-centered Church or "Creation Covenant spirituality" includes diverse groups, such as, the Native Americans, African Religionists, Buddhism, Hinduism, Islam, Judaism. Anonymous Christianity covers those who have never heard the gospel of Christ. It also refers to those who have rejected both the Incarnate Christ and historical Christianity because it was misrepresented, corrupted and presented to them in a distorted or a culturally objectionable, irrelevant and meaningless manner.

Therefore, the various morally responsible, humane, self-confessed atheists who obey and do God's will, but reject the idolatry and hypocrisy of organized religions and corruption in the Church, also qualify to go to heaven under this mode of Christianity. In this mode of spirituality, positive moral action and good deeds which enhance life, peace and harmony in the community, are the criteria for true godliness. In this respect, Karl Marx is God's social prophet and saint of justice, equality and brotherhood.

Secondly, Rahner's second category of Christianity is that of the explicit divine temporal revelation in the Apostolic historical Christianity. This is the traditional Christian mode of the conventional, cultural, hierarchical, institutional and missionary Christian Church in the world. This ethnocentric, self-righteous, confessional Church is by its essential Apostolic faith and kerygmatic nature, creed oriented and dogmatic.

Therefore, it self-consciously conformist to the creeds and the Apostolic teachings as recorded in the New Testament. It both rejects religious or theological pluralism and despises any other religious groups whose creeds or confessions or liturgical procedures are different. This Church is Incarnational and Jesus-centered. This is therefore a Jesus-Covenant Church and spirituality.

In this soteriological complexity, it is helpful to view God's universal gratuitous activities of creative and redemptive self-communication to the world in two moments. The first moment of revelation being that of "God the Father" in creation. This is the era or moment of the divine "Universal Transcendental Otherness," which is non-cognitive, ethical, remote, transcendent, law and mystical experiences that tend to occur on "the mountain-tops." These mystical experiences are known to take place in other isolated quiet places, such as monasteries, convents, deserts, forests or woods, caves, along rivers, sea or lake shores, islands and solitary hermits cabins.

This is an experience of the radically Transcendent God of Moses and the African Religion. He is experienced as the remote Creator, holy, wrathful, Law-Giver and Cosmic Judge. In this radical divine transcendence, heaven or sky, sun (Ra, Kazoba), moon, high mountains and the horizon are employed as God's symbols. Holy mount Kenya, Kilimanjaro, Birunga, Rwenzori, Sinai, Fugi, Tibet, Himalayas and St. Helena are famous examples. These symbols and temples of God are analogous to the Christian symbols of the cross and the Church. In both cases, the symbols for God are treated with reverence, but they are not worshipped as God. Only God is worshipped in these traditions.

However, excessive reverence for the holy symbols is often mistaken by the outsiders as both polytheistic worship and idolatry. This radical divine transcendence is universal and represents the first, divine moment of self-disclosure to the world. It constitutes the divine universal and inclusive "Creation Covenant" or Old Testament. This moment is characterized by natural revelation, nature oriented wholistic religions and theocentric ethics. The religions at this level are redemptive for both humanity and the environment.

In other words, God as cosmic Creator is as concerned about the well-being and redemption of human beings, as that of animals, plants and the world. Shintoism, African-Religion, Native-American Religion, Hinduism and Buddhism are the best examples of this positive affirmation of human beings, ecological balance and harmony as God's will, and part of God's acts of free grace both in creation and redemption.

Thus, heaven as the paradise of "Happy Hunting Grounds" with lots of buffalos was an ideal theological-ecological conception of heaven in Native American Religions. Both the Islamic and traditional concepts of heaven as paradise or the restored primordial lost "Garden of Eden" is not far from this ideal ecological-theological understanding of God, humanity and God's kingdom as God's reign on earth and the world, in this present moment.

The second moment is that of the awareness of the Incarnation, immanence, Agape, parenthood (*Abbaship*) of God Hypostatic in the Union. This is the moment in which the human being apprehends himself or herself as the reconciled child of God. The best example of this dual nature of God-human nature and God-human self-consciousness was explicitly found in Jesus-Christ.

Accordingly, Jesus as the Christ would declare that God and himself (Jesus) were one and that whoever has seen him has also seen God (John 12:44-50; 14:6-21). This is the case since by virtue of his obedience and complete openness to God, God was present in him more fully than he is in other sinful and rebellious human beings.

This mode of divine self-communication in the Incarnation of the Logos-Christ in the world as Jesus-Christ, the man of Nazareth, constitutes a historical, cognitive, thematic, ethical and mystical model for explicit or missionary Christianity. The second moment is complementary and fulfilling to the first moment rather than being its abolition or negation, as Jesus himself affirmed: "Think not that I have come to abolish the law and the prophets; I have come not to abolish them but to fulfill them."[3] Similarly, the writer of the Letter to the Hebrews also saw the continuity of these two moments of God's self-communication to the world and put it as follows:

> In many and various ways God spoke of old to our fathers by the prophets; but in these last days he has spoken to us by a Son, whom he appointed the heir of all things, through whom also he created the world. He reflects the glory of God and bears the very stamp of his nature, upholding the universe by his word of power.[4]

However, the second moment of God's self-disclosure, being cognitive and historical in nature, can only be mediated historically through the teaching of the Church and its missionary teachers and preachers. This is a very slow process as judged by the example of Jesus himself, who taught and made converts by the personal exemplary way of life of the teacher touching his students at the innermost core of their being by his own life, love, words and deeds.

In this sense the Gospel of God in Christ is also Incarnational in that it is the love of God addressed to human beings through the embodiment of another human being. This is a slow and time-consuming process. Therefore, there will always be people who will not be effectively reached by this Gospel message of the Incarnation and evangelized.[5]

Nevertheless, these unreached people will not be in any way excluded from God's salvific grace. This is because God is already active world-wide in an impartial manner to effect his will and salvation for all those who hear his Word or Logos-Christ and obey. God is ever through the cosmic Logos-Christ ever inviting all human beings to come to him in his Mystery. As the very Transcendent Mystery, God is the one that guides each positively responding individual towards salvation as the fullness of authentic being and the full individualistic uniqueness of being a person.

Since this process is enabled by Christ as the Cosmic divine Logos that mediates and energizes this dual coextensive process of humanization and salvation, and outside of which this process is unable to take place, Karl Rahner correctly designates those people who experience this divine humanization process as Christians and those responding to God at the level of the first moment of "implicit faith" as "anonymous Christians," and those responding in the second moment of the explicit faith in the Gospel as "explicit" or "confessing" Christians.[6] Rahner epitomizes this as follows:

> Until the gospel actually enters the historical situation of a certain person, a non-Christian religion contains not only elements of a natural knowledge of God mixed with depravation caused by original sin and human elements, but also supernatural elements, of grace. It can therefore be acknowledged to be a legitimate religion even though in different gradations...Non-Christian religion may be said "a priori" to contain supernatural elements of grace...As Christians, we must profess the dogma that God wills the salvation of all men even in post paradisal period of original sin. On the one hand this salvation is specifically Christian for there is no salvation apart from Christ...God truly wants all men to be saved...Man is exposed to the influence of divine grace, which offers him communion with God, whether he accepts it or not...True we cannot hope that religious pluralism will disappear in the foreseeable future; nevertheless, Christians themselves may well regard the non-Christian world as an anonymous Christendom.[7]

Rahner, having declared the non-Christian world to be an "anonymous Christendom,"[8] then, goes on to repudiate the notorious Catholic doctrine of *extra ecclesiam nulla salus* as follows:

> It follows, therefore, that today the Church will not so much regard herself as the exclusive community of candidates for salvation, but rather as the avant-garde, expressing historically and socially the hidden reality which, Christians hope, exists also outside her visible structure. The Church is not the community of those who possess God's grace as opposed to those who lack it, but the community of those who can confess explicitly what they and the others hope to be.[9]

1. Anonymous Christianity and its Theological and Societal Implications for the World

Undoubtedly, the affirmation of this concept of "anonymous Christianity" is an essential component for any useful or practical and inclusive post-modern Christian theology. The affirmation of African Traditional Religion as part of this "anonymous Christianity" in Africa is very meaningful.

However, this positive affirmation of African Religion as a redemptive channel of God's grace and salvation has serious implications for both the people and the Church in Africa. It is also important for the Western world which has traditionally negatively viewed and despised Africa as a benighted pagan continent both lost to God and civilization, apart from the civilizing influence of Western Christian missionaries and colonial agents.

Tragically, the world has become seriously divided chiefly on the basis of religion, race, ethnicity, socio-economic and political ideologies. It is also further divided along other lines and societal systems which tend to be deeply grounded in this chaotic and competitive religious milieu, and sometimes expend a great deal of energy and resources fighting each other in the name of God and misguided ethnocentric religious missionary or erroneous mutually exclusive soteriological doctrines, and trying to convert one another both by word and sword!

Africa has become a fertile ground for all this Western religious missionary activity and conflict due to bigoted and intolerant missionaries who form the main bulk of the missionary personnel. Unfortunately, the local converts internalize this negative and warlike, mutually intolerant form of missionary Christianity as the truth and ignorantly and tragically recreate to some degree a kind of "mini-African" Northern Ireland or Lebanon.

As a tragic consequence, Africa has become the battle ground not just for Western economic and political ideological conflicts and wars, but also for religious crusades and wars. Uganda, Sudan and Nigeria are typical African examples of these religious Western and locally inspired ethnic, and mutually destructive religious intolerance, violent conflicts and wars. Therefore, the affirmation of "anonymous Christianity," implies the correction and the negation of this myopic religious exclusivism and bigotry that both divides humankind and negates humanity itself. If we are to avoid the tragic morally deficient and bigoted exclusivist religious and ethnocentric xenophobic cultural unhealthy backgrounds which have created many serious problems and evils in the world.

These religiously or ideologically related evils and problems include the crusades, the inquisition, jihads, religious divisions, communism, fascism, apartheid and the like, we have to develop a more inclusive broader or universal concept of God's unmerited free cosmic creative and redemptive Grace, the brotherhood and sisterhood of all humanity, the universality of sin, and God's universal unmerited free salvation, for all human beings who respond to God's universal invitation for salvation, full humanization and fulfillment.

Therefore, we have to affirm that any human being, anywhere and everywhere, who responds to God's invitation to a fuller life and positive self-actualization in love and repentance, or those men and women of good-will who desire and seek to live a just life both in peace and harmony with their neighbors and other human beings and the rest of God's creation, that they too, have effectively found God's efficacious redemptive grace and are thereby in fellowship with the Creator God and have been effectively redeemed by God.

2. Anonymous Christianity as a Critique of Narrow-Minded Exclusive Ecclesiology:
Uganda as an African Example

The human being as created in God's image or *imago Dei*, is God's specially appointed representative in the cosmos, and as the high priest, or sarcedotal mediator and advocate for creation before the Almighty God, the Cosmic Creator and Redeemer. This being the case, the human being is therefore, by quintessential constitutive special nature, a religious creature.

In this inclusive Christian theological system, each human being has been viewed appropriately, as essentially religious and as the "hearer," "bearer," "embodiment" and voluntary obedient respondent and proclaimer of God's Word both by "word and deed." Along with Karl Rahner, we also positively affirm that God's universal salvific will and efficacious grace are freely bestowed on each human being anywhere and everywhere in the world. This is God's free gift to humanity, and it cannot be rejected by any human being, since it is bestowed on each human being by God at the moment of creation. This divine gift is supernaturally conferred on humanity in the permanent form of an "*a priori*" quintessential supernature which is housed in the evolutionary finite humanity, as God's elect, unique finite being and temporal vehicle for God's own self-expression and supernatural activities in the temporal world.

The divine Incarnation of God's creative and redemptive Logos or the Christ into humanity, the cosmic processes and history, is the universal testimony that humanity is special and divine in nature, despite its temporality. The Apostolic Christian creedal confession, and positive affirmation that God's eternal Logos has in Jesus of Nazareth become a complete finite human being, just like us in all respects, except sin, is the explicit human affirmation and declaration that humanity had finally evolved and returned into the Godhead from which it had started at the moment of creation.

Accordingly, the eternal divine Logos as the Cosmic Christ, is the effective universal agent of God's activities of creation, salvation and redemption of his creation. Therefore, the Incarnation as a human being is the maximum positive human affirmation the universal, irrevocable, permanent reconciliation, communion and union of God and humanity. This is to affirm that all human beings everywhere, indiscriminately and without exceptions, have by God's unmerited grace and unconditional love, all become irrevocably, symbolically and mystically united with God.

Correlatively, and mystically, therefore, all human beings everywhere, and anywhere in the cosmos, just like Mary the Mother of Jesus, have become the embodiments or the "body of Christ" and the bearers of God in the world. This is the kind of inclusive Christian perspective that has inspired, directed and informed most of this book.

Therefore, just like our minds and actions testify of who and what we are, likewise, our religious views, doctrines and moral values ultimately shape and mold us into the kind of people we become. Obviously, religion and its myths shape our world-views, our modes of existence, our ideals, goals, values, hopes and utopias, in the same way, also shape the nature of our dislikes, fears, egotism, guilt, associations and dissociations.

In some extreme cases, this leads to the tragic incidents of religious fanaticism, bigotry and intolerance for religious diversity and theological or religious pluralism. For instance, due to religious bigotry and intolerance, and therefore, in the quest for religious and cultural monolith structures, destructive religious wars were fought in Uganda between 1885 and 1889.

Nevertheless, many Ugandans appear not to have learned from the bitter history. Obviously, many young Ugandan Church and political leaders have not effectively learned from the lessons of Uganda's wars and historical nasty experience. This appears to be the case since the ancient religious wars and feuds have continued to be fought today in the guise of the modern party politics. Accordingly, the previously defeated Roman Catholics are also predominantly the members of the disenfranchised Democratic Party

(DP), which is the majority party, and once again, there is a ruling minority Anglican party whose are membership comes from the former Peoples Congress Party (UPC).

Unfortunately, religious fanatics and bigots do not take seriously the religions and cultures of members of other religions which are different from their own. Religious bigots are universally intolerant of other people who members of other religions or have different religious views, theological philosophies and religious practices which differ from their own. Unfortunately, most of these prejudiced and intolerant people also very often naively, tragically exclusively equate their own religion as the only true or right one for all people to join if they wish to be saved by God.

These kinds of religious fundamentalists, fanatics and religious ethnocentric bigots, also generally consider their own religious views as universally definitively true, orthodox and binding on everybody. Consequently, their own religion is zealously and confidently proclaimed to the rest of the world as the only divinely approved path and channel of supernatural grace and salvation. Without becoming converted to this religion or Church, its fundamentalist members infallibly affirm in the name of an infallible God, Christ, scriptures, Church or Pope or other religious leader, that there is no other way to God in heaven and the authentic, since the Church or religion constitutes God's ordained medium of redemptive grace and ultimate or definitive universal divine salvific revelation of God in the world.

This is the tragic claim of the Catholic dogma of *extra ecclesiam nulla salus*, prior to Vatican II. In pre-Vatican II Catholic theology, this kind of attitude was articulated in the guise of what was then acceptable as the doctrine of *extra ecclesiam nulla salus* before it was repudiated by the Vatican II. This theological repudiation of a popular doctrine, especially among the laity and less theologically sophisticated clergy, was reluctantly carried out by the Vatic Council at the prompting and theological direction of the more open-minded Catholic theologians and ecclesiologists like Karl Rahner and Hans Kung, who were among the major scholarly consultants and theological advisors of bishops at the Vatican II.

Unfortunately, the type of Catholic doctrine, theological teaching and Catholicism which is found in much of Africa today, and particularly, among many Catholic fundamentalists of Uganda, is still largely pre-Vatican II. It is very exclusive of other Christian traditions, conservative and reactionary to both modernism and postmodernism in religion. Ugandan Catholicism is so unorthodox and conservative, that in the rural parishes, converts from Anglicanism are still rebaptized as if they were converts from Islam or the African Traditional Religion.

Obviously, many naive Catholics and poorly educated parish priests in Uganda, generally, do not regard Anglicans as authentic Christians. In many cases, Anglicans and their clergy are negatively viewed within the anachronistic theological context of nineteenth century Catholic theology and Papal conflicts with the Church of England in his quest to force the Anglicans to return to unity with the Catholic Church. In order to scare and force the Anglicans to return to the Roman Church, Pope Leo XIII (in *Apostolicae Curae*, 1896) who called them heretics and declared Anglican ordinations invalid, void and without efficacy for their recipients. This papal action caused more Anglican resentment and hostility against Rome than was anticipated by Pope Leo XIII and his religious and political advisors.

Therefore, the Anglican sacraments, were also correlatively negatively viewed as invalid and void by many Catholics. Pope Leo XIII rejected Anglican orders and sacraments due to religious politics, and what he considered improper liturgical language and inadequacy of the Anglican sacramental formula for ordinations.

Pope Leo XIII declared that Anglican ordination formula was liturgically defective. He observed that it was deficient in the essential intention for ordination of Anglicans priests to a valid sacrificial priesthood. As a result, he argued that the Anglican priests would not be able to confect the mass or to cause a mystical transubstantiation to occur, thus transforming the ordinary elements of bread and wine into efficacious eucharistic elements of the sacrificial atonement of the true body and blood of Christ.

The Pope affirmed that this was the case since the Anglican priest was not ordained as a "sacerdotal priest" to "confect the mass" into a real sacrifice. Pope Leo XIII only wanted to scare the Anglicans to rejoin the Catholic Church. Therefore, the doctrine of sacraments and the subsequent invalidation of the Anglican holy Orders and sacraments was designed to scare them into returning to the Mother Church. Unfortunately, this political-theology misfired, and has now caused unnecessary theological complexity between the Vatican and Lambeth than Pope Leo XIII had anticipated.

Tragically, within this context and spirit of theological rivalry, political religious intrigue, hostility and competition between the Roman Catholics and Anglicans for African converts, the Catholic converts were often taught to by their priests and spiritual directors to disregard and despise the Anglicans and other protestants as being less than true Christians. Since, sacramental theology and the question of sacraments did not make sense to lay people. The Catholic teaching focused on Christianity itself being either true or false.

The theological problem between Anglicanism and Catholicism were so simplified that it was taught that if you were a Catholic you were a true Christian believer, and if you were an Anglican you were an infidel and a follower of Luther the "archheretic," and therefore, an enemy of Christ, the Pope in Rome and to be repudiated as anathema to both God and Christianity. Meanwhile, the protestants were teaching that the Catholics were not true Christians, and that they idolatrously worshipped images, the Pope and saints, instead of worshipping God and Jesus-Christ.

Meanwhile, Muslims were accusing Catholics and Protests of idolatry, since both denominations preached and worshipped Jesus-Christ as God. For Muslims, Jesus was a mere prophet and a human being who could never be worshipped as God. This Christian controversial doctrine of Christology and the Trinity constituted heresy, blasphemy and a crime against the holy God, to be seriously punished by his faithful followers. Christians themselves were united in their teaching that Islam and the African Religion were false religions which were abominable to God.

As a result, in many parts of Africa, particularly, Uganda and Nigeria, a Northern Ireland type of hostility and religious intolerance was tragically irreversibly introduced by these Western religious fanatics and war-faring missionaries. Consequently, the European Catholic missionaries, especially those from Northern Ireland and Italy, encouraged their African converts to view Protestants as inferior heretic sectarians who were heading for eternal damnation and hellfire! Unfortunately, the Ugandan Anglicans were also negatively taught to regard Catholics as heretic "papists" who worship "images" of the saints, Mary the blessed Mother of Jesus, and the Pope.[10]

This kind of background has led to religious hostility, rivalry and conflicts. And in the unforgettable past has led to real military confrontations between the Anglicans and the Catholics and between these two groups and the Muslims.[11] And it is no secret that the D.P. (Democratic Party) and U.P.C. (Uganda People's Congress) are disguised forms of an ancient religious-political rivalry, which is now a conflict between Catholicism and Anglicanism in an acceptable modern conventional warfare of modern times, and which is mitigated only by tribalism, especially in Buganda.[12]

Therefore, Rahner's inclusive, positive theology of the Church and the availability of supernatural salvation outside the conventional Church, made such exclusive religious bigotry and mutual anathematization appear to be pathological anachronism. But as we know, this kind of anachronistic and misguided religious understanding is possesses great potentiality for religious division, uncharitable conflicts, violence, and some kind of inquisition, especially among religious fundamentalists such as the rigorous Balokole of Uganda and Shiite or other fundamentalist Muslims.

In a sense, Rahner's concept of the "anonymous Christianity" is serious critique of the Church and its pride, mutually denigrative sectarian theology and exclusive ecclesiology, as well as its failure for recognition and an acknowledgment of the universality of God as Agape and to appreciate his gratuitous activities in cosmic creation, and redemption.

However, God is Agape and *Sola Gratia*. His free redemptive grace are visibly expressed in God's own universal self-communication in gratuitous grace for the salvation of every human being who will respond to this supernatural invitation to a fuller life of self-actualization and complete humanization by God. This is what is fully symbolized and articulated in Christ's incarnation and the Hypostatic Union as the divinization of the human being, since authentic humanity is possible only through the supernatural elevation of the human being by the divine salvific grace.

Since the historical Church cannot by itself represent all the cosmic divine salvific activity, therefore, it cannot be the sole container and dispenser of God's salvation nor can it hold any valid claim of being the exclusive community, the sole divine medium, embodiment and dispenser of this supernatural salvation, which by God's gratuitous grace transcends time, human culture, technology, language, sins, understanding and exclusiveness.

As a result, no individual religious group can ever validly claim to possess salvation in its exclusive totality to the exclusion of non-members, who must join this one Church group, denomination or religion in order to gain God's favor and access to supernatural salvation, which is somehow now thought to be encapsulated in this specific community, which usually has become analogous to "Noah's Ark,"[13]. The affirmation was that outside of Noah's Ark nobody survived and likewise, nobody can ever obtain any supernatural salvation outside the Church, since it is today's "Divine Ark" of salvation which is delicately suspended in a sinful and perishing world.

Unfortunately, this has been the kind of destructive anti-earth and anti-world attitude as the domain of the devil, instead of God's kingdom and beloved world (cf. John 1-3). This has been the explicit enthusiastic teaching of some groups of Christians in Uganda, mainly the Balokole, who are mostly low-Church Anglican in origin and membership. For instance, the

Balokole have made it known that non-Balokole people will never go to heaven and that they are all candidates for hellfire! This has of course alienated the non-Balokole Anglicans in the same Church and the Catholics, who are despised and disliked by the Balokole because, although they claim to be Christians, to the horror of the Balokole, they drink beer openly, dance and smoke! They do the very things which the Balokole have repudiated as deadly sins which only lead to hell and destruction, instead of heaven and happiness!

However, it can be argued that the Balokole have misunderstood the Gospel of Christ to mean self-denial for everybody, which is an error and uncharitably mean; they insist that all should confess their sins publicly and should become ascetic like them in order to gain their fellowship and, most important of all, in order to gain eternal life. What is often overlooked, however, by the Balokole, like most of us human beings, is the Biblical warning not to judge anybody, as judgment is the sole prerogative of God, the holy impartial, omniscient Creator and gracious, redemptive God:

> Therefore, you have no excuse, o man, whoever you are, when you judge another; for, in passing judgement upon him you condemn yourself, because you, the judge, are doing the very same things. We know that the judgement of God...will be revealed. For he will render to every man according to his works: to those who by patience in well-doing seek for glory and honor and immortality, he will give eternal life; but for those who are factious and do not obey the truth...there will be wrath and fury. There will be tribulation and distress for every human being who does evil, the Jew first and also the Greek [everyone else], but glory and honor and peace for everyone who does good...For God shows no partiality.[14]

If God is the Creator, loving Savior and impartial, omniscient, merciful Judge of human beings, then anyone who usurps this divine prerogative is attempting some kind of *coup de Dieu*. We can never be completely sure that the individual is totally lost to God, even when society may condemn that very individual to death as a criminal, and therefore we cannot know who is "saved" and who is lost. The implication is that we should treat all human beings as potential candidates and heirs of supernatural salvation.

The values of God and the values of society might sometimes be opposed to each other and might be in conflict, and therefore in this case what would be regarded as a sin and a criminal offense by human beings might prove the reverse with God. For instance, Jesus was executed on the cross as a criminal by self-righteous and intolerant theologically monolithic human beings.

However, the scriptures consistently claim that he was innocent and that his trial and consequent execution were a travesty of justice.[15] The Scriptures also point out that one of the two criminals that were crucified along with Jesus was granted eternal life by Jesus, regardless of the fact that he was being put to death as punishment for the sin and crime of theft![16]

We also know that during his earthly ministry, Jesus was in constant opposition and conflict with the religious priests, scribes, and the rigorous, self-righteous and legalistic Pharisees who were pious adherents of the law, observing it diligently to its minor details. Instead, Jesus commended sinners, the tax-collectors, harlots, and outcasts, because they were more open-minded and receptive to his teaching of the good news of salvation.

Unlike the self-righteous Pharisees, priests and religious leaders, these sinners were receptive of God's Word ready to hear God's redemptive proclaimed and Incarnate Word, to repent and experience God's mystical and supernatural touch of his healing power that transforms men and women into new beings and saints of God's by faith, hope, obedience and practice of agape. Accordingly, Jesus would affirm that the first in this life would be last and the last first in God's kingdom.

For such a receptiveness, spiritual hunger, and openness to God's grace and transformation is the right kind of faith which is required by God as basis for his wonders of new creation and transformation of the sinner to newness, wholeness and restoration to God or salvation through Jesus as the Incarnate Christ. Like the anonymous woman in the crowd who touched Jesus in faith and hopeful anticipation of wholeness and salvific healing and who was made whole, similarly, every man and woman everywhere, and at any time, may also touch the same Cosmic Christ by faith, and be healed.

Through faith in God and Christ, and by praxis of love in hopeful anticipation for salvific divine mysteries, God can mystically affect healing of body, mind, social relationships, the community and the world. As such, the mission and symbol of Jesus-Christ is that of agape, forgiveness, simplicity and mutual human total restoration to newness and wholeness in the name of God, as the loving and caring heavenly parent (*Abba*).[17]

Therefore, the affirmation of "anonymous Christianity" brings us back to the authentic teaching of Christ and the Apostles as we find it in the New Testament. Jesus and the Apostles never excluded other people outside their original small community from divine salvation. Indeed, the Jews and the Gentiles (pagans included) were all thought to be equal candidates for this supernatural salvation. For instance, St. Luke dramatizes this fact by recording the "Song of Simon," known in the Anglican and Catholic liturgy as the "*Nunc Dimittis*:"

> Lord, now lettest thou thy servant depart in peace, according to thy word; For mine eyes have seen thy salvation, Which thou hast prepared before the face of all people, To be a light to lighten the Gentiles, and to be the glory of thy people Israel.[18]

Or the "Song of the Lamb" (*Dignus es*):

> Worthy art thou For thou wast slain and by thy blood didst ransom men for God. From every tribe and tongue and people and nation and hast made them a kingdom. And priests to our God and they shall reign on earth.[19]

And the "Song of the Redeemed" (*Magna et Mirabilia*):

> O ruler of the universe, Lord God, great deeds are they that you have done, surpassing human understanding. Your ways are ways of righteousness and truth, O King of all the ages. Who can fail to do you homage, Lord, and sing the praises of your Name? for you only are the holy One. All nations will draw near and fall down before you because your just and holy works have been revealed.[20]

These liturgical texts are sung or said for "daily office" in the in main-line churches, such as the Catholic and Anglican Churches. But how seriously are they taken or understood? It is probably amazing, then, that one can read these Biblical texts, sing them, meditate prayerfully upon them as it is supposed by the liturgy, and yet still remain blind to the fact that God's salvific activity is by nature and scope universal, proffered to all human beings everywhere in the world and through all the ages. This cosmic dimension of God's love compels us then, as his redeemed people, to think, to love and to act like our God in a cosmic fashion.

This probably means that we have to be more open minded, discerning, patient and tolerant in order to see and appreciate this divine cosmic dimension of God's salvific activity, as we have to look at the Traditional African Religion's believer, the Muslim, the Jew, the Hindu and Buddhist transcendentalist in order to see it, for that is where it is happening. It might not be the kind of spirituality with which we are familiar and expect to find. Nevertheless, there is something of God's work going on there, even when the forces of evil are also seen to be actively at work in the same locus.

Moreover, our own spiritual life can be further deepened by learning from other peoples and other religions: new religious truths, new ways of thinking, worship, meditation, or a fresh way of viewing the world and the supernatural. Similarly, these other religions and people, too, can learn from us. And therefore, be able to supplement their own deficiency to a certain extent (e.g. concerning unconditional love for the neighbor, concern for human value and human rights, providing and taking care of those in need, such as the poor and the victims of disasters).

Hopefully, through this delicate interfaith, and interreligious dialogue, or the ecumenical process of mutual religious, socio-economic and political exchange, and explicit missionary endeavors, the "anonymous Christendom," can gradually, but significantly move toward the more explicit Apostolic Christianity. This is only desirable in its general outlook and socio-political basic emotional religious values, and self-understanding.

This is positive inasmuch as the Apostolic Christianity is in itself faithful to the Christ's definitive and non-negotiable commandment of the unconditional love for the neighbor. Agape or its non-self-cognitive or implicit praxis as in the case of altruism, is the universal definitive moral and theological grounding for all the good Christian theology, sound humanistic values and sound moral actions in the community and the world, both in politics and the economy (cf. Matt. 25:31-46, Jam. 2:1-26).

3. The Theological Problem of the Exclusive Sacrament of Christian Baptism

The exclusive Sacrament of Christian Baptism, like the Mosaic prerequisite for circumcision in orthodox Judaism, has become a stumbling block for theologians who wish to include non-baptized, good and loving people among the saints of God, the Church, salvation and the kingdom of God. God requires obedience and works of Agape. God never requires baptism as a prerequisite for salvation or godliness. For the gracious and loving Creator-Redeemer God, baptism is merely an optional pius ritual. It does not bind God to offer or deny salvation to anyone. Ultimately, God's salvation is free for all who obey his call and in faith and Agape come into his fellowship of love which includes all obedient people everywhere.

Nevertheless, for many Christian thinkers and laity, baptism is considered important and a necessary rite for salvation. It is understood in the same way as circumcision was considered essential for salvation by some

Jews at the time of Paul's ministry (cf. Acts 15). This becomes the case when baptism or circumcision are equated with gates of heaven.

However, that is a false analogy and misleading symbolism since even in Judaism women were never circumcised, and yet they were considered to be members of the Covenant and heirs of eternal life if they obeyed God's commandments. Likewise, the exclusive affirmation of the Christian sacrament of baptism and the Church as the Ark of Noah which is only universally accessed through the gate of Christian confession and baptism is another false and misleading metaphor, analogy and paradigm or model for God's inclusive Agapic work of salvation in the world.

This is the case since salvation is universal and coextensive with any meaningful, harmonious and loving human life and healthy societal relationships and good life enhancing human actions. God's concrete redemptive actions of salvation take place through people as God's vehicles of grace, redemption and salvation. This takes place within the community of created beings, nature, life and the cosmos as God's work and self-manifestation in the eternal abyss of nothingness, darkness and chaos.

In the process of affirming the universal redemptive existence, and reality of God's supernatural free grace in the Logos, we also correlatively affirm the traditional Christian doctrine of God's inclusive universal divine salvific will. We also accept the traditional Christian that in broad terms God's will is efficacious and irresistible by sin and evil, including evil men and women, regardless of whether they are ignorant lay people or malicious clergy. This is also true for God's work including those of free cosmic creation and salvation. As such, although the traditional theologians of the Apostolic Church have often narrowly viewed historical Church and her sacraments as being necessary for salvation, especially baptism, God's universal salvific will for all human beings, within or outside the Church can be sinfully nullified by any human being.

Therefore, any human religious sinful ethnocentric and exclusive Christian theological or religious bigoted clergy and theologians cannot nullify God's inclusive Agape, and unmerited free cosmic grace which are operative in both unmerited divine cosmic creation and universal redemption of this cosmos. Ultimately, God always finds a way to perform his works of unconditional love in the world despite the creaturely finitude, ignorance, sin and limitations of his human chosen agents and agencies, including the Apostolic Church, and her popes, bishops, clergy, and theologians.

Whether they are formulated by an infallible pope or a great theologian like Rahner, Tillich, Barth, or by a religious reformer like Luther, Calvin or Wesley or prophet like Moses, Buddha, Jesus and Muhammad, or formulated by a great philosopher, such as Socrates, Plato, Aristotle, Hegel and Whitehead, ultimately, no human doctrines are ever binding on God. As such, no human fraudulent teaching or exclusive doctrines can truly limit God's free grace and cosmic activities of creation and gratuitous redemption.

Therefore, the task of any good Christian theologian and any sound doctrine should try to decipher God's inclusive will in cosmic free creation, preservation, redemption and fulfillment of all his creatures, without any prior conditions. As such, faith, agape and worship, are merely human appropriate responses to what God has already done in the world for them. The rituals and sacraments of the Church are also mere celebrations of God's work which is already effected. This includes the sacraments of circumcision in Judaism and baptism in Christianity. These rituals celebrate the free redemptive works of God in the covenants.

God's supernatural salvation for all people that he has created exists prior to the establishment religion, the Church, and the administration of sacraments and other religious rituals, which human beings mistakenly equate with God's effective offer redemptive grace, media of God's redemptive action in the world and salvation.

Contrary to much of the traditional Catholic mechanical and mystical sacramental theology of "*ex opere operantis*" these religious rituals and Church sacraments are in themselves mere public testimonials of faith and intentions to keep God's holy commandments, which constitute the covenants. As such, keeping the commandments is the path to God, a good life and salvation. The sacraments are in this respect mere public confessions of faith and collective celebrations of redemptive activities in the world. As such, no one can ever transformed into a more godly or better person by the mere reception of these sacraments.

Conversely, true obedience to God's moral law and praxis of God's definitive commandment of agape, ultimately, transforms the sinner into a saint and establishes harmony and peace in the world. Within the traditional Christian theological context, the concept of a redemptive informal "anonymous Christianity" which exists outside or beyond the traditional confines of the historical Church, and confer salvation without the benefit of the Church's central atonement rituals, particularly, the administration of the sacrament of baptism in order to wash away the primordial Adamic or the original sin, and its guilt, can become a major theological problem.

However, God's cosmic Word or the primordial cosmic creative and redemptive Word as the pre-Incarnate Christ, was same eternal cosmic

Logos-Christ who was carrying out God's cosmic activities in the world without being limited or confined to the Apostolic Church or monopolized by any religion. God's activities of creation and redemption are free and cosmic in nature. As such, God's free universal blessings of creation, life, agape, grace, redemption, peace, and salvation are available everywhere and anywhere in the world with or without the aid of the Church.

These universal free divine activities transcend the Church and any religious tradition. After all, the transcendent holy Creator-Redeemer-God is infinite and too great to be fitted into a single Church or religious tradition. Accordingly, Jesus warned his hearers that the common sinners such as prostitutes, tax collectors and other outcasts would enter God's kingdom first. However, as Origen the great African theologian in University of Alexandria realized in the early Church, the theology of Church and the sacraments and, particularly, baptism, can present a political, social and theological great hurdles in the acceptance of the doctrine of salvation outside the Church.

Christian baptism is analogous to the sacrament of circumcision in Judaism. Circumcision became a major theological hurdle for the Apostles and theologians of early Church (cf. Acts 10-15). As such, the Church today can learn from this early Church's pain and inclusive theological venture as it opened the Church to the Gentiles and eliminated the prerequisite of the Mosaic law and circumcision as being necessary for entrance into the church and for salvation. Consequently, it can also become a serious hindrance, preventing the Church from seeing God's salvific activity that is taking place world-wide even among the unbaptized.

As we know, even in explicit Christianity it is recognized that conversion and the outpouring of the Holy Spirit and divine salvific grace can precede baptism, as St. Peter to his shock discovered at the house of Cornelius, a Gentile non-Christian whom he had regarded as an outsider to God's salvific community until God visibly contradicted him by sending the Holy Spirit upon Cornelius and the whole of his household, indiscriminately.[21] This indicates how God's salvific activity can work apart from and independent of the Church and the sacraments such as baptism. Christians are like the ancient Jews, who were very reluctant to admit that God can and does act redemptively and graciously outside the covenant, which was marked by circumcision regarding Judaism and now by baptism in regard to Christianity.[22]

Therefore, St. Paul's remarks on the irrelevancy of the external Jewish rite of circumcision, in contrast to unconditional love and good deeds as the essence of true religion, can also apply to baptism in our general argument and context of "anonymous Christianity." For instance, if Paul was writing his Letter to the Romans today, Chapters 2:12-3:2 would read as follows:

> All who have sinned without the Gospel will also perish without the Gospel and all who have sinned under the Gospel will also be judged under the Gospel. For it is not the hearers of the Gospel that are righteous before God, but the doers of what the Gospel teaches are the ones who will be justified. When non-Christians who have not yet heard the Gospel do by nature what the Gospel requires, they are a Gospel unto themselves, even though they do not have the written Gospel of Christ Jesus. They show that what the Gospel requires is written on their hearts, while their conscience also bears witness and their conflicting thoughts accuse or excuse them on that day when, according to my gospel, God judges the secrets of men by Christ Jesus.

Paul would probably continue his theological letter to the well boastful Christians in Rome as follows:

> But if you call yourself a Christian and rely upon the Gospel and boast of your relation to God and know his will and approve what is excellent, because you are instructed in the Gospel, and if you are sure that you are a guide to the blind, a light to those in darkness...you then who teach others, will you not teach yourselves?...You who boast of the Gospel, do you dishonour God by not living according to the Gospel? For it is written, "The name of God is blasphemed among the non-Christians because of you."
>
> Baptism is indeed of value if you obey the Gospel; but if you disobey the Gospel your baptism becomes unbaptism. So, if a man who is unbaptized keeps the precepts of the Gospel will not his unbaptism be regarded as baptism? Then those who are physically unbaptized but keep the Gospel will condemn you who have the written Gospel and baptism but fail to live by it. For he is not a Christian who is one outwardly, nor is true baptism something external and physical. He is a Christian who is one inwardly, and real baptism is a matter of the heart, spiritual and not literal. His praise is not from men but God (cf. Rom. 2:12-3:12).

Then what advantage has the Christian? Or what value is baptism? Much in every way. To begin with, The Christians are entrusted with the explicitly proclaimed Word of God and the written Gospel of Christ.[23]

If baptism by itself does not confer eternal life (*ex opere operant*) and neither does its absence exclude anybody from God's unconditional love and gratuitous universal efficacious salvific grace, then why should the Church insist on it? The answer to this difficult question may be found in sociology as well as theology. Sociologically the Church as a voluntary social community needs a "rite of passage" for making the initiation and entry of new members into its own community and membership.

The best illustration of the social element is perhaps infant baptism, which is usually a time of social gathering and party-making at the child's home.[24] The christening party following the infant's baptism has little religious significance, if it has any. It is on the whole just another social function like a wedding, Thanksgiving, Christmas or Independence Day.

Theologically, baptism is more difficult to discuss, as it is a very controversial subject within Christianity itself. For instance, some Christians such as the Baptists contend that infant baptism is invalid and spiritually meaningless since the candidates for baptism should be old enough or mentally alert in order to make a personal decision to accept and confess Jesus-Christ as Lord and personal Savior.

However, other major Christian traditions, such as the Catholic, Anglican, Eastern Orthodox churches' doctrines, infant baptism is strongly commended as the beneficial ritual entry into the Church as God's redeemed community. It is also required as a ritual and mystical means for washing away, and negating the original or Adamic sin and both its correlative existential evil consequences and divine penalties. In this case, the sacrament of baptism is treated as if it was of an automatic intrinsic value in itself, thus mechanically functioning as *ex opere operant* in the life of the baptized child until the child grows up to affirm his or her own faith in the confirmation ceremony.

Therefore, the adoption of a more flexible view of baptism, as the concept of "anonymous Christianity" demands as its necessary prerequisite the repudiation not only of the old-fashioned and anachronistic doctrine of *extra ecclesiam nulla salus*, but also of the underlying Augustinian view of the universality of the original sin that can only be cleansed by Christian ritual baptism.[25]

Nevertheless, the Augustinian predestination, if looked at from a cosmic point of view, need not be opposed to the view of "anonymous Christianity." It would rather enhance it in that in every age or nation God would have to find a way of saving those elected to supernatural salvation, including the era before the Incarnation and the arrival of the Gospel in each given area or individual people.[26]

Theologically, baptism is the initiation of a person into the mystery of Christ's life, passion, death and resurrection, and into communion of all those people that acknowledge Jesus as Christ the Lord and Savior.[27] This means that baptism, if clearly understood, is not a denominational entry rite or affair; rather it is a symbolic ritual entry into mystical union with Christ and the saints past, present and future, and a symbol that one belongs to a particular institutional church as temporal local expression of this universal belonging and union with the universal (Catholic) Church, which is the aggregate sum of all the presently divided traditional and denominational churches.

Ultimately, it was within this symbolic sacramental context that Thomas Aquinas solved this problem of sacramental physicalism and literalism. His solution was that sacraments are symbolic and they effect mysteries that symbolize through faith and not by magically partaking in the physical elements, as if they were pills of medicine or magic potions.

Rahner went on to argue that since the sacraments were mystical in their function, that a person with either implicit or explicit faith could gain the efficacy of the sacraments of baptism and the eucharist by an implicit or explicit desire for them. As such, the anonymous Christians can on this basis truly qualify to become the true beneficiaries of the Apostolic Church and her redemptive sacraments. Accordingly, for Rahner, anonymous Christians can gain God's salvation, through the Incarnate historical Christ and his Church, without ever stepping into the Church building, for the physical administration of baptism and the eucharist (cf. John 1:1-18; Matt. 7:13-27; 25:31-46).

4. Anonymous Christianity as Constructive Theological Background and Context for Ecumenism

Most African Christians, especially those of Ugandan, must learn to accept divine truth that they are all Christians and God's redeemed people, irrespective of whether they are Balokole, Catholics or Protestants. If they cannot accept each other as Christians who share one common baptism in the triune God, then, how can they accept the authentic humanity of non-Christians as expressive of an "anonymous Christianity" or God's salvation?

In addition, if some Christians like those in Uganda, insist on the absurd idea that Anglicanism and Catholicism are two religions rather than two branches or denominations of the same Religion or Faith, and if they could affirm the existence of "anonymous Christianity," then they could find it easy to accept each other at least on the level of "anonymous Christianity!" This approach would circumvent the problems of doctrine, orthodoxy and heresy that have been major stumbling blocks in the current ecumenical discussions for unity and joint religious ventures in education, community service and development projects.

Most of this bigotry and denominational pride and exclusiveness could be constructively dealt with if "anonymous Christianity" got positively affirmed. Life would change in many cases, if we taught the ordinary Christians to be inclusive of the people of other religions as God's children and beneficiaries of God's kingdom with us now and in the life to come. As such, one has to both effectively and constructively teach about the moral or religious common ground and need religious inclusion of non-Christians in a way that would not cause them to lose their own faith.

One has to teach this inclusive doctrine in constructive ways that would enable people to see God and one another in new agapic ways. This includes the cosmic free redemptive grace and inclusiveness of God's incomprehensible, infinite Mystery and diverse cosmic activity causes pluralism in religious systems, knowledge, experiences, hopes, beliefs and practices. As a societal and theological redemptive consequence of this teaching, people would be able to be more sensitive to and tolerant of the religious views and practices of other people, even when they are apparently quite different or seem to be opposed to our own cherished religious or philosophical views, cultural values and moral principles! This requires the true praxis of agape.

There is always a possibility that one's own religious beliefs and practices could be erroneous or distorted, too, so that the condemnation of the beliefs and practices of others could also be a condemnation of one's very own. There is no basis or guarantee on this crucial point that the religion, religious beliefs, hopes, objectives and practices of the other people will always be wrong and that our own will always be right.

Furthermore, we can always mutually benefit through mutual acceptance of each other's traditions and exchange of ideas. We can grow to understand better, and work or live with one another more peacefully by learning from each other, rather than engaging in negative and uncharitable mutual destructive behaviors such as resenting, hating and fighting with each other. Moreover, God does not seem to be bothered by diversity, since he has created it in its plentiful richness and colorful splendor. Accordingly, difference, diversity or pluralism are our God-given gifts to be celebrated rather than condemned and rejected in favor of a global monolithic life, religious and cultural conformity. This would be a sin against the Cosmic Creator God and an impossible task for human beings to achieve, since it defies God and his natural laws of biodiversity and evolution.

Therefore, there is no good theological reason why we should seek religious conformity rather than well-informed diversity in the unity of understanding and appreciation. Conformity can be understood to be mainly required by those people and groups who are insecure and afraid of variety or change, whereas the diversity of religious views and practices can only be accepted by those people and churches that are secure in their faith that is fully grounded in the triune Creator and Redemptive God that is the *mysterium tremendum* behind the beauty, variety, diversity and individuating uniqueness in the world.

Surely, such a God that is behind the rich variety and diversity in this world would not like to be understood, glorified and worshipped in the unison of religious conformity! Therefore, it would seem that religious fundamentalist rigorous conformity is preferably understood as a manifestation of human insecurity and lack of sufficient faith in God as Agape or the God of infinite unconditional love, gratuitous salvific grace, the very same cosmic Creator and Redemptive God that desires us to become the unique selves that he has created us to be.

This is as true of individuals as it is also true for nations and races or ethnic groups of people in their uniqueness and diversity, and yet together constitute a global unity of one all-embracing common humanity and one human race. Analogously, human religions, religious views, beliefs and cultic expressive practices, are likewise ideally diverse within the unity of one common objective. This primary unitive objective in life is to live a most meaningful and fulfilling life, as long as possible.

This objective for ultimate self-fulfillment and eternal happiness in life remains an open gaping infinite reality which is never filled by any finite material goods or personal successes and achievements. This underlying human openness and incompleteness drives human beings into the eternal journey and quest for the infinite or God as the true Object of fulfillment and happiness. Buddha, Moses, David, Jesus, Paul and Gandhi are examples of this journey unto God.

In general and universally, most human beings are inwardly individually and collectively driven to mystery, contemplation, prayer or the practice which we call "religion" and "worship." This pre-existing innate drive to religion or mystery is in itself supernatural.

However, universally, this innate or indwelling supernatural drive in the human being "*qua* human being as *imago Dei*", occurs in all "*homo sapiens*" or thinking and free moral beings (moral agents) as a natural part of their "*a priori*" true human nature. the worship and adoration of God as the Infinite Mystery at the center of our being and the cosmos, the Ultimate Source and Destiny of our lives, and his Logos-Christ as the cosmic mediator of our own lives to God, and those of others in the quest of meaning and direction for a more satisfying future divine action.

5. Ecumenism and the "Venture in Mission" to the "Anonymous Christians"

The implication for Christianity is that God can be served best by the Church when it is diverse in practice and theology, but united in faith, love, worship, witness and missionary outreach. Our own destructive religious divisions, conflicts, fights, and mutual Christian anathematization and excommunication are a great Christian theological scandal to the Church of God and the commandment of agape. This mutual religious intolerance and hate is also a great moral impediment and stumbling block to our Christian witness and missionary outreach in the world, since uncharitable deeds to each other negate words of God's love in Christ.

Christian ecumenism and unity will, therefore, not only enhance fellowship and love for each other as brothers and sisters in Christ, but it will also give more credibility in the world as a consequence of joint witness and venture in mission. Moreover, resources and expertise can be pooled in the cause of world Christian mission, in order to bring "anonymous Christianity" to cognitive explicit Christianity, and specifically to personal acknowledgment and confession of Christ as Lord and Savior and unconditional love of neighbor. This is the apex of explicit Christianity.

Therefore, "anonymous Christianity" should also be brought to full cognitive espousal in its mature, explicit Christian expression. In order to speed up this historical growth process, all missionary endeavors should be undertaken by the Christian Church in an attempt to bring it about quickly.

However, the very notion of "anonymous Christianity" should serve to warn all Christian missionaries of the need for the appropriate missionary strategies that take into account the people's notions of integrity, dignity and freedom, local religious traditions and cultural religious practices. These local elements should be approached with respect as the prior divine groundwork preparation for the new, that is the Gospel, that has to be taught in light of this given background, and therefore, must be linked with the old that is already known.

Accordingly, all attempts should be made to avoid condemnation of what is found there, but rather, like St. Paul, to look for the "altar of the unknown God" as St. Paul did on his missionary journey in "pagan" Athens.[28] Certainly, Paul saw the numerous "pagan" temples, statues and idols that abounded in the city. But he chose not to start his preaching on a negative note by attacking or even possibly demolishing these idols and other false gods. Paul being tactful, chose wisely, to begin positively by focusing local people's attention on the good news he was bringing them in fulfillment of what they already imperfectly and anonymously knew, and had worshipped as the Unknown God! So Paul, standing in the middle of the Areopagus, where the people were always gathered to hear enlightening public lectures and other educated kinds of discourses, said:

> Men of Athens, I perceive that in every way you are very religious. For as I passed along, and observed the objects of your worship, I found also an altar with this inscription, "To an unknown god." What therefore you worship as unknown, this I proclaim to you. The God who made the world and everything in it...[29]

The main objective for Christian missions should not be to make people feel more guilty than they already feel about their sins and failures. But rather, it is to bring them the good news of their free unmerited acceptance, forgiveness, hope and unconditional love of God in Christ's Incarnation, life, teaching, passion and resurrection.

This approach is certainly the reverse of the former missionary strategy and approach in Uganda. Missionaries like Alexander Mackay of the Church Missionary Society thought that everything that was African, such as dress, music, dance, names, marriages, religious practices, morals and customs, were all barbaric and pagan. This being the case, Mackay understood the Christian mission as the downgrading and destruction of the African culture, or at least to achieve local individual conversion, which he equated with the total break with the past and the encompassing and constitutive African culture that he equated with barbarism and heathenism.

In his own understanding, there was no divine activity going on prior to the arrival of the Anglican missionaries. He was convinced that the African Traditional Religion, Islam and Catholicism, which arrived two years later after the initial arrival of the Anglican missionaries in 1877, were all devilish! For instance, of the local East Africans, Mackay wrote the following in his letter to Wigram:

> East Africans are generally savage...sunk in low state of barbarism, low intellect and low in morals. Their names are those of animals or deities or

they bear some grotesque meaning on the face of them causing the owner to blush with shame when a European pronounced the word...It was necessary to make a clean break with names of 'things indecent and obscene.'[30]

Did it ever occur to Mackay that the Europeans terribly mispronounced these African names, causing a total change in the meaning, thus grossly changing the identity of the people who bore the names, and thereby causing them embarrassment?[31] It seems that in his ethnocentric missionary approach and fundamentalist Christian bigotry, he ignored the cultural and linguistic barrier and consequently there were frequent misunderstandings between the European missionaries and their local African converts.

Christian boarding school education for the young was one of the missionary maneuvers to cut the young converts from their relatives and community and to uproot them from their African Traditional Religion and culture, that they regarded as an unredeemable pagan, in a misguided attempt to make them "good Christians" or "Black-European Christians" at best! This kind of ethnocentric and assimilitionist British missionary approach was similar to the French colonial policy of "assimilation" in Africa that proved to be a great failure. Obviously, the targeted African subjects for brainwashing, Western enculturation and de-Africanization rebelled and "naturally failed" to turn into "Black Frenchmen or Europeans" as it had been naively hoped. Likewise, Mackay's imperialist-missionary venture of turning the East Africans into "Black Anglican Englishmen" was also bound to fail.

Mackay, being in charge of the Anglican Church Missionary Society's (C.M.S.) work in Uganda, was terribly upset that the Catholics, also had decided to come and do some missionary work in the same country. Instead of welcoming them as allies and fellow Christian laborers in this wide unharvested vineyard of God, he became annoyed and resentful. Consequently, he lamentedly wrote back home to England as follows:

It seems to me that God has allowed these false teachers to come...Oh, that we could and use the short time we have, more to God's story. We did what we could to keep the tares from being sown when the Papists [Catholic missionaries] turned up, but we failed and now they will settle in the country beside us. Well as Christ himself taught, let the tares grow up along with the wheat and on harvest day God will gather them separately.[32]

Christianity and the Church in Uganda were established within this tragic context and background of religious rivalry, intolerance, exclusivism, hostility and bigotry that have bedeviled the people and Church of Uganda since that time. How was Mackay sure that the Catholic missionaries and their converts constituted the tares in the wheat? Were the Anglicans then the wheat? Could Mackay ever work together in love with the Catholics he regarded tares, and as such fuel for the eschatological hellfire?

Obviously, for Mackay the Anglicans and only "those born again," (Balokole) were the wheat and the rest,particularly the Catholics whom he referred to simply as "the Papists," were the tares that the devil was sowing in Uganda by the mediation of the "anti-Christ" Catholic missionaries!

It is hardly surprising, therefore, that just ten years later, this religious intolerance, hostility and rivalry grew worse as the local converts to both these denominations that were mutually opposed to each other. Consequently, an open religious military conflict took place between the Anglicans and the Catholics, thus turning the previous religious, verbal "cold war" into a real, protracted, military and bloody one.

Obviously, the Lord's obligatory commandment for his followers to love one another and all human beings unconditionally, even inclusive of one's enemies, is the quintessence and the only veritable measure of authentic Christianity or any other truly redemptive religion. Therefore, unconditional love is the only true criterion and universal Christocentric definitive standard measure of who is either an authentic Christian and a false one, and who is saved from sin and lives a life of salvation in the fellowship of Agape with God and the neighbor.

Subsequently, faith and not agape is the path to God and salvation. Faith and courage in God's grace and power are the means and equipment required to make this difficult life and path of agape to God through the neighbors' heart possible. Since Agape demands personal and societal positive transformation and material mutual care, in a Western materialistic and capitalist economy, this central Christian doctrine and Commandment has been effectively negated and ignored.

On the contrary, Christians in the West and abroad have preferred individualism and the acquisition of personal wealth, power, fame and control over others, rather than obey God's commandment in Jesus-Christ and practice the redemptive virtues of Agape. Instead, Christians world-wide have fallen from the authentic redemptive universal social Gospel of God as taught by Jesus-Christ.

By this human rebellion against God in Christ and his redemptive positive social moral of the Unconditional Love for the Neighbor or Agape, the world has voluntarily undergone a second fall and alienation from God.

This has been concretized by the rebellious Christian Church and greedy materialist Christians who have chosen to repudiate agape in favor of sola fide (salvation by faith alone). By so doing, many of these Christians have also fallen into the destructive demonic moral evils, individualistic, negative, and unchristian materialistic modes of life.

These evil modes of life are characterized by mundane, uncharitable, wickedness, greed, selfishness, slavery, ethnocentrism, xenophobia, rape, theft, oppression, malice, deceit, racism, sexism, tribalism, violence, crusades, inquisitions, genocide, warfare and bloodshed. Ironically, some of these evils, such as the crusades, inquisition, genocide (Native American), and colonialism were sometimes committed by the naive Christians in order to demonstrate their personal deep commitment and love for both Jesus Christ and God his heavenly Father.

Therefore, one can validly ask if it ever occurred to these Western Christian missionaries or their converts that this religious warfare and bloodshed in the name of Christ/God might actually be the very negation of authentic Christianity? The same question is still valid today, since this religious milieu is still basically the same, despite the current positive attempts at ecumenism, joint translations of the Holy Scriptures, religious educational syllabi and educational programs.

These pioneering joint programs are a great Christian idea and positive godly witness that should be promoted in order to minimize the negative effects of the initial Christian missionaries, who sowed the harmful seeds of religious hatred, intolerance, division, bigotry, and war, instead of bringing the Gospel of the good news of forgiveness, unconditional love and reconciliation with God and the neighbor.

There is great hope that the negative state of affairs will also change with good, positive, sound teaching of the Gospel and its underlying essential obligation for unconditional love for the neighbor. Therefore, it is also hoped that this kind of uncharitable, harmful religious background that has been fatefully inherited from these European ethnocentric bigoted, and factious Christian missionaries can be either neutralized or negated by the African Religion and traditional theocentric community.

The African traditional orientation to love, openness, community and inclusiveness of diversity and religious pluralism can in this case become the backbone for an African inclusive theology and Christianity. This noble African background has great potentiality for greater factual Christian successful ecumenism and Christian unity. However, at the moment this ecumenical process is still moving slowly because of the presence of large numbers of Western missionaries still in Africa.[33]

Therefore, the Church in Africa would do better if it became independent of Western traditions and structures. This is also necessary in order to distance itself from Western entrenched Christian ethnocentrism, cultural imperialism, materialism, racism, European nationalism, ideological or political conflicts and denominational rivalry which Africa has no business getting engrossed in as if they were of its own creation.

It is self-evident that Christianity in Africa will continue to become more meaningful, unitive, holistic, reconciliatory and redemptive to the African people if it is allowed to become authentically African. In other words, if Christianity is appropriately contextualized and rooted within the African milieu, and within the African life itself, both correlatively and coextensively with this process, God will also have become truly Incarnate in African life in Jesus Christ, not as a Jew, but as an African, in order to address the Africans within their own language, symbols, world-view, historical experience, cultural and philosophical-religious context.

6. Anonymous Christianity and the Universal Cross of Christ

"Anonymous Christianity" should not be looked upon with disdain or even rejected as "anti-Christian missions" or an "easy back door to divine salvation."[34] Salvation may be gratuitously given to all human beings by God, regardless of what they are or where they are.

However, human beings have to work out their salvation daily in the course of ordinary day-to-day living with this divine assistance. Even then living is not easy, and this is precisely where the cross of Christ comes into focus in the process of human life and salvation. This pain of the cross that is encountered and experienced in the course of living, like "anonymous Christianity," transcends the barriers of conventional historical Christianity.

It can also be argued that in the same way "anonymous Christianity" was in existence even prior to the Incarnation of Christ, as preparatory anticipation of Christ's Incarnation, the cross was also implicitly present as an anticipation of the passion event. This means also that wherever and whenever human beings have stood up strongly for justice, righteousness, or truth, they often have been persecuted and sometimes even executed by their own communities that could not bear hearing them. Here, good examples include the Jewish prophets, and the most climactic of all, the crucifixion of Jesus as a blaspheming subversive religious teacher.[35]

Obviously, John the Baptist, the forerunner of Jesus, had been arrested, imprisoned and beheaded for his religious teachings and activities. He was not a conventional Christian, since he lived and died shortly before the founding of historical Christianity by Jesus his cousin.

Nonetheless, can we then as Apostolic Christians, validly claim that John the Baptist, actually never shared Christ's mission, self-sacrificial atoning sufferings nor experienced the redemptive cross, just because he preceded Christ in time? And can we validly theologically continue to argue that non-Christians are eternally lost to God? For instance, can we affirm that since John the Baptist or Abraham, Moses and King David, preceded Jesus-Christ and his crucifixion, that as a result, they were all eternally lost to God and his salvation? The answer is "NO." Only a very poorly trained and an unsophisticated Christian theologian and clergy person or naive lay Christian would actually and unequivocally dare to answer these kinds of questions in the affirmative.

One can also both theologically ask and soteriologically wonder about the fate of non-Christian saints, such as Buddha, Prophet Muhammad or more recently, Mahatma Gandhi, whose life was entirely dedicated to the unconditional loving, self-sacrificial non-violent mobilization for the freedom and independence of his own people of India that led to his unjust arrests, torture and imprisonment by the British imperialist officers in India. Can we say that he did not participate in the sufferings of Christ and experience of the cross of Christ just because he was a Hindu? The definitive answer to these kinds questions is definitely, "NO!"

Ultimately, human obedience to God's moral laws of Agape and nonviolence is not easy. This is partly because unlike the passivity of mere empty faith, obedience to Agape requires concrete positive moral action in the community and in the world. The positive moral action has consequent correlative good and just deeds which may be resented and opposed by evil-doers, who constitute the majority of the citizens in the local community, society and the world. This is the case, since it easier and more financially lucrative to do evil than good. For instance, it is easier to get rich by prostitution, stealing or selling illegal drugs than by working for minimum wage at the local gasoline station or fast food restaurant.

Therefore, doing good, and other works of justice may oppose and expose the evils done by the other people. This may cause friction, conflict and require the Christian "to bear his or her cross." Agape in its praxis as concrete moral actions of good works, holiness, compassion and peace-making, are by God's universal efficacious redemptive grace. As such, they are God's concrete universal efficacious media of grace, and salvation, since they transcend the human erected sinful barriers of religious creeds, exclusive boundaries of religious affiliations, Church denominations, race and gender.

Accordingly, it is theologically valid, to maintain that whenever and wherever human beings are persecuted for what they believe and where they stand on issues involving truth, religion, gender, race, color, nationality, sexuality, justice, human rights, equality, freedom, independence and self-determination in order to become what God has created them to become. Accordingly, if one stands for the truth, and refuses to compromise this perceived truth, there is the cross of Christ "being carried" and there may follow a crucifixion for that individual by the society.

Nevertheless, some religious people, such as Christian and Islamic fundamentalists, seem to relish such a social-religious conflict in the name of God. Some of these religious zealots and moral fanatics or "puritans" believe that they will be united with God in heaven if they experience some kind of personal participation in the same kind of socio-religious rejection, persecution, and innocent suffering Jesus and Prophet Muhammad under-went for the sake of obedience to the redemptive divine truth, election for special divine mission in the world, and unconditional love for fellow human beings. Therefore, for some of the Apostolic Christians, participation in this redemptive moral venture, in which suffering is inevitable because of the presence of evil, human moral failure and sin in the world, is also equivalent to participation in the cross of Jesus-Christ. This is regarded to be the case, regardless of time, geographical location, creed, nationality, race and level of technology.

In this symbolic and metaphorical sense, the cross of Christ transcends the barriers of time, culture, age, race, and therefore can be said to preceded the actual crucifixion. As such, Abraham, Joseph, Moses, David, Socrates, Buddha, Muhammad, Chief Sitting Bull (one of the Native American Chiefs), Gandhi and others, can be affirmed to have both efficaciously experienced and painfully carried this redemptive cross of Christ for themselves and their people.

This can be validly theologically affirmed to be the case even when these people, like Jesus himself, were not conventional Christians. As such, conventional Christianity does not nullify God's work of grace, unconditional love, mercy and universal salvation, in the world, both inside and outside the conventional Church. Likewise, God's agents and prophets are not only chosen from the Jews, they are chosen from every race, tribe, color and nationality of all God's people. Likewise, God's redemptive revelation, truth, and efficacious free grace in unconditional love are also bestowed on the entire world by God. This is God's cosmic free creative and redemptive work of unmerited grace and unconditional love.

This is consistent with Jesus-Christ's central theological and moral teachings. He definitively taught that it is the doers of God's will, specifically, those who do the works of unconditional love for the neighbor, and not those with unproductive faith, as mere confessors of his name, that shall enter the kingdom of God or heaven. For instance, St. Matthew reports Jesus' own definitive universal standard measure and criteria for God's eschatological judgement of true godliness, and qualification for God's salvation and the kingdom as follows:

> Beware of false prophets, who come to you in sheep's clothing but inwardly are ravenous wolves. You will know them by their fruits. Are grapes gathered from thorns, or are figs from thistles? So, every sound tree bears good fruit, but the bad tree bears evil fruit. A sound tree cannot bear evil fruit nor can a bad tree bear good fruit...Not everyone who says to me, "Lord, Lord" shall enter the kingdom of heaven, but he who does the will of my Father who is in heaven. On that day many will say to me, "Lord, Lord, did we not prophesy in your name, and cast out demons in your name, and do many mighty works in your name?" And then I will declare to them, "I never knew you; depart from me, you evil-doers."[36]

According to Jesus human beings and their moral well-being are analogous to a fruit-tree which can only be judged to be good or bad by the quality and nature of its fruits. God is the farmer and the planter and owner of the fruit trees. The world is God's garden in which the trees have been planted by God. In this analogy, the leaves are analogous to faith, whereas good fruits are analogous to good deeds of charity or agape. As such, the godly person must also bear the corresponding good deeds as the explicit evidence and necessary spiritual fruits of a new life of positive transformation, new being, grace, sanctification, agape and salvation (cf. Gal. 5:15-22).

Therefore, conventional and confessing Christians who ignore the cross of Christ as it is carried and experienced in living in unconditional love for the neighbor and active self-sacrificial activity in the world's mundane or temporal processes. This saintly service and positive practical involvement in the daily affairs of the world is what God requires of all his loving and caring saints. This is the meaning of God's incarnation in the world. Jesus-Christ spent most of his time in the world serving men and women. He taught the ignorant, healed the sick and fed the hungry as an example for his followers to imitate.

All obedient religious people, particularly, the Christians who are called upon to become the agapic or loving servants of God in the world, just like the saintly examples of Jesus, Gandhi, Martin Luther King, Jenani Luwum and Mother Theresa. This benevolent, non-violent saintly involvement in the world on God's behalf is needed in order to achieve freedom and justice for the oppressed, to feed the hungry, clothe the naked, defend the defenseless or powerless, and to speak on behalf of the silent or voiceless poor masses of oppressed powerless people in the world, will have also ignored Christ and his fundamental redemptive mission in the world (Luke 4:16-20).

These evil and oppressive existential conditions or other desperate situations in the world are the very places and redemptive contexts where Christ and God's redemptive work are naturally most needed and best experienced and appreciated as Jesus-Christ clearly affirmed in his definitive sermon on the mountain, particularly, in the beatitudes regarding God's blessings for the poor and the oppressed (cf. Matt. 5-7).

Therefore, within the context of these conditions of injustice, abuse, oppression and despair is also where Christ and his unconditional love, forgiveness, self-sacrificial salvific activity are to proclaimed and effectively mediated by God's saints and ambassadors of God's redemptive or healing love, justice, forgiveness and salvation.

Sister Theresa of Calcutta is a perfect modern example of this infinite loving selfless dedication and service to others. She has diligently served the poor masses and the needy street dwellers of the overcrowded Indian cities in order to serve Christ in them. This praxis of agape or the unconditional loving service to all human beings should be treated as the true bearing of the cross of Christ and the very criterion of authentic humanity and salvation. This is also the ultimate criterion for the irrevocable and definitive divine eschatological judgment. St. Matthew again reports the following words of Jesus about this subject:

When the Son of Man comes in glory, and all the angels with him, then he will sit on his glorious throne. before him will be gathered all the nations and he will separate them one from another as a shepherd separates the sheep from the goats ...Then the King will say to those at the right hand, "Come, O blessed of my Father, inherit the kingdom prepared for you from the foundation of the world; for I was hungry and you gave me food, I was thirsty and you gave me drink, I was a stranger and you welcomed me, I was naked and you clothed me, I was lonely and you visited me, I was in prison and you came to me." Then the righteous will answer him, "Lord, when did we see thee hungry and feed thee or thirsty and give thee drink? And when did we see thee a stranger and welcome thee? And when did we see thee sick or in prison and visit thee?"

This parable teaches the principle or the idea of "anonymous Christianity" in the sense that the righteous seemed not to be aware that they were serving God and they were as surprised as the self-righteous who found themselves very unexpectedly rejected. Jesus goes on to give a definitive measure by which all human beings will be eschatologically measured and judged by God. He answered the above question as follows:

And the King will answer them, "Truly, I say to you, as you did it to me." Then he will say to those at his left hand, "Depart from me, you curse...for I was hungry and you gave me no food, I was thirsty and you gave me no drink, I was a stranger and you did not welcome me, naked and you did not clothe me, and in prison, you did not visit me." Then they also will answer, "Lord, when...?" Then he will answer them, "Truly, I say to you, as you did it not to one of the least of these [people], you did it not to me." And they will go away into eternal punishment, but the righteous in eternal life.[37]

This is the very quintessence and epitome of soteriology and Christianity in its overlapping two-fold dimensions, the explicit, cognitive and confessional Christianity on one hand, and yet, on the other hand, being the implicit, non-cognitive, unaware or unconscious of itself, and therefore, completely incognito and "anonymous" both to itself and others as "Christianity." The latter form of spirituality may be anonymous Christianity to itself and the world in which it practiced, however, it is not so with God.

Ultimately, God is transcendent; and therefore, unlike finite human beings, God does not care about the specific religious names and theological labels which human beings put on their various religions and forms of spirituality. What God has commanded is the imperative observation of Agape and justice. This is what matters to God. God is the loving and merciful impartial judge, who does not judge by external appearances of human beings and their actions, but rather the true judge of human hearts and motives for their actions (deeds) both good and bad.[38]

These words of Jesus-Christ reveal that the only sure key to unconditional love and charitable generous service and treatment of our fellow human beings, most especially during their time of need when they are most open and receptive to both God and their fellow beings. For this is the opportune time when they are most eager to see, hear and experience the divine word of Love, Life and Hope acted out both in word and deed through us as Christ's missionaries and God's ambassadors of life, forgiveness, love, hope and reconciliation by the power of the Holy Spirit.[39]

However, in order to achieve this and to become God's effective missionaries and ambassadors in this temporal world of religious, cultural, economic, and socio-political ideological pluralism, we have to be humble, flexible, open-minded, inclusive and loving to all human beings without any conditions. This means working jointly with all men and women of good will regardless of their creed, race, color, political views, ideology and party or religious affiliation in the world, so as to serve God best and our fellow human beings (or our neighbor) more effectively. Above all, this approach will greatly insure global harmony, justice, peace and careful development and equitable utilization of the world's natural resources for the general welfare of all the earth's inhabitants.

7. The Affirmation of Anonymous Christianity
Requires a New Theological Reflection

The affirmation of the existence of "anonymous Christianity" will inevitably require a new theological reflection in light of this new broad, universal context. It requires not only the repudiation of narrow and exclusive theological doctrines such as *extra ecclesiam nulla salus*, but it will also mean a review of other key doctrines on the sacraments, most especially baptism, the Eucharist and matrimony, questioning religious intermarriages.

Furthermore, there has to be an indigenous African theology which is expressive of the Gospel in a locally meaningful mode of thought, understanding, practice and liturgical worship. That means allowing the African man or woman to think, act and worship as an African Christian *vis-a-vis* the Western missionaries who brought Christianity to the local area.

It is difficult for an ordinary African to worship God in a foreign liturgy and to sing Western hymns, even those with references to winter, snow and spring, when in reality most Africans have never seen snow! For Christianity in its explicit form to become the meaningful and the divine vehicle or medium for daily salvific guidance and influence on the lives of the African masses, as the traditional religion still does, Christianity has to become African. It has to emphasize love, wholeness, healing, forgiveness and release from guilt.

In addition, many would urge that Western missionary Christianity has to shed its superficial marks and trappings of the Western cultural elements that have no value or meaning in Africa, such as Western Christian art, music and musical instruments, architectural designs of church buildings, clerical robes, liturgical garments and vessels, wedding dress and order of ceremony, and the use of bread and wine for the Eucharist instead of local staple food and drink. These foreign practices, they would argue, can be adapted locally without necessarily making a radical change in theology.

However, the problem lies in human reluctance to change and, most of all, the lack of belief that the African cultural and traditional elements are truly fitting vessels and media for communicating God's Word in the proclaimed message and consecrated local food and drink to become by the power of the Holy Spirit the true efficacious symbols of Christ's mystical body and blood, for the maintenance of life now and, mystically, in the world to come.

Perhaps most important of all, Christology and the theories of the Atonement have to be reviewed in the light of "anonymous Christianity" and in a broader universal context as the arena of God's unconditional self-communication in efficacious grace for the salvation of every human being regardless of time and space, creed, tribe, nationality, race or level of technological development. Following the example of St. John, Christ's centrality in both creation and salvation would have to be strongly affirmed for all places and in all ages.

Therefore, those people experiencing and enjoying salvation before the Incarnation and before the arrival of the explicit historical institutional Christianity can be validly termed "anonymous Christians," since their salvation is possible only through and by the presence and mediation of Christ, as there is no salvation possible anywhere except through Christ as the cosmic pre-existent divine creative and redemptive Logos/Word which is the very Logos of God that became temporal in the Incarnation and was historically manifested to the world in history as Jesus of Nazareth.[40]

It is this temporal Logos as Jesus that becomes the founder of the historical, agapic and Apostolic Christianity. It is because of its emphasis of God's agape and unmerited grace for the free forgiveness of all human sins, that this Christocentric moral ethos of unconditional love and free forgiveness for the neighbor as God's redemptive healing power for all unloving, estranged and sinful broken humanity and the culture of alienation in the world, is to be historically proclaimed as a superior form of divine revelation, God-consciousness and mode of existence in the world with fellow human beings, since agape promotes peace, harmony and fellowship of all God's people irrespective of differences or diversity of people, cultures, religions and values.

Agape being the primary essence and moral virtue of God's goodness constitutes a superior and highest level of God's revelation and divine message of spiritual and moral reconciliation with the neighbor, God and the world as God's good and evolutionary process of creation and redemption (cf. 1 John 4:7-21). This divine redemptive agape, unmerited grace and free forgiveness of sins will finally be mediated to all human beings through personal contact of loving and forgiving Christians, and the collectively organized Christian Church missionary outreach. Loving, caring and forgiving missionaries are God's historical and temporal "christs" and "incarnations" to the people to whom they come to serve. This is the kind of historical Christianity which was coextensive with both the early Church and the medieval Europe and its Christendom.

However, in this world, there will always be a mutual co-existence and overlapping of the universal "anonymous Christianity" and historical Christianity. The former form of Christianity being deficient in agape and self-consciousness as Christianity. It is only aware of the immanent and omnipresent, eternal cosmic, transcendental and pre-Incarnate Christ as the divine Logos.

On the contrary, the explicit historical Apostolic Christianity is extremely self-conscious as God's definitive cosmic revelation. As a direct, result Apostolic Christianity is very dogmatically exclusive of other religions. It is also traditionally very derogatory of other world religions as being inferior and non-redemptive. As we have already seen, until Vatican II, the Roman Catholic Church officially taught *"extra ecclesiam nulla salus"* to mean that there was no salvation outside the holy Roman Catholic Church, and the obedience to the sound Christian doctrines as formulated by her infallible Pope in Rome.

The Apostolic Christianity is self-celebrative as the complete embodiment, special God's temporal sacrament or vehicle and instrument for redemptive work in the world. That is, the Apostolic Church is sharply aware of itself as the temporal mediation of God-consciousness, therapeutic agape, universal efficacious divine grace, free divine forgiveness for sins, redemptive self-disclosure and it is missionary in order to convince all human beings of that fact as the authentic redemptive truth and apex of God's revelation to the world.

The explicit, apostolic and historical missionary Christianity is grounded in the Incarnation, life, teaching, passion, death, resurrection and ascension of Jesus Christ. This teaching is outlined in the Gospels and the Letters to the Romans and Hebrews, as being the ideal form of Christianity, but both of them possessing salvific efficacy despite the glaring deficiencies to be found in "anonymous Christianity." It is therefore, mandatory that Christian missionary activity must be undertaken by the Church in order to remedy these dehumanizing shortcomings in the world. In this way the institutional Christian Church, being the temporal embodiment as well as the historical redemptive mediation of the fullness of God's unconditional love, would be the main temporal divine medium of the fullness of freedom, authentic humanization, and supernatural salvation in this world.[41]

NOTES

1. John 1:1-5, 9, 10. There are many texts in the Bible that can be used to support this concept of "anonymous Christianity," since it affirms that only God creates, judges and redeems the world and all the people in it. Cf. Gen. 1-12:3, Isa. 52-61, Rom. 1-5.

2. John 1:1-5, 9-14.

3. Matt. 5:17.

4. Heb. 1:1-3a.

5. According to David Barrett's statistics in *World Christian Encyclopedia: A Comparative Survey of Churches and Religions in the Modern World, A.D. 1900-2000*, only 33 percent of the world is Christian. Even more sinister, he found that whereas Christianity was losing ground in terms of percentage of world population growth! Significantly, in 1995, the statistics had not changed much. This was because the birth rate among non-Christians in India, China and Africa tends to be higher than the rate of Christian conversions.

6. Rahner acknowledges the problem of the term "anonymous Christianity." But, he also criticizes his critics, such as Kung, Jungel and Henri de Lubac for not coming up with a better term that would include all human beings experiencing God's salvation without being objectionable or offensive to anybody. See Rahner, "Observations on the Problem of the 'Anonymous Christian'," *Theological Investigations* 14:280-294, and Karl-Heinz Weger, *Karl Rahner: An Introduction to His Theology*, 112-141.

7. Karl Rahner, *Grace in Freedom* (New York: Herder and Herder, 1969), 83-85.

8. David Barrett, *World Christian Encyclopedia*, 1-33.

9. Rahner, *Grace in Freedom*, 85-86.

10. For an example, see Ssemakula Kiwanuka, *A History of Buganda*, 155-180.

9. Rahner, *Grace in Freedom*, 85-86.

10. For an example, see Ssemakula Kiwanuka, *A History of Buganda*, 155-180.
11. Ibid.

12. For instance, during the Ugandan national elections of 1980, most of the Baganda, regardless of political party or religious affiliation, voted D.P. mainly for tribal reasons, and in protest against Dr. Obote, who is a Northerner and from a non-Bantu ethnic group.

13. Cf. Gen. 6-11 and Cyprian's the doctrine of *extra ecclesiam nulla salus* in his *De catholicae ecclesiae unitate*, 6: "If anyone was able to escape outside of Noah's ark... also escapes...outside the doors of the Church."

14. Rom. 2:1-3, 6-11.

15. Luke 23:13-25; Matt. 27:1-31; Mark 15:1-20; Acts 3:13-14, 18:38-40, 19:14-15.

16. The story of Jesus and the criminal who got redeemed on the cross should keep us all humble. The thief went to heaven whereas the self-righteous were rejected by God.

17. Cf. Luke 8:43-48.

18. Luke 2:29-32.

19. Rev. 5:9-10.

20. Rev. 15:3-4.

21. See Acts, 10.

22. See, e.g., Rom. 1-4.

23. Baptism in Christianity is an equivalent" of circumcision in Judaism, similarly, Gentile to be the equivalent of "non-Christian," the Jewish Torah/Law to be the Christian equivalent of the Gospel, especially the Lord's commandment of Agape as Unconditional Love for the Neighbor (cf. Lk. 6:27-36; Jn. 13:34-35, 15:9-17; 1 Cor. 13; 1 Jn. 4:8-21).

24. This is a common practice in Africa including Uganda. Baptism is regarded as a supernatural birth, and like a natural birth, is regarded as a time for rejoicing and festivity in order to celebrate the addition of new life to the family and the community as a whole.

25. See: *On Free Choice of the Will*, 19-25; *Confessions*, X; *De Civitate Dei*, X.

26. See Augustine, Epistle 217 (427) to Vitalis (which deals with prevenient grace) and irresistible grace in *De corruptione et gratia; De dono perseverantiae* (428).

27. Cf. Rom. 6:3-11; Col. 2:6-15.

28. See Acts 17:22-32.

29. Acts 17:22-23.

30. Asavia Wandira, *Early Missionary Education in Uganda: A Study of Purpose in Missionary Education* (Kampala: Makerere Un. Dept. of Education, 1972), 109.

31. For instance, the religious name "Hategikimana," which means that "God reigns." However, if mispronounced with a short *a* in the last syllable, the word changes to mean "the vagina reigns!"

32. Kiwanuka, op. cit., 171.

33. In 1976 Hastings estimated that there were more than 40,000 Christian foreign missionaries in Africa, of which 25,000 were Roman Catholic missionaries; cf. Hastings, *African Christianity*, 20-21, 31-34. This large Catholic number of missionaries represents a serious Catholic effort to win African converts to Catholicism.

34. As Hans Urs von Balthasar claimed in protest to Karl Rahner's concept of "anonymous Christianity," which Balthasar saw as an unacceptable Christian relativization; see Karl Heinz Weger, *Karl Rahner*, 118 ff., Rahner, "Observations on the Problem of the 'Anonymous Christian,'" *Theological Investigations* 14:280-294; "Anonymous Christians," *Theological Investigations* 6:390-398; "Anonymous Christianity and the Missionary Task of the Church," *Theological Investigations* 12:161-178.

35. See, Matt. 22:66-71, 26:61-68, 27:32-50.

36. Matt. 7:15-23.

37. Matt. 25:31-46. Having lived in exile for many years, I know from personal experience the centrality of Agape to life and godliness. Help in time of my greatest need has usually came from unexpected people. My great disillusionment with Western Christianity was experienced in Eldoret in western Kenya. My wife and I got stranded on our flight from Idi Amin in Uganda on April 4, 1977. Our bus-fare was short by half a dollar. To our disillusionment, an Italian Roman Catholic nun uncharitably refused to aid us. Ironically, it was an anonymous poor man on the street who gave us help. For me the incident was revelatory of God's mystery and anonymous redemptive deeds which are only known to God and to human beings through positive and Agapic revelatory actions.

38. Cf. Rom. 2:1-11.

39. Cf. 2 Cor. 5:16-20.

40. Cf. John 1:1-5, 9-14.

41. See: Karl Rahner, "Anonymous Christianity and the Missionary Task of the Church," *Theological Investigations* 12:161-178; "Church, Churches and Religions," *Theological Investigations* 9:30-49; "The Church's Commission to Bring Salvation and Humanization to the World," *Theological Investigations* 14:295-313.

X

GOD'S INSEPARABLE COSMIC TWIN ACTIVITIES OF GRATUITOUS GRACE AND AGAPE IN UNMERITED CREATION AND FREE REDEMPTION

God as the creative Agape and "*Sola Gratia*" is also quintessentially both the unconditional cosmic Creator and Redeemer. From beginning to end both creation and salvation are unmerited free divine cosmic activities of grace and unconditional love or agape. No human being or creature ever deserves to be either created or redeemed and saved by God, apart from God's own unmerited mercy, love, grace and free will to act as he or she wills.

Therefore, out of his unmerited grace and unconditional love, God created the world and all its natural creatures. God has created the human being and endowed this creature with a special gift of mind which results from the special equipment in the form of a larger brain which God has given to the human being, so that the human being could become God's own representative in the material world and its history. This special divine gift of intelligence or mind makes the human being the finite mirror and incarnation of God in creation, the world and the cosmic history.

As a result of this human-divine gift of mind, thinking, freedom and moral agency, the human being is not only the mirror of God, but also the image of God in creation (*imago Dei*). The human being is a multi-intelligent creature. For instance, the human being is a free, social or intra-personal, thinking, knowing, God-self contemplative, loving and moral creature who is gratuitously endowed with special talents, gifts and a unique body. The human body allows great flexibility to allow intricate arts of dance, delicate eye-hand and brain coordination to facilitate great and complex surgical skills and other technological designs or art work.

Unlike the other primates, the human being as the "*homo sapiens*" also possesses the greatly enhanced special biological apparatus for great verbal and analytical thinking capacities, which in turn facilitate both speaking and writing to occur.

The human being is also logical, rational, mathematical, analytical and intuitive thinker. This special mental aptitude enables the human being to build complex technological structures and systems which other animals cannot match. The visual and spacial gift lets human beings see various colors and appreciate beauty more than most other animals. This gift enables human beings to appreciate the great complex beauty, wonders and mysteries of the creation or the cosmos, and give due praise to its benevolent ingenious Designer and Maker or God.

In this respect, the God of religion and as a creation of the human imagination, intellect, fears and needs for Ultimate meaning, and redemption from evil, chaos, pain and death. However, this does not mean that God is a mere mental illusion as some atheists and agnostics, such as Feuerbach, Marx, Nietzsche, Durkheim, and Freud have erroneously claimed. On the contrary, in religion, worship or theological-philosophical reference to God or the Creator of the cosmos, these theologians and religious people, both ancient and modern and like the Bible writers, Thomas Aquinas, the Africans and Native Americans, simply mean whatever Mystery that has created the cosmos.

Subsequently, for most religionists and worshippers of God, God is a term that names and refers to the nameless Transcendent Creative Mystery which has caused the universe and mind in the form of the loving and self-transcending human being evolve and come into meaningful orderly being, and to maintain this cosmos against the strong destructive powers of entropy, nothingness and chaos. Therefore, in religion, the incontrovertible evidence for God's existence as the object of worship and praise is the very existence of creation itself, which is regraded as his work and dwelling temple (cf. Gen. 1-12; Palms. 14, 23, 90, 119; Isa. 31-33, 45). A god who is not the Creator of the universe is a mere idol and an illusion or the mere figurement of the human imagination.

Therefore, it is to this perceived great Cosmic Creator, that the obedient and thankful human being sings praises, dances in celebration of life, beauty, love, and prays for protection and deliverance from evil as both the unpleasant experiences or events and imagined and real threats of evil in the form of chaos, conflict, meaninglessness, boredom, anxiety, loneliness, hate, malice, disease, aging, pain, and premature death. This universal experience of human mortality or finitude and evils or threats of chaos may be variously experienced at different times in relationship to one's life, family members, friends, the community and the world.

This human finitude and the correlative existential anxiety or fear of eternal death, is experienced more acutely by the human beings more than any other creatures. This is the case despite the fact that all creatures constantly live precariously in the presence and fear of death or being eaten in the case of the other animals in the wild. As a result, survival of the fittest, quickest and most cunning seems to be the natural law that governs life in the jungle.

Nevertheless, human beings suffer more from finitude, existential anxiety and fear of death than the other creatures because the human being is able to think more analytically and project the possibilities of his or her life into the future and in the present moment be able to anticipate this future with both its eventualities and confusing many open alternative possibilities.

This special divine-human capacity to think and to visualize potential future events scares the human being. In turn, the human being seeks for the Creator-Redeemer God for concrete deliverance from the present and future predicament. Accordingly, most of the human life is lived in this perpetual quest for redemption from evil, imperfection, incompleteness, ignorance, sin, guilt, fear of death, anxiety and pain.

Therefore, it is not surprising that Jesus as the Christ and Incarnate God came into the world as a carpenter (designer, builder and repairer of broken things), moral teacher or Rabbi, healer (physician of mind and body) and forgiver of sins or priest. This wholistic ministry of Jesus took care of all human anxieties, including the destruction of death by raising the dead and later by his own resurrection.

The human being as the finite historical spirit who is most akin to God in the cosmos, is in many perspectives like God (*imago Dei*). Therefore, like God the human being is able to transcend himself or herself by the virtue of being akin to God his or her creator and also being the embodiment of God in the material world. However, because of human rebellion against God and refusal to listen to God's Word or the Logos and the Holy Spirit which speak from within the mind and soul of the obedient and contemplative person, human beings have become deaf to God's Word and guidance. As a result, human beings have become alienated from the center of their own being and from God who resides within as his holy temple in the cosmos. Moreover, all human beings are aware of their personal and collective disobedience against God and separation from him or her and the fountain of eternal life and happiness which is found in God's eternal presence.

Subsequently, all human beings everywhere and in every generation are aware of their own finitude, natural limitations, threats of chaos, pain and death. As a result, all human beings are to some degree engaged in the same quest for security, food, shelter, harmony with others and the universe, peace, fellowship with others or love, and happiness.

Accordingly, all human beings tend to be religious in their ultimate quest for meaning and lasting self-fulfillment. This quest for the ultimate meaning, satisfaction in life and happiness is an essential religious quest for the Transcendent Creator-Redeemer and Fulfiller of creatures. This is the Mystery that we call God. Accordingly, our institutionalized quest for this Ultimate meaning and happiness and Destiny is what we also call religion.

In this understanding all religions are human invented paths (*yogas*) to God. Since God is everywhere in the cosmos, there is no need for a path in order to go on a pilgrimage in order to find God. God does not dwell in some remote holy place on special mountains, in the deserts or in special holy places in the Middle East. On the contrary, the omnipresent God is everywhere and resides within each human being as his or her holy temple, physical embodiment and incarnation in the local culture, place, community and human history. As such, those who wish to see God should look within the innermost depths of their own humanity, mind, freedom, spirit, and moral values.

However, if they cannot see God there because of the noise and pollution of sin, then they should clean their own inner being until they can see God reflected within. This is possible because each obedient and loving person, by an *a priori* quintessential divine-human nature as *imago Dei*, a good temporal mirror of God which faithfully reflects God's true image, goodness, justice and agape to the world, and particularly, to those people and institutions around him or her. As such, if a person finds it difficult to see God within, then he or she should look at the saints and their obedient holy agapic lives, around him or her, in order to see God's image and work within the world.

Therefore, for the Christians a holy, agapic godly life as the universal path to God and saintliness lies in the diligent praxis of agape in obedience to God's commandment to love the neighbor and forgive those who sin against us without any prior conditions.

Accordingly, an obedient saintly or redeemed life in God, is a humane and loving life of free forgiveness, justice and altruistic service of our fellow human beings, irrespective of condition, and for both explicit and implicit or "anonymous Christians," just because God has in Christ and the Incarnation become historically and mystically permanently united with all humanity, and therefore, has become universally present in every human being in the world. This is a reaffirmation of the central Christian traditional Christological teachings, the Apostolic and Nicene creeds, and the Chalcedonian Christological Dogma or formulation that God has become inseparable from humanity everywhere by virtue of Christ's Incarnation, and the irrevocable "Hypostatic Union."[1]

In short, Rahner argues that human authentic existence as divine gratuitous salvation, which is also the divine humanization of the human being, is universally given freely by the loving God, the Transcendent Infinite Mystery, to every human being who lives in full openness to the world and loves the neighbor, and that such a person is in essence an authentic human being saved by God, regardless of whether he/she calls himself/herself a Muslim, a Hindu, a pagan, a communist or even an atheist.

Furthermore, Rahner believes that such a person should be termed an "anonymous Christian," because this salvation occurs through the pre-existent, cosmic divine Logos that also becomes incarnate in the temporal world and history in Jesus Christ, and that such a divine universal self-communication in gratuitous grace constantly takes place for the salvation of every human being, everywhere in the world and in every age, in order to enable human beings to become ever more loving, forgiving, humane, generous, creative and personally responsible.

The affirmation of this Rahnerian inclusive Christian concept of "anonymous Christianity," though seemingly radical for a "conventional Christian," is actually in line with the biblical message of gratuitous divine salvation. It can even amplify Jesus Christ's teaching, particularly, on constant forgiveness and the unconditional love for God and one's fellow human beings, including even one's enemies. Jesus' teaching on the Good Samaritan and association with the traditionally non-acceptable people, such as the "tax collectors and sinners," can be viewed as laying the foundation for such a broad and inclusive Christian teaching on the universal divine free salvation.

This universal and inclusive soteriological teaching is what Karl Rahner has sought to expound by his apparently controversial Christian teaching on universal mystical supernatural salvation and union with God through the cosmic Logos-Christ. This salvation is achieved through obedience to God and the practice of agape as an implicit universal redemptive spirituality and concrete positive mode of life based on obedience to God as universally revealed and communicated through the cosmic Logos-Christ. Therefore, for Apostolic and Christocentric Christians, this form of inclusive soteriological spirituality is both religiously ethnocentrically and Christologically referred to as an "anonymous Christianity."

This Rahnerian inclusive Christian teaching is particularly attractive to those who are trying to discern how God's gratuitous salvific activity could have been previously at work in East Africa prior to the arrival of Western Christian missionaries at the end of the last century. Furthermore, this Rahnerian Christian teaching may help them to realize that God is even at work among our Muslim neighbors. This is the traditional Christian affirmation that the incomprehensible transcendent Cosmic Mystery that we call God, "moves in mysterious ways in the cosmos, his wonders to perform."[2]

Accordingly, this is also the correlative positive affirmation that even when some people like the Hindus of India, Native American people, along with the Karamojong and the Masai, nomadic cattle keepers of East Africa, who are still largely considered "unreached by the Gospel of Christ," are not entirely lost to God, but are saved by obedience to his moral law as revealed in cosmic creation, their own religions and moral consciences.[3]

Probably most important of all, is that the affirmation of "anonymous Christianity" requires that we must inclusively and positively view and humanely treat all human beings as the beloved, and redeemed children of God. This must be done irrespective of creed or color. We must treat all human beings everywhere in the world with both love and respect, without any prior conditions for this agapic, humane and just treatment. This is the universal and unalienable God-given right of every human being as a Child of God. This is the basis of many religious egalitarian doctrines and political movements and historical documents, such as, the Magna Carter, the French Declaration of the Rights of Man, the American Declaration of Independence, and the United Nations' Universal Declaration of Human Rights of 1948.

Ultimately, this new global noble mutual human acceptance of one another, and all human beings as the redeemable children of God can in itself be a redemptive and divinizing factor. It can become a fundamental universal human ethic and moral common ground for human interaction with one another and peaceful co-existence. To this end, it can most effectively serve as a common unitive philosophical theological ground for handling religious diversity and socio-political pluralism at national and international levels to enhance dialogue, mutual understanding, reconciliation and mutual peaceful co-existence.

However, unconditional love for the neighbor is still required to enable this mutual peaceful co-existence to endure the challenges of conflicts that usually arise in such a pluralistic context. Since it also appears that the world is getting even more pluralistic, both religiously and socio-politically, it can be also argued that there should be a great emphasis placed on Johannine and Rahnerian types of Christocentric unconditional love for the neighbor and, co-extensively, the realization that each human being is potentially a "child of God," and is therefore, to be socially and religiously reverently treated as such, a special and divine being.

In the final analysis, this book represents an Africanist Christian theological, theocentric-Christocentric or Logos Christian theology in a serious academic attempt to explicate, defend and adopt Rahner's Christian teaching for the world, and particularly Africa today. Africa serves as a mere Christian theological example of this inclusive Rahnerian universal Christian doctrine of salvation. Accordingly, in this book, I have drawn a lot from Rahner's broad teaching on God's universal self-communication in gratuitous salvific grace, and unconditional love for every human being, in order to effect the individual's unique, God-ordained special divinization process of positive growth, complete humanization, love, faith, freedom, good works, humaneness and personal responsibility in the exercise of personal freedom.

"Anonymous Christians" is Rahner's Christocentric Christian theological term for those people whom God has saved outside the Apostolic Church. These are the redeemed saints of God, or those people in the world, who have responded positively to God's cosmic free invitation for all human beings to hear God's Word of Life (the Logos or the Christ) and live according to agape, and obedience to God's will in creation, and thereby, they are able to actualize themselves most positively. This is possible if they actualize themselves most meaningfully in love, peace, simplicity, and fellowship with both God and the neighbor. As result, they are able to experience maximum self-fulfillment, love, fellowship, peace and happiness in the community as God's universal redemptive Church and the kingdom.

Therefore, this inclusive universal divine call to an authentic humanization and meaningful human existence, is a call to constant openness to the transcendent Infinite Mystery in hope and love for the neighbor. As such, as the mystics, such as Moses, Buddha, and Gandhi have clearly and correctly theologically illustrated to the world, one does not have to be an official member of the Apostolic Church, Islam, or Judaism in order to be redeemed and saved by God.

Human beings, everywhere in the cosmos, have been freely endowed with God's special, efficacious indwelling redemptive grace and intrinsic divine power to be able to positively respond to God's free universal invitation to supernatural salvation. For Muslims, those people are called "Muslims," such as Adam, Abraham, Moses, David and Jesus. Similarly, for the Christians those people who are saved outside the Church, such as Abraham, Moses, Jesus and Gandhi are Christians or "anonymous Christians," since they may not be explicitly aware of themselves as "Christians," or for various reasons happy with being referred to as Christians. Although this term itself is problematical and controversial, it can be discarded in favor of a better terminology.

Nevertheless, the fundamental doctrinal affirmation of "anonymous Christianity" is attractive and intellectually meaningful to a selectively well educated, inclusive and post-modernist theologians, mystics and other interreligious or interfaith thinkers or inclusive pastoral care-givers. This is a noble inclusive soteriological and theological Christian and an interreligious practical theological and moral "common ground" for all those people, who are truly interested and committed in finding an inclusive Christian soteriological understanding, and an inclusive working model or paradigm.

This constructive doctrine of theological and religious inclusiveness is essential in order to unite members of various religious traditions into God's redeemed, harmonious, one inclusive happy family or Church, in the world and his kingdom. The inclusive paradigm of the "anonymous Christianity," is best formulated, inclusive and flexible enough to achieve this theological global soteriological inclusiveness and religious unity. This is due to the fact that this universalist inclusive theological paradigm takes seriously the world's religious pluralism into theological account, yet without compromising the uniqueness of historical Christianity and its special message of the Incarnation, and Jesus Christ's commandment of unconditional love for the neighbor.

Therefore, this book has attempted to show that for those who seek to discern God's free salvific activity in traditional Africa, Rahner's inclusive Christian concept of "anonymous Christianity" can be a useful guide for their own inquiry, and theological contextual reflection, without negating the central message of the Bible and the Gospel of Christ. This is particularly true, since the emphasis is rightly placed on Jesus Christ's definitive commandment of the moral and religious obligation of unconditional love for the neighbor as the quintessence of Christianity, and the universal criterion of all true godliness, justice, peace and divine salvation (cf. Matt. 7:13-21; 25:31-46).

In this global theocentric inclusive soteriological understanding of God, humanity, and the world, and because of the correlative all-encompassing Cosmic Christological view of the intrinsic inseparable interrelatedness of God's free Cosmic creation and redemption in the Logos or Christ, universal divine salvation for non-Christians becomes God's "agapic moral duty." This is the case, since redemption is an inseparable component of God's active universal free grace in both creation and the creature's concrete causal free will, freedom, choice and moral action. This means that the finite and imperfect human being is ever standing inadequate, and therefore, constantly in need of God's grace, moral guidance, and redemption from evil, hate, meaninglessness, despair or existential anxiety (angst) chaos, and premature death.

Therefore, regardless of religious, theological and moral condition, like a loving and caring mother takes care of her children, and protects them from self-destruction or external evil, analogously, God as the Cosmic Parent of each human being is ever keeping benevolent and redemptive vigilant watch over his or her children everywhere in the cosmos. Within this global context of real consequential personal moral freedom, love, conscience, choice and capacity to do either good or evil, a meaningful theological teaching on salvation has to include the normative value for definitive self-determining freedom, choice and the voluntary praxis love or agape.

Therefore, being consistent with the quintessential, agapic inclusive universal soteriological, moral teachings of Jesus as based on his universal definitive commandment to love God and the neighbor, without condition, I have subsequently, illustrated in this work that an inclusive interreligious theological study of the scriptures and the correlative critical analysis of the diverse religious traditions yields a rich global religious quest for God, happiness and salvation, and that these are effectively also found in God, through following an apparent variety of seemingly divergent paths and even conflicting religious traditions.

Nevertheless, the different paths and religions end up converging in the "common ground" or transcendent and omnipresent Cosmic Mystery or God whose unmerited and unconditional free universal grace and agape are externally concertized in the free universal creation and redemption of the world. However, only human beings as his intelligent creatures are conscious of these divine actives and free gifts, and only his obedient people, and saints everywhere, and in every age respond to God in free praise, thanksgiving, active love, and justice for their fellow human beings and respect for the rest of God's creation.

This general human religious quest for God's fulfillment, validation and completion as a happy and most fully positively self-actualized and immortalized or divinized human being, is a characteristic universal human phenomenon. This universal insatiable human quest for divinization or deification and divine salvation in God, is both implicitly and explicitly formulated or expressed in the human quest for meaning, self-affirmation, self-fulfillment, self-completion, goodness, justice, love, peace, fellowship and happiness.

These are the divinizing noble virtues and ultimate answers which are eagerly sought after by both Christians and non-Christians. This is a natural universal human quest that is intrinsic in every normal finite human being everywhere in the cosmos. It is God's "a priori" gracious free orientation of the human being in creation towards himself as the source of life, happiness, fulfillment, completion and salvation or peace from the threat of finitude, chaos, imperfection and existential anxiety.

Just like fish or other aquatic creatures are naturally oriented to water at the moment of birth, human beings are permanently oriented to God, at the moment of creation. The human mind and spirit are created as God's mirrors and echoes God to the cosmos. As such, the human being is God's concrete ambassador in the material cosmos. Therefore, the human mind and spirit are uniquely created by God so as to be simultaneously both supernaturally and naturally oriented and attuned to hear God's Word and reflect God to the rest of the material and non-intelligent cosmos. Consequently, the human quest for God is prompted by the conditions of finitude and imperfection, the cure for them is projected into God and heaven by the ideal positive virtues which are also correlatively abstracted from the temporal world, idealized and projected into a more perfect utopian future in heaven.

Therefore, since these heavenly conditions are idealized earthly states of being, and because God's grace is active in the world as God's kingdom, therefore, these heavenly conditions can be fully realized and concertized on earth, if we let God's reign become normative in our lives. Therefore, if the majority of the religious people shifted their religious emphasis from seeking to gain salvation through the path of faith alone or "*sola fide*," in a future life, and instead, obey Christ's practical commandment to love and forgive the neighbor unconditionally, this world would become effectively transformed into "God's kingdom on earth as it is in heaven."

Ultimately, the diligent religious and moral observation Agape, and good works which are a result of the true praxis of agape constitute the righteous, holy, just true path of salvation as the road to God, eternal life, happiness, peace and fellowship with the neighbor. Good deeds as the practice of these virtues and as the fruits of grace and agape, constitute a universal redemptive moral path which leads to a concrete positive mode of a redeemed supernatural life and heaven on earth in Agapic fellowship with God, and the neighbor.

This mystical and Agapic kingdom of God or heaven on earth takes the beatific form of true unconditional love (Agape), compassion, peace and reconciliation and fellowship with God. This is necessarily the case, since in the Incarnation of God in the world, God has become a true human being and therefore, our concrete neighbor, as God is now permanently inseparable from any other human being as the neighbor. Accordingly, to love the neighbor unconditionally is to love God, and conversely, to be loved unconditionally by the neighbor and be forgiven unconditionally, is truly to be loved and forgiven unconditionally by God.

Within this inclusive global theological complexity of religious diversity, and theological pluralism, the practical viable universal criterion and measure of a God-centered or an authentic human existence and true Christianity, is considered to be the personal self-expressive exercise of responsible freedom and unconditional love for the neighbor, inasmuch as it is St. John's affirmation that "Love is of God, and one who loves is of God and knows God...for God is Love"[4] is universally true and applicable or definitive for all religious experiences and practices in all eras.

Given this theological context and inclusive universal understanding of God as "*Sola Gratia*" or as the cosmic Creative-Redemptive Agape, the praxis Agape universally and effectively replaces the theological centrality of faith and the sacrament of baptism. The praxis of Agape becomes the new universal criterion, efficacious and explicit vehicle for any true and societal beneficial or redemptive godliness.

According to this complex religio-societal context and constructive new theological understanding, Agape or its praxis becomes the real universal God's open gate, means or path, divine redemptive power, foundation, origin and destiny of God's salvation in the world. This true inasmuch as supernatural salvation is also a concrete or real personal and societal experience of positive openness to God, one another, mutual acceptance, fellowship, positive transformation, harmony, and peace. And peace or divine salvation being correctly theologically understood as a concrete temporal state of mutual peaceful neighborly co-existence in the community, work and the world in which we all share and live with one another as God's adopted children, and therefore, as brothers and sisters in God's family and fellow citizens in God's kingdom.

Thus, true obedience to God's ultimate and definitive universal commandment of Agape transforms the local community into God's true Church and transforms this world of strife and conflict into one God's harmonious pluralistic and inclusive kingdom of Agape and reign of peace. This is the kind of ideal society that Martin Luther King referred to as the "beloved community" in the course of his writings, speeches and most especially in his most famous speech: "I Have a Dream" which was delivered on 28 August, 1963 as the keynote address of a Civil Rights March on Washington, (D.C.) District of Columbia.

Ultimately, to exercise agape and truly participate in the concrete divine-human agapic fellowship, or the loving and forgiving harmonious human community, is truly to participate in God, and the fellowship of his kingdom of love. To accept God's definitive redemptive and divinizing principle of agape and to live by its good works, is to gain divine supernatural salvation and experience on earth, the real beatific bliss or heaven. This also means that one has to live on earth as fully as living in God's kingdom, since both are inseparable to God and for all God's true agapic saints in the world.

Therefore, the true practical obedience to God's commandment of obligation of observing societal unconditional love and forgiveness of our fellow men and women as our concrete neighbors in both Christ and God is the true path to God, peace, salvation, and heaven or God's kingdom. Jesus-Christ as the incarnate Logos, and thereby becoming the embodiment of God, Agape, divine oracle and theophany of God in human history, has showed us that to be God-like.

According to Jesus-Christ, to be godly, redeemed by God, and to become God-like, consists in obedience to God and to receive God's free gift of Agape and to exercise it diligently in relationship to the neighbor in who God has become eternally present and inseparable by the virtue of the incarnation of God in humanity through the Logos and the Holy Spirit. Therefore, it is not by virtue of "faith alone" (*sola fide*) or "Christian sacrament of baptism" that human beings are redeemed by God and transformed from their sins and evil deeds into positive loving and responsible moral agents. On the contrary, it is through obedience to God's commandment of Agape, and the praxis of this agape that God both redeems and saves the community from self-destructive malice and violence and sets it on the path of peace and happiness.

It is by God's Agape and the human obedience which is concretely expressed through the praxis of Agape, that any obedient human beings anywhere in the world or in any era, truly become redeemed and divinized to become "God-like" or "Christ-like." It is also through Agape that God's people can in God's holy name, most effectively and positively work together irrespective of the sinful barriers of religious affiliation or creed, race, culture and socio-economic class to transform this imperfect, war and strife torn wounded world into the temporal "God's kingdom."[6]

This kingdom of God on earth is unique and negates much of the human ethnocentric and xenophobic attitudes and behaviors which divide human beings into various mutually hostile and competing groups based on exclusive natural or local traits and unique traditions or history. In contrast, God's temporal kingdom or membership is characterized by in human mutual inclusive unconditional love and acceptance of one another as God's children irrespective of gender, race, color, class, culture, creed, sexual orientation, marital status and level of technological development.

This ideal harmonious human mutual acceptance of one another as the beloved children of God will in itself lead to the redemption of the world. It will facilitate the establishment of God's kingdom on earth as it is in heaven. The praxis of Agape promotes fellowship mutual love, societal, global peace and true happiness. This is because the true praxis of agape is the only condition that fulfills the commandment of God in Christ. The universal moral imperative of God or Agape for all human beings in the world is the moral obligation to become humane, just and loving like God. And also to become more loving and forgiving like our heavenly "Father or Mother" loves and forgives us without condition.

This universal divine moral imperative requires either an explicit or implicit or anonymous obedience to God's explicit commandments or moral law as universally revealed in nature (cf. Rom. 1:17-31). Agape also demands that human beings must become like God, and then, like God they must also love and forgive one another without conditions (Matt. 5-7; 25:31-46; Luke 15; John 13:34-35; 1 John 4:7-21). This is also the universal divine commandment or moral imperative and obligation.

Regardless of creed, color, nationality, race, gender, class and level of technological development and sophistication, the world's people must obey to some reasonable and practical degree, unless, like fools they wish to perish. And become extinct through an existential hell or self-destructive and terminal state of human voluntary mutual hatred, intolerance, environmental pollution, suicidal nuclear wars or "self-destruct" in other tragic ways.

Ultimately, in order to avoid disaster and extinction, despite human differences, and evils of greed, sin, hate, hubris and ethnocentrism, all human beings must inevitably learn to live harmoniously together in this world, in order to survive together if they do no wish to perish together as fools. Optimistically, these human beings may even learn to obey God's cosmic moral law of harmony, symbiosis, justice, and finally, by the praxis of agape to effectively transform it into God's peaceful kingdom on earth, where there is an enduring state of harmony and peace.[6]

NOTES

1. Cf. Karl Rahner, *Grace in Freedom*, 261.

2. *The Hymnal of the Protestant Episcopal Church in the United States of America*, 1940, #310 (written by William Cowper, 1774).

3. See Rom. 1:17-32. St. Paul was sure that God had freely bestowed his own free sufficient redemptive grace and revelation in nature and creation. As a result, Paul affirmed that no human being has any excuse not to know God, worship him and perform good deeds for his or her neighbor as the fulfillment of all the moral law and righteousness (cf. Rom. 13:8-11 and 1 Cor. 13). Paul's teaching is in line with what Jesus taught as the prerequisite for heaven (cf. Matt. 5-7; 25:31-46; Jn. 14:6-21).

4. 1 John 4:7-8 and John. 14:21. The New Testament has put it most definitively that God is LOVE, and that those who do not love do not know God. It is very clear that those who love like God loves are his redeemed people, and it is of no consequence to what Church or even religion these people belong to! Wherever and whatever they are, all human beings as "*imago Dei*" and by the virtue of the divine Incarnation into humanity, are God's own chosen, obedient and redeemed people, and nothing can change that except God himself. We may be Christians, Jews, African Religionists, Muslims, Hindus, monks, nuns, cab-drivers, soldiers, janitors or kings, nevertheless, the religious test and requirement for salvation is the same, namely, the unconditional love for both God and the neighbor.

5. God's kingdom has already been effectively established here on earth in both creation and redemption. However, because of human sin, it now exists in a state of imperfection. Sinful human beings resist God's reign by disobedience to his will and moral laws as explicitly revealed in the Old Testament through Moses or Jesus teachings and Law of voluntary Agape and free forgiveness of sins. As result, Jesus taught his followers to practice Agape and pray for God's kingdom to be fully established on earth as it is in heaven; see Luke 11:3.

6. This eschatological kingdom of God in both its present "realized" imperfect state in the world now, and also in its potential for future perfection, is based on concrete human voluntary good deeds of grace and agape. In this respect, Jesus as the Christ affirmed that God's eschatological judgement would also be based on this criteria of agape and divine expectation of altruistic good works by all his obedient saints in the world. Of this final eschatological judgement of the world, as the final separation of God's people between the sinful, disobedient evil doers from God's obedient and holy saints, Jesus-Christ affirmed the following principles and criteria for universal ethical, "moral correctness," godliness and guidelines for an acceptable, good moral life required in God's kingdom as follows:

> When the Son of Man comes as King and all the angels with him, he will sit at on the royal throne, and the people of all nations will be gathered before him. Then he will divide them into two groups, just as a shepherd separates the sheep from the goats. He will put the righteous people at his right hand and the wicked at the left.
>
> Then the King will say to the people on his right, 'Come, you that are blessed by my Father! Come and possess the kingdom which has been prepared for you ever since the creation of the world. I was *hungry*, and you *fed* me, *thirsty* and you gave me a *drink*; I was a *stranger* and you *received me in your homes*, *naked* and you *clothed* me: I was *sick* and you *took care of me*, in *prison* and you *visited* me.'
>
> The righteous will then answer him, *'When, Lord, did we ever see you hungry and feed you, or thirsty and give you a drink*? When did we ever see you a stranger and welcome you into our homes, or naked and clothe you? When did we ever see you sick or in prison, and visit you?
>
> The King will reply, 'I tell you, *whenever you did this for one of the least of important of these brothers of mine, you did it to me.'*"
>
> "Then the King will say to those on his left, 'Away from me, you evil doers who are under God's curse! Away to the eternal fire which has been prepared for the Devil and his angels! *I was hungry but you did not feed me, thirsty, but you would not give a drink; I was a stranger, but you did not welcome me in your homes, naked but you would not clothe me; I was sick and in prison but you would not take care of me.'*
>
> Then the wicked will answer, 'When, Lord, did we ever see you hungry or thirsty or a stranger or naked or sick or in prison, and we would not help or serve you?'
>
> Then the King will reply, 'I tell you, *whenever you refused to help or serve one of these least important ones, you refused to help me*' (cf. Matt. 25:31-45) [Emphasis added].

This universal divine requirement for good works as the free praxis of agape as the path to both salvation, the kingdom of God, a good life, moral perfection, a humane world, peace and happiness should constitute the central gospel message and redemptive proclamation of Christian Church, all redemptive religions and all God's prophets and saints in the world.

To this end, Gandhi, Martin Luther King and Mother Theresa are God's modern examples of true prophets and saints. Jesus as the Christ and definitive God's messenger of agape, free divine redemptive grace, in the free forgiveness of all sins and a self-sacrificial life in the service of humanity, has set a good example for all God's saints to aim at in their lives. And also to imitate as they try to work together to transform this world into God's temporal kingdom mutual unconditional acceptance as God's children, unconditional love, free mutual forgiveness and peace.

See also, Twesigye, *The Global Human Problem*, 1-124, 147-234, 249-258; Jam. 2:12-26; I Cor. 13; 1 John 4:7-22; Rom. 1:17-32. The Hebrew Scriptures and the New Testament are in full agreement that a satisfying, good and ethical life in the world for God's saints is inseparable from their good works as evidence of the presence of the invisible indwelling power of God, personal commitment to God's work of love, mercy and justice in the world, that of God's goodness, beauty and creativity in the world.

Finally, since God is Agape, holy, just, merciful and good, so must be all God's obedient people, ambassadors and saints in the world. This is irrespective of gender, creed, religious affiliation, nationality, race, color, or class. These human barriers and categories do not count in God's consideration or kingdom, because transcends all of them. Only Agape and its praxis matters to God and shapes the actual historical and existential nature of his kingdom in the world, history and human affairs. Unloving people like Hitler and Idi Amin destroy the world whereas God seeks to redeem it through the positive deeds and self-sacrificial unconditional love of his obedient people and the saints, like Gandhi, King and Mother Theresa.

Appendix A

AUTHENTIC HUMAN EXISTENCE AND SALVATION:
A Theological Comparative Study of Christianity, Buddhism and the African Religion

by Trent Bryce Collier
A Term Paper Researched and Written under the Direction of
Professor Emmanuel K. Twesigye
as Partial Course Fulfillment for
RE 50: Radical and Liberation Theologies

> Give up your self and you will find your real self. Lose your life and you will save it. Submit to death, death of your ambitions and favorite wishes every day and death of your whole body in the end: submit with every fibre of your being, and you will find eternal life. Keep...nothing. (C.S. Lewis, *Mere Christianity*).[1]

One of the great functions, and perhaps missions, of religion is to teach us how to live authentically. This means how to view the world, ourselves, and each other from a theocentric perspective. This begins with the law; enough, at least, to show us how to behave. Our great teachers then show us that Mosaic and natural law are not enough. Our Christs, and Buddhas teach us that we are saved or damned by our spirit. Our actions are important, but they're just a reflection of our heart, mind and spirit. What counts, more than our actions, are our desires, our fears, our transgressions of thought. What counts, most of all, is our love.

As followers of religion, we believe it is possible to live authentically. More than that, we believe authentic existence has been embodied in our religious teachers: Christ, Mohammed, Buddha, and so on. Then we attempt to follow the path they have made for us, to imitate them, act as they did, and understand what they have taught. However, some religious traditions don't have one specific example of righteousness and true consciousness; neither do they have scripture. These religions are rich in myth and cultural tradition, passed orally through many, many generations. There is a common understanding of what it means to live authentically, or to be truly human. For instance, the people of Native American and African cultures, have as rich an understanding of authenticity and righteousness as our Western and Eastern religions.

It is self-evident that there is a unity in many of these religious traditions. Granted, there are major differences in faith; some religions focus on a personal God, some have no interest in God at all. Some worship Christ, some are still waiting for the Christ to come. They are almost unified, however, in their ideal of authentic existence. Perhaps true humanity for one religion is no different from true humanity in another.

In order to address this issue, I have focused on three religions: Christianity, Buddhism, and African Traditional Religion. Christianity was chosen because it is a major Western religion and since I am a Christian, it served as a point of reference for me. Buddhism is a major Eastern religion, and is very different in theology and focus from most Western traditions. African Traditional Religion has no Scripture, no prophets, and no "great teachers" such as Mohammed or Christ. It does, however, have a profound understanding of humanity and the Divine.

1. Buddhism and its Theology

> I think it is only important to love the world, not to despise it, not for us to hate each other but to be able to regard the world and ourselves and all beings with love, admiration and respect. (*Siddhartha*).[2]

Goutama Siddhartha Buddha, in the Benares Sermon, identified two extremes[3], two unauthentic modes of existence, that his disciples are to avoid. The first is a preoccupation with material things, sensuality and passions. He says, "It is a low and pagan way, unworthy, unprofitable, and fit only for the worldly minded." The second extreme is asceticism. The ascetic places himself in difficult and uncomfortable positions and maintains this for a long time as an act of prostration and proof of devoutness before the gods.

The Buddha saw this as false spiritualism is more like an act of show than one of true spiritual worth. He taught that one should follow the middle path between these extremes, that this path would lead to true understanding and peace of mind. The Noble Eight-fold Path is the way of the monk; it consist of right views, right aspirations, right speech, right conduct, right livelihood, right effort, right mindfulness, and right contemplation.[4]

The Buddha gave many instructions to the laity about righteous existence.[5] He taught: "Let him [a monk] not kill, nor cause to be killed any living being, nor let him approve of other killing." Buddhists are to abstain from stealing, from telling untruths, and are commanded to be chaste. If chastity is not possible, "...let him not transgress with another man's wife." Intoxication is forbidden, as are overeating and vanity. Buddha teaches: "Let him dutifully maintain his parents, and practice an honorable trade."

The Buddha also lectured about proper conduct for the monk.[6] He called for restraint and discipline of the body. A monk is to dwell, delight and meditate in the law; he is to speak calmly, teaching "the meaning and the law." He is not to despise, not to envy. Monks are instructed to act with kindness: "Let him live in charity, let him be perfect in his duties." Most importantly, he is to disassociate himself from material things, from natural desires, from his physical needs, and to empty himself of passion and hatred and fear. "O monk, empty this boat! If emptied, it will go quickly."

The Buddha taught that a transgression in thought is as sinful as a transgression in act: "All that we are is the result of what we have thought." Buddhists also preach a rule very much like the law of agape: "...hatred does not cease by hatred at any time. Hatred ceases by love; this is an old rule."[7] The Buddha also emphasized the necessity of thinking, reflecting, and meditating. "As rain breaks through a poorly thatched house, passion will break through an unreflecting mind."[8] Authentic existence is a life of prayer and devotion. Like the Buddha, our spiritual journey must focus inward.

It is not by knowing the law but by following it that one is a true disciple. The Buddha taught: "The thoughtless man, even if he can recite a large portion (of the law), but is not a doer of it, has no share in the priesthood...The follower of the law, even if he can recite only a small portion, but, having forsaken passion and hatred and foolishness, possesses true knowledge and serenity of mind, he caring for nothing in this world or that to come has a share in priesthood."[9]

The Buddhist teachings on authentic existence can be divided into two realms. First, there is the law. It is the Buddha's instruction to his laity, monks and nuns. The Buddhist must aim for moderation, abstinence, honesty, and respect for others. These teachings are natural law; similar dictates can be found in most cultures. The second realm deals with the "spiritual" side of authentic existence. Though this realm is made concrete in human temporal existence, it is exceedingly hard to achieve and observe.

The Buddha teaches that we must accept everything; all is good and all is necessary. Some observers of the Buddhist tradition see this as detachment, but this is far from true. Acceptance is an active process. It is a welcoming of all, a universal blessing, and unconditional love of all things. The Buddhist cherishes sorrow, pain, and death, as much as he or she cherishes joy, pleasure, and life. Furthermore, the Buddhist must achieve enlightenment through self-discipline and great commitment. Only in this way can one live authentically and then achieve Nirvana.

For the Buddhist, "salvation" is achieved through personal effort which results in the union and full realization of the Truth. It results from union with the divine, self-knowing and understanding or seeing first hand as God sees and knows us. This differs from the Western idea that salvation is a gift of God resulting in eternal life. Buddhists find salvation inwardly, and it radically affects their temporal life.

Salvation is a complete departure from previous forms of consciousness and existence. In this respect, divine salvation is an utterly new point of view of the self, other creatures and the cosmos. This enlightenment is so enriching that it permeates every aspect of life. There is no more dualism; no more right and wrong, no more just and unjust, no more good and evil. One who has achieved Nirvana no longer separates the secular from the holy, the body from spirit, or the temporal from the eternal. Authentic existence is the recognition that all is truth, is one, all is good, and all is necessary.

In *The Power of Myth,* Joseph Campbell describes the *Bodhisattva* as is the Buddhist name for "one who knows immortality, yet voluntarily enters into the field of the fragmentation of time and participates willingly and joyfully in the sorrows of the world."[10] The *Bodhisattva* is one who has achieved Nirvana, but chooses to share the sorrows of others. Campbell says: "Compassion is the awakening of the heart from bestial self-interest to humanity."[11] This "awakening of the heart to humanity" is one of the most profound understandings of what it means to be an authentic human being or a true *imago Dei*.

2. Christianity and its Theology

Do not suppose that I have come to abolish the Law and the prophets; I did not come to abolish, but to complete. I tell you this: so long as heaven and earth endure, not a letter, not a stroke, will disappear from the Law until all that must happen has happened...I tell you, unless you show yourselves far better men than the Pharisees and the doctors of the Law, you can never enter the kingdom of Heaven (Matt. 5:17-20).

When Jesus spoke these words, he was speaking of the Mosaic Covenant, of the dictates in Israel dealing with circumcision, cleanliness and food. He was fighting the false sense of spirituality of self-righteousness of the "Pharisees and doctors of the law." They followed the Mosaic law with an obsessive attention to detail, but sacrificed any real understanding of what it means to live authentically. The law isn't enough.

Jesus gave new emphasis to the God's moral law. Not only were our actions important, but so were our secret desires and emotions. Matthew 5:23-28 says: "You have learned that our forefathers were told 'Do not commit murder'...but what I tell you is this: Anyone who nurses anger against his brother must be brought to judgment. You have learned that they were told, 'Do not commit adultery.' But what I tell you is this: If a man looks on a woman with a lustful eye, he has already committed adultery with her in his heart." Salvation exceeds our physical actions. Our hearts and wills must also be with Christ.

According to Matthew (7:22) Jesus says "Many will say to me, 'Lord, Lord, did we not prophesy in your name, cast out devils in your name, and in your name perform many miracles?' Then I will tell them to their face: 'I never knew you.'" Perhaps the reverse is also true: *"You never knew me!"* The Gospel shows again and again that, not only must our actions be Christ-like, but our spirit must follow Christ's example as well.

What does it mean, then, for our spirit to follow Christ? It means we must follow the law of agape. Christ taught: "'Love the Lord your God with all your heart, with all your soul, with all your mind.' That is the greatest commandment. It comes first. The second is like it: 'Love your neighbor as yourself.' Everything in the law and the prophets hangs on these two commandments" (Matt. 22: 34-40).

Christ definitively taught that: "Do good to those who hate you; bless those who curse you; pray for those who treat you spitefully. When a man hits you on the cheek, offer him the other cheek, too...Treat others as you would like them to treat you" (Lk. 6:28-31). Jesus calls us to be selfless, self-sacrificing, to put others' needs before ours. We must forgive and love unconditionally. This is how we must be "far better men that the Pharisees." Not only must we not harm or steal from others, but we must put their interests before ours.

It is important to note that Jesus Christ never de-emphasized the importance of our actions. According to Luke 6:43 Jesus Christ says: "There is no such thing as a good tree producing worthless fruit, nor yet a worthless tree producing good fruit...A good man produces good from the store of good within himself; and an evil man from evil within produces evil. For the words that the mouth utters come from the overflowing of the heart." If one truly loves his or her neighbor, that love will naturally be manifest in action. Jesus' message is that we must love with mind, heart, spirit, and actions.

In *A Theology of Liberation,* Gustavo Gutierrez writes: "Salvation is totally and freely given by God, the communion of men with God and among themselves. It is the inner force and the fullness of this movement of man's self-generation which was initiated by the work of creation."[12] His definition of salvation is profound.

Salvation is the completion of creation. Just as we grow out of childhood, we grow out of hate, jealousy, lust, and our "animal" nature. Just as we grow into maturity and responsibility, we grow into communion with God and our neighbor. According to St. John (1 John 3:14): "We know that we have passed out of death into life, because we love the brethren. He who does not love remains in death." Our "self" dies and we become a "new being" in Christ. Roger Schmidt writes that salvation is not self-improvement and positive transformation.

Paul Tillich defined sin as separation from ourselves, from others, and from God.[13] Karl Rahner described the feeling of incompleteness that plagues us uneasiness and the feeling that something is missing.[14] Salvation, then, is the abolishment of self and unification with God, with our neighbor. It is the abolishment of sin, and the completion of ourselves. For the Christian, authentic existence is a life of agape. Jesus said we can "tell a good tree by it's fruits," the concrete manifestation of God's grace is a transformation of spirit. Christ said: "You cannot tell by observation when the kingdom of God comes. There will be no saying, 'Look, here it is!' or 'there it is!'; for in fact the kingdom of God is among you" (Lk. 17: 20-21).

3. African Traditional Religion

May you grow many foods and many crops. May you live in good houses, May you moreover live in a beautiful village. Don't quarrel with one another. Don't pursue another's spouse. Don't mock the invalid passing in the village. And he who seduces another's wife will be killed! Accept the chief. Fear him. May he also fear you. May you agree with one another, all together, no enmity in the land nor too much hate. May you bring forth tall and short children-- in so doing you will bring them forth for the chief. From *The Mwindo Epic* of the Nyanga people[15]

The study of African morality and humanity differs in many ways from the study of the established religions of the East and West. In Africa, there are no scriptures. Wisdom and common law are carried in folktales and myth. Religion and philosophy are written in the actions and expressions of the African people. In a culture where there is no distinction between the sacred and the profane, one must look to everyday life and interactions to find what it means to be authentically human.

African religion also differs from Eastern and Western religion in its attitude toward the individual. African scholar John Mbiti writes: "I am because we are and, since we are, therefore I am."[16] One is an individual only in relation to the community, and is defined by the social group to which he or she belongs. Though African philosophy does recognize the uniqueness of individual personality given by the Creator, the community defines where one comes from, who one is, and what one may become. It is not surprising, then, that what makes an act "good" or "evil" in African Philosophy is its effect upon relationships, not any intrinsic value. Mbiti demonstrates this very clearly: "Kindness is not a virtue unless someone is kind; murder is not evil until someone kills another person in his community. Man is not by nature either 'good' or 'bad' except in terms of what he does or does not do."[17]

Following the customs of the society and co-existing peacefully with one's community is pleasing to God. Likewise, the offense of an individual is, in God's sight, the offense of the social group, and is punished with "locusts, floods, or other calamities," in Mbiti's words.[18] Authentic existence depends on harmony and peaceful co-existence with one's temporal neighbor. Although "evil" acts depend solely on their effects upon relationships, African theology does have specific examples of what "good character" consists of. Mbiti lists these in *African Religion and Philosophy:* "chastity before marriage and faithfulness during marriage; hospitality; generosity, the opposite of selfishness; kindness; justice, truth, and rectitude; avoiding stealing; keep a covenant and avoiding falsehood; protecting the poor and weak; avoiding hypocrisy."[19]

Indeed, the focus of African morality is the community, not necessarily the spirit. Mbiti calls it "a morality of conduct rather than a morality of being."[20] African religion does have a spiritual aspect, however, and does move beyond one's temporal actions to the root of those actions. In *Common Ground*, Professor Emmanuel Twesigye discussed at length the African Bantu philosophy of authentic existence.

In this philosophy, *obuntu* is the essence of authentic being, and *omuntu* is one who lives authentically. It is a state of agape, of true love and concern for one's brothers and sisters. Twesigye writes: "*Omuntu* is...a human being who is essentially humane, considerate, loving, social, able-bodied, and a willing participatory member of the respective human community."[21] There is emphasis on one's actions, especially in terms of the community, as well as emphasis on one's spirit. One must *love* the neighbor, as well as behave in a loving manner.

One is created incomplete *(abantu)*, and living authentically and humanely constitute the societal process of divine salvation. In this context, divine salvation is the acquisition of agape *(obuntu)*. This is complete humanization within the concrete societal context and in relation to the community. *Obuntu* is essential for good relationships, trust, solidarity, and, in Professor Twesigye's words, "harmony and cohesion."[22]

True humanity, for the African, also precludes a spiritual orientation. The community consists of ancestral spirits and other supernatural forces, as well as the "human" community. *Obuntu* is openness, awareness, and receptiveness to God. Authentic human existence, for the African, is positive orientation to God *through* one's neighbor.

4. The Wonder of God

"But I don't want comfort. I want God, I want poetry, I want real danger, I want freedom, I want goodness, I want sin." "In fact," said Mustapha Mond, "you're claiming the right to be unhappy." "All right then," said the Savage defiantly.

"I'm claiming the right to be unhappy," he added. "Not to mention the right to grow old and ugly and impotent; the right to have syphilis and cancer; the right to have too little to eat; the right to be lousy; the right to live in constant apprehension of what may happen tomorrow; the right to catch typhoid; the right to be tortured by unspeakable pains of every kind." There was a long silence. "I claim them all," said the Savage at last. Mustapha Mond shrugged his shoulders. "You're are welcome," he said. (Aldous Huxley, *Brave New World*.)[23]

The great mythological scholar Joseph Campbell once said, referring to Jesus, Buddha, and Muhammad: "These heroes of religion came back with the *wonder* of God, not with the blueprint of God."[24] Perhaps this is the best definition of authentic humanity, which is the temporal embodiment of the wonder, majesty, and universality of God. It is the transcending of the image of "reality" that we have built up; getting past our image of what and who we are to what is eternal and divine in each of us. Christ and Buddha are the personification of the Divine. *Obuntu* is the African equivalent of *imago dei*, the image of God in man.

We must first transcend our image of "self." To love one's neighbor is to make the neighbor's wants, needs, fears, and joys our own. Joseph Campbell writes that, in order to "love thy neighbor as thyself," one must recognize that the neighbor *is* "thyself."[25] In African religion, the community acts as a whole before God. For the Buddhist, salvation hinges upon harmonious coexistence with all creation. Christ's two commandments are to love God and love one's neighbor. In all three traditions, divine salvation is recognizing that, above all, one is simply a part of the community of God and living in communion and unconditional acceptance of all creation.

Secondly, one must transcend dualistic thinking. The achievement of this transcendence is Nirvana lies in the recognition that nothing is "good" or "bad" but that everything simply *is*. In African philosophy, there is no separation of the divine from the profane; God is present in all. For the Christian, this requires a radical shift from looking for God's kingdom in some eschatological afterlife to finding the Kingdom of Heaven *here* and *now,* as Christ taught us to. It is to see the pain and suffering that comes with simply being alive as among the greatest of God's blessings.

Authentic human existence is acceptance of the God within. It is a concrete and positive manifestation of agape, which is the most wonderful gift of God's kingdom and divine salvation. True humanity is present in every religious tradition. We have similar laws, similar philosophies, but different images and symbols. Carl Jung spoke about our "collective unconscious," that which is written on the soul of every human being. Since we are all children of the same God, it is not surprising that we should have the same goals and dreams, the same fears, and the same need of communion with our God, each other, and ourselves.

NOTES

1. C.S. Lewis, *Mere Christianity*, 175.
2. Hermann Hesse, *Siddhartha,* 119.
3. Robert E. Van Voorst, *Anthology of World Scriptures,* 83.
4. Ibid. 83.
5. Ibid. 89-91.
6. Ibid. 88.
7. Ibid. 90.

8. Ibid. 91.
9. Ibid. 91.
10. Joseph Campbell, *The Power of Myth*, 201.
11. Ibid. 201.
12. Gustavo Gutierrez, *A Theology of Liberation*, 159.
13. Paul Tillich, *The Shaking of the Foundations*, 25-35.
14. As noted by Emmanuel Twesigye in *Common Ground* (1987), Chapter Two.
15. Roger Abrahams, *African Folktales*, 294.
16. John Mbiti, African Religion and Philosophy, 214.
17. Ibid. 214.
18. Ibid. 206.
19. Ibid. 212-213.
20. Ibid. 214.
21. See, Twesigye, *Common Ground*, Chapter Four.
22. Ibid. Chapter Four.
23. Aldous Huxley, *Brave New World*, 246-247.
24. Joseph Campbell, *The Power of Myth*, 173.
25. Ibid. 139.

REFERENCES

Abrahams, Roger D. *African Folktales*. New York: Pantheon Books, 1983.
Campbell, Joseph. *The Power of Myth*. New York: Anchor Books, 1988.
Gutierrez, Gustavo. *A Theology of Liberation*. Maryknoll, New York: Orbis, 1973.
Hesse, Hermann. *Siddhartha*. New York: New Directions Publishing Co. 1957.
Huxley, Aldous. *Brave New World*. New York: Harper Collins Publishers, 1932.
Kierkegaard, Soren. *Attack Upon "Christendom."* Princeton: Princeton Uni. Press, 1944.
Lewis, C.S. *Mere Christianity*. New York: Macmillan Company, 1943.
Mbiti, John S. *African Religions & Philosophy*. New York: Praeger Publishers, 1969.
Monk, R.; Hofheinz, W., et al. *Exploring Religious Meaning*. New Jersey: Prentice-Hall, 1973.
Oduyoye, Mercy Amba. *Hearing and Knowing*. Maryknoll: Orbis, 1986.
Price, James. L. *Interpreting the New Testament*. New York: Holt, Rinehart, 1961.
Ray, Benjamin C. *African Religions*. New Jersey: Prentice-Hall, Inc., 1976.
Schmidt, Roger. *Exploring Religion*. Belmont: California: Wadsworth, 1980.
Tillich, Paul. *The Eternal Now*. New York: Charles Scribner's Sons, 1963.
_____. *The New Being*. New York: Charles Scribner's Sons, 1955.
_____. *The Shaking of the Foundations*. New York: Scribner's Sons, 1948.
Twesigye, Emmanuel K. *Common Ground*. New York: Peter Lang, 1987.
----------. *God, Race, Myth and Power*. New York: Peter Lang, 1991.
----------. *The Global Human Problem*. New York: Peter Lang, 1988.
Voorst, Robert E. Van. *Anthology of World Scriptures*. Belmont: Wadsworth, 1994.

Appendix B

A GLOSSARY OF SOME KEY WORDS
AND AFRICAN TERMS

(Most of these words are Bantu words taken from East and Central Africa. Most words come from Lunyoro, Luganda, Rukiga-Runyankole, Runyarwanda, and Swahili, unless otherwise noted.)

Abafumu: Medicine people, prophets and visionaries. These charismatic gifts and powers are attributed with supernatural powers to heal, bless or curse.

Abantu/Bantu: Human beings. This category includes only those who are alive. It does not include the living-dead or the ancestors. However, the community of the "*abantu*" includes the ancestors, even when they are no longer alive. This an African form of immortality. The living people immortalize the dead through libation or sacrifices, and the positive perpetuation of their names and memories. (See "*Bantu*" below).

Balokole: Luganda word meaning literally "the saved ones" or those "born again." The Balokole are the major Evangelical group in East Africa. The Balokole tend to be fundamentalist and religiously conservative. They are theologically and liturgically akin to the American Southern Baptists.

Bantu: Human beings; the African people of most of East Africa, Central and South Africa who speak related languages employing the root word *NTU* for a human being or another form of being. Nevertheless, these concepts are similar to those of West Africa, but under different names. However, different names for God or concepts, do not mean different religions, as some people very naively tend to think. Only those who are living are referred to as *Abantu/Bantu* or people. The dead or "living-dead" are the departed, ghosts, "*mizimu*" or ancestors. The good people (*Bantu*) who die become the venerated ancestors and the wicked ones turn into hated *mizimu*.

Buntu: Human qualities that make human beings (*Bantu*) humane, such as love, kindness, patience, and gentleness. *Buntu* constitute the *Bantu*.

Bachwezi: The legendary founders of the ancient East African empires and kingdoms. They are now part of the Traditional Religious cult in most of Uganda, Rwanda and Burundi, serving the benevolent role of watchful ancestral spirits and guardians of statehood.

Categorial: This is Rahner's technical term for the finite human existential condition. This condition includes the dimensions of time, history, location, space and concreteness. Temporal has been employed in this work, in order to capture some central aspects of Rahner's usage of the term.

Dini: A Swahili word for (foreign) religion. This word was introduced by the Arabs because the Africans generally lacked a separate word for religion. This absence of the word for religion was largely due to the fact that in African thinking and ontology, to be truly a human being was the same as being religious. This was the case since in African understanding, each person was considered to be theocentric by an *a priori* intrinsic nature, and as such a religious being, by essential nature "*qua* being." As such, there are no atheists in Traditional Africa. Every human being is religious by essential basic "divine" or theocentric constitutive nature, essence, cultural and moral conditioning or humanization.

Subsequently, the African Religion has no special separate name for itself apart from humanity, and culture. Therefore, in African thinking, the local African Religion's name or identity is the same as that of the local people of which it is co-extensive. This is the case since religion and human modes of existence are one and the same inseparable theocentric dimensions of African human existence, and self-consciousness. Therefore, for the African life is a sacred reality which intrinsically inseparable from both God and godly living or religion.

Eiguru/Iguru: Sky or heaven; God's dwelling place. It is supposed to good. It is the source and destiny of time, creation, human beings and happiness. Kintu (Adam) and Nambi (Eve) came from God in heaven, and they returned there after death as spirits and ancestors of humankind.

Emizimu/Mizimu: The spirits of the dead. The bad "*mizimu*" are those of the dead wicked people. These possess people in order to carry out their malicious activities or vengeance. The *"Bafumu"* (Priests) and medicine people are consulted to come and exorcise or "bust them." In reality, Africa has always had its own "Ghost Busters" in the form of the *"Bafumu."*

Ensi/Nsi: World, the Earth; land as opposed to sky or heaven; the human dwelling place. Human beings and living creatures were created to live there as their heaven; that is if they obey the natural and moral laws of God.

Imaana/Imana: Runyarwanda word for God. The same as "Amun" or "Amen" in ancient Egypt. God is the Creator is a Cosmic Mystery. Some people think that God dwells in the impenetrable mountain cloudy tops, and terrifying fires of the Birunga volcanic mountain ranges. Evil people are thought to be judged and thrown into the fire in the volcano or hell as punishment for disobedience, sin and evil.

Juju: A kind of West African form of Voodoo. It is a kind of witchcraft by remote control. It is also the exercise of supernatural power for negative purposes, so as to cause harm, death or other kinds of evil.

Katonda: Luganda word for the cosmic transcendent Creator or God. *"Katonda ye atonda."* God is the one who creates. God who does not create is a mere created secondary power or an idol. Only the Creator is worthy of worship.

Kazoba/Kazooba: The Great Light; the Enlightener; the Cosmic Seer or the Omniscient; the Sun the Creator; Amen-Ra in the case of Egypt. The Sun was thought to be God's cosmic visible symbol of light, power, warmth, growth, health, goodness, creativity and productivity. However, the less sophisticated villagers tended to believe that the Sun was God in itself, since without it, the world gets engulfed by darkness, evil, fear, hidden dangers, unproductivity and death.

Kucwa: To curse; to ostracize or excommunicate a guilty person from the humanizing fellowship of the human community. This amounts to social death. The ritually ostracized person is considered both socially and spiritually dead. Therefore, the ostracized person is also regarded as both socially and religiously unclean and untouchable. Roman Catholicism has very effectively replaced this African traditional practice with excommunication. The religious and social consequences for the unfortunate victims of "*Kucwa*" and excommunication are comparably similar.

NTU: Bantu term which means "Being" in Tillich or Heiddegar's usage of the term. It is the underlying and cosmic omnipresent Essence, Vital Force or Ultimate Reality in which all beings participate in order to obtain their own being or reality.

    As *NTU* the Ultimate Reality Cosmic Creative Force, *NTU* is the same as God in the philosophical and theological teachings of Justin Martyr, Origen, Thomas Aquinas, Hegel, Paul Tillich, and Rahner. It is the totality of Infinite Being in which beings merely participate for their own concretization and finite being. *NTU* is existence. It is the cosmic creative force or vitality. God and human beings are the self-consciousness of "*NTU.*" *UNTU* is the fundamental reality or essence of existence and cosmic divine creativity. See *Ozovehe*.

Obuntu/Buntu: The same as "*Buntu.*" The essence of humanity or being humane, and humanized. The good qualities that constitute humaneness.

Omuntu/Muntu: Singular of "*Bantu.*" Human being. The embodiment of mind of "*NTU.*" The human being as "*Omuntu*" is "*imago Dei*" because of participation and embodiment of *NTU* or God.

Omunsi: In the world; belonging to the world; mundane.

Omwiguru/Gulu: In heaven; belonging to the heavenly or divine. Being with God. The sky. A place where God dwells. The opposite of "*omunsi.*"

Ozovehe: This is a West African term which almost means the same thing as *NTU*. It stands for God and the cosmic ultimate essential force of creativity. It denotes God as the cosmic spiritual ground of material being or creation, and the correlative natural processes of concretization and animation or spiritualization.

Ruhanga/Nyamuhanga: The Supreme Being; the Creator; God. The same as "Katonda" or "Mungu" in Swahili.

Sasa: Swahili word meaning the present time. Sasa also means the present state of affairs or present reality. Sasa covers several months. It covers both the vivid or immediate past as well as the immediate future. This is the very arena of African life. For the African, life is meaningfully lived within this perimeter of the present time. Time as reckoned by the events of daily life and measured by major events, therefore, events which are either too far in the past or in the distant future is are irrelevant and meaningless for the ordinary traditional African. As result, it has no appeal for the average African. Therefore, it is important to note that in most African languages, there is no native word for the distant future, and in some cases, there is no word for time beyond tomorrow!

Shalom/Salaamu: God's transcendent peace. The African Muslims use the word as a greeting and as benediction or prayer for peace. In this respect, the Muslims identify themselves explicitly as the people of peace. As a result, the Muslims are referred to as "*Aba-Salaamu*" (those of peace).

However, in some Bantu languages and cultures of East Africa, the term "*sala*" also means to cut or "mutilate." Consequently, "*Abasalamu*" can be used negatively as a derogatory term. In this pejorative sense the word "*Musalamu*" can be used to mean those who mutilate themselves (i.e. those who circumcise).

Since some Africans groups, such as many Bantu groups of East Africa, Central and Southern Africa generally believe that it is unfortunate for the body to be mutilated in anyway, or for the male genital to have a big opening (*empaari*), in the parts of Africa both the practice of circumcision and Islam are generally despised. However, with exposure to Western secular values, Christianity and gradual dying out of some of these traditional African customs, Islam is beginning to have greater appeal to these Africans due to its greater promises for Arab fiscal assistance, wealth and polygamous practices.

Zamani: Time in African Ontology: Swahili word meaning the past. This may refer to the events of just a few years or the antiquity. John S. Mbiti's contention is that African life is oriented to the known past or *Zamani*. *Zamani* constitutes heaven as the glorious lost paradise.

Like in the biblical book of Genesis, this *Zamani* as heaven or Garden of Eden was lost to humanity due to human rebellion, sin and the fall or expulsion by God from the realm of immortality, perfection, happiness and plenty to the life of imperfection, finite, disease, pain, scarcity and death. Subsequently, in Africa, there are more glorious stories of the past, the despair at the present time and little planning for the unseen and unknown future.

Therefore, most of the serious problems of Africa today, are largely due to a lack of sound vision and lack of access to modern technology. As a result, most of Africa suffers from poverty, poor education, and incompetent poor leadership. Lack of vision and sound agenda has led to the familiar general poor planning for the future and the mismanagement of the economy and other important resources, including the citizens.

Since, the remote future is meaningless, therefore, most African leaders, just also characteristically plan in a traditional African mode, which leads to political incompetence and economic underdevelopment. They fail to fit into a global world order and the economy, because these leaders plan for survival "today/now and tomorrow as the immediate future," instead of the decades and centuries still to come.

Consequently, most of the African recurrent chronic major problems, such as famine and food shortages, can be more effectively dealt with, if Africa shifts from a *"Zamani"* oriented mode of life, and adapts a more practical future oriented one.

Obviously, Africans need to develop a better future dimension of time. This is essential in order to create better future-oriented and more effective development time-tables, agendas, dreams and utopias. This is desirable as a mechanism to project them more successfully into the future as the unknown, unmarked and unexplored territory or dimension, which requires some kind of planning maps, which have been marked with the guiding lights over the horizon, which are ever beckoning and inviting the Africans to come closer to a better mode of technology and experience of life. By this clear vision of the future, and more effective socio-economic planning Africa can, thereby, travel forward and toward more meaningful development, self-fulfillment, and perfection in the future mode of life and positive eschatological recapture of heaven, which was lost in the primordial time of *"Zamani"* or the "Garden of Eden."

This process of practical or technical education in agriculture, sciences, technology, medicine, global economy, and effective planning for economic development and better medical programs should be the foundation of any meaningful post-colonial Western Christian missionary activity in Africa and other parts of the world where Anonymous Christianity has already done a good job to redeem the human spirit, yet, the physical body and environment still need God's care, redemption and restoration to wholeness.

BIBLIOGRAPHY

Selected Primary Works by Karl Rahner

The Church and Sacraments. New York: Herder and Herder, 1963.

Christian at the Crossroads. New York: Seabury Press, 1975.

Encyclopedia of Theology: The Concise Sacramentum Mundi. New York: Seabury, 1975.

Faith Today. London: Sheed and Ward, 1967.

Foundations of Christian Faith. New York: Seabury Press, 1978.

Grace in Freedom. New York: Herder and Herder, 1969.

Hominization: The Evolutionary Origin of Man as a Theological Problem. New York: Herder and Herder, 1965.

Karl Rahner: A Reader. Edited by Gerald A. McCool. New York: Seabury Press, 1975.

On the Theology of Death. New York: Herder and Herder, 1961.

Opportunities for Faith. New York: Seabury Press, 1974.

Prayers and Meditations. Edited by John Griffith. New York: Seabury Press, 1980.

Revelation and Tradition. New York: Herder and Herder, 1966.

Spirit in the World. New York: Herder and Herder, 1968.

Theological Investigations 1: "God, Christ, Mary and Grace." London: Darton, Longman and Todd, 1961.

Theological Investigations 2: "Man in the Church." London: Darton, Longman and Todd, 1963; New York: Seabury Press, 1975.

Theological Investigations 3: "The Theology of the Spiritual Life." London: Darton, Longman and Todd, 1967; New York: Seabury Press, 1974.

Theological Investigations 4: "More Recent Writings." London: Darton, Longman and Todd, 1966; New York: Seabury Press, 1974.

Theological Investigations 5: "Later Writings." London: Darton, Longman and Todd, 1966; New York: Seabury Press, 1975.

Theological Investigations 6: "Concerning Vatican Council II." London: Darton, Longman and Todd, 1969; New York: Seabury Press, 1974.

Theological Investigations 7: "Further Theology of the Spiritual Life 1." London: Darton, Longman and Todd, 1971; New York: Seabury Press, 1972.

Theological Investigations 8: "Further Theology of the Spiritual Life 2." London: Darton, Longman and Todd, 1971; New York: Seabury Press, 1972.

Theological Investigations 9: "Writings of 1965-1967 1." London: Darton, Longman and Todd, 1972; New York: Seabury Press, 1973.

Theological Investigations 10: "Writings of 1965-1967 2." London: Darton, Longman and Todd, 1973; New York: Seabury Press, 1973.

Theological Investigations 11: "Confrontations 1." London: Darton, Longman and Todd, 1974; New York: Seabury Press, 1974.

Theological Investigations 12: "Confrontations 2." London: Darton, Longman and Todd, 1975; New York: Seabury Press, 1975.

Theological Investigations 13: "Theology, Anthropology, Christology," trans. David Bourke. New York: Seabury Press, 1975.

Theological Investigations 14: "Ecclesiology, Questions in the Church, The Church in the World," trans. David Bourke. New York: Seabury Press, 1976.

Theological Investigations 16: "Experience of the Spirit; Sources of Theology," trans. david Morland, O.S.B. New York: Seabury Press, 1979.

Theological Investigations 17: "Jesus, Man, and the Church," trans. Margaret Khol. New York: Seabury Press, 1981.

Theological Investigations 20: "Concern for the Church," trans. Edward Quinn. New York: Seabury Press, 1981.

Ed., *Sacramentum Mundi: An Encyclopedia of Theology.* 6 vols. New York: Seabury Press, 1968-1970.

Selected General Bibliography

Abbott, Walter M., S. J., and Gallagher, Very Rev. Msgr., eds. and trans. *The Documents of Vatican II*, with an Introduction by Lawrence Cardinal Shehan. Chicago: Association Press/Follet Publishing Company, 1966.

Abraham, W. E. *The Mind of Africa.* Chicago: University of Chicago Press, 1962.

Achebe, Chinua. *Arrow of God.* New York: John Day, 1964.

Aquinas, Thomas. *Providence and Predestination.* Indiana: Regnery/ Gateway, 1961.

_____. *Summa Theologica: 4 vols.* Rome: Vatican Press, 1948.

_____. *Summa contra Gentiles.* Rome: Vatican Press, 1934.

Athanasius. "On the Incarnation of the Word." *Christology of the Later Fathers.* Edited by Edward Rochie Hardy. Philadelphia: The Westminster Press, 1954.

Atterbury, A. P. *Islam in Africa.* New York and London: G. Putnam's Sons, 1899.

Baeta, C. Gonsalues. *Christianity in Tropical Africa.* London: Oxford Uni., 1968.

Banks, John G. *Healing Everywhere.* Richmond: St. Luke's Press, 1980.

Barnette, Donald and Njama, Karari. *Mau Mau from Within.* London: MacGibben and Kee, 1966.

Barr, J. *Fundamentalism.* Philadelphia: The Westminster Press, 1978.

Barrett, D. B. *Schism and Renewal in Africa: An Analysis of Two Thousand Independent Churches.* Nairobi: Oxford Press, 1968.

_____, ed. *World Christian Encyclopedia: A Comparative Survey of Churches and Religions in the Modern World A.D. 1900-2000.* London: Oxford Uni., 1982.

Barrett, David B. *African Initiatives in Religion.* Kenya, Nairobi: EAPH, 1971.

Barrett, William. *Irrational Man: A Study in Existential Philosophy.* New York: Doubleday & Co., Inc., 1962.

Barth, Karl. *Church Dogmatics: A Selection.* Introduction by Helmut Gollwitzer. Translated by G. W. Bromley. New York: Harper & Row, 1961.

_____. *Church Dogmatics.* Vol. 3. New York: Scribner's Sons, 1960.

_____. *Dogmatics in Outline.* London: S.C.M., 1949.

_____. *The Epistle to the Romans.* London: Oxford University Press, 1933.

_____. *Evangelical Theology: An Introduction.* New York: Holt& Winston, 1963.

_____. *The Humanity of God.* Richmond, Va.: John Knox Press, 1960.

_____. *Protestant Theology in the Nineteenth Century.* NY: Harper & Row, 1959.

Bascom, William. *Ifa Divination: Communion between Gods and Men in West Africa.* Bloomington: Indiana University Press, 1968.

Baxter, P. T. W. "The Kiga," *East African Chiefs.* Ed. by A.I. Richards. New York: Praeger, 1959.

Beattie, John, and Middleton, eds. *The Banyoro*. New York: APC, 1964.

_____, eds. *Spirit Mediumship and Society in Africa*. New York: APC, 1969.

Beetham, T. A. *Christianity and the New Africa*. New York: Fred. A. Praeger, 1967.

Beier, Ulli. *African Mud Scripture*. Cambridge: Cambridge University Press, 1963.

_____. *African Poetry: An Anthology of Traditional African Poems*. Cambridge, England: Cambridge University Press, 1969.

_____. *Contemporary Art in Africa*. Pall Mall Press, 1968.

_____. *Introduction to African Literature*. London: Longmans, Green, 1967.

p'Bitek, Okot. *African Religions in Western Scholarship*. Kampala: EALB, 1970.

_____. *Religion of the Central Luo*. Nairobi: East African Literature Bureau, 1975.

_____. *The Song of Lawino*. Nairobi: East African Publishing House 1960.

Booth, Newell S. *African religions: A Symposium*. New York: NOK Publishers, 1977.

Brother-Andrew. *Battle for Africa*. London: Marshall Morgan and Scott, 1977.

Brown, Collin. *Philosophy and the Christian Faith*. Downers Grove, ll.: IVP, 1968.

Brunner, Emil. *Man in Revolt*. Philadelphia: Westminster Press, 1948.

_____. *Moral Man and Immoral Society*. New York: Scribner's Sons, 1960.

Bultmann, Rudolf K. *Modern Theology: Selections from Twentieth Century* Ed. with Introduction and notes by E. J. Tinsley. London: Epworth Press, 1973.

_____. *Jesus and the Word*. New York: Charles Scribner's Sons, 1934.

_____. *Kerygma and Myth*. New York: Harper & Row, 1961.

_____. *Theology of the New Testament*. New York: Charles Scribner's Sons, 1955.

Buscaglia, Leo. *Love*. New York: Fawcett Crest, 1972.

Chadwick, O. *The Victorian Church: An Ecclesiastical History of The Church*. London: Oxford University Press, 1950.

Church, J. E. *Awake Uganda*. Kampala: Uganda Bookshop Press, 1954.

Clark, Gordon H. *Thales to Dewey: A History of Philosophy*. Massachusetts: The Riverside Press, 1957.

Cobb, John. *Christ in a Pluralistic Age*. Philadelphia: The Westminster Press, 1975.

_____. *Christian Natural Theology: Based on the Thought of Alfred North Whitehead*. Philadelphia: The Westminster Press, 1965.

_____. *God and the Word*. Philadelphia: Westminster Press, 1969.

_____. *The Structure of Christian Existence*. Philadelphia: Westminster Press, 1967.

Cousins, Ewert H., ed. *Hope and the Future of Man*. Philadelphia: Fortress Press, 1972.

_____, ed. *Process Theology: Basic Writings by Key Thinkers of a Major Modern Movement* New York: Newman Press, 1971.

Desai, Ram. *Christianity in Africa as Seen by Africans*. Denver: Allan Swallow, 1962.

Dewart, L *The foundations of Beliefs*. New York: Herder, 1969.

Dickson, Kwensi, and Ellingworth, P. *Biblical Revelation and African Beliefs*. London: Lutterworth Press, 1969.

Dumery, henry. *The Problem of God in Philosophy of Religion*. Translated by Charles Courtney. Northwestern University Press, 1964.

Edel, M. M. *The Chigga of Western Uganda*. London: Oxford University Press, 1957.

Evans, Christopher Francis. *Is Holy Scripture Christian?* London: CM Press, 1971.

Evans-Pritchard, R. *Nuer Religion*. Oxford: Oxford University Press, 1956.

_____. *Theories of Primitive Religion*. Oxford: Clarendon Press, 1965.

Fagg, W. B. *African Tribal Images*. Cleveland: Cleveland Museum of Art, 1968.

_____. *Tribes and Forms in African Art*. New York: Tudor, 1965.

Fagg, W. B., and Elisafon, Eliot. *The Sculpture of Africa*. New York: Praeger, 1958.

Fallers, Llyod A., ed. *The King's Men: Leadership and Status in Uganda on the Eve of Independence*. London: Oxford University Press, 1964.

Farley, Edward. *Ecclesial Man: A Social Phenomenology of Faith and Reality*. Philadelphia: Fortress Press, 1975.

Feuerbach, Ludwig. *The Essence of Religion*. Translated by Ralph Manheim. New York: Harper & Row, 1967.

Findlay, John. *Hegel: A Re-examination*. New York: Oxford University Press, 1958.

Finney, G. *Revivals of Religion*. London: SCM Press, 1954.

Forde, Daryll, ed. *African World: Studies in the Cosmological Ideas and Social Values of African Peoples*. New York: Oxford University Press, 1968.

Fortes, Meyer, and Dieterlen, G., eds. *African Systems of Thought*. New York: Oxford University Press, 1965.

Foucault, Michael. *The Order of Things: An Archaeology of the Human Sciences*. New York: Vintage Press, Random House.

Froelich, J. Claude. *Les Musulmans dans l'Afrique noire*. Paris: de l'Oriente, 1964.

Fuller, R. H. *The Mission and Achievement of Christ*. London: SCM Press, 1959.

_____. *Foundations of New Testament Christology*. New York: C. Scribner, 1965.

Gaba, Christian. *Scriptures of an African People: The Sacred Utterances of the Anlo*. New York: NOK Publishers, 1973.

Gelpi, Donald, S. J. *Light and Life: A Guide to the Theology of Karl Rahner*. New York: Sheed and Ward, 1966.

Gilkey, Ladon. *Catholicism Confronts Modernity: A Protestant View*. New York: Seabury Press, 1975.

_____. *Message and Existence: An Introduction to Christian Theology*. New York: Seabury Press, 1980.

Graham, B. *World Aflame*. New York: The Worlds Word, Ltd., 1966.

Green, M., ed. *The Truth of God Incarnate*. London: Hodder and Stoughton, 1977.

Greenburg, J. *The Influence of Islam on a Sudanese Religion*. NY: Augustine, 1947.

Guilleband, L. *A Grain of Mustard Seed*. London: C.M.S. Press, 959.

Guthriew, W. K. C. *The Greek Philosophers: From Thales to Aristotle*. New York: Harper & Row, 1950.

Gutierrez, Gustavo. *A Theology of Liberation: History, Politics and Salvation*. Translated and edited by Sister Cardidad Inda and John Eagleson. New York: Orbis, 1973.

Hardy, Edward R. *Christology of the Later Fathers*. Phila.: Westminster Press, 1954.

Harrelson, Walter. *The Ten Commandments and Human Rights*. Philadelphia: Fortress Press, 1973.

Harris, Lyndon P. *Islam in East Africa*. London: Uni. Mission to Central Africa, 1954.

Hartshorne, Charles. *The Divine Relativity: A Social Conception of God*. New Haven: Yale University Press, 1978.

Hastings, A. *African Christianity*. New York: Seabury Press, 1976.

_____. *Christian Marriage in Africa*. London: S.P.C.K., 1959.

_____. *Church and Mission in Modern Africa*. London: Burns and Bates, 1967.

_____. *The Faces of God*. London: Geoffrey and Chapman, 1975.

Hatch, Edwin. *The Influence of Greek Ideas on Christianity*. Gloucester, Mass., 1970.

Hayward, Victor E. W., ed. *African Independent Church Movements*. London: Edinburgh House Press, 1963.

Hegel, G. W. F. *The Christian Religion: Lectures on the Philosophy of Religion Part III (The Revelatory, Consummate, Absolute Religion)*. Edited and translated by Peter C.

Hodgson, based on the edition by George Lasson. American Academy of Religion: Scholars Press, 1979.

————. *Phenomenology of Spirit*. Translated by A. V. Miller, with Analysis of the text and Foreword by J. N. Findlay. New York: Oxford University Press, 1977.

Heidegger, Martin. *Being and Time*. Translated by John Macquarrie and Edward Robinson. New York: Harper & Row, 1962.

————. *The Question Concerning Technology and other Essays*. Trans. and with Introduction by William Lovitt. New York: Harper & Row, 1977.

————. *What Is a Thing?* Translated by W. B. Barton, Jr., and Vera Deutsch. Analysis by Eugene T. Gendlin. Chicago: Gateway, 1967.

Hick, John. *Evil and the God of Love*. New York: Harper & Row, 1978.

Hewitt, G. *The Problems of Success: A History of the Church Missionary Society 1910-1942*. London: C.M.S. Press, 1960.

Hillman, E. *Polygamy Reconsidered*. London: Orbis, 1975.

Hobley, Charles W. *Bantu Beliefs and Magic*. London: Franklin Cass, 1967.

Hodgson, Peter C. *Jesus—Word and Presence: An Essay in Christology*. Philadelphia: Fortress Press, 1971.

————. *New Birth of Freedom: A Theology of Bondage and Liberation*. Philadelphia: Fortress Press, 1976.

Holmes, Urban T. *To Speak of God*. New York: Seabury Press, 1974.

————. *What is Anglicanism?* Wilton, Conn.: Morehouse-Barlow, 1982.

Hughes, Langston. *Poems from Black Africa*. Bloomington: Indiana Uni. Press, 1963.

Hunter, David E., and Whitten, Philip, eds. *Encyclopedia of Anthropology*. New York: Harper & Row, 1976.

Idowu, E. Bolaji. *African Traditional Religion: A Definition*. Maryknoll: Orbis 1973.

————. *Towards an Indigenous Church*. London: Oxford University Press, 1965.

Ignatius of Loyola, St. *The Spiritual Exercises of St. Ignatius*. Edited by Louis J. Puhl. Chicago: Loyola University Press, 1951.

Ilogu, Edmund. *Christianity and Igbo Culture*. New York: NOK Publishers, 1973.

Jahn, Jahnheinz. *Muntu: An Outline of the New African Culture*. New York: Grove Press, 1961.

James, William. *The Varieties of Religious Experience: A Study in Human Nature*. Introduction by Reinhold Niebuhr. New York: Collier MacMillan Publishers, 1974.

Janzen, John and MacGaffey, Wyatt. *An Anthology of Kongo Religion*. Lawrence, Kans.: University of Kansas Press, 1974.

Jessop, T. E., Brunner, Emil, et al. *The Christian Understanding of Man*. New York: Willett, Clark & Co., 1938.

John of the Cross, St. *The Collected Works of St. John of the Cross*. Trans. by Kieran Kavanaugh and O. Rodriguez. Washington: Institute of Carmelite Studies, 1960.

Johnston, William. *The Inner Eye of Love: Mysticism and Religion*. New York: Harper & Row, 1978.

Kagame, Alexis. *La Philosophie Bantu-Rwandaise de l'Etre*. Brussels: Academie Royale des Sciences Coloniales, 1956.

Kaggwa, Apolo. *The Kings of Buganda*. Translated with an introduction by S. Kiwanuka. East African Publishing House, 1971.

Kant, Immanuel. *Groundwork of the Metaphysic of Morals*. NY: Harper & Row, 1956.

————. *Prolegomena to Any Future Metaphysics*. Indianapolis: Bobbs-Merrill Educational Publishing, 1979.

Kasemann, E. *New Testament Questions for Today*. Philadelphia: Fortress Press, 1969.

Kaufmann, Walter. *Existentialism from Dostoevsky to Sartre*. New York: A Meridian Book, New American House, 1975.

_____. *Systematic Theology: A Historical Perspective*. New York: Scribner, 1968.

Kenyatta, Jomo. *Facing Mount Kenya*. New York: Random House, 1962.

Kierkegaard, Soren. *Philosophical Fragments*. Translated and Introduced by David Swenson. Princeton: Princeton University Press, 1974.

King, Noel Q. *Religions of Africa: A Pilgrimage into Traditional Religions*. New York: Harper & Row, 1970.

Kivengere, Festo. *When God Moves*. Accra: Asempa, 1970.

Kiwanuka, S. M. *A History of Buganda from Early Times up to 1900*. Nairobi: Longmans, 1972.

_____. *Mutesa*. Nairobi: East African Literature Bureau, 1968.

Kiwanuka, Semmakula. *A History of Buganda: From the Foundation of the Kingdom to 1900*. London: Longman Group Ltd., 1971.

Kritzeck, James, and Lewis, William H., eds. *Islam in Africa*. New York: Van Nostrand-Reinhold, 1969.

Kung, Hans. *The Church*. New York: Image Books, Doubleday & Company, Inc, 1976.

_____. *On Being a Christian*. New York: Pocket Books, 1966.

Lanternari, Vittorio. *The Religions of the Oppressed: A Study of 1990 Modern Messianic Cults*. New York: Knopf, 1963.

Latourette, S. K. *The Expansion of Christianity* 1-8. London: Zondervan, 1970.

_____. *A History of Christianity*. London: Eyre and Scottiwoode, 1954.

Laye, Camera. *The Dark Child*. London: Collins, 1955.

Leakey, Louis S. B. *Mau Mau and the Kikuyu*. New York: John Day, 1952.

Leaver, Robin A. *Luther on Justification*. St. Louis: Concordia Publishing House, 1975.

LeFevre, Perry, ed. *Philosophical Resources for Christian Thought*. New York: Abingdon Press, 1968.

Lienhardt, G. *Divinity and Experience; the Religion of the Dinka*. Oxford: Oxford University Press, 1961.

Lewis, I. M., ed. *Islam in Tropical Africa*. London: Oxford University Press, 1966.

Lonergan, Bernad. *Method in Theology*. Darton: Longman and Todd, 1972.

_____. *A Second Collection*. Darton: Longman and Todd, 1974.

Low, A. D. *Buganda in Modern History*. London: World University Press, 1970.

Macquarrie, John. *Principles of Christian Theology*. New York: Scribner's Sons, 1977.

_____. *Twentieth Century Religious Thought*. London: SCM Press, 1976.

Mair, Lucy P. *An African People in the Twentieth Century*. New York: Russell, 1965.

_____. *Witchcraft*. London: World University Press, 1969.

Malik, Charles H. *The Wonder of Being*. Texas: World Book Publishers, 1974.

Macquet, Jacques. *Africanity. The Cultural Unity of Black Africa*. London: Oxford University Press, 1972.

Martin, Marie-Louise. *Kibangu*. London: Blackwell, 1975.

Marty, I. *African Theology: Inculturation and Liberation*. Maryknoll: Orbis Books, 1993.

Matthews, R. *English Messiahs*. London: Methuen, 1936.

Mbiti, John. S. *African Religions and Philosophy*. London: Heinemann, 1969.

_____. *Akamba Stories*. Oxford: Clarendon Press, 1966.

_____. *Concepts of God in Africa*. New York: Praeger, 1970.

_____. *New Testament Eschatology in African Background*. London: Oxford University Press, 1971.

_____. *The Prayers of African Religion*. New York: Maryknoll, Orbis Books, 1976.

McGavran, A. D. *Understanding Church Growth*. Grand Rapids: W.B.Eerdams, 1970.

McVeigh, Malcolm J. *God in Africa: Concepts of God in African Traditional Religion and Christianity*. Cape Cod, Mass.: Claude Stark, 1974.

Melland, Frank H. *In Witch-Bound Africa*. London: Frank Cass, 1967.

Mendelson, Jack. *God, Allah, and Juju: Religion in Africa Today*. New York: Nelson, 1962.

Merriam, Alan P. *An African World: The Basongye Village of Lupupa Ngye*. Bloomington: Indiana University Press, 1974.

Metz, J. *Theology of the World*. New York: Herder and Herder, 1969. Middleton, John, and Winter, E. H., eds. *Gods and Rituals*. Garden City, N.Y.: The Natural History Press, 1967.

_____. *Magic, Witchcraft and Curing*. Garden City: The Natural History Press, 1967.

_____. *Myth and Cosmos*. Garden City, N.Y.: The Natural History Press, 1969.

_____. *Witchcraft and Sorcery in East Africa*. London: Rowledge and Kegan Paul, 1963; New York: The Natural History Press, 1967.

Moltmann, Jurgen. *Man: Christian Anthropology in the Conflicts of The Present*. Translated by John Sturdy. Philadelphia: Fortress Press, 1979.

Montagu, A. ed. *Culture and Human Development*. Englewood: Prentice-Hall, 1974.

Moore, Basil, ed. *Black Theology, the South African Voice*. London: Hurst, 1973.

Mulago, V. *Une Visage Africaine du Christianisme*. Paris: Presence Africaine, 1962.

Niebuhr, R. H. *Christ and Culture*. New York: Harper & Row, 1951.

_____. *The Purpose of the Church and Its Ministry*. New York: Harper & Row, 1956.

_____. *The Social Sources of Denominationalism*. Cleveland: World Publishing Medidian Books, 1965.

Niebuhr, Reinhold. *The Nature and Destiny of Man*. 2 vols. NY: Scribner's Sons, 1964.

Neill, S. C. *Christian Missions*. London: Pelican, 1966.

_____. *Colonialism and Christian Missions*. London: Lutterworth Press, 1966.

_____. *Twentieth Century Christianity*. London: Collins, 1962.

Neill, S. *The Christian Society: Theology and Philosophy*. London: Lutterworth, 1972.

Neuner, Joseph, and Roos, Heinrich. *The Teaching of the Catholic Church as Contained in Her Documents*. Ed. by Karl Rahner. New York: Alba House, 1965.

Newlands, George M. *The Theology of the Love of God*. Atlanta: John Knox, 1980.

Ngugi, James. *A Grain of Wheat*. London: Heinemann, 1967.

_____. *The River Between*. London: Heinemann, 1965.

_____. *Weep Not Child*. London: heinemann, 1964.

Norris, Richard A., Jr., trans. & ed. *The Christological Controversy*. Philadelphia: Fortress Press, 1980.

Northcott, Cecil. *Christianity in Africa*. London: S.C.M. Press, 1963.

Nygren, Anders. *Commentary on Romans*. Philadelphia: Fortress Press, 1980.

O'Grady, John F. *Christian Anthropology: A Meaning for Human Life*. New York: Paulist Press, 1976.

O'Donovan, Leo J., ed. *A World of Grace: An Introduction to the Themes and Foundations of Karl Rahner's Theology*. New York: The Seabury Press, 1980.

Oliver, R. *The Missionary Factor in East Africa*. London: Longmans-Green Co., 1952.

Olupona, Jacob, K. *African Traditional Religions in Contemporary Society*. New York: Paragon House, 1991.

Osthuizen, G. C. *Post Christianity in Africa: A Theological and Anthropological Study*. Grand Rapids: William E. Eerdmans.

Outler, A. C. *The Christian Tradition and the Unity We Seek*. New York: Oxford University Press, 1957.

Pannenberg, Wolfhart. *Human Nature, Election, and History*. Philadelphia: The Westminster Press, 1977.

_____. *Jesus-God and Man*. Trans. by Lewis L. Wilkins and Duane A. Priebe. Philadelphia: The Westminster Press, 1968.

_____. *What Is Man? Contemporary Anthropology in Theological Perspective*. Translated by Duane Priebe. Philadelphia: Fortress Press, 1970.

Pannenberg, Wolfhart, et al. *Spirit, Faith and Church*. Phila.: The Westminster, 1970.

Parker, William R., and Aldwell, Enid. *Man: Animal and Divine*. L A: Scribner, 1970.

Parrinder, Edward Geoffrey. *African Mythology*. London: Paul Hamly, 1967.

_____. *African Traditional Religion*. Westport, Conn.: Greenwood Press, 1970.

_____. *Religion in an African City*. London: Oxford University Press, 1953.

_____. *West African Religion*. London: Epworth Press, 1961.

_____. *Witchcraft: European and African*. New York: Barnes and Noble, 1963.

Patricia, St. John. *The Breath of Life*. London: Norfolk Press, 1971.

Pelikan, Jaroslav. *The Christian Tradition: A History of the Development of Doctrine, Vol. 1: The Emergence of the Catholic Tradition (100-600)*. Chicago: The University of Chicago Press, 1971.

Pittenger, Norman W. *The Christian Understanding of Human Nature*. Philadelphia: The Westminster Press, 1964.

Ramsey, M. A. *An Era in Anglican Theology: From Gore to Temple*. New York: Charles Scribner's Sons, 1960.

Ranger, T. and Kimambo, I. N., eds. *Christian Independence in Tanzania*. Dar Salaam: Historical Association of Tanzania, 970.

_____. *The Historical Study of African Religion*. Berkeley: Uni. of Ca. Press, 1972.

Ranger, T., and Weller, J. *The African Churches of Tanzania*. Dar Salaam: Historical Association of Tanzania, 1969.

_____. *Themes in the Christian History of Central Africa*. London: Heinemann, 1975.

Ray, B. C. *African Religions: Symbol, Ritual and Community*. Englewood Cliffs, N.J.: Prentice Hall, 1976.

Richardson, C. C., ed. *Early Christian Fathers*. New York: MacMillan, 1970.

Robertson, E. H. *Man's Estimate of Man*. Richmond, Virginia: John Knox Press, 1958.

Roberts, Louis. *The Achievement of Karl Rahner*. New York: Herder and Herder, 1967.

Rogers, Carl. *On Becoming a Person*. Boston: Houghton Mifflin Co., 1961.

Roscoe, J. *The Baganda*. London: Frank Cass, 1965.

_____. *The Bagesu and Other Tribes*. Cambridge: Cambridge University Press, 1924.

_____. *The Bakitara or Banyoro*. Cambridge: Cambridge University Press, 1923.

_____. *The Danyankole*. Cambridge: Cambridge University Press, 1925.

_____. *The Northern Bantu*. Cambridge: Cambridge University Press, 1915.

Russell, Bertrand. *Has Man a Future?* Baltimore: Penguin Books, 1961.

_____. *Why I Am Not a Christian and Other Essays on Religion and Related Subjects*. New York: Simon and Schuster, 1957.

Russell, J. K. *Men Without God*. London: The Highway Press, 1966.

Sabatier, Auguste. *The Religions of Authority and the Religions of the Spirit*. New York: Williams & Norgate, 1904.

Sangree, Walter H. *Age, Prayer and Politics in Tikiri, Kenya*. New York: Oxford, 1966.

Sawyer, Harry. *God: Ancestor or Creator*. London: Longman, 1970.

_____. *The Christian Faith*. Philadelphia: Fortress Press, 1976.

Shepherd, W. *Man's Condition: God and the World Process*. New York: Herder, 1969.

Shorter, Aylward. *African Christian Theology*. London: Geoffrey and Chapman, 1975.

_____. *African Culture and the Christian Church*. London: Geoffrey-Chapman, 1973.

_____. *Prayer in the Religious Traditions of Africa*. London: Oxford Uni., 1975.

Sithole, Ndabaningi. *Obed Mutezo, the Mudzimi Christian Nationalist*. London: Oxford University Press, 1970.

Smith, Edwin. *African Ideas of God, A Symposium*. London: Edinburgh House, 1961.

Smith, Huston. *The Religions of Man*. New York: Harper & Row, 1965.

Stock, E. *A History of the Church Missionary Society*. London: C.M.S. Press, 1899.

Stott, J. *Men Made New*. London: Inter Varsity Press, 1966.

Sundkler, Bengt. *Bantu Prophets in South Africa*. London: Lutterworth Press, 1948.

_____. *The Christian Ministry in Africa*. London: S.C.M. Press, 1960.

_____. *Zulu Zion*. London: Oxford University Press, 1976.

Tanner, Ralph E. S. *Transition in African Beliefs: Traditional Religion and Christian Change*. Maryknoll, N.Y.: Maryknoll Publications, 1967.

Taylor, J. V. *Christianity and Politics in Africa*. London: Harmondsworth, 1957.

_____. *The Christians of the Copperbelt*. London: S.C.M. Press, 1963.

_____. *The Church Growth in Buganda*. London: C.M.S. Press, 1958.

_____. *The Cross of Christ*. London: MacMillan and Co., Ltd., 1956.

_____. *The Primal Vision*. London: S.C.M. Press, 1963.

Teilhard de Chardin, Pierre. *The Phenomenon of Man*. New York: Harper & Row, 1975.

_____. *The Prayer of the Universe*. New York: Harper & Row, 1973.

Tempels, P. *Bantu Philosophy*. Paris: Presence Africaine, 1959.

Temple, William. *Nature, Man and God*. London: MacMillan, 1934.

TeSelle, Eugene. *Christ in Context: Divine Purpose and Human Possibility*. Philadelphia: Fortress Press, 1975.

Temu, A. J. *British Protestant Missions*. London: Longman Group Limited, 1972.

Tillich, Paul. *The Courage to Be*. New Haven: Yale University Press, 1969.

_____. *Dynamics of Faith*. New York: Harper & Row, 1957.

_____. *The New Being*. New York: The Scribner's Sons, 1955.

_____. *Systematic Theology*: 3 Vols. Chicago: Chicago University Press, 1960.

Tracy, David. *Blessed Race for Order: The New Pluralism in Theology*. New York: Seabury Press, 1978.

Trimingham, J. S. *The Christian Approach to Islam in the Sudan*. London and New York: Oxford University Press, 1948.

_____. *Christian Church and Islam in West Africa*. London: S.C.M. Press, 1955.

_____. *The Influence of Islam upon Africa*. New York: Praeger, 1968.

_____. *Islam in East Africa*. New York: Friendship Press, 1962.

_____. *Islam in Ethiopia*. New York: Barnes and Noble, 1965.

_____. *Islam in the Sudan*. New York: Barnes and Noble, 1965.

_____. *Islam in West Africa*. London: Oxford University Press, 1961.

Tucker, A. R. *My Eighteen Years in East Africa*. London: Edward Arnold, 1908.

Tuma, Tom, and Mutibwa, Phares. *A Century of Christianity in Uganda, 1877-1977*. Nairobi: Uzima Press Limited, 1978.

Twesigye, Emmanuel Kalenzi. *"Anonymous Christianity" and Human Existence in African Perspective: A Study based on Karl Rahner's Philosophical Theology*. Ann Arbor and London: UMI, 1983.

_____. *Common Ground: Christianity, African Religion and Philosophy*. New York: Peter Lang, 1987.

_____. *The Global Human Problem: Ignorance, Hate, Injustice and Violence*. New York: Peter Lang, 1988.

_____. *Martin Lurther King and W.E.B. DuBois as Foundations for Afrocentric Teaching*. Nashville, Fisk University Press, 1989.

_____, ed. *In Quest for Knowledge and Truth: Fisk University Faculty Lecture Series*, Vols. 1-2. Nashville: Fisk University Press, 1989.

_____. *God, Race, Myth and Power: An Africanist Corrective Research Analysis*. New York: Peter Lang, 1991.

Vidler, A. R. *The Church in an Age of Revolution*. London: Penguin, 1961. Vorgrimler, Herbert. *Karl Rahner: His Life, Thought and Works*. Translated by Edward Quinn. London: Burns & Oates, 1965.

Warren, A. M. *Revival: An Inquiry*. London: C.M.S. Press, 1954.

_____. *Social History and Christian Mission*. London: S.C.M. Press, 1967.

Weber, M. *The Sociology of Religion*. Boston: Beacon Press, 1964.

Webster, J. B. *West Africa Since 1800*. Ibadan: Longmans, 1968.

Welbourn, F. B. *East African Christianity*. Nairobi: Oxford Press, 1967.

_____. *East African Rebels: A Study of Some Independent Churches*. London: S.C.M. Press, 1961.

_____. *Religion and Politics in Uganda, 1952-1962*. Nairobi: Oxford Press, 1965.

Welbourn, F. B. and Ogot, B. A. *A Place to Feel at Home*. London: Oxford Uni., 1965.

Welch, Claude. *Protestant Thought in the Nineteenth Century, Vol.: 1799-1870*. New Haven: Yale University Press, 1972.

Werner, A. *Myths and Legends of Bantu*. London: Oxford University Press, 1933.

Whitehead, Alfred North. *Adventures of Ideas*. New York: MacMillan, 1933.

_____. *Process and Reality*. New York: MacMillan, 1978.

_____. *Religion in the Making*. New York: MacMillan, 1926.

_____. *Science and the Modern World*. New York: MacMillan, 1925.

Willet, Frank. *African Art: An Introduction*. New York: Praeger, 1971.

Williamson, S. George. *Akan Religion and the Christian Faith*. Accra: Shane, 1965.

Willis, J. J. *An African Church in Building*. London: C.M.S. Press, 1925.

Willoughby, William Charles. *The Soul of the Bantu: A Sympathetic Study of the Magico-Religious Practices and Beliefs of the Bantu Tribes of Africa*. Garden City, N.Y.: Doubleday and Doran, 1928.

Wilson, Bryan R., ed. *Magic and the Millennium: A Sociological Study of Religious Movements of Protest among Tribal and Third World Peoples*. New York: Humanities Press, 1975.

_____. *Patterns of Sectarianism: Organization and Ideology in Social and Religious Movements*. London: Heinemann, 1967.

_____. *Religious Sects*. London: Weidenfield and Nicholson, 1970.

Wilson, C. J. *Uganda in the Days of Bishop Tucker*. London: MacMillan & Co., 1955.

Wilson, Monica. *Communal Rites of the Nyakyusa*. London: Oxford University, 1949.

_____. *Good Company: A Study of Nyakyusa Aged Villagers*. Boston: Beacon, 1963.

_____. *Rituals of Kingship among the Nyakyusa*. London: Oxford Uni. Press, 1949.

_____. *Religion and the Transformation of Society: A Study in Social Change in Africa*. Cambridge: The University Press, 1971.

Wiredu, Kwasi. *Philosophy and African Culture*. London York: Cambridge Uni., 1980.

Wright, Richard A., ed. *African Philosophy: An Introduction*. Washington: University Press of America, 1979.

SUBJECT INDEX